AF535054

Published on the occasion of the exhibition

THE EDWARD R. BROIDA COLLECTION

A SELECTION OF WORKS

at the Orlando Museum of Art

March 12, 1998 - June 21, 1998

EXHIBITION CURATED BY:

Sue Scott, Adjunct Curator of Contemporary American Art and

Betsy Gwinn, Assistant Curator

The Orlando Museum of Art is member supported

and sponsored in part by United Arts of Central Florida, Inc.

and the State of Florida, Department of State, Division of

Cultural Affairs, and the Florida Arts Council.

Accredited by the American Association of Museums

Printed in the United States

ISBN# 1-880699-05-2

Library of Congress Catalog Card Number: 97-68828

2416 North Mills Avenue

Orlando, Florida 32803-1483.

(407) 896-4231

THE EDWARD R. BROIDA COLLECTION

A SELECTION OF WORKS

Orlando Museum of Art

TABLE OF CONTENTS

SPONSORS

PRESENTING SPONSOR

AT&T

CONTRIBUTING SPONSOR

Absolut Vodka/Seagram Americas
City of Orlando
Faison

SPONSOR

Gary and Barbara Sorensen
Lynn and Charles P. Steinmetz
Art and Sherry Zimand

PARTNERS IN EXCELLENCE

Sustaining Partner—A. Friends' Foundation
Contributing Partner—Enterprise Rent-A-Car
Partner— Fannie Hillman & Associates, Inc., Randolph H. Fields,
The Raymond E. and Ellen F. Crane Foundation

FOREWORD

The Orlando Museum of Art is committed to presenting exhibitions of national and international importance which relate to its permanent collections of 19th- and 20th-century American, Pre-Columbian, and African art. The Edward R. Broida Collection is a leading collection of contemporary art, and featuring it is consistent with the Museum's commitment to collect and exhibit the finest art available.

The Orlando Museum of Art is privileged to present the first exhibition of works from the Edward R. Broida Collection. Prior to this exhibition, Mr. Broida loaned works to important museum exhibitions worldwide, but this will be the first major exhibition of selections from his exquisite collection.

Mr. Broida began collecting art in the late 1970s. Often cited by *ArtNews* and *Art and Antiques* magazines on their lists of top collections, the Edward R. Broida Collection is a comprehensive survey of contemporary art, consisting of over 600 works, spanning the last one hundred years.

This exhibition includes 168 highlights of the Edward R. Broida Collection which are representative of its breadth and depth. In addition to the works displayed in the Museum, ten monumental sculptures will be on long-term loan and installed in the picturesque park surrounding the Museum. The extension of this exhibition into public places creates a wonderful dimension which can be enjoyed by thousands of motorists passing Orlando Loch Haven Park, as well as visitors to the Museum.

The Orlando Museum of Art is deeply grateful to Mr. Broida for lending works from his collection for this landmark exhibition. To work with a collector like Mr. Broida, who has a genuine love of art, the eye of an art connoisseur, and the desire to share his treasures with the public, has been an extraordinary experience.

We want to thank the following for their support of this exhibition: Presenting Sponsor — AT&T; Contributing Sponsors — Absolut Vodka/Seagram Americas, the City of Orlando, and Faison; and Sponsors — Gary and Barbara Sorensen, Lynn and Charles P. Steinmetz, and Art and Sherry Zimand. In addition, we want to thank the Partners in Excellence, United Arts of Central Florida, Inc., the State of Florida, Department of State, Division of Cultural Affairs, and the Florida Arts Council for their support. All of these donors recognized the importance of this exhibition and gave generously to ensure its success.

We encourage everyone to seize the rare opportunity to see this exhibition. Without a doubt, it is of world-class importance and one not to be missed.

Marena Grant Morrisey
Executive Director

ACKNOWLEDGMENTS

Ed Broida has been central to all aspects of this presentation, from the initial planning and selection of works through the catalogue design and installation of the exhibition. His guidance and input have been invaluable, and his generosity in opening up his entire collection during the selection process has ensured the excellence of this exhibition. For all of this, the staff of the Orlando Museum of Art is extremely grateful.

I would like to thank the numerous artists and galleries who provided photography, biographical material, and other necessary information. I am particularly indebted to Bob Kane; Renee and David McKee and Bruce Hackney of McKee Gallery, New York; Paula Cooper Gallery, New York; and Kimberly Davis of L.A. Louver, Santa Monica. Mr. Broida's Registrar, Trish Berube, was essential in ferreting out necessary documentation and photography and dealing with loan agreements and transportation. It has been a pleasure working with her. Special thanks to catalogue designer Meredy Jenkins whose creativity and collaboration has brought much to the project.

The staff of the Orlando Museum of Art has worked tirelessly in presenting this exhibition. Betsy Gwinn, Assistant Curator for this exhibition, was key to the success of the project. She worked diligently to perfect the checklist and the exhibition layout and to produce the catalogue. I would like to thank Andrea Farnick, Registrar, for her attention to detail throughout the project as well as for her work on loan agreements and shipping arrangements. Kimberly Heitzman, Exhibitions Assistant, has been invaluable for her support in all areas, particularly in procuring copyright permission. Hansen Mulford, Curator of Exhibitions, has given his assistance from the start to facilitate the logistics of this challenging installation with added help from Kevin Boylan, Preparator.

As with any presentation of this scale, this exhibition would not have been possible without the financial support of the private and business communities. I would like to thank Executive Director Marena Grant Morrisey, Trustee Francine S. Newberg, and Development Director Wrenda Goodwyn for their tireless efforts in fundraising and publicity, and Sharon Miller, Development Coordinator, for her assistance in this effort. I am indebted to Charles Meiner, Gary and Barbara Sorensen, Lynn and Charles P. Steinmetz, and Art and Sherry Zimand, not only for their financial support but for their ongoing generosity and commitment to the arts. Frank Holt, Public Art Coordinator for the City of Orlando, generously gave his time to assist with the installation of the outdoor sculpture.

It is with great pleasure and pride that we present this exceptional collection to the people of Central Florida.

Sue Scott
Adjunct Curator of Contemporary American Art

Eyes Open Wider:
The Collection of Edward R. Broida

THE BEGINNING

On October 5, 1978, Ed Broida with his former wife, Joyce, visited McKee Gallery in New York on the advice of his uncle, Sydney Feldman. A collector himself, Feldman knew the added dimensions that collecting art had brought to his own life. He felt that his nephew, an architect and recently retired real estate developer in Los Angeles, was primed for the experience. Since Feldman had bought a few fine works at McKee Gallery, he felt it was a good place to start.

By chance, McKee Gallery was featuring a retrospective of the drawings of Philip Guston, and Broida, with his training in architecture, responded not only to the drawn line but to the boldness of the work. Renee and David McKee were struck by his confidence and open-mindedness, and they showed him a number of large Guston paintings. After many hours of looking, talking, and thinking, Broida purchased *Source*, 1976 and *Rug*, 1976, two very large and challenging paintings. Aptly named, *Source* is a portrait of Guston's wife, Musa, rising out of the horizon like some giant sunburst with her eyes open wide. *Rug* is easily as tough for the uninitiated, a group of skinny legs, knobby knees, and shoes resting on a rug and wooden floor. "I got stuck on shoes," Guston once said. "Shoes on the floor. I must have done hundreds of paintings of shoes.... And the more I did, the more mysterious these objects became."[1]

A novice to the art world, Broida had no background on Guston and consequently no baggage or expectations from the artist's earlier abstractions. He was able to respond directly to the strength of these paintings. "The more unusual the work, the more he seemed to accept and enjoy the breadth of Guston's imagination," recalled David McKee. "Whatever it was that Philip put into it, he seemed to continue the process. Appreciating it. And art needs that process to occur."[2]

Again by chance, Philip Guston came that day to the gallery, which he rarely did unannounced. It was at a time when his figurative paintings were not selling well, and he was surprised and thrilled to find out that someone, unknown to him, had just purchased two paintings. A bottle of whiskey was found in a drawer in the back room and, as Broida recollects, they sat on the floor in the gallery passing the bottle around in celebration. "I can remember Philip saying, 'It's so wonderful, he gets it,'" said McKee. "It was obvious everybody was connected. It cemented something." For Guston, "getting it" translated as an innate understanding of what he was trying to do. "I think that probably the most potent desire for a painter, an image-maker, is to see it," he once said, "to see what the mind can think and imagine, to realize it for oneself, through oneself, as concretely as possible."[3]

Before day's end, Broida had also purchased a painting by Katherine Porter. He came back the following morning to buy four Guston drawings before returning to Los Angeles. It was during this visit to New York that Broida mentioned how much he liked one of the small sculptures in his Uncle Syd's apartment. McKee knew the work and said he would keep an eye out. Within two weeks, Broida received a letter saying that a sculpture by the same artist was coming up at auction, and he should consider bidding on it. The sculpture was *Jurassic Bird* by David Smith. A picture of it was on the cover of the auction catalogue. Although Broida immediately fell in love with it, he also worried that it was too much too fast. The price was twice what he had spent on a Guston painting, and he didn't know who Smith was. After several sleepless nights, he called the Los Angeles County Museum of Art and was connected to Stephanie Barron in the Contemporary Art Department. He explained his earlier purchases and his current dilemma, and asked her if she had ever heard of an artist named David Smith. "She could have killed me at that moment I was so fragile," remembered Broida. "I've thanked her so many times that she didn't destroy me. Instead, she proceeded to tell me who he was and the importance of his work, and I knew I was on safe ground."[4] Broida purchased the sculpture at auction, and from that moment on he moved forward with more confidence.

THE COLLECTION

These two experiences in a sense encapsulate Broida's approach to collecting, which is based both on intuitive response and in-depth analysis. "Ed is passionate and intuitive," said Renee McKee. "But he's also logical and reasoned. It's not just a gut reaction; it's a very studied reaction." This catholic sensibility, penchant for analysis, and as artist Bob Kane pointed out, "an extremely developed eye,"[5] has enabled him to put together a collection numbering over six hundred works during the last nineteen years that is marked not only by diversity of style and medium, but by radical variations in size and scale. Works in this collection span the century from a Brancusi *Kiss* completed in 1908 to a 1997 sculpture by Peter Shelton. The works vary in size from a small Léger drawing to Mark Di Suvero's *Mahatma* with its thirty-foot span. There are both established masters and lesser-known young and mid-career artists. There is abstraction and realism as well as variations on the two. The aesthetic ranges from Carl Andre's minimalist floor piece to the brightly colored exuberance of Pierre Alechinsky and Bob Kane to a crocheted umbrella by Valerie Favre. Some artists have a single representation of their work. Others, like Claes Oldenburg, Vija Celmins, Joel Shapiro, Mark Di Suvero, Jake Berthot, Jonathan Borofsky, and Philip Guston, are collected in-depth. No single movement is focused on and few are excluded; one can find examples of Pop art, Neo-Expressionism, Abstract Expressionism, Minimalism, and artists who defy categorization.

As a result of this diversity, it is difficult if not impossible to categorize or qualify Broida's collection. The aesthetic that ties the works together is more ethereal than tangible, more visual than intellectual. Still, there are common threads that run through the collection and one cannot help but look.

An obvious beginning is the work of Philip Guston, which Broida continued to collect obsessively from the first day he was introduced to his work. He is one of several artists whom Broida collected backwards, later adding a 1938 painting entitled *Gladiators*, a stylized rendition of children fighting that recalls Picasso's *Guernica*,[6] as well as two abstract paintings *Zone*, 1953-54 and *The Mirror*, 1957. *Zone*, with its figure/ground delineation and central webbed mass of paint is a subtle harbinger of Guston's later, figurative paintings.

From the moment Broida and Guston met in McKee Galley in 1978, they established a friendship that was to continue until Guston's untimely death in 1980. On numerous occasions, Broida visited Guston at his home and studio in Woodstock, New York. He sometimes bought en masse. On one visit he sat quietly with Guston, each in a chair, a table with a bottle of wine between them, as an assistant brought in painting after painting for them to view. Little was said, but the following day Broida appeared at McKee Gallery with a list of five paintings he wanted: *A Day's Work*, 1970, *Midnight Pass Road*, 1975, *Web*, 1975, *Green Rug*, 1976, and *Ladder*, 1978. He tried several times to buy a 1976 painting entitled *Cherries*, but Guston repeatedly resisted. Then, on one trip upstate with the McKees, they stopped to buy provisions for a picnic where Broida happened on a flat of cherries displayed in the window. He bought the entire flat and presented it to Guston upon their arrival. By the end of the day, *Cherries* was his. He continued to buy paintings, prints, and drawings and soon became known as "The Guston Man." On numerous occasions Guston himself introduced Broida as "My Arensburg" in reference to Walter Arensburg, the Los Angeles collector and patron of Marcel Duchamp.

Whether it was Broida's own eye and training in architecture, or the effect of collecting so many of Guston's works in a relatively short time, one can see throughout his collection Guston's aesthetic—a love for the painterly, a thick build-up of paint, and a strong internal structure. As Renee McKee pointed out, "There is something of the sculptural in many of his paintings and something linear in his sculptures." This is particularly apparent in the fragmented canvas of Elizabeth Murray's *More Than You Know*, 1983, one of her earliest shaped and painted canvases. "Philip Guston would be the artist I would think about more than Cézanne," Murray once noted in an interview. "When I was doing the shoe paintings it hit me like a ton of bricks just how much I owe to Guston."[7] Tad Wiley's shaped and painted wall sculpture *Wave Eater*, 1987 and Jill Giegerich's *Untitled (Figure with Arch of Industry)*, 1983 also share these qualities. Broida's love for the plastic surface is as apparent in smaller paintings such as Melissa Meyer's *Ophelia*, 1985, Spencer Gregory's *Underneath*, 1986-87, and Alfred Jenson's *Interval in Six Scales*, 1963, as it is in the larger, gestural works by Neil Jenney and the monumental painterly geometric abstractions of Sean Scully.

Susan Rothenberg has said that her paintings come right out of the targets of Jasper Johns, but one can also see Guston's influence in her expressive brushstrokes and use of imagery—fragmented heads and hands and myriad variations of the horse. Like Guston, the images come from an intuitive place. "The way the horse image appeared in my paintings was not an intellectual procedure," she said; "most of my work is not run through a rational part of my brain. It comes from a place in me that I don't choose to examine. I just let it come. I don't have any special affection for the horse. A terrific cypress will do it for me too. But I knew that the horse is a powerful, recognizable thing, and that it would take care of my need for an image."[8] Two of Rothenberg's paintings in Broida's collection, *Triphammer Bridge*, 1974 and *Black in Place*, 1976, are prototypes from this period. Perhaps even more telling is Rothenberg's naming of a 1985-86 lithograph printed at ULAE, *Stumblebum*, referencing Hilton Kramer's derisive moniker given during a review of Guston's figurative works from the 1970s.

Jake Berthot is an artist whose work Broida supported early on and has continued to collect over the years. Because the works in this selection range from 1971 to 1997, one has the opportunity to trace the development and growth of this "painter's painter." *Greenpoint*, 1971, for instance, is minimal in its aesthetic, and yet one experiences the artist's love for surface, color, and texture. In *Anawanda*, 1985 Berthot contrasts field painting with gesture, exploring what lies below the surface (he once said he painted a certain painting to "get to that red, that green, that orange")[9], while in *Nymph*, 1991 the play seems to be more about the relationship of figure and ground. These works point the way to his most recent work *Off Lower Bone Hollow*, 1997. Preceded by a move from New York City to the country, this painting, a landscape, is a departure for Berthot, but like his earlier work is a sumptuous study in color and composition.

Broida's collection is an organic outgrowth, the result of buying what he liked when he saw it, regardless of the whims of the art world. However, there is one aspect of his collection that was more studied. The idea, encouraged by the McKees, was to collect a few choice historical pieces that would help make sense of a contemporary collection. In addition to the early Gustons, there are several key examples of Abstract Expressionism. Prime among them are Mark Rothko's *Homage to Matisse*, 1954, a glowing field of orange and blue, and two paintings by Franz Kline, which together show his two sides: the black and white of *Luzerne*, 1956 and *Washington Wall*, 1959, a painting with color gracing the black structure.

Kline is an artist whose work was known to and admired by Broida from his college days, probably because of the inherent architectonic qualities of the paintings. He was determined, if possible, that Kline would be one of the artists he would collect, and as it turned out, Kline was one of the few artists he pursued in earnest. Early in his collecting career, Broida attended an exhibition at the Phillips Collection in Washington D.C. entitled *Kline in Color*. During the exhibition, Broida fell in love with *Washington Wall*. The painting was owned at the time by a Washington D.C. collector who was unwilling to sell, but Broida, through David McKee, expressed his continued interest, and within a year, the painting was his.

A number of the more historic sculptures, Jean Arp's *Sculpture de Silence Corneille*, 1942-64; Henri Laurens's *Le Matin*, 1944; Joan Miró's *Femme Verte*, 1968; Barbara Hepworth's *Figure (Ascending Form)*, 1956; and Jacques Lipchitz's *Benediction I*, 1942, reveal much about the tug-of-war between figuration and abstraction that sculpture experienced during the latter half of the twentieth century. Constantin Brancusi engaged in this tug-of-war while working with primal shapes—the egg, the cone, the circle, the square—and experimenting with and juxtaposing a variety of materials. *The Kiss*, 1907-08, is not only quintessential Brancusi, but as the earliest work in the collection, seems to be a paradigm for many of the sculptures Broida collected.

Bryan Hunt cites Brancusi as one of his fundamental influences, particularly for his bronze lakes which resemble in conformation and aesthetics Brancusi's wooden cups. Like the cups, Hunt's waterfalls and airships are simultaneously objects and sculptural forms. If it was the primal shapes of Minimalists such as Carl Andre and Robert Morris (both have works in this exhibition) that inspired the young Martin Puryear, one can also see in his work references to Brancusi with his fusion of folk craft and the historical tradition of sculpture. Puryear's sculpture in this exhibition, *Verge*, 1987 is at once referential—one thinks of a giant clunky shoe or a pipe—and abstract in configuration. Likewise, in the freestanding columns and the curved or serrated wall sculptures of John Duff one can see, or more to the point, feel, the effect of the primal shapes of Brancusi.

Christopher Wilmarth was also tremendously affected by Brancusi, as much conceptually as formally. As Laura Rosenstock, curator of Wilmarth's retrospective at the Museum of Modern Art, noted in her essay, "Brancusi's love of rough-hewn wood, his tendency to conjoin wood with polished metal or stone, and his infusion of metaphysical significance into simple reductive forms had a strong impact on Wilmarth."[10] In most of his works included in this exhibition, from the monumental *Tina Turner*, 1970-71 to the more subtle *Baptiste (Longing) #2*, 1984, with its ovoid forms recalling Brancusi's *Sleeping Muse*, it is the poetry of light that he seeks to convey. Brancusi once said, "My hands are the last hands to touch my work."[11] Wilmarth's sculpture *Last Hands*, 1969 is not only a marked reference to this statement, but as it was created during a time when Conceptual and Minimal art were the reigning styles, it stands as an homage to sculpture where the hand of the artist is very much in evidence.

One of England's most well-known sculptors, David Nash, brings a new insight to the use of natural materials. Early in his career he carved wooden planks, later evolving to the use of entire tree trunks and limbs which he would often carve in situ. The three sculptures by Nash in this exhibition reveal the full spectrum of shapes and conceptual references he is able to coax from a single tree.

Black Column, 1983, made of burnt sycamore, brings to mind the *Endless Column* of Brancusi; *Rising Boat*, 1986 evokes the movement of a ship while *Three Cogs*, 1987 is a conceptual conundrum referencing industry in its shape and nature in its material.

Obviously not all the sculptors in Broida's collection come from the lineage of Constantin Brancusi. Mark Di Suvero, for instance, is closer to the welded steel tradition of Julio Gonzalez (in fact one of his sculptures is titled *Homage to Gonzalez*, 1973) and David Smith. Di Suvero's vocabulary of industrial materials— I beams, steel, rubber tires, found objects, and wood—has resulted in a body of work that is as diverse and fantastic as any sculpture produced in the twentieth century. Broida's collection, which has the most in-depth holding of work by Di Suvero in the country, is unique in that it enables the viewer to comprehend the diversity of Di Suvero's work. Compare, for example, the 1961 work *Eatherly's Lamp* to *Mahatma*, 1978-79. *Eatherly's Lamp* is a small pedestal piece, lit from within and resembling some weird archaic artifact (Eatherly was the bombardier on the *Enola Gay*), while *Mahatma* is a giant steel toy that balances, rocks, and turns 360 degrees on a single I beam column. As diverse as these two works may seem, the aesthetic of whimsy or storytelling as well as a transformation of materials, is encoded into both and is a thread that weaves through much of Di Suvero's work.

A number of artists continue the figurative tradition of sculpture. Peter Shelton, influenced by David Smith probably more than any other artist, is interested both in the body and architecture, often focusing on the way the body occupies space. In *allarms*, 1990-96, for instance, two spindly arms snake out of a trunklike torso, reaching ten feet in opposite directions. As a result, this somewhat minimal piece can be read on many different levels, from the humorous undertones to the play between realism and abstraction to the notion of how something small, when projected into space, can occupy the same area as a larger counterpart. Likewise, Jonathan Borofsky mines the human figure and psyche for its inherent humor and social commentary. His figures, flying, fighting, or dancing as clowns, are the ordinary made extraordinary.

Daisy Youngblood also works somewhere in between abstraction and realism, her sculptures of animals are as beautiful for their abstract qualities of surface and composition as for the emotions they communicate. Youngblood often works in low-fire clay, a medium that conveys an ancient quality to the pieces, as if they are as much about ritual as representation. Like Youngblood's animal sculptures, Judith Shea's empty bathing suit in *The Crawl*, 1983 exists as a stand-in, a surrogate for that which is not present.

The two sculptures in this exhibition by William Tucker indicate the extraordinary distance an artist can travel within the context of his own work. Seen together they reveal an interest both in the figure and the place of the figure. *The House of the Hanged Man*, 1981, made from wood salvaged from a used ventilator system on the top of Tucker's studio, is both a structure and a line drawing in space. *Gymnast II*, 1985 is a study in balance and movement with its off-axis v-shape bringing to mind a torso, not just bent, but in the act of bending. The surface treatment, modeled and gestural, covers the bronze with a skinlike veneer, a softness belying the solidity of the bronze.

Minimalism is an aesthetic one would not necessarily ascribe to Broida's sensibility, and yet there are some exceptional examples of Minimalism in this collection, among them Carl Andre's *64 Steel Square*, 1967, made from squares of hot rolled steel. Andre rejected both the pedestal and upward thrust of traditional sculpture, unlike one of his counterparts, Joel Shapiro, who embraced a reductive version of the human form. Shapiro's many permutations of the figure, running, standing, falling, headless, or simply a torso, are studies in essential form. In her floor sculpture, *Stevens' Bouquet*, 1991, Roni Horn riffs on both Minimal and Conceptual art by not only paring down the "flowers" to aluminum forms but by "naming" their colors—yellow, black, red, orange, white, and pink.

Expressive figuration is another loose grouping into which a number of artists in Broida's collection can be placed. Many are international. The German artist Horst Antes, who sees himself as an anthropologist of his own imagination, created his own brand of figuration called the "gnome people." Rendered in heightened colors, these characters, two of which occupy the painting *Mother and Child*, 1973-74, have such a distinct physiognomy they seem to have a shared gene pool. Represented here by his signature work, Francis Bacon gives full reign to his sense of line and composition in *Two Figures*, 1961. This leading master of London's figurative school shows a painterly ease of brushstroke that defines his paintings from this period. Katherine Porter casts her expressive eye for brushstroke and composition on the city. *The City at Night*, 1983 reflects an ongoing theme for Porter, a simultaneous love for the city and a commentary on the disharmony with nature found in city dwelling.

Pop art is a movement that has little representation in Broida's collection, except for the work of Claes Oldenburg, which he collected in depth. *Model: Rope Garden*, 1969 has the wonderful raw edge of material and form found in many of Oldenburg's early works when he was still working his way out of Abstract Expressionism into the coolness of Pop art. It is not surprising that Broida, a great baseball fan, collected three Oldenburg works—two bats, a standing batcolumn, and a mitt and glove—on that theme.

Vija Celmins's early 1960s paintings of objects from her studio—a hot plate, lamp, or heater—resulted in critics associating her with California Pop artists like Ed Ruscha and Joe Good. Since then, she has gone on to create works so original in concept and execution, it is difficult if not impossible to place her work in a specific category. Broida's idea of collecting an artist in-depth is not just about quantity, it is about having representation from all periods of an artist's oeuvre. His extensive holdings of Celmins's work—ranging from the early objects and realistic paintings of airplanes and guns to drawings of the ocean and paintings of the galaxy—clearly illustrate this philosophy. The sculptural piece *To Fix the Image in Memory*, 1977-82, is one of Celmins's masterpieces and encapsulates her approach to art making. By juxtaposing real rocks collected in New Mexico with identical objects made from cast bronze (not unlike Johns's cast bronze ale cans), she forces the viewer to both look and see, to compare that which is real to that which is man-made. "Part of the challenge of exhibiting them together with the real stones was to create a challenge for your eyes," she has said "I wanted your eyes to open wider."[12]

CONCLUSION

By 1982 Broida's collection had grown to mammoth proportions, and he began making plans to open a museum in New York City. He bought a building in SoHo in December of 1982 and moved to New York in the spring of the next year. For close to three and a half years, he worked nonstop to open the museum, but for myriad reasons and complications, it was not to be realized, and he stopped the operation in March of 1986. Although he has continued to lend to exhibitions around the world, this is the first time a selection of works from his collection has been exhibited together. It represents just over one-fourth of his holdings.

The evolution of Ed Broida's collection, like his collecting habits, continues to be both intuitive and unplanned. From the moment he purchased his first Guston painting to his most recent purchases—a Berthot landscape and a small Di Suvero sculpture among them—he has bought what he liked, driven neither by the art market nor current trends. "One aspect of collecting contemporary art is problem solving," he once said. This philosophy has enabled him to collect regardless of physical considerations of storage or display and allowed him to envision the possibilities of this exhibition.

For Broida, collecting is not just about acquiring. It reflects a lifetime commitment. "Collecting changes your life," he said recently, "your friends, events in your home town. Even the reason for your travel changes. It is something that, once you get the bug, once you're bitten, you'll do it until you die. It's a vocation and an avocation, all wrapped up into one. It's remained an important part of my life. Uncle Syd was right."

Sue Scott
Adjunct Curator of Contemporary American Art

1 Christine Stiles and Peter Selz, eds., *Theories and Documents of Contemporary Art. A Sourcebook of Artists' Writings* (Berkeley: University of California Press, 1996), p. 250.
2 All quotes from Renee and David McKee are from an interview with the author on November 4, 1997.
3 Stiles and Selz, p. 250.
4 All quotes from Ed Broida are from an interview with the author on November 6, 1997.
5 All quotes from Bob Kane are from an interview with the author on November 3, 1997.
6 Dore Ashton, *A Critical Study of Philip Guston* (Berkeley: University of California Press, 1976), p. 47.
7 Joan Simon, *An Interview with Elizabeth Murray* (New York: PaceWildenstein Gallery, 1997), n.p.
8 Stiles and Selz, p. 264.
9 Dore Ashton, *Jake Berthot* (New York: David McKee, Inc., 1982), n.p.
10 Laura Rosenstock, *Christopher Wilmarth* (New York: Museum of Modern Art, 1989), p. 11.
11 Ibid.
12 Chuck Close with William S. Bartman, eds., *An Interview with Vija Celmins* (New York: Art Press, 1992), p. 17.

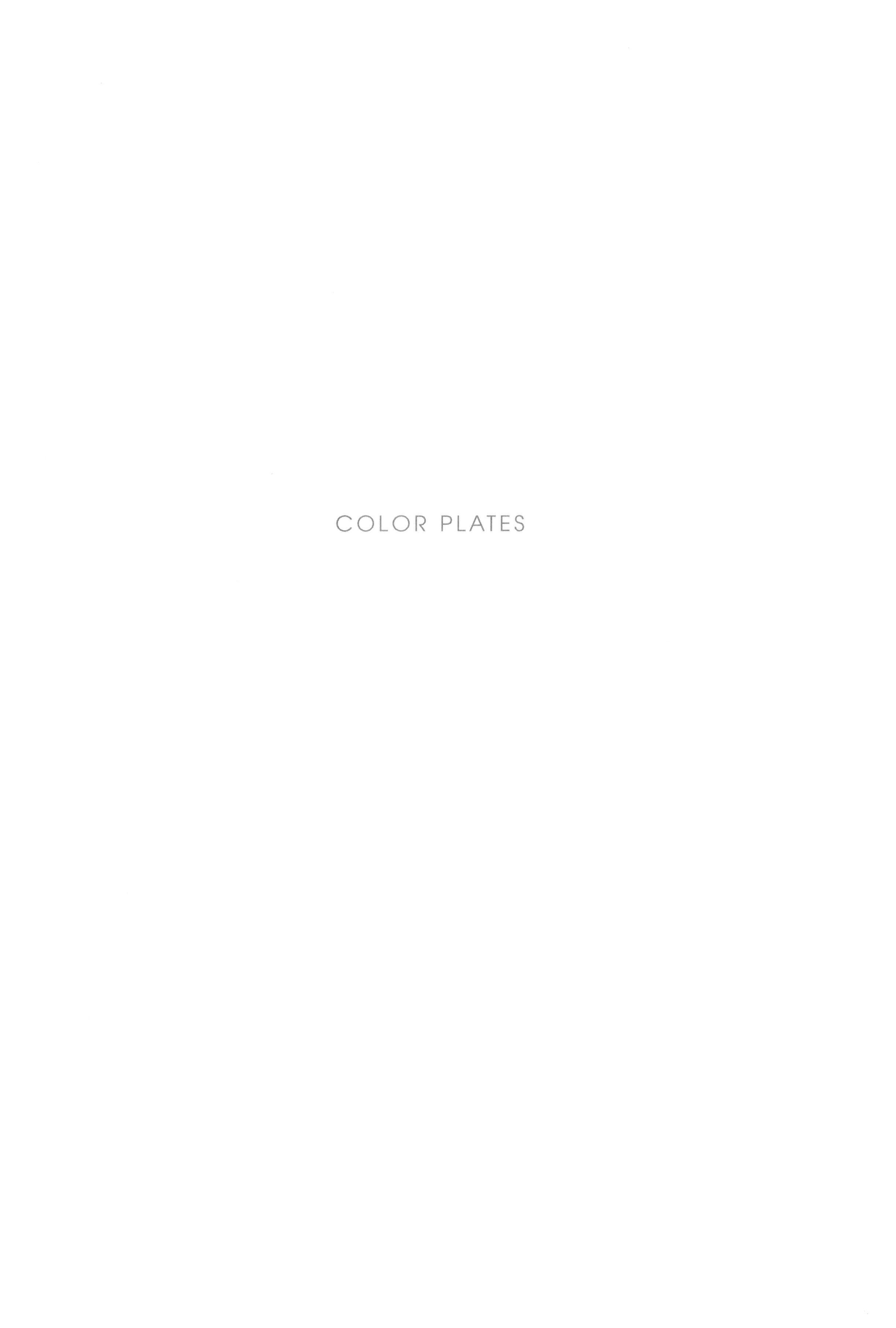

COLOR PLATES

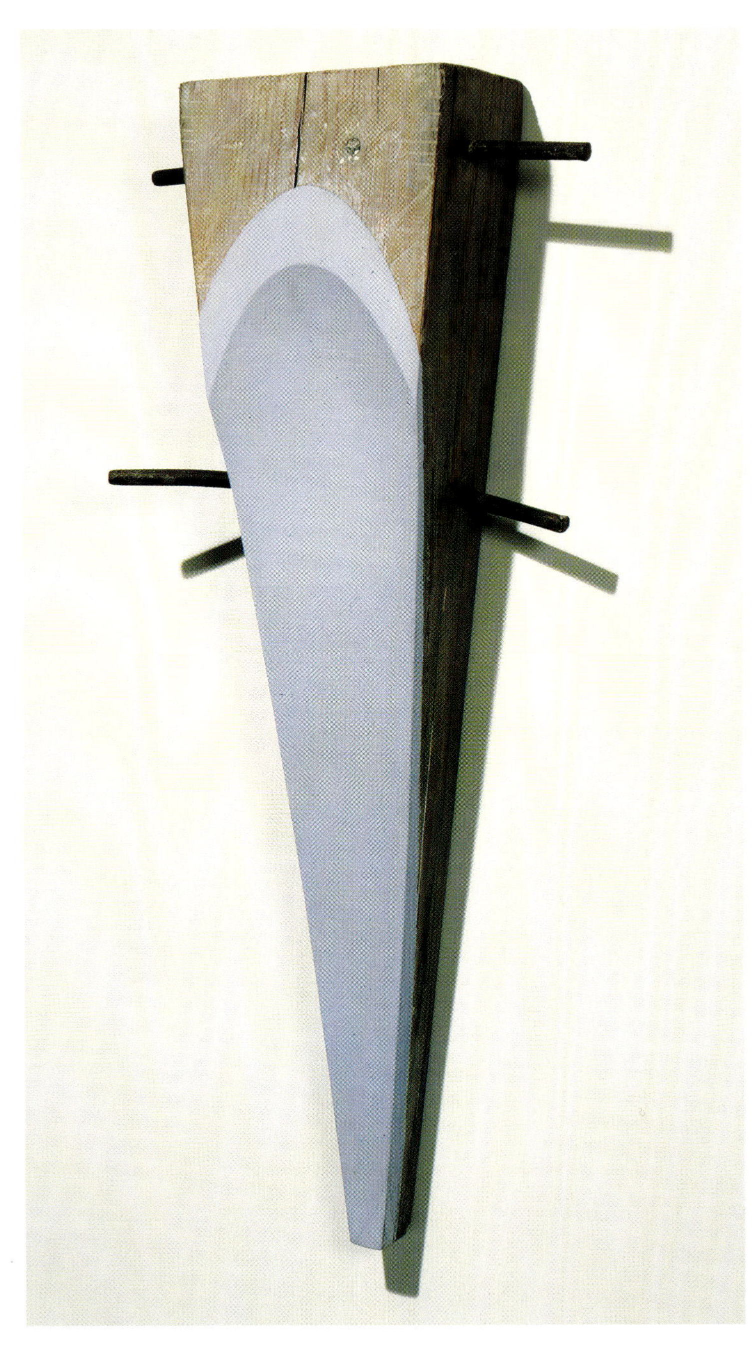

HANNO D. AHRENS, UNTITLED, 1985

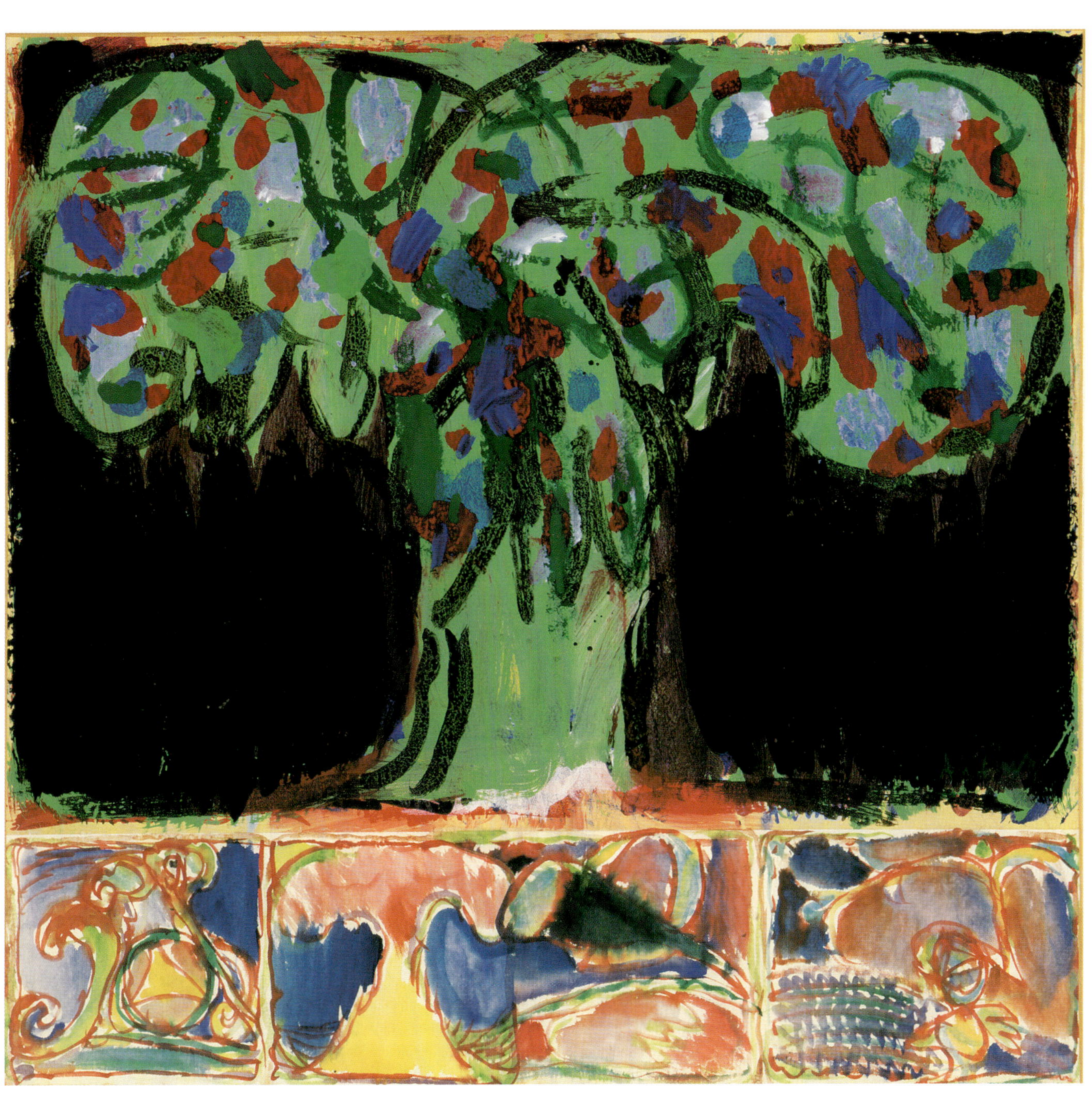

PIERRE ALECHINSKY, L'ARBRE EN ACTIVITE, 1973

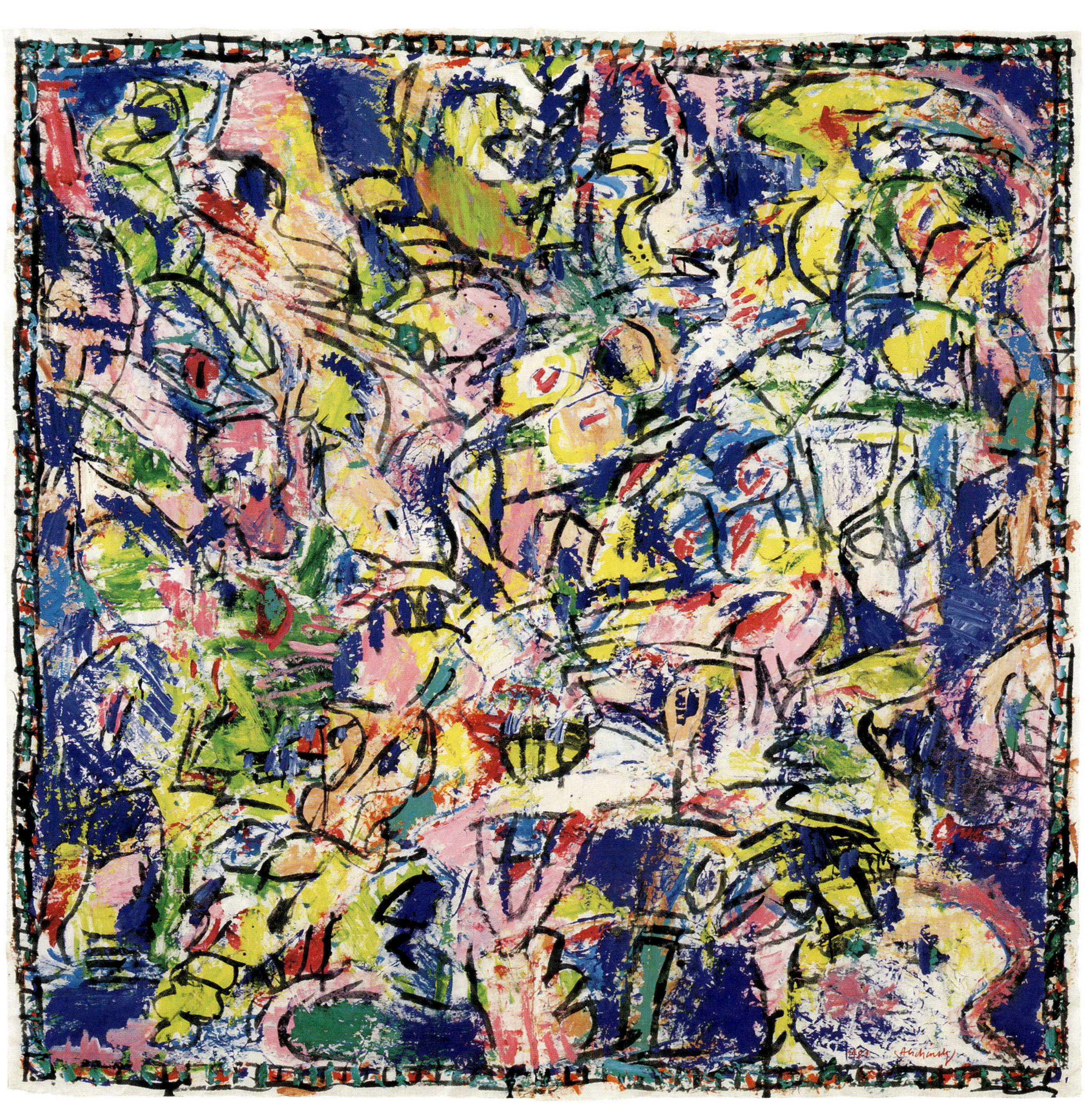

PIERRE ALECHINSKY, TO THE FOUR WINDS, 1981

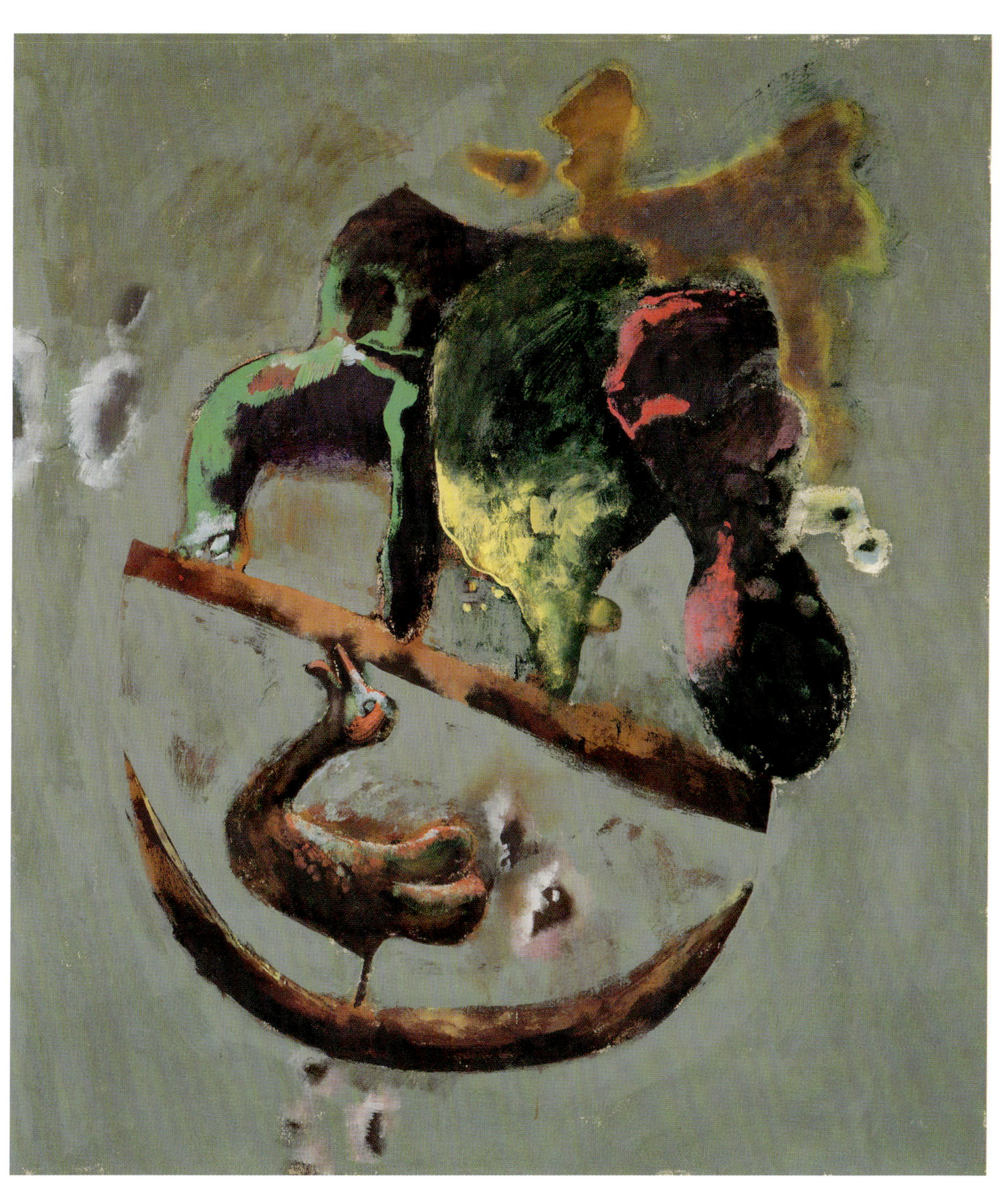

JOHN ALTOON, HAIRCUT #2, 1965

JOSEPH AMAR, UNTITLED, 1986

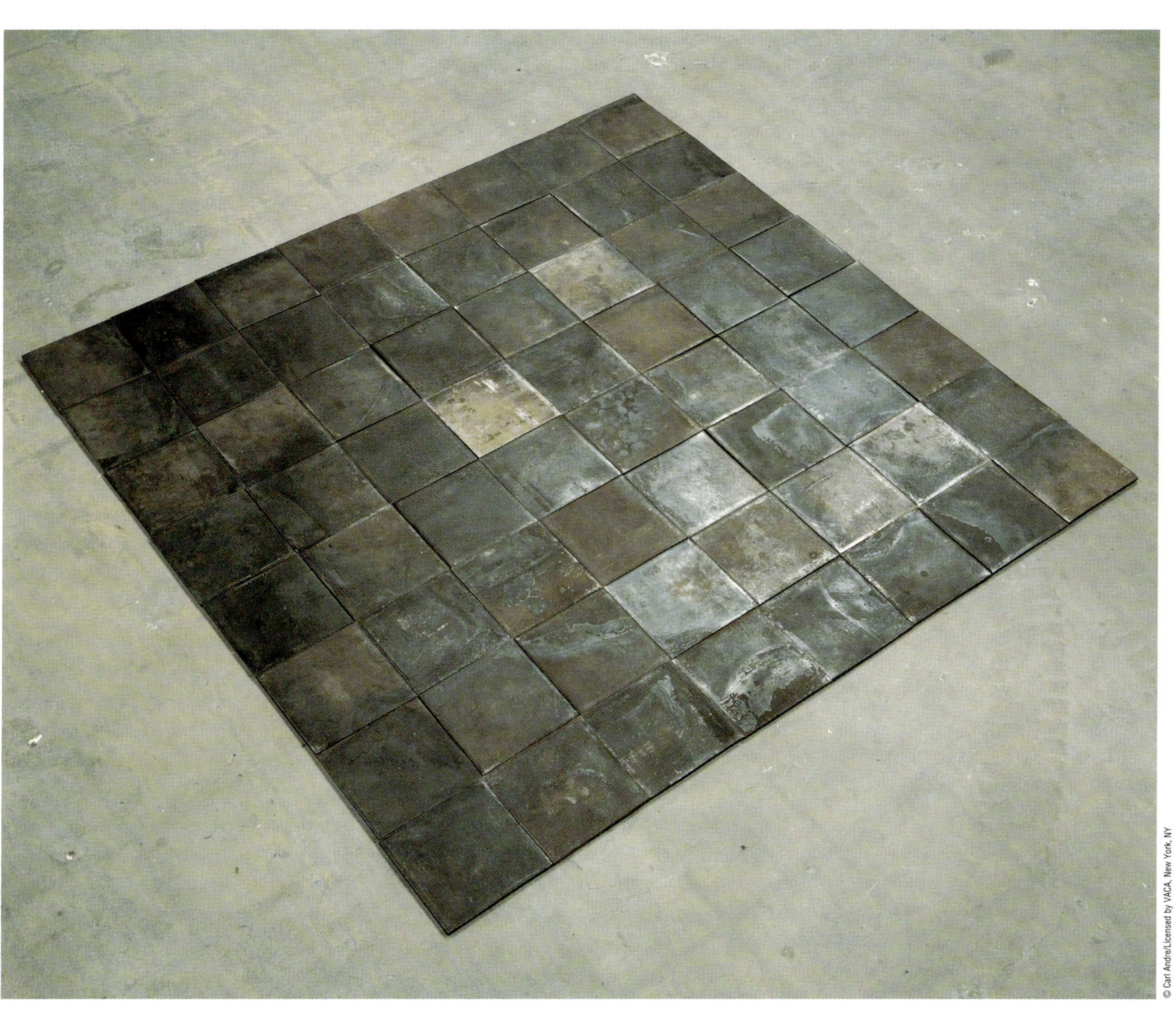

CARL ANDRE, 64 STEEL SQUARE, 1967

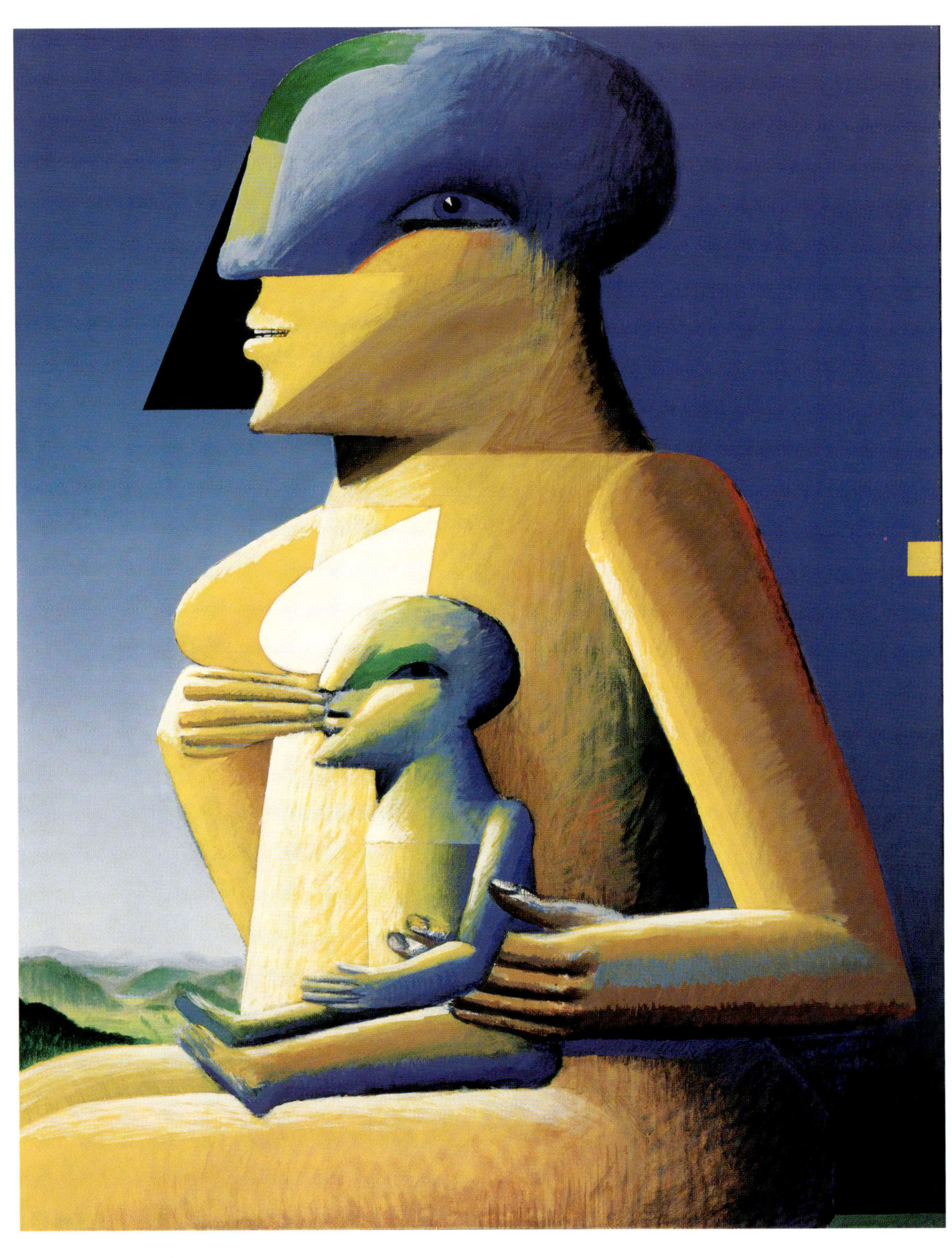

HORST ANTES, MOTHER AND CHILD, 1973-74

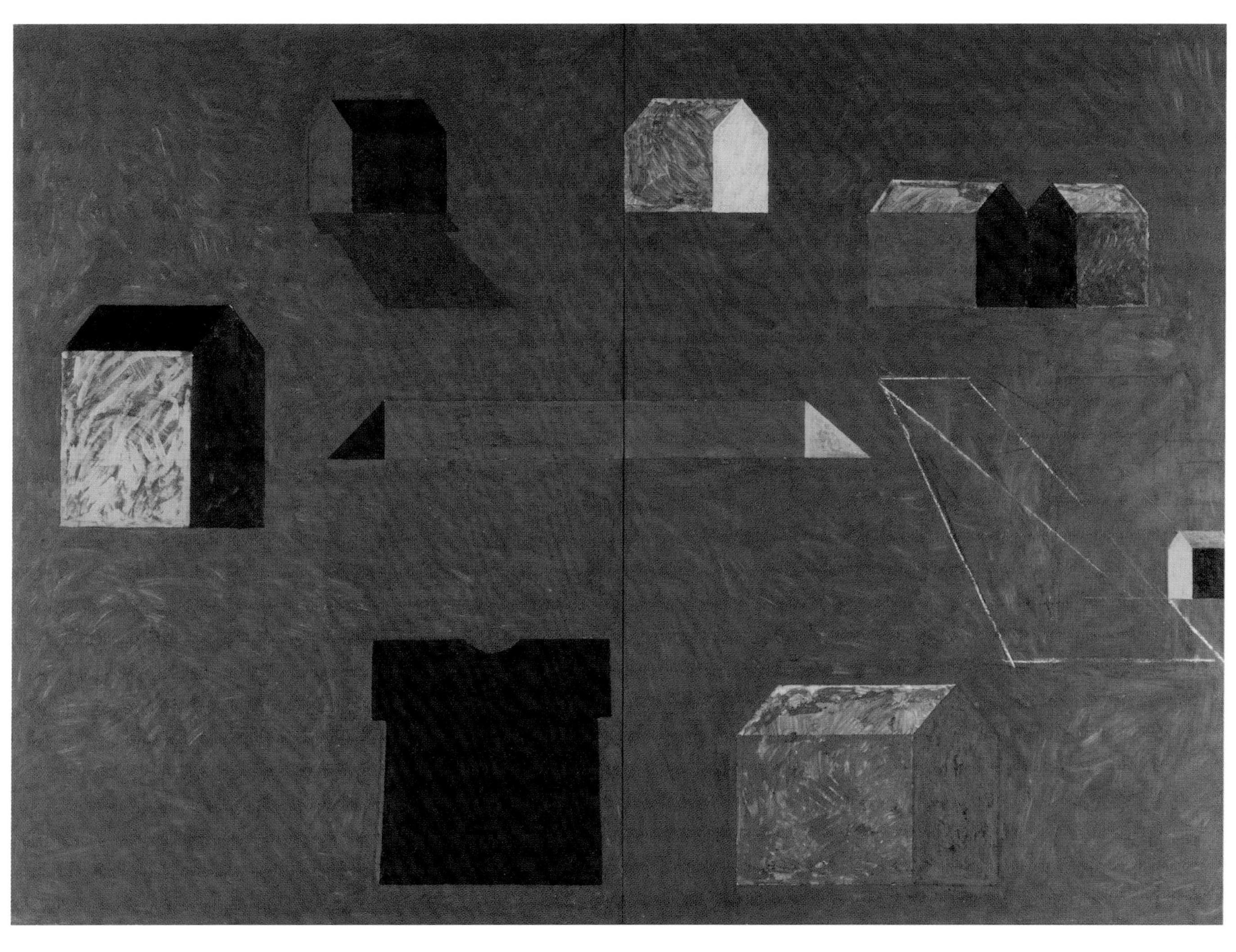

HORST ANTES, 7 HÄUSER, 2 HEMDEN, 1993

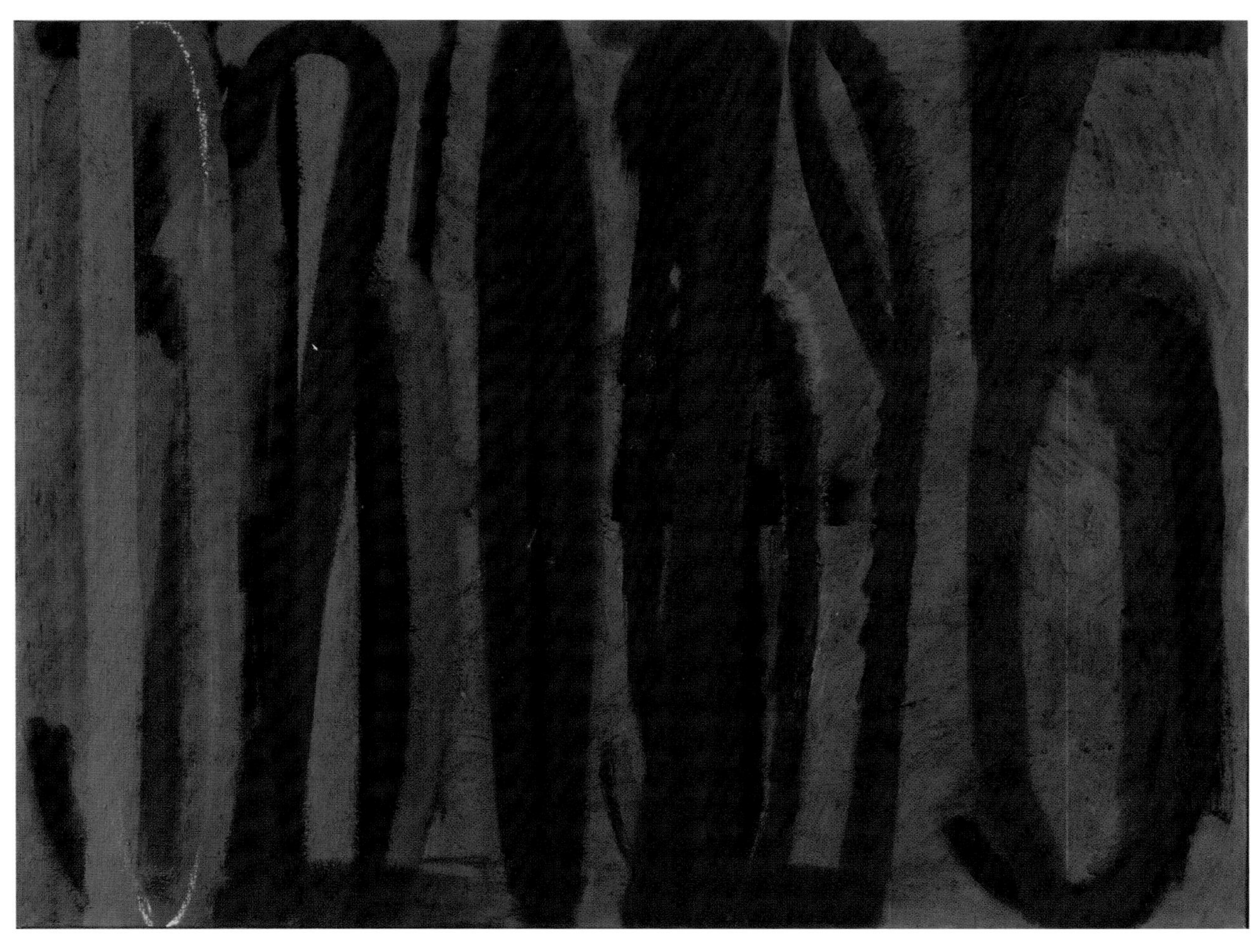

HORST ANTES. 14.2.95/15.2.95/16.2.95/17.2.95/09.3.95/28.4.95/30.4.95/01.5.95/02.5.95/03.5.95/4.5.95/15.5.95/16.5.95/17.5.95/18.5.95/19.5.95/20.5.95/21.5.95/24.6.95/25.6.95/27.6.95/28.6.95, 1995-96

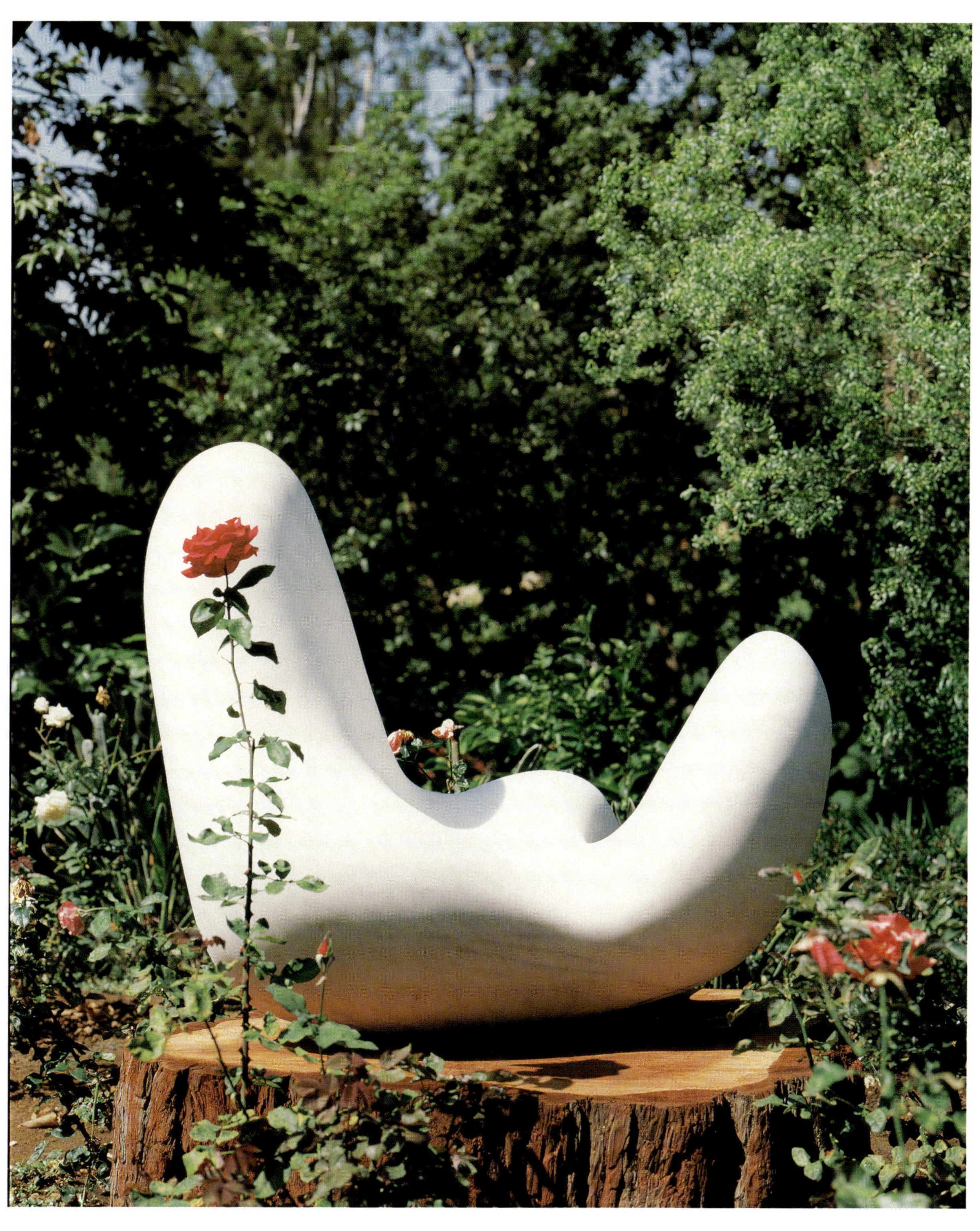

JEAN ARP, SCULPTURE DE SILENCE CORNEILLE, 1942-64

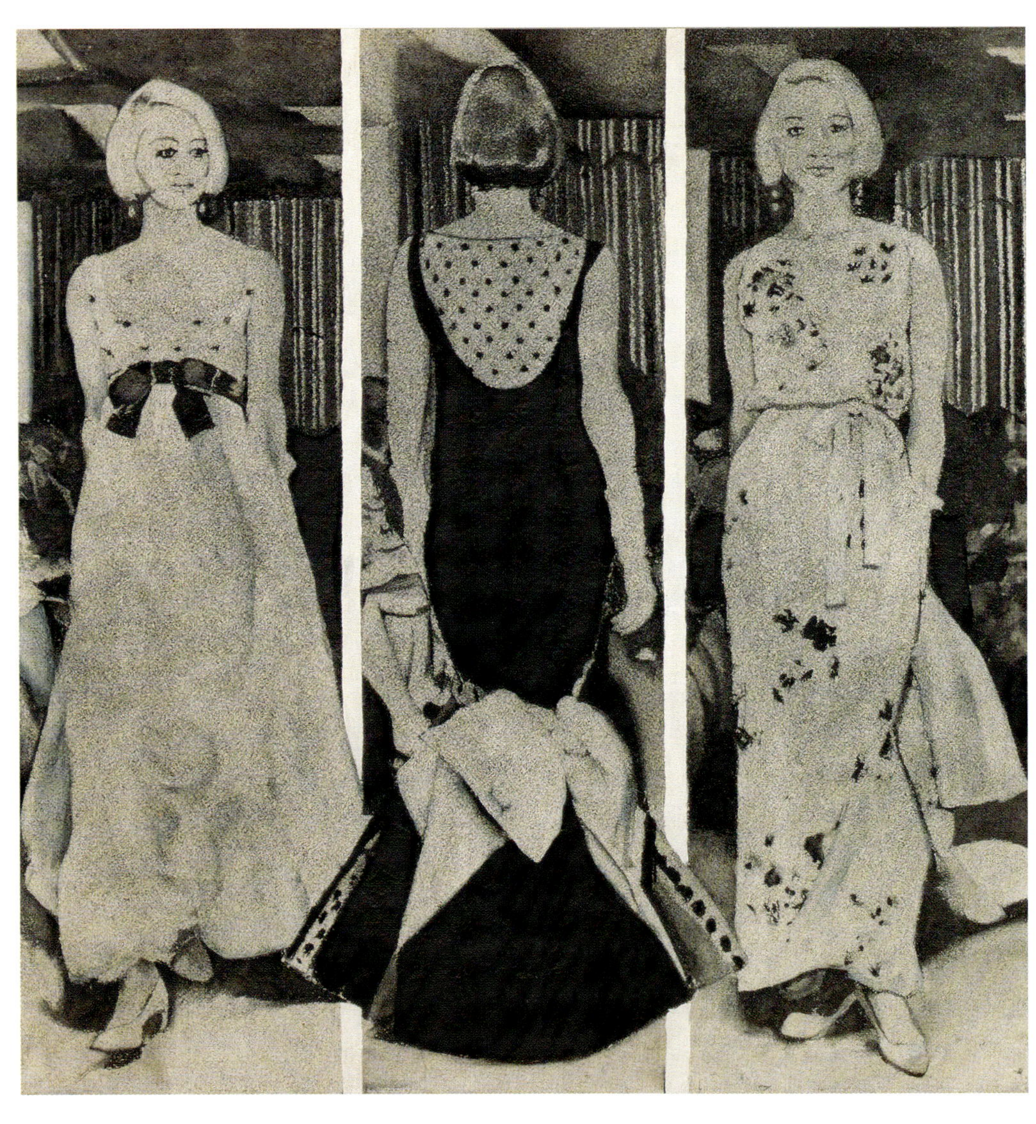

RICHARD ARTSCHWAGER, *WOMAN*, 1963

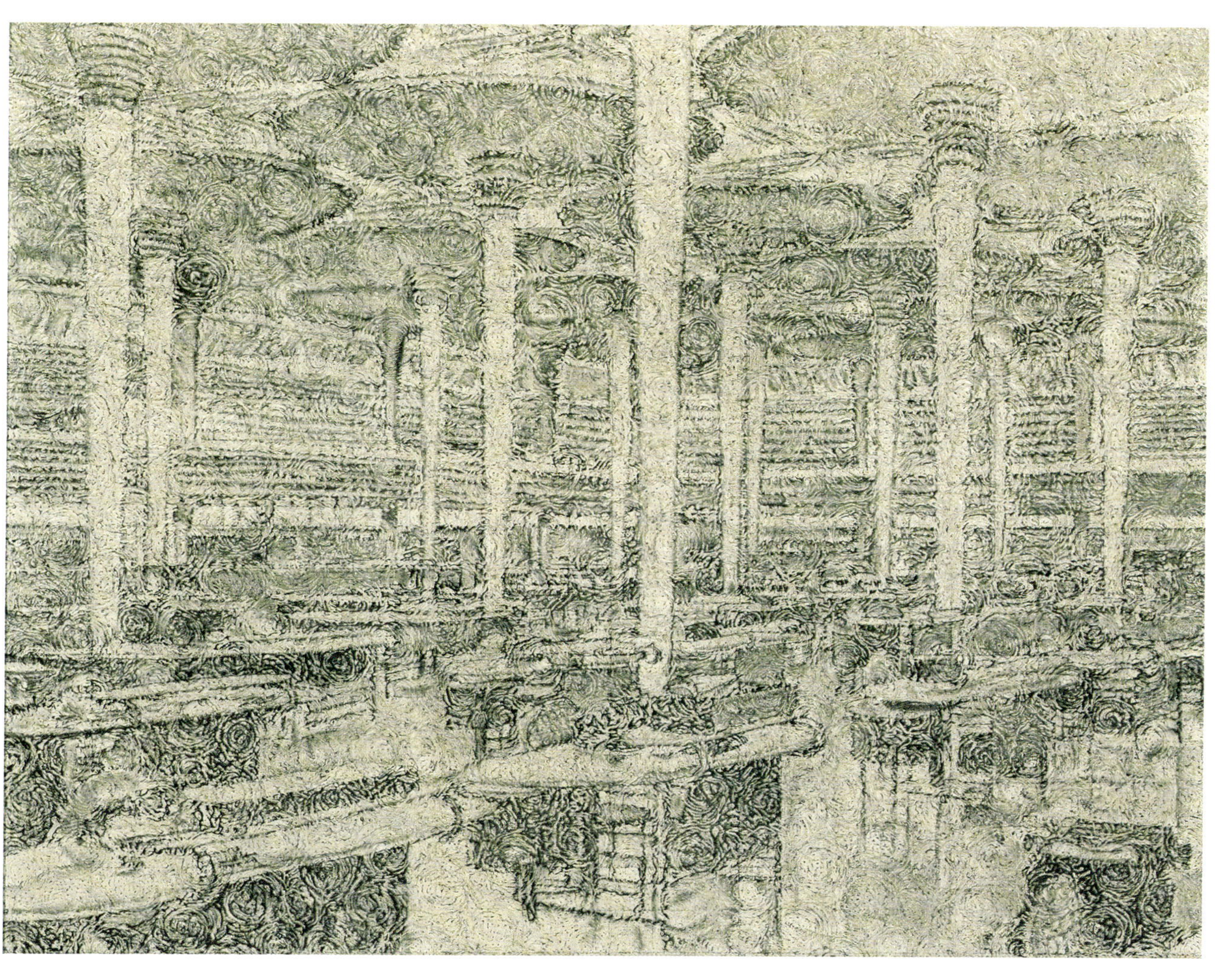

RICHARD ARTSCHWAGER, JOHNSON WAX BUILDING, 1974

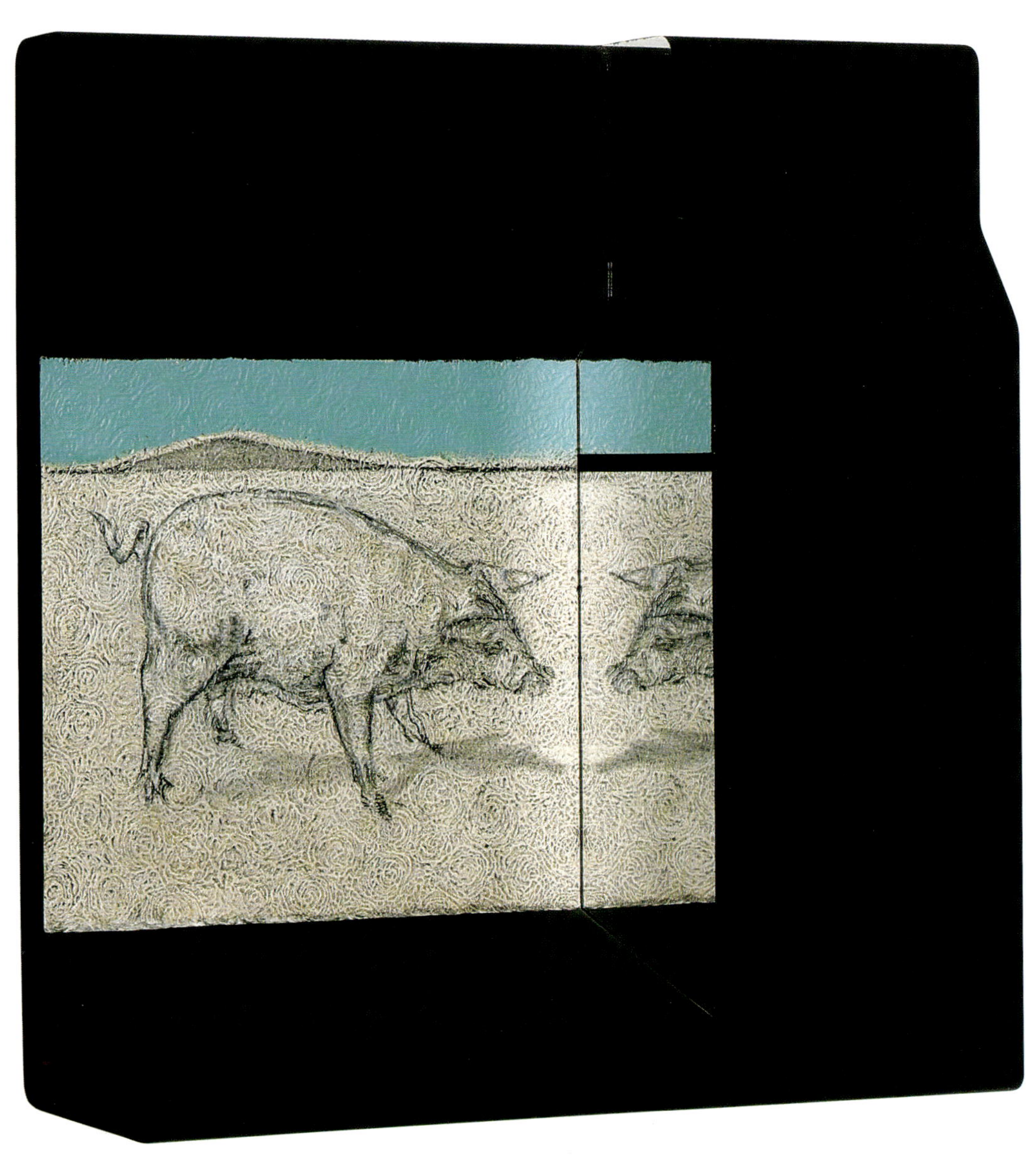

RICHARD ARTSCHWAGER, PIG PIG, 1984

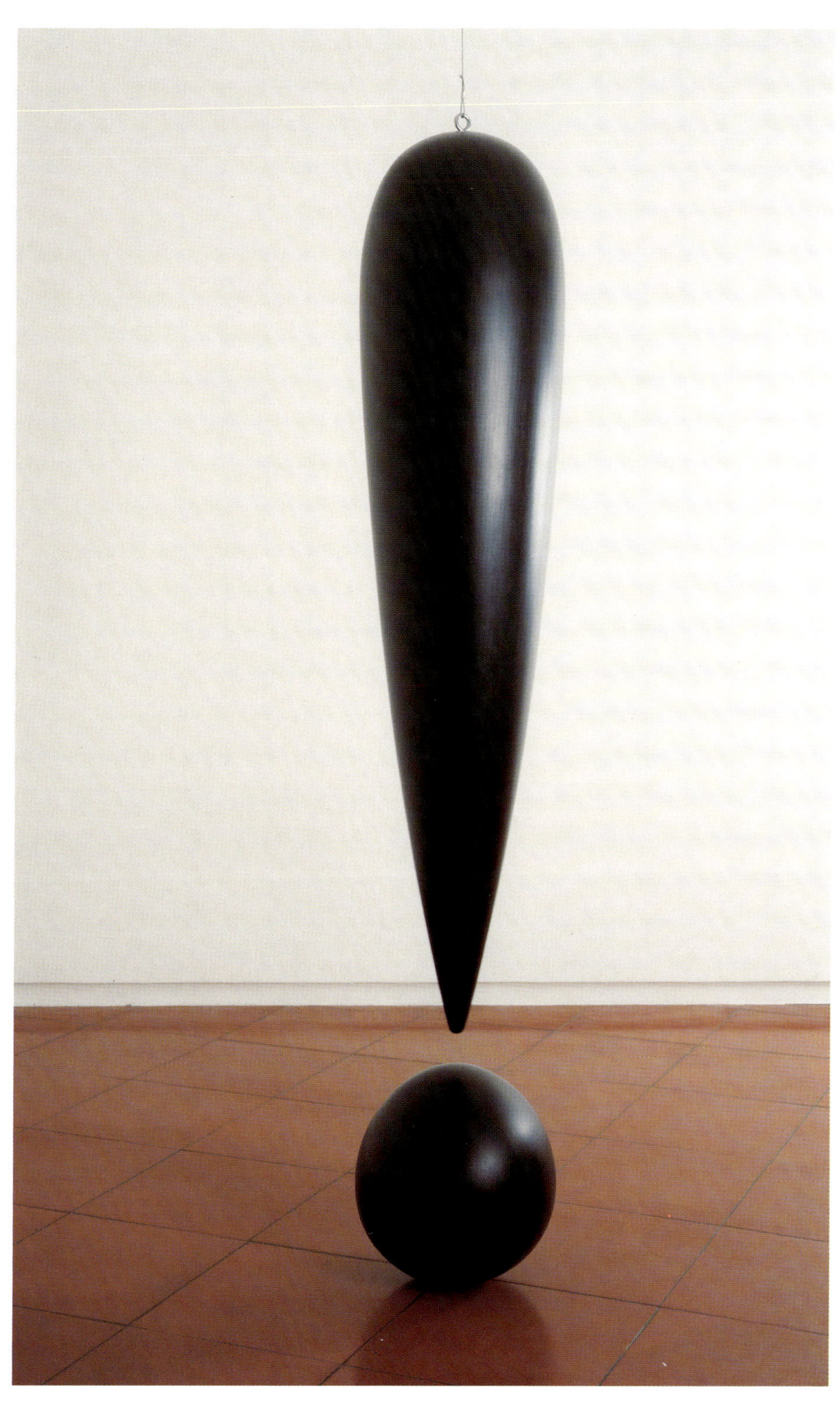

RICHARD ARTSCHWAGER, EXCLAMATION, 1994

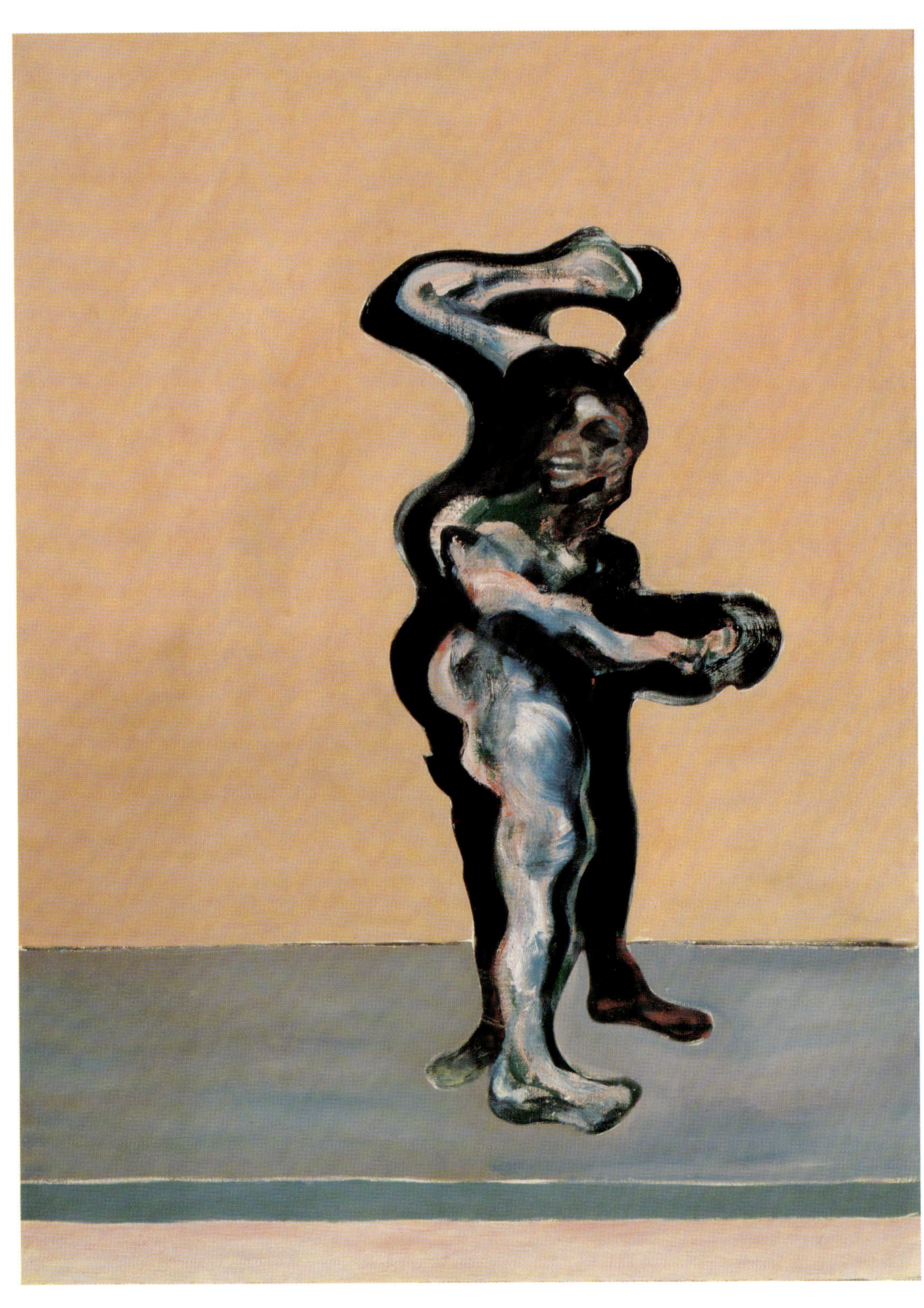

FRANCIS BACON, TWO FIGURES, 1961

JAKE BERTHOT, GREENPOINT, 1971

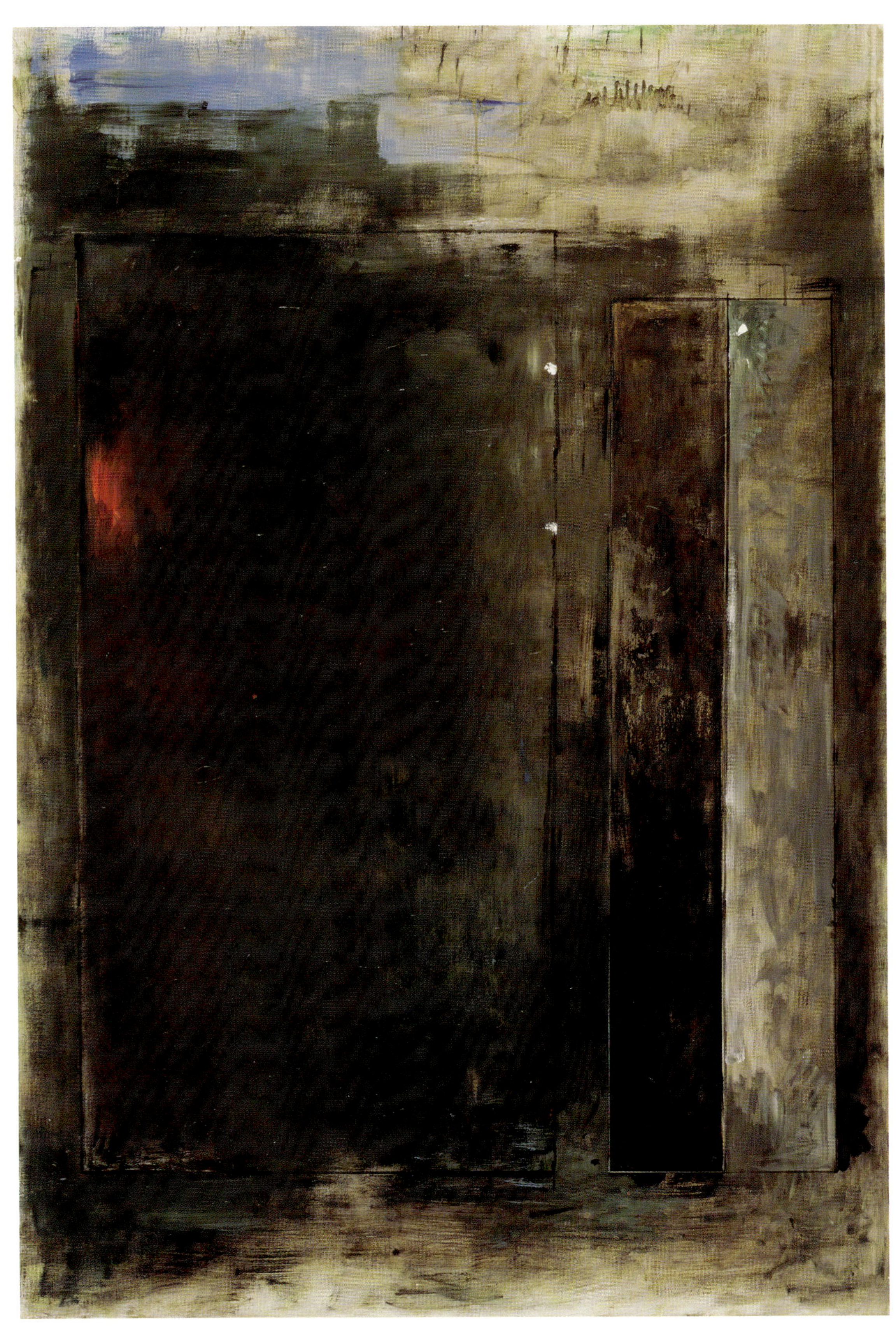

JAKE BERTHOT, BELFAST, 1981

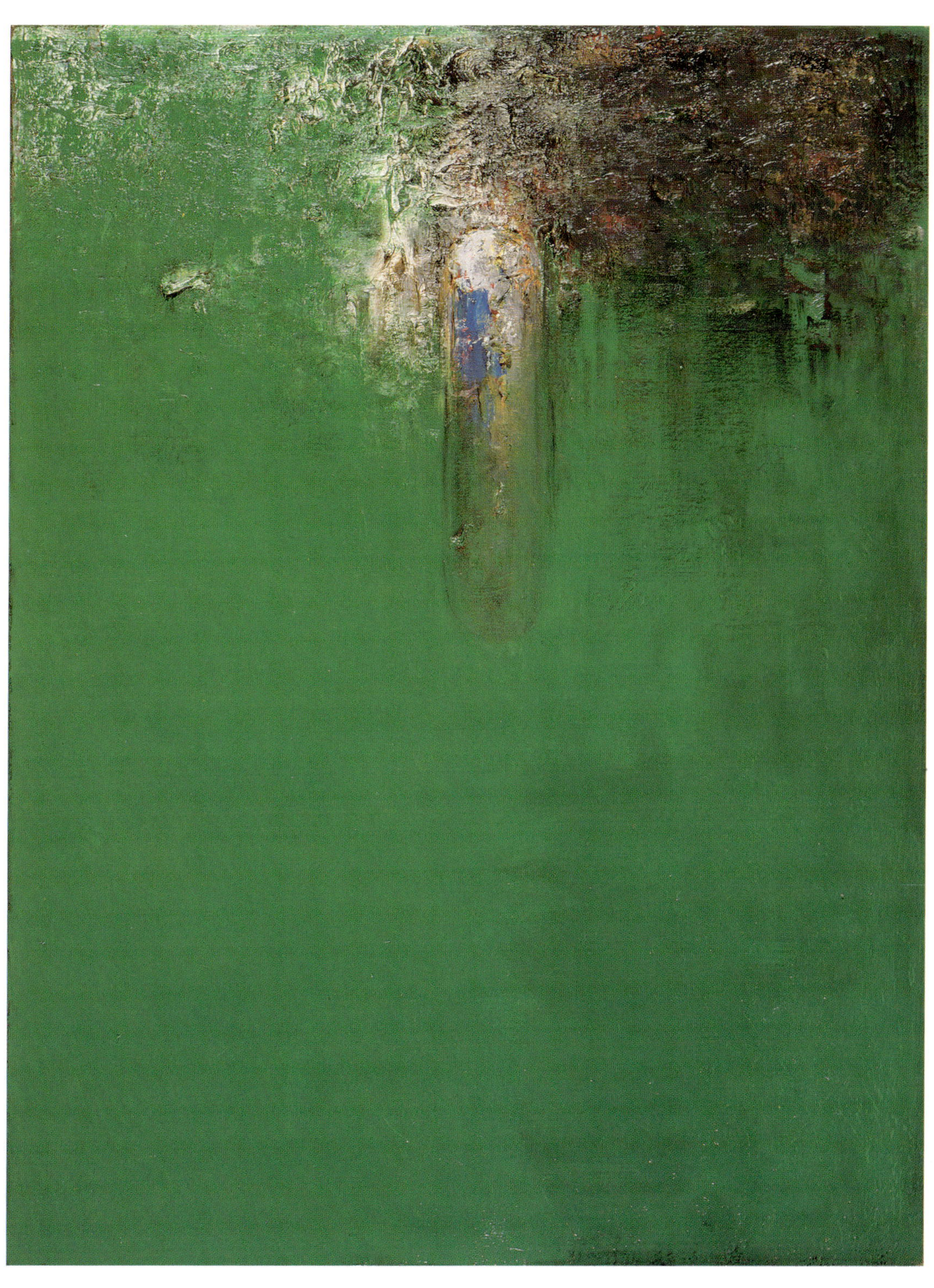

JAKE BERTHOT, ANAWANDA, 1985

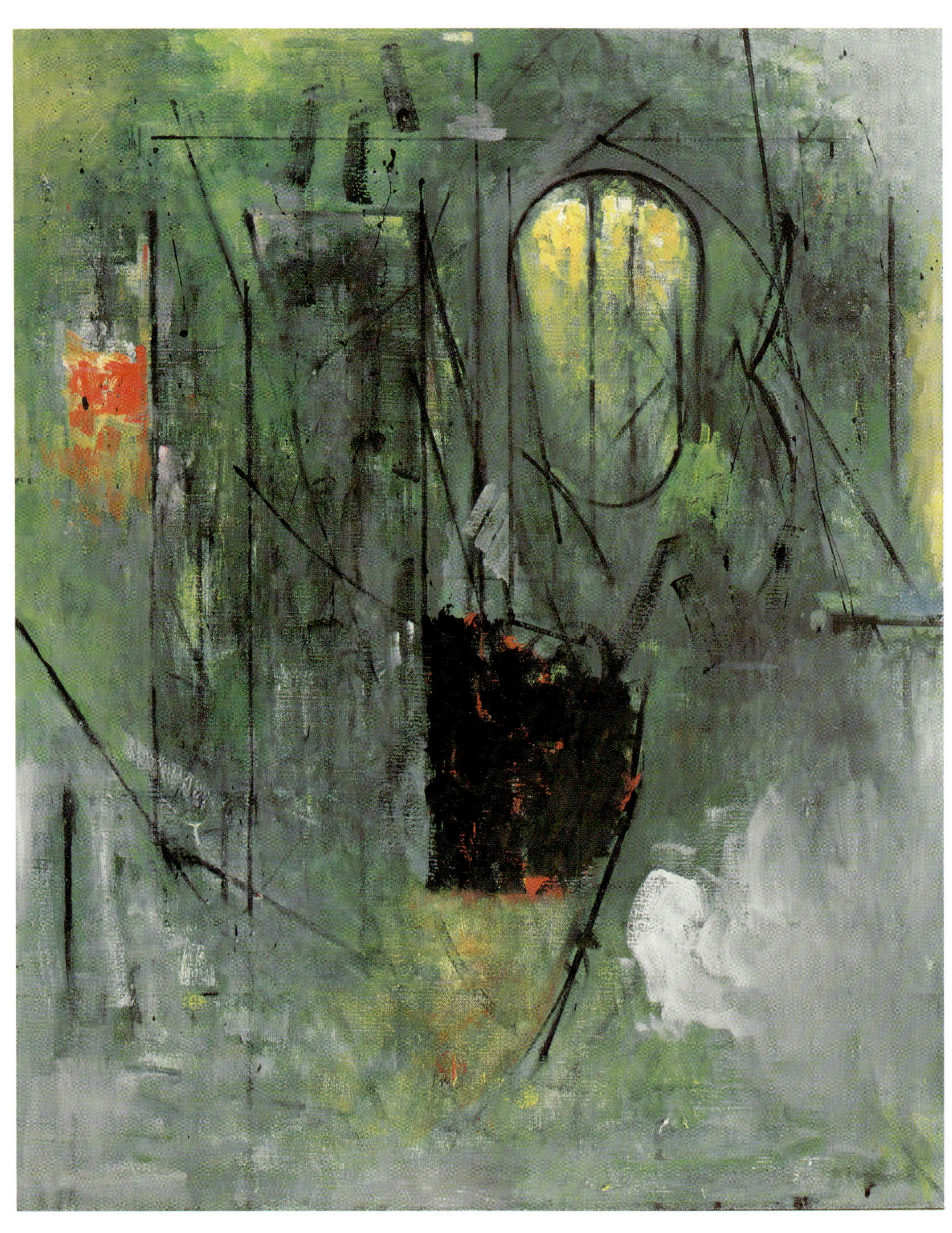

JAKE BERTHOT, NYMPH, 1991

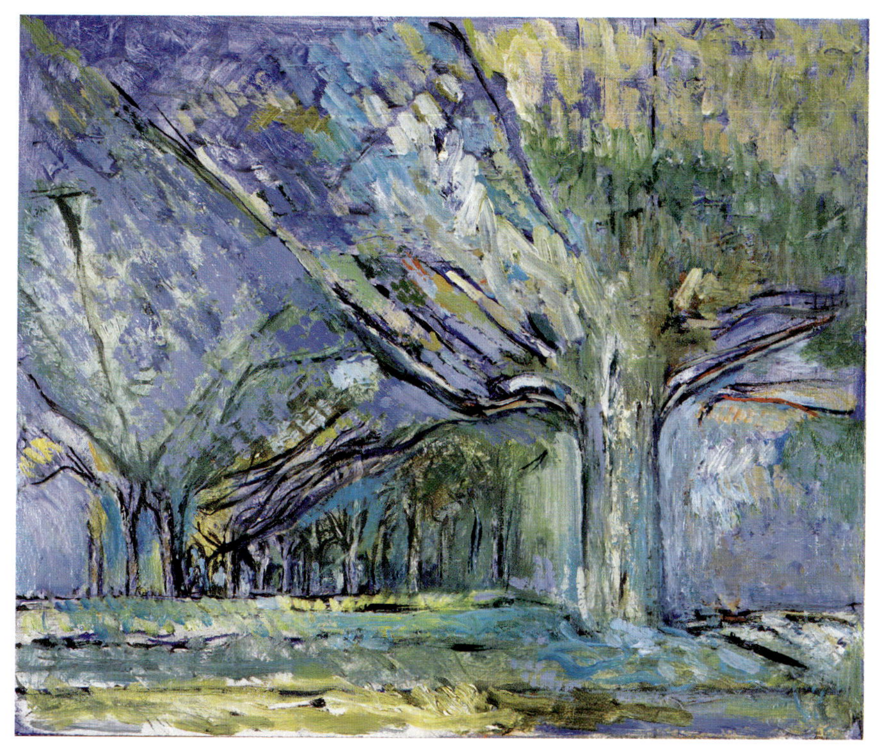

JAKE BERTHOT, OFF LOWER BONE HOLLOW, 1997

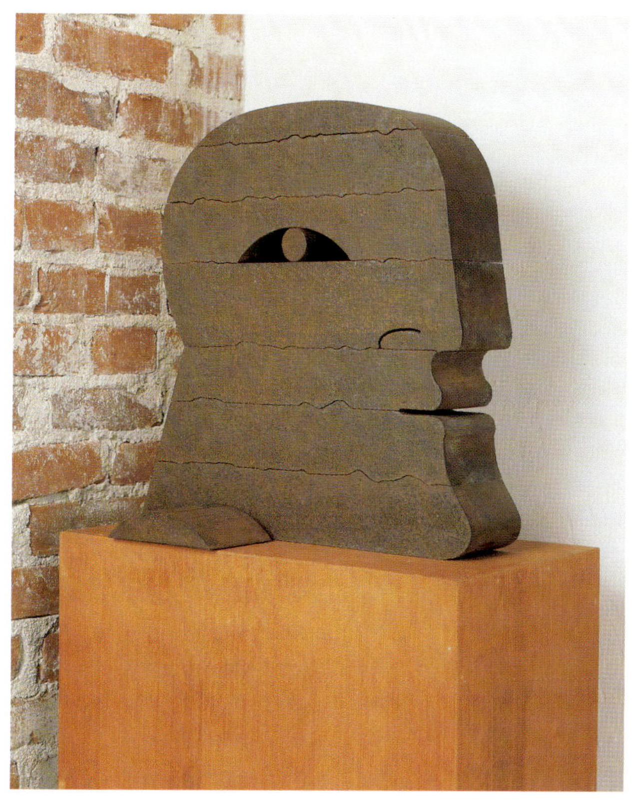

HORST ANTES, HEAD CONSISTING OF NINE SEPARATE PARTS, 1979

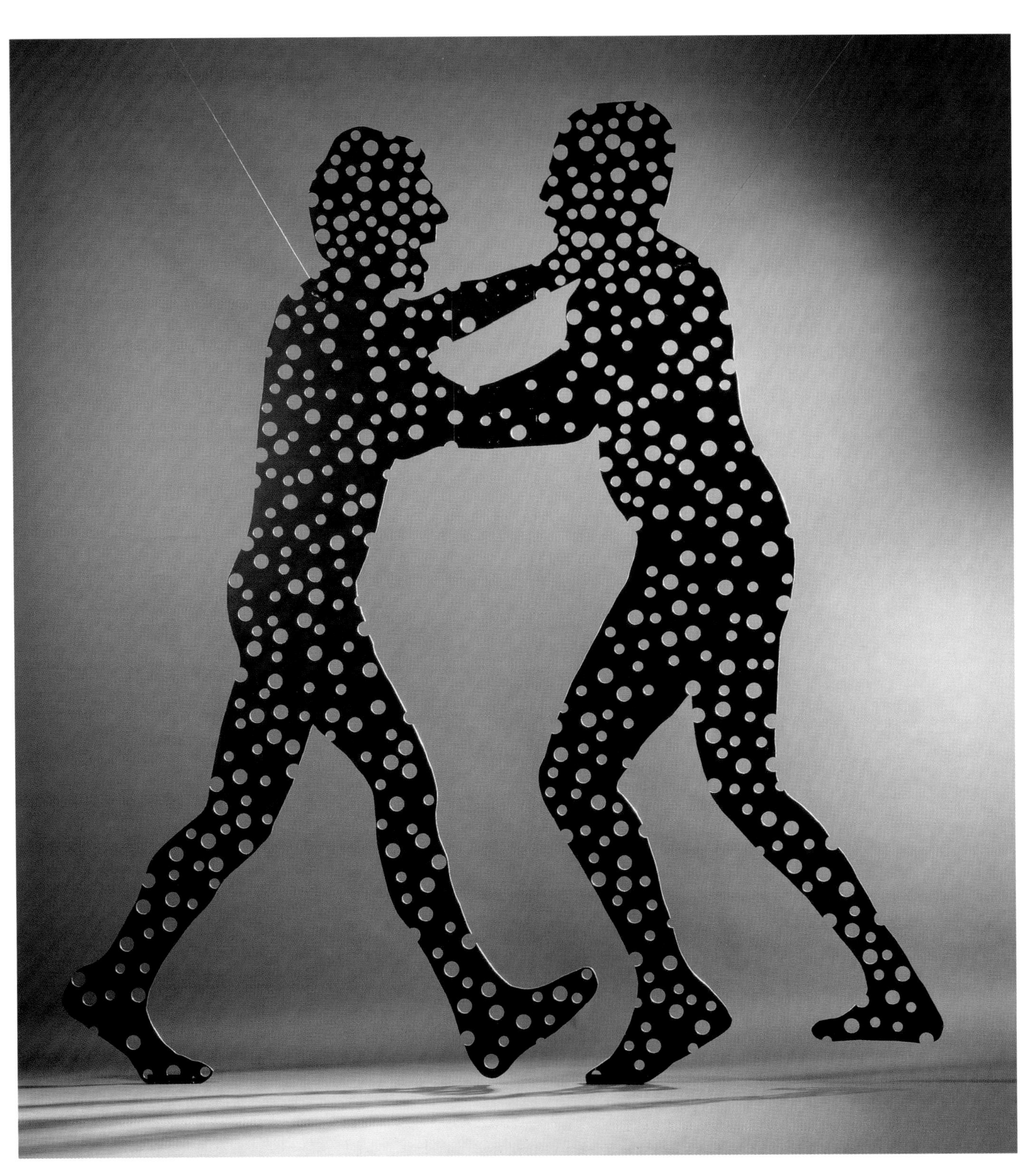

JONATHAN BOROFSKY, 2,845,318 MOLECULE MEN, 1982-83

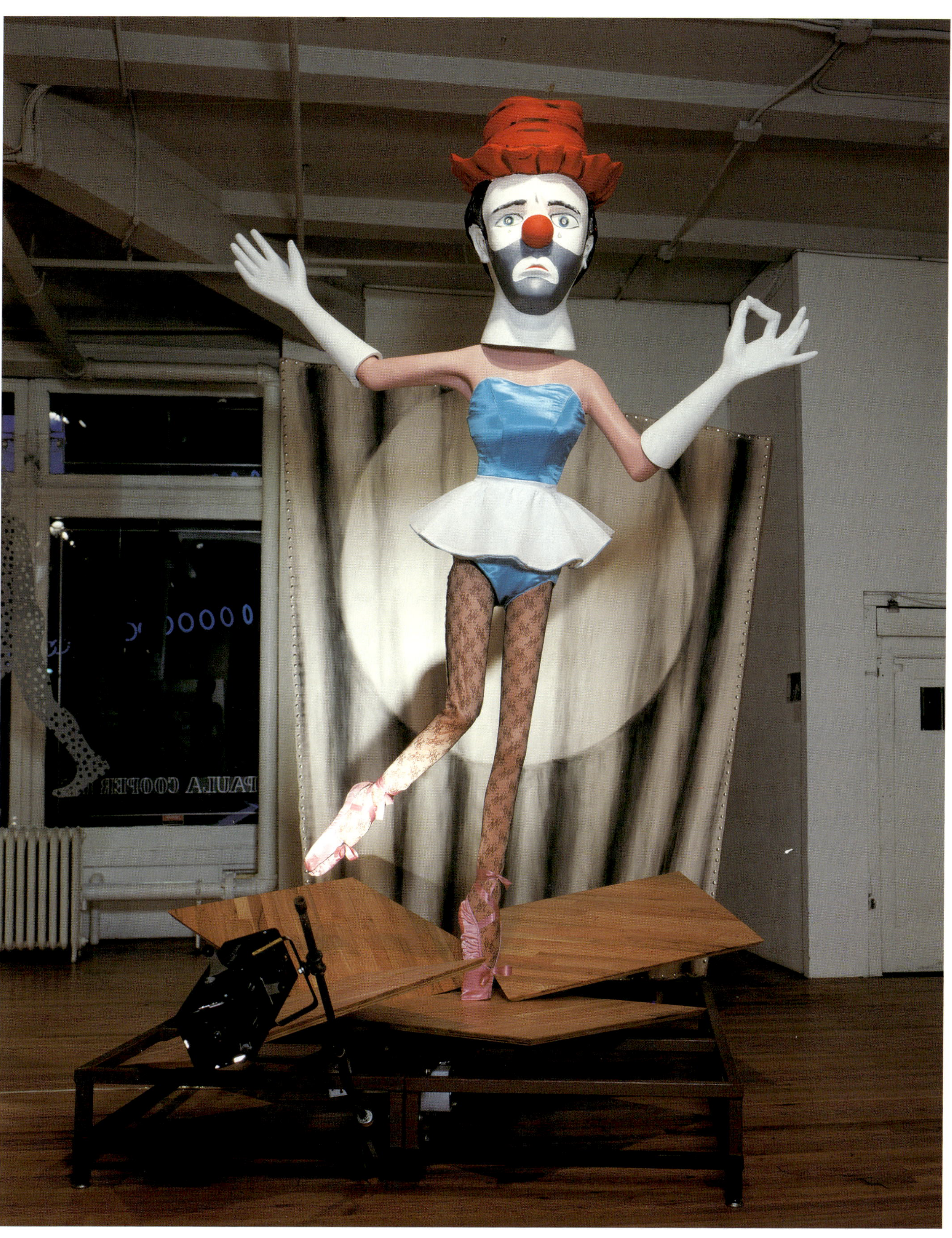

JONATHAN BOROFSKY, THE DANCING CLOWN AT 2,845,325, 1982-83

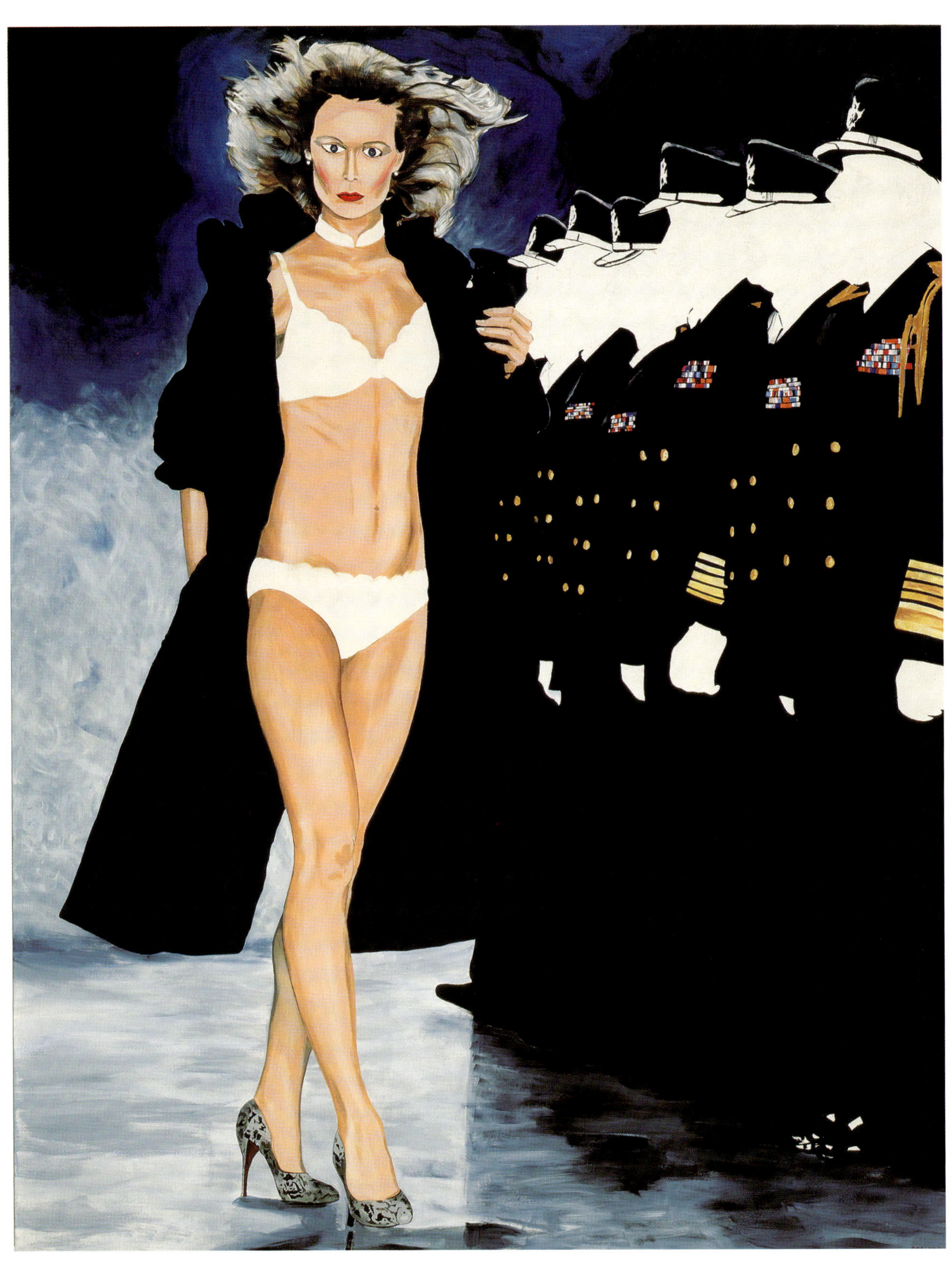

JONATHAN BOROFSKY, 2,841,779 MAIDENFORM WOMAN, YOU NEVER KNOW WHERE SHE'LL TURN UP, 1983

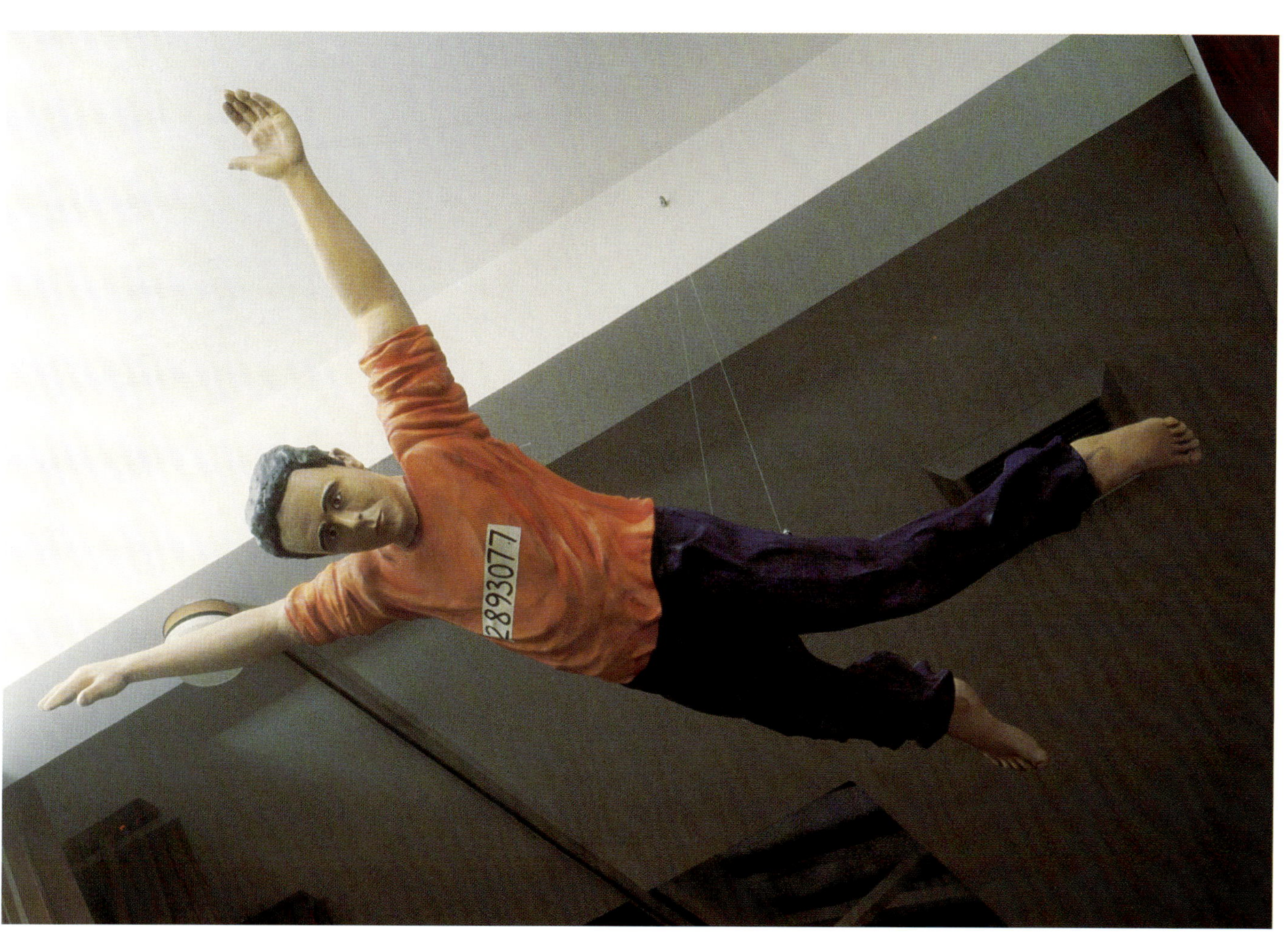

JONATHAN BOROFSKY, I DREAMED I COULD FLY AT 2,893,007, 1984

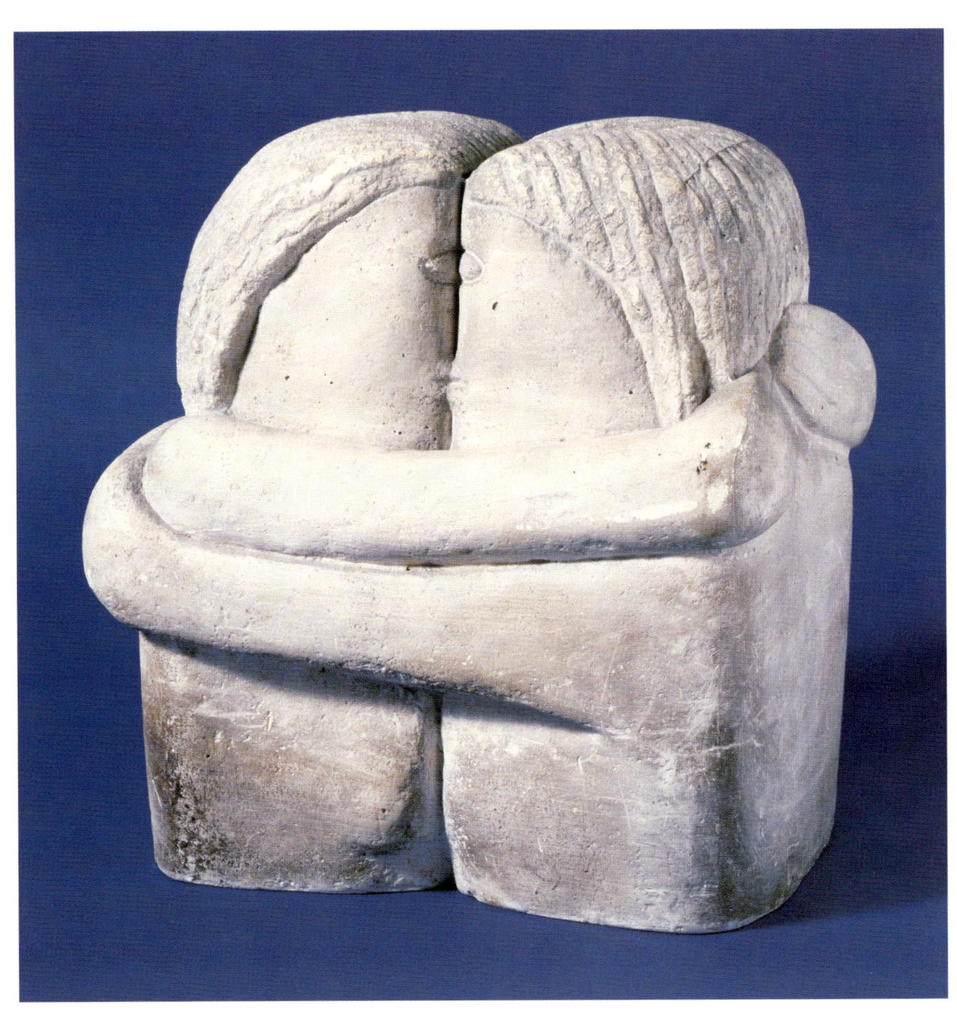

CONSTANTIN BRANCUSI, THE KISS, 1907-08

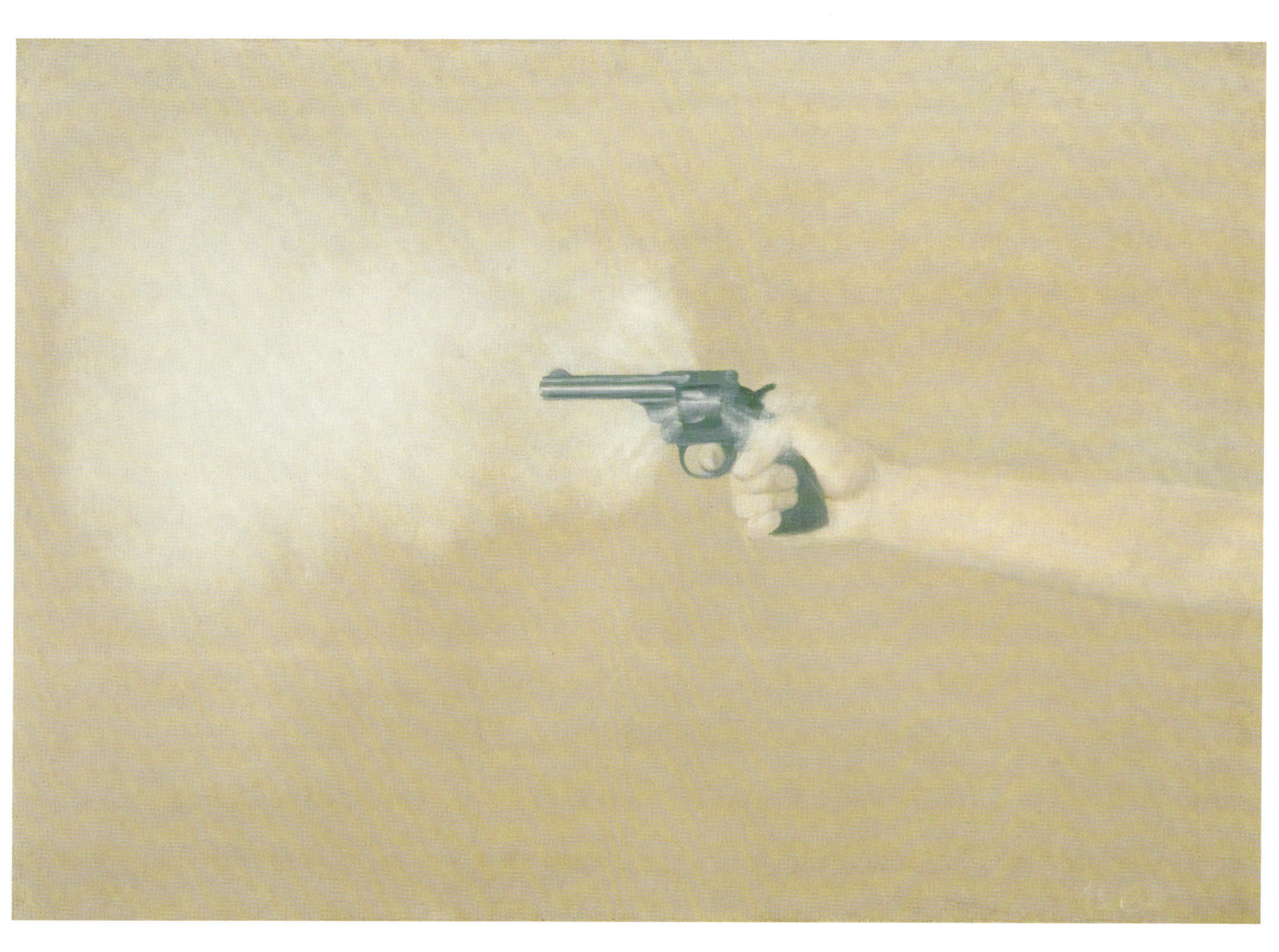

VIJA CELMINS, GUN WITH HAND #1, 1964

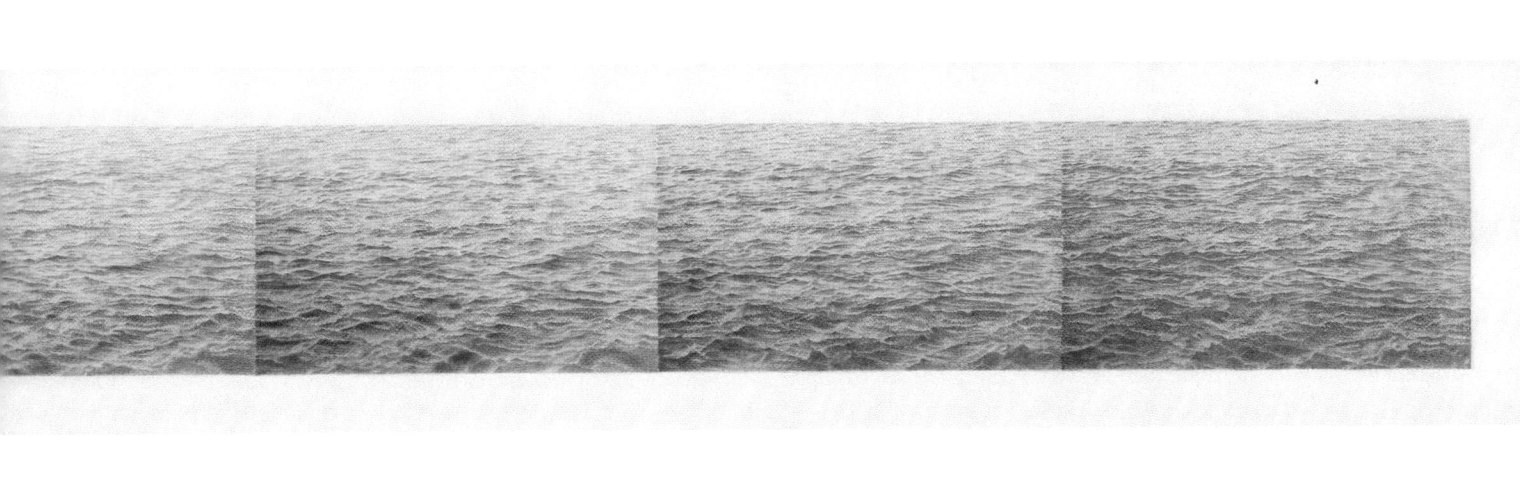

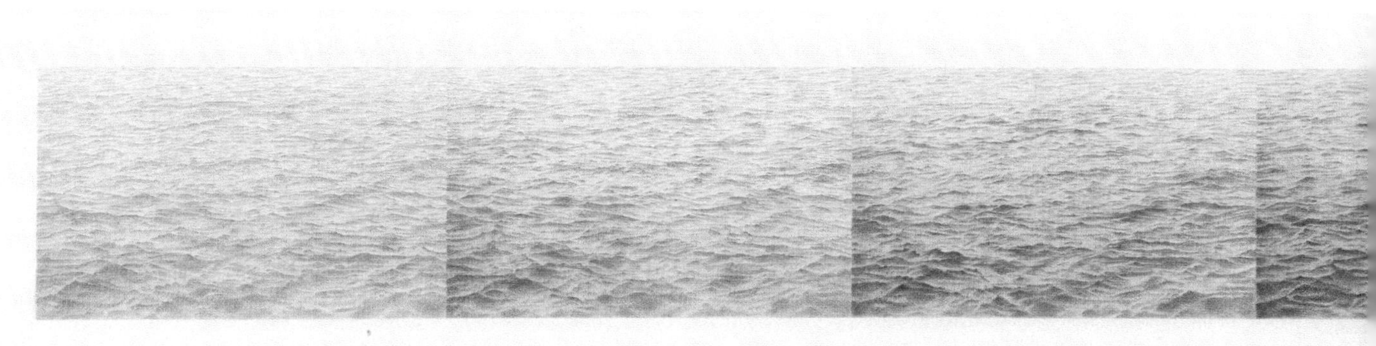

VIJA CELMINS, OCEAN, 7 STEPS #2, 1972-73

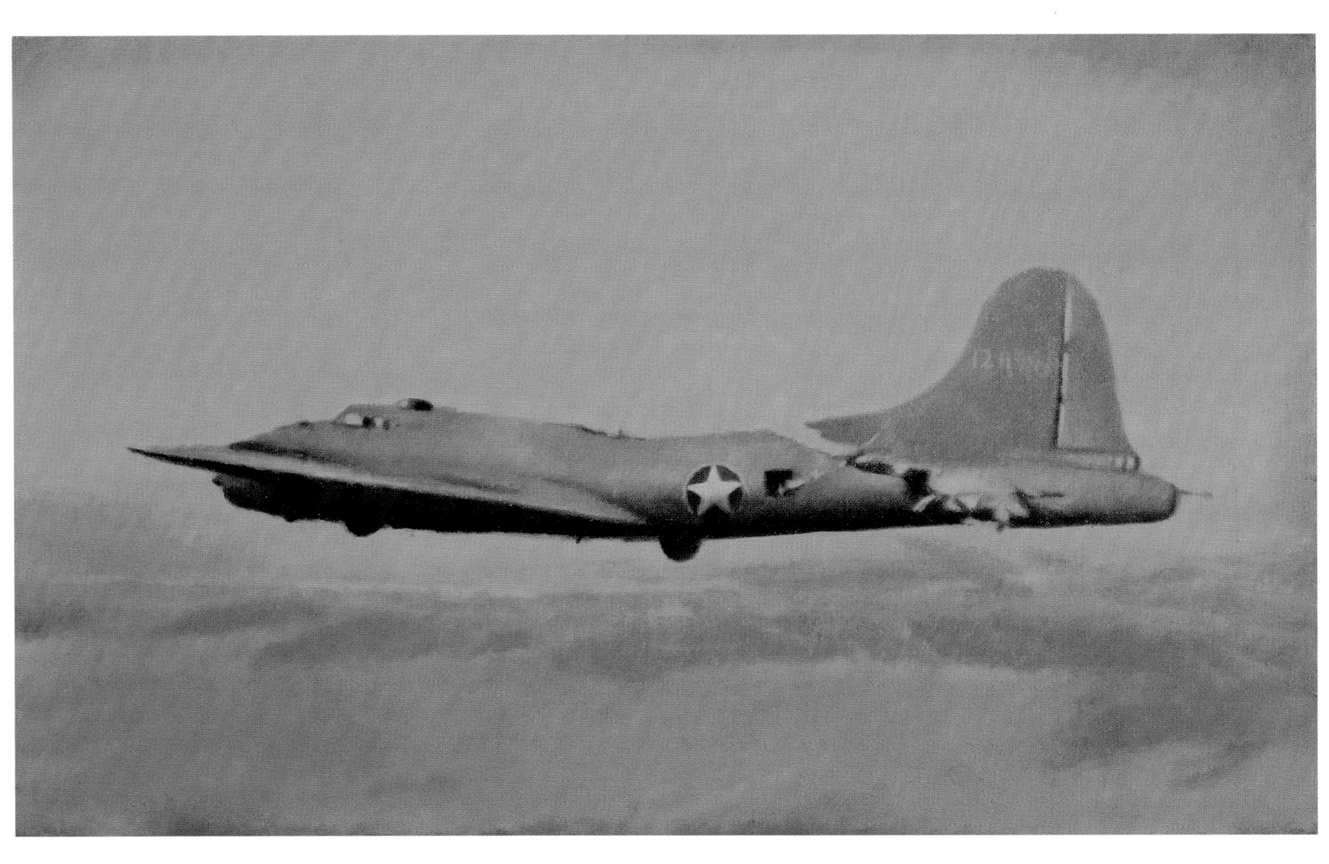

VIJA CELMINS, FLYING FORTRESS, 1966

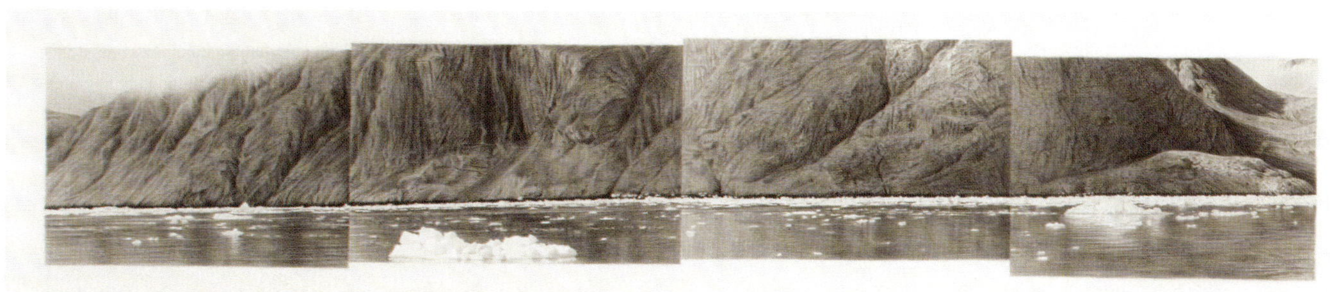

VIJA CELMINS, GLACIER BAY, 1975

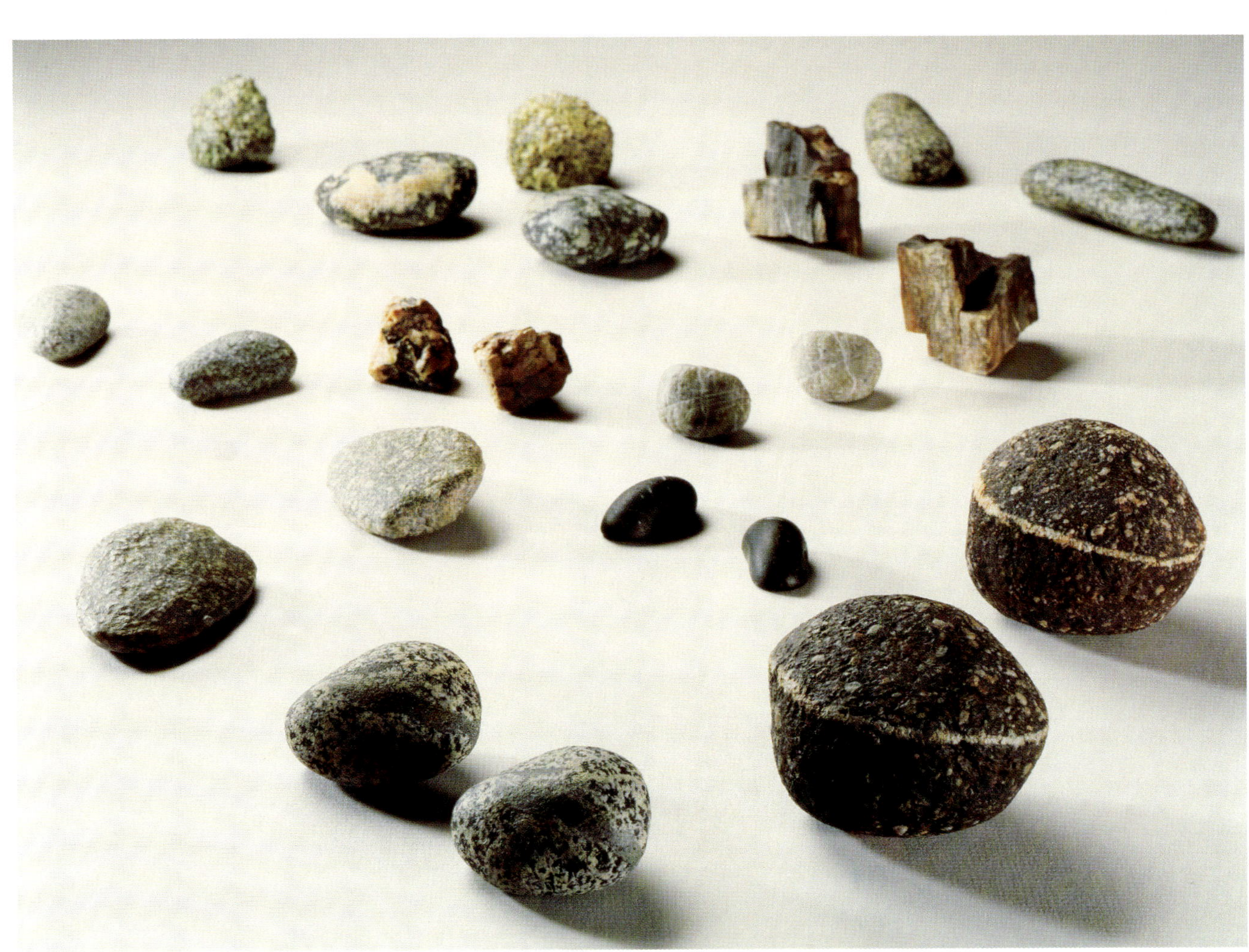

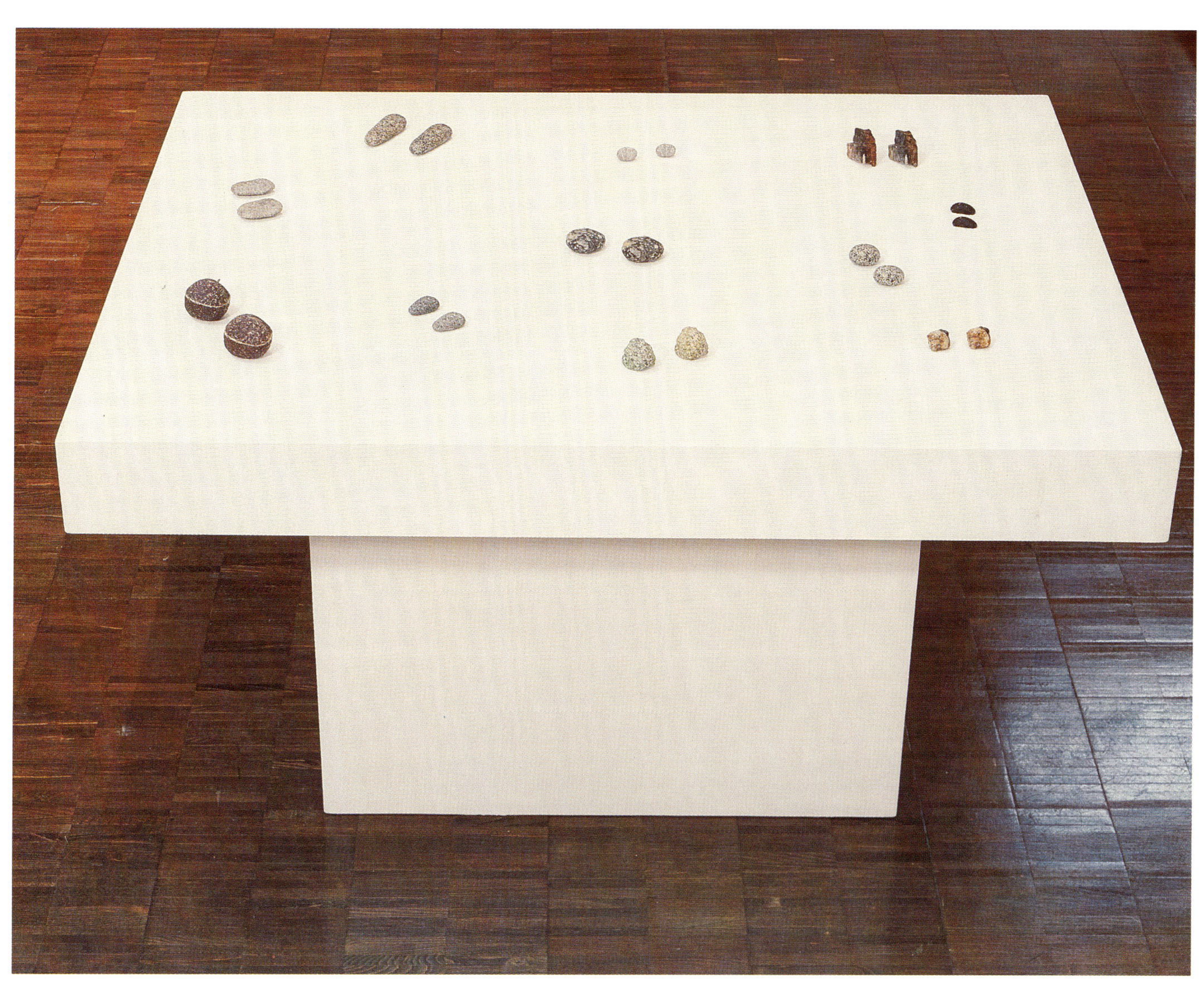

VIJA CELMINS, TO FIX THE IMAGE IN MEMORY, 1977-82, (INSTALLATION AND DETAIL)

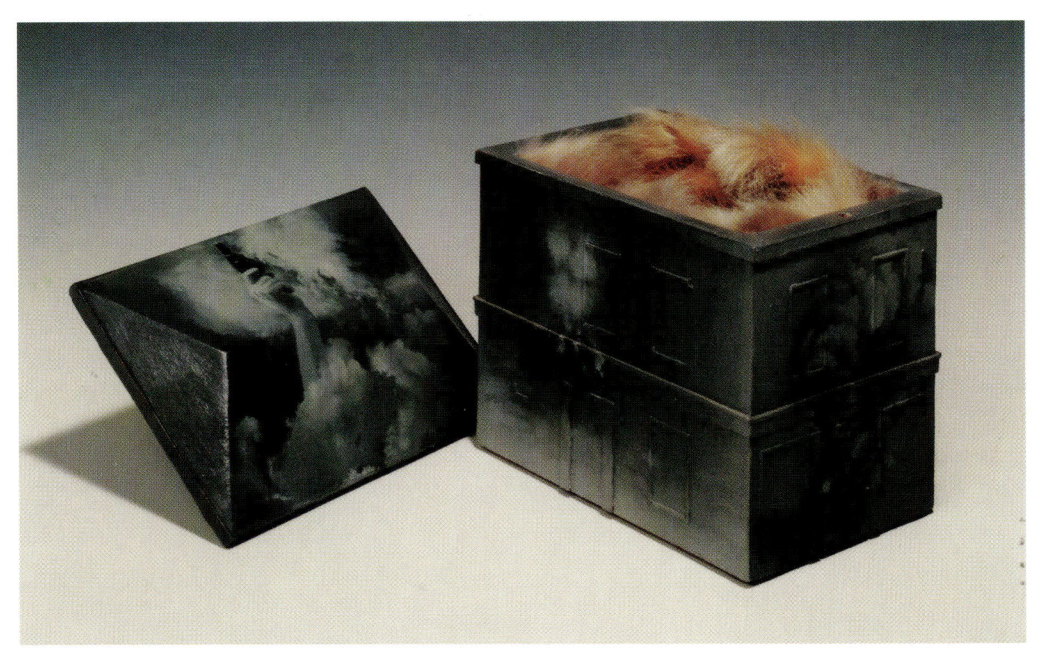

VIJA CELMINS, HOUSE #1, 1965

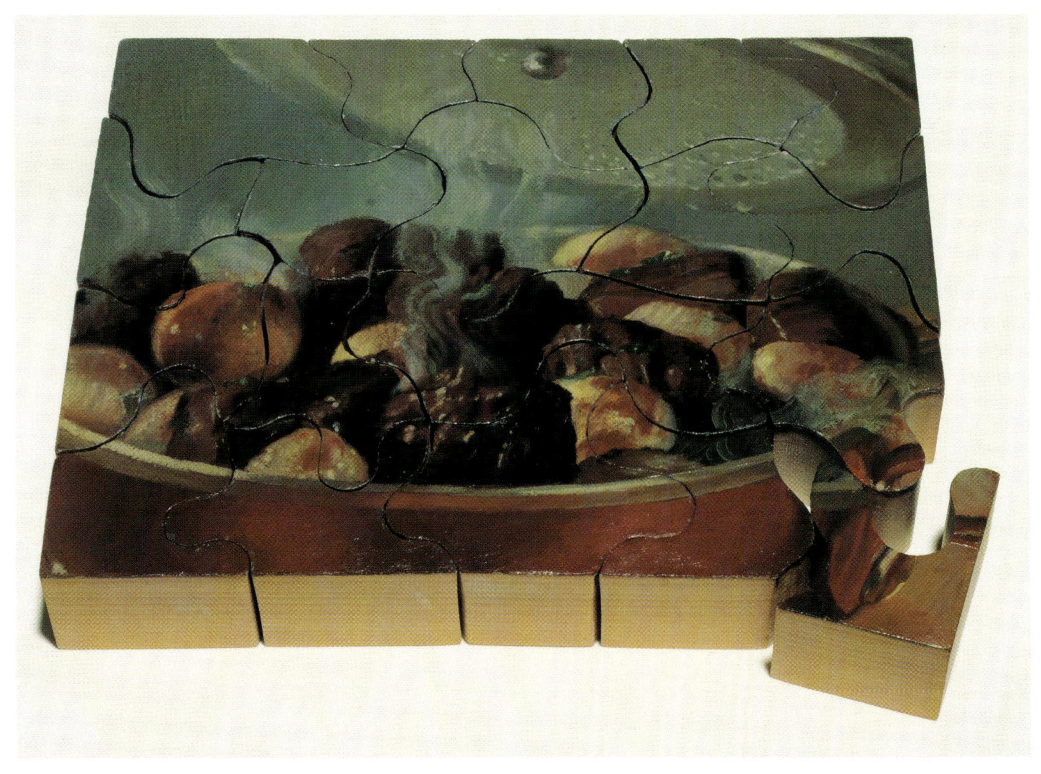

VIJA CELMINS, PUZZLE, 1965-66

VIJA CELMINS, UNTITLED (COMET), 1988

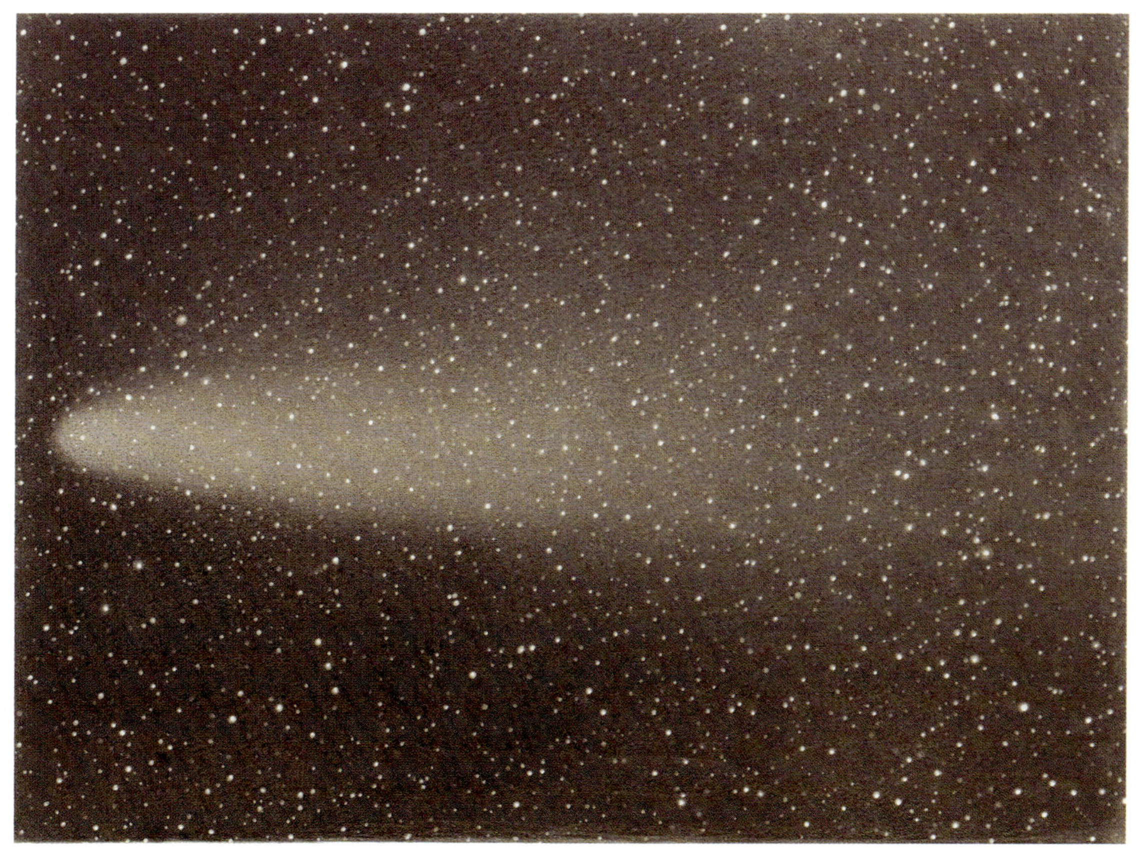

VIJA CELMINS, UNTITLED #13, 1996

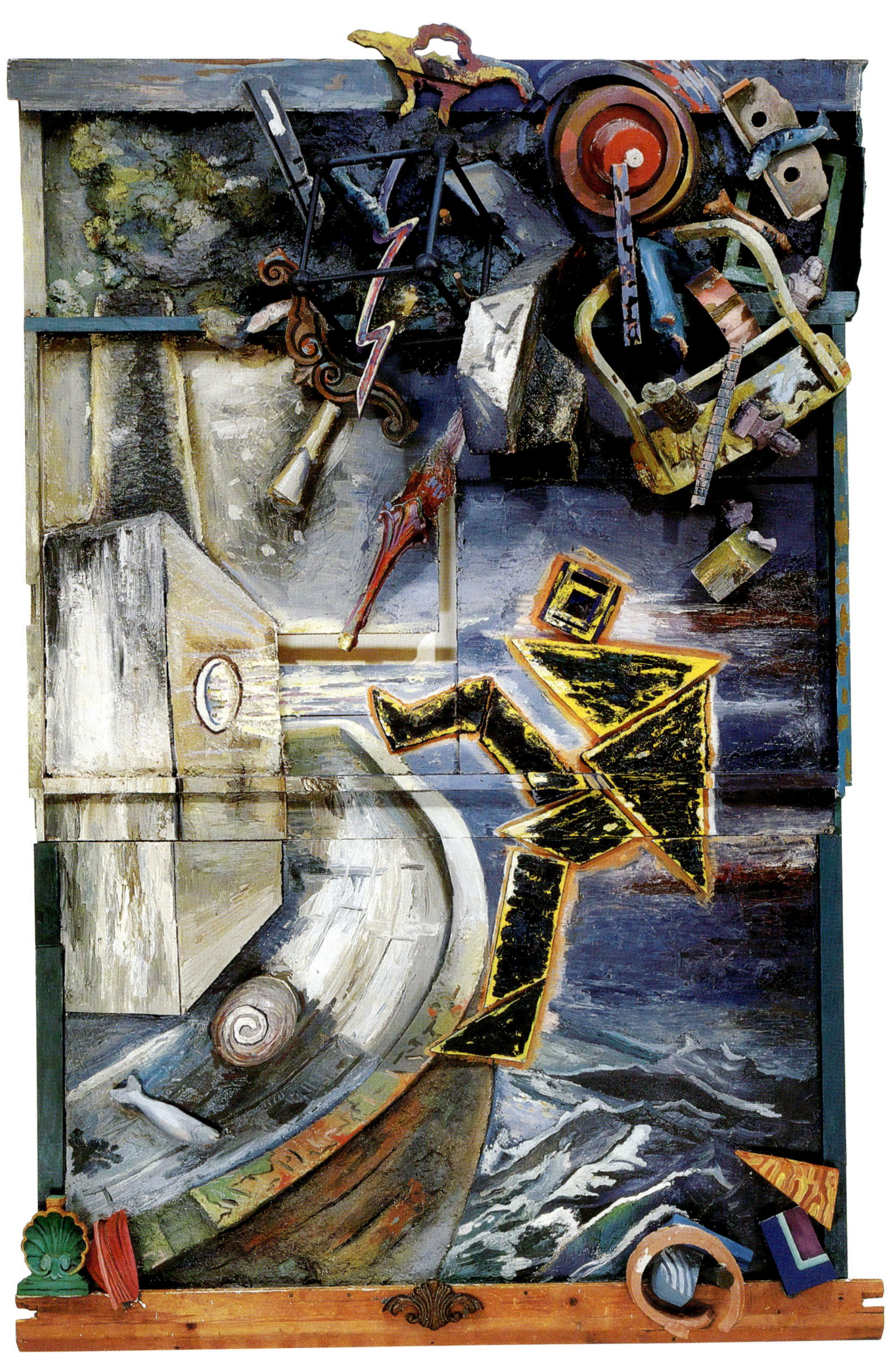

STUART DIAMOND, NIGHT FALLS, 1984

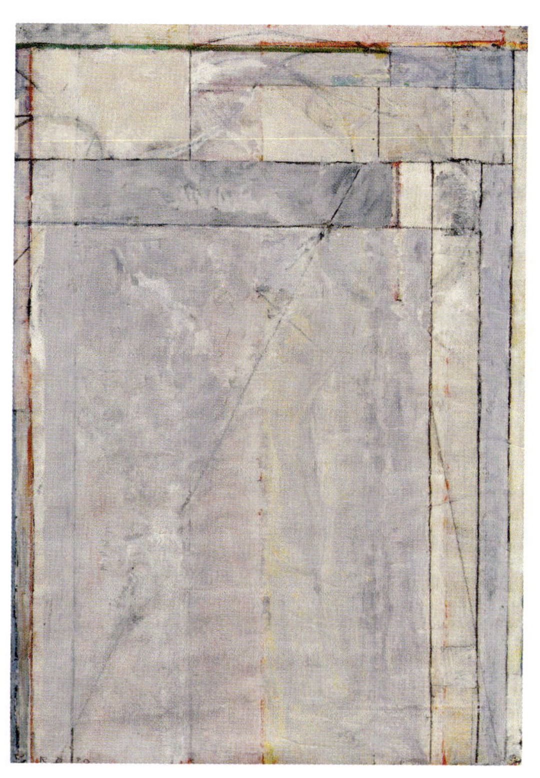

RICHARD DIEBENKORN, UNTITLED, 1980

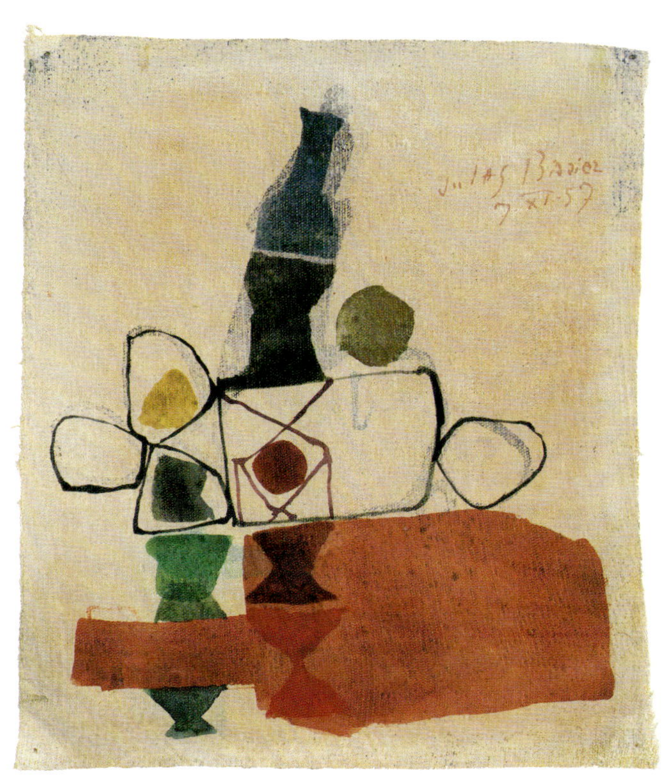

JULIUS BISSIER, 7.XI.57, 1957

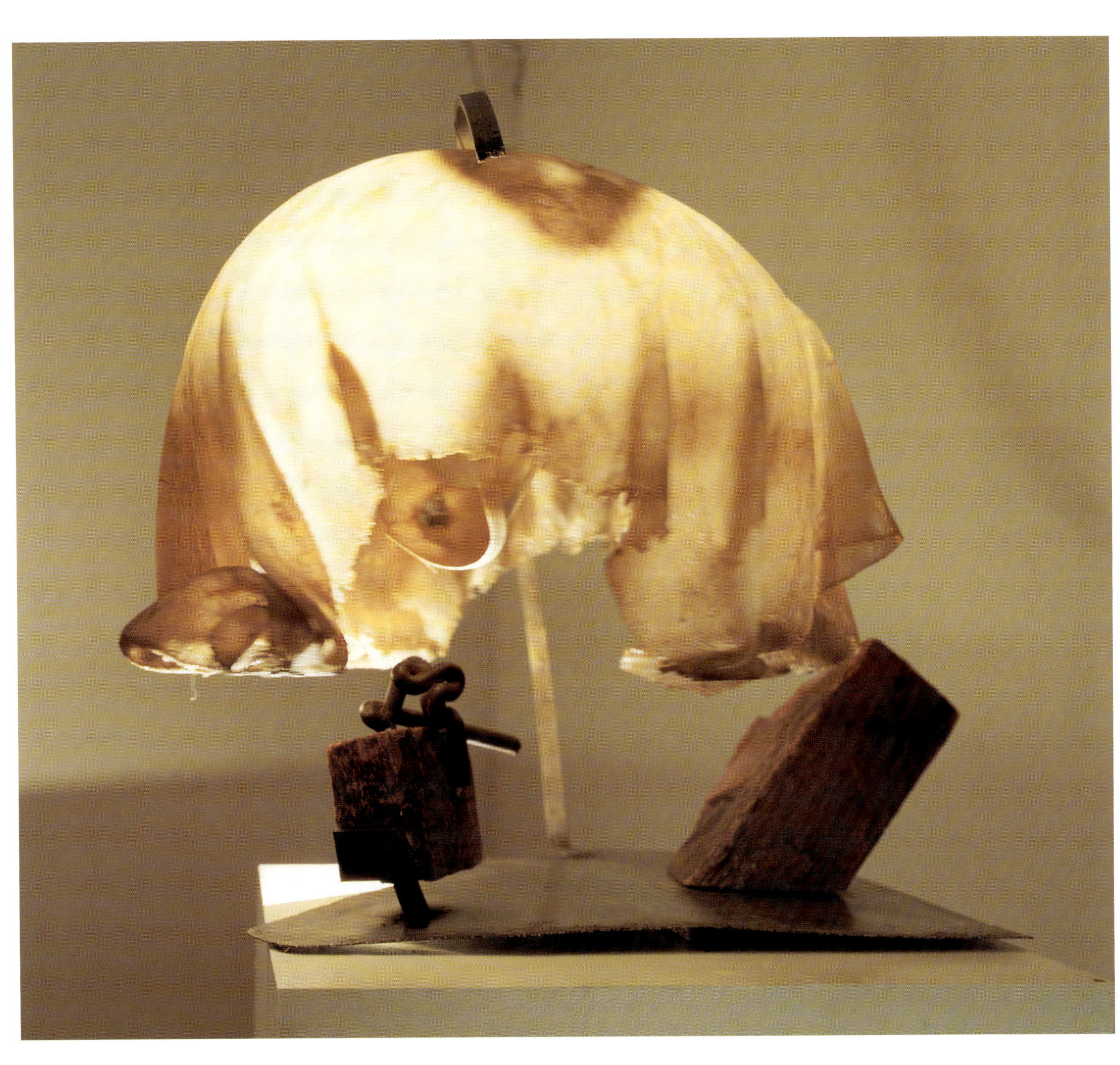

MARK DI SUVERO, EATHERLY'S LAMP, 1961

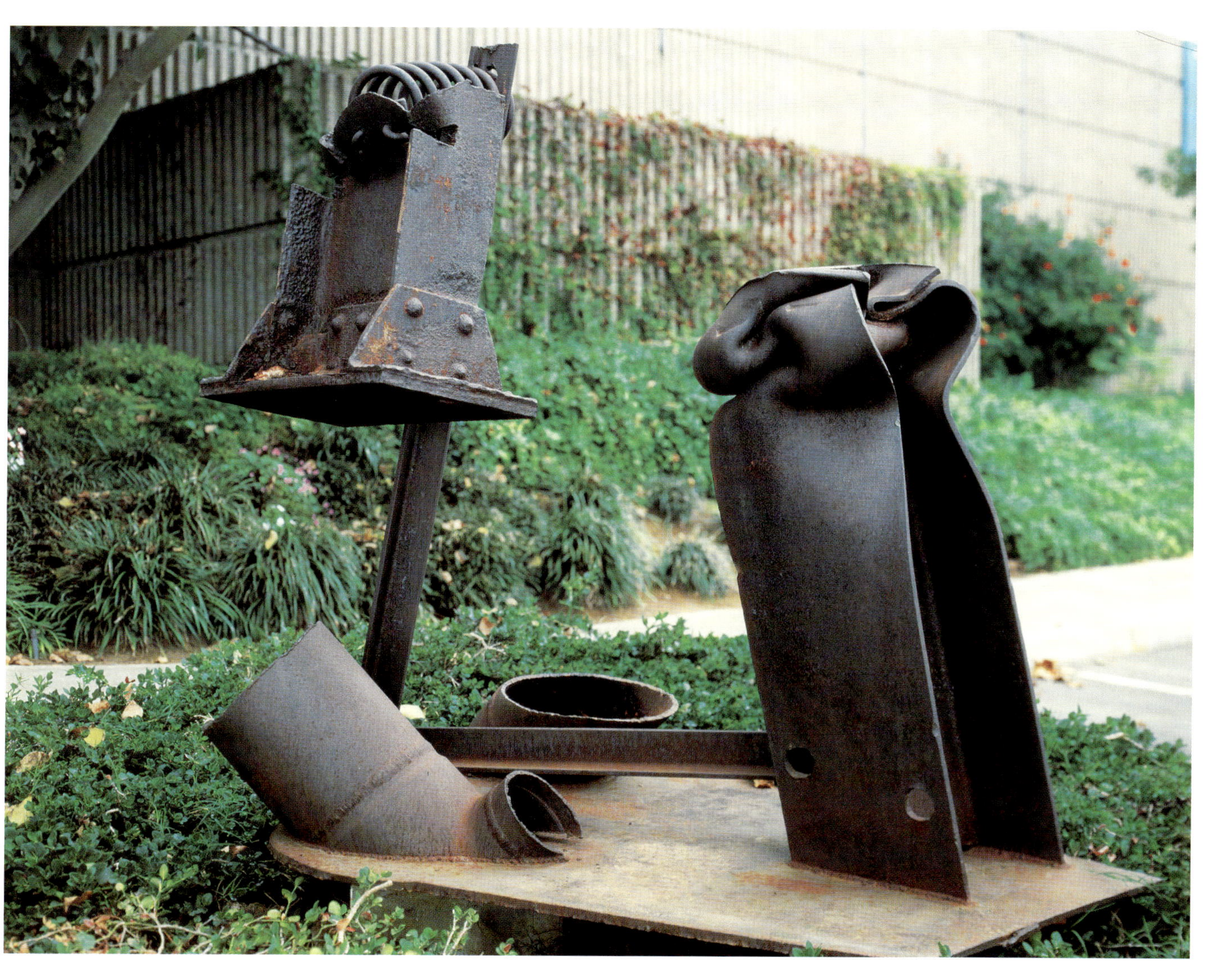

MARK DI SUVERO, BOOBER, 1965

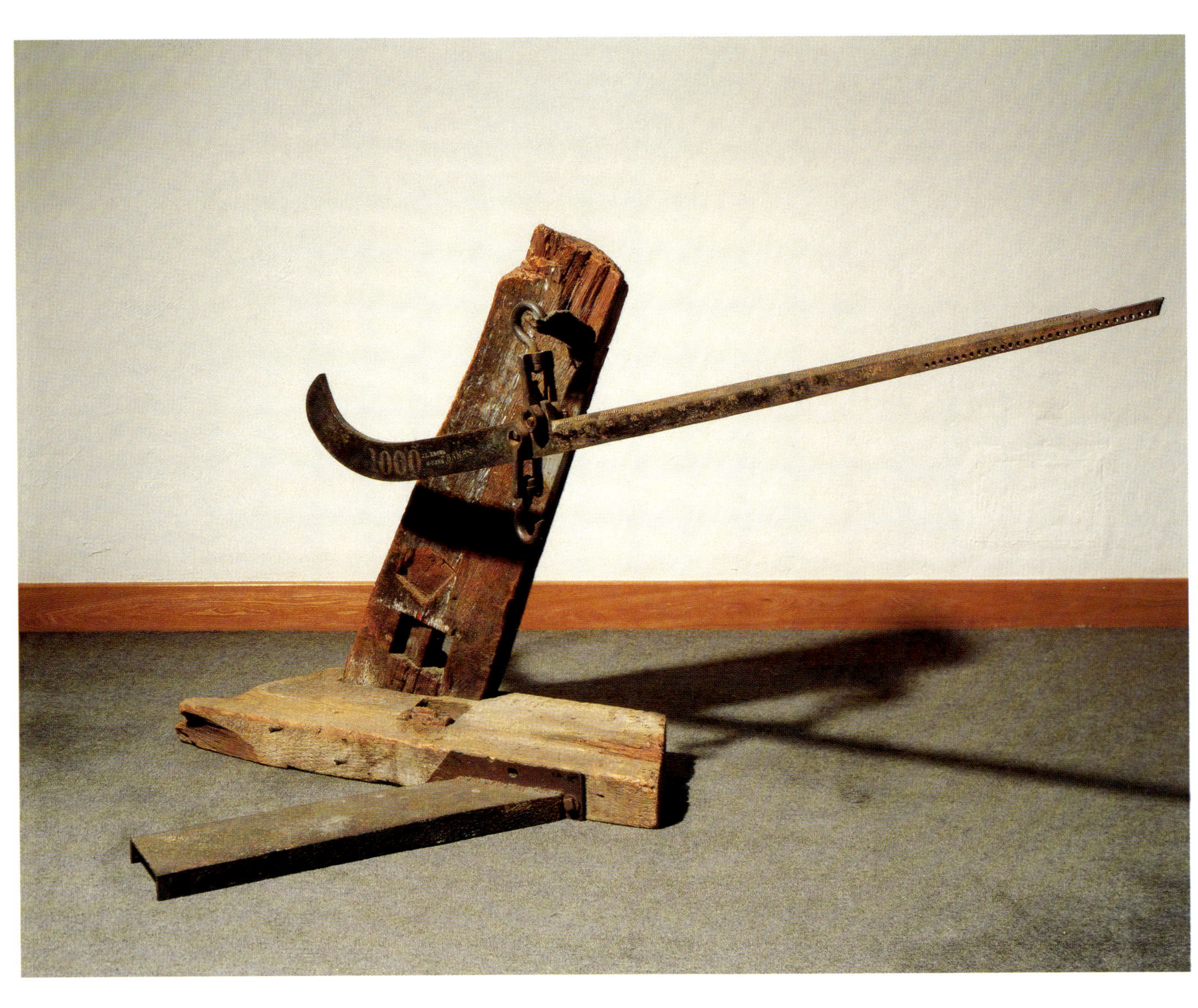

MARK DI SUVERO, MEASURE PIECE, 1967

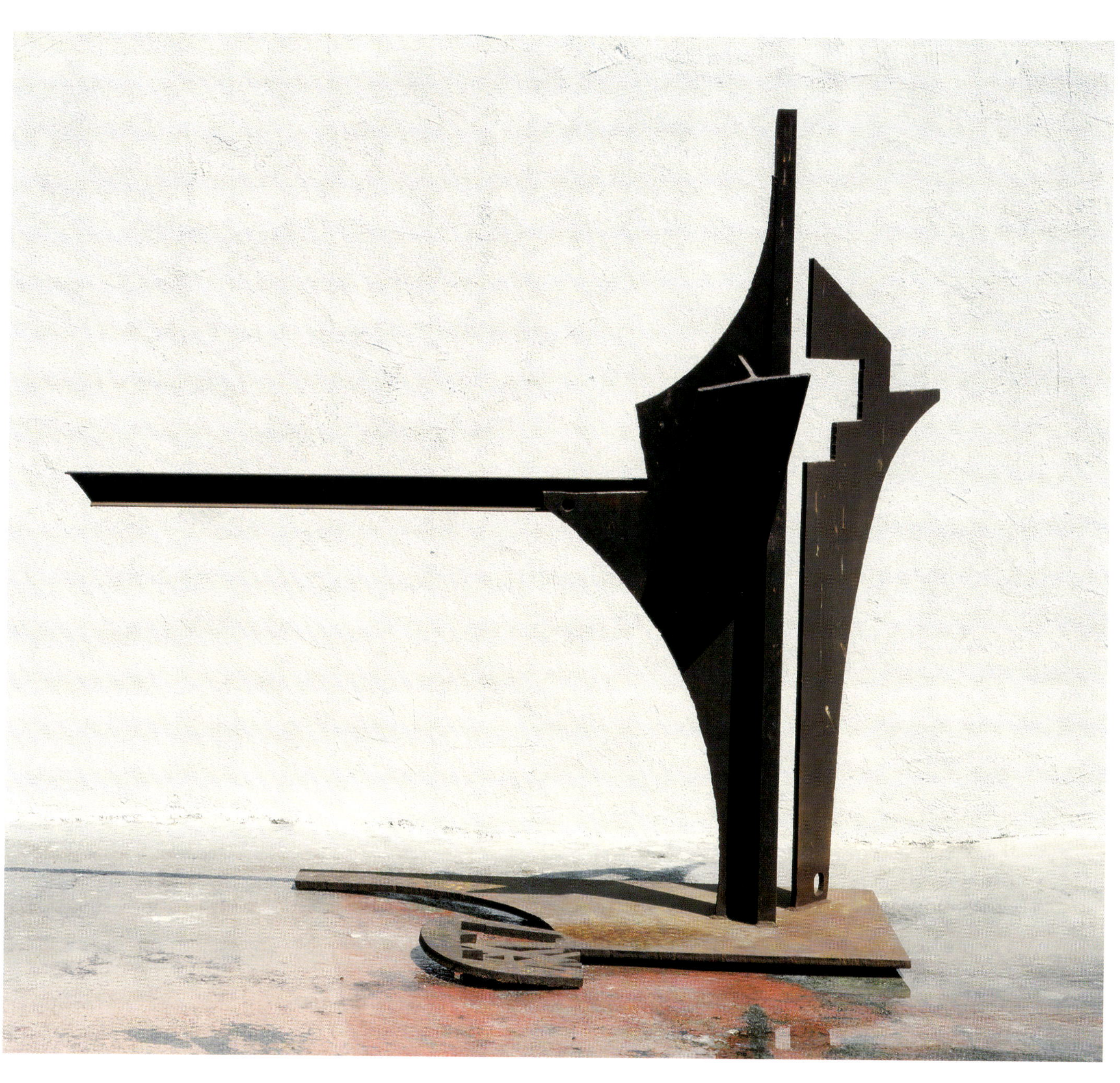

MARK DI SUVERO, HOMAGE TO GONZALEZ, 1973

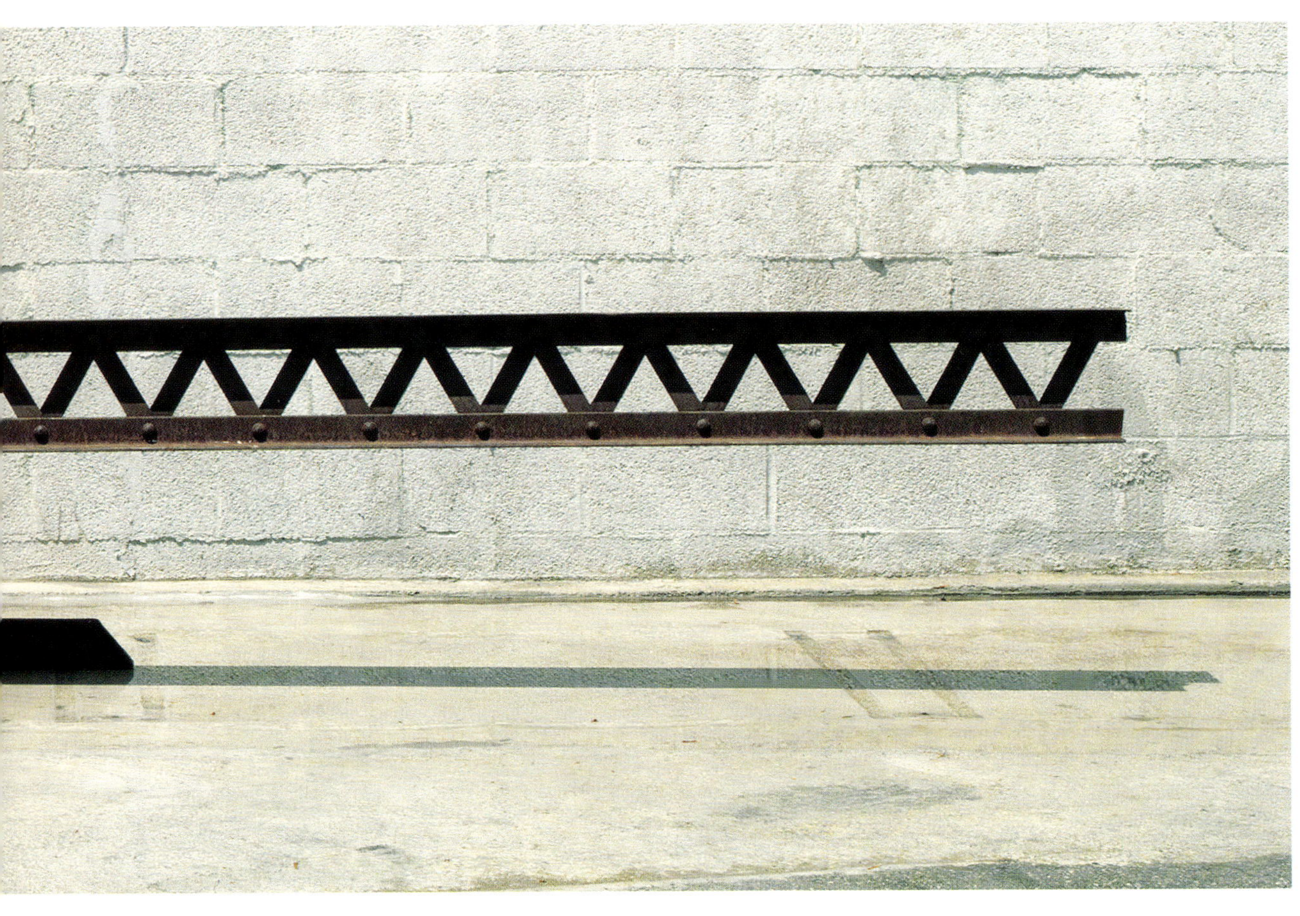

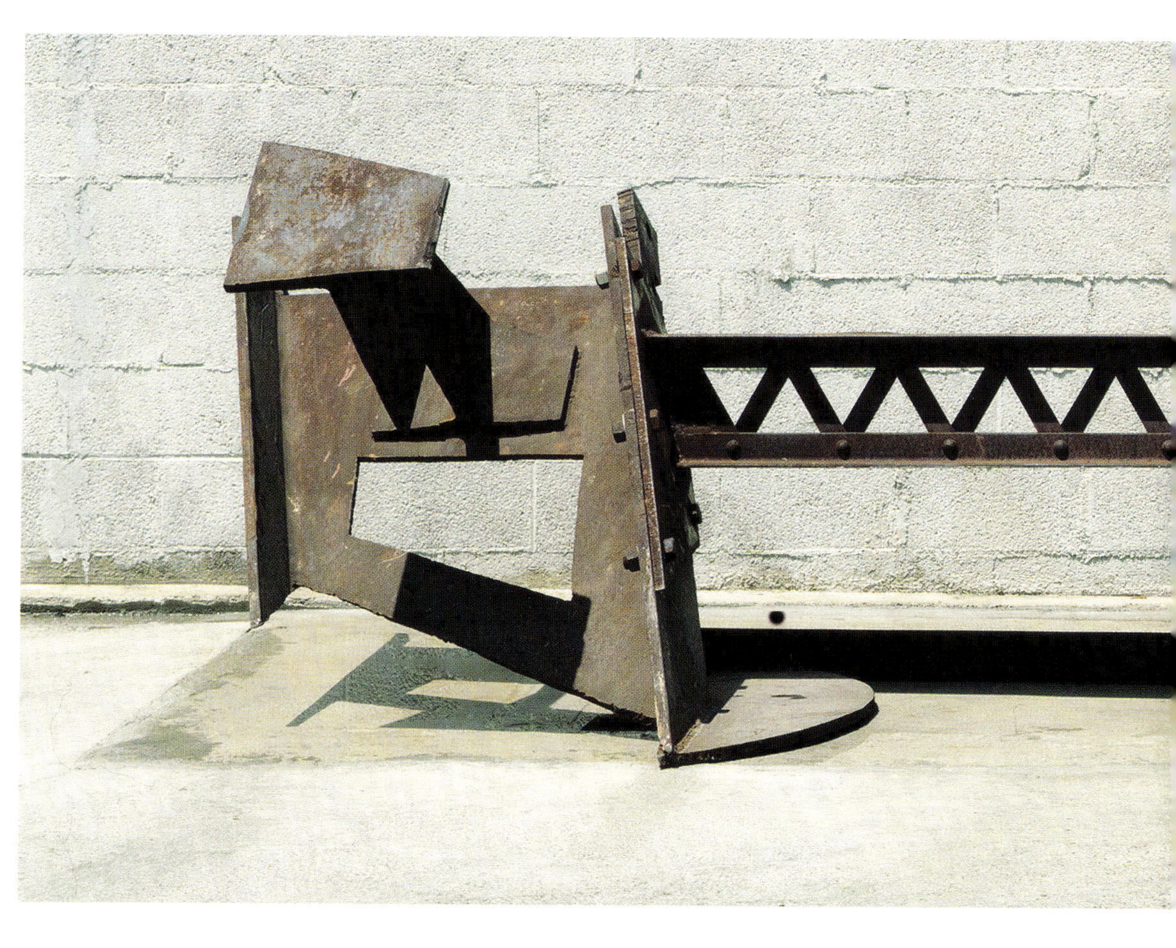

MARK DI SUVERO, TRUSSPIECE, 1975-76

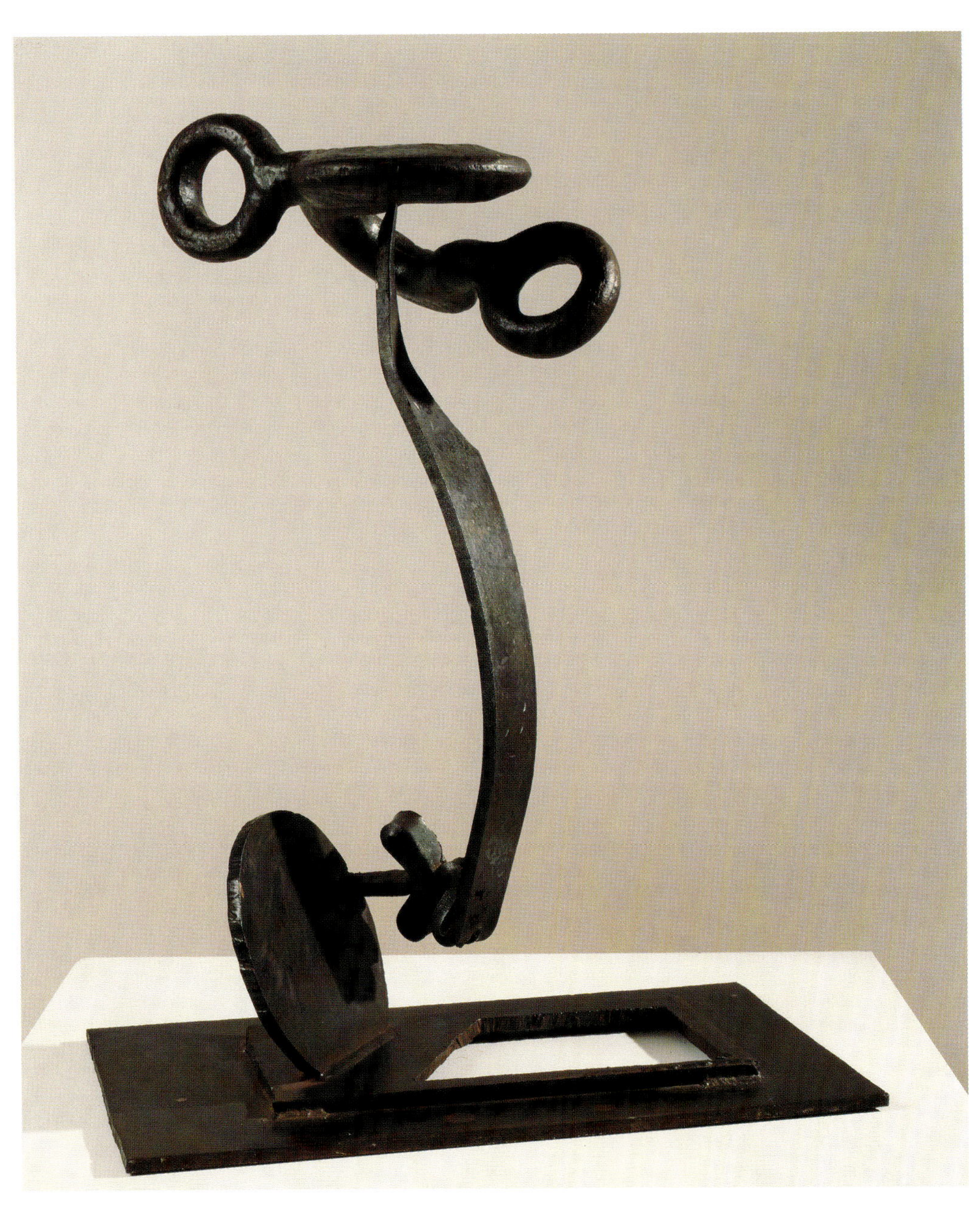

MARK DI SUVERO, 2 HOOKS, 1971-82

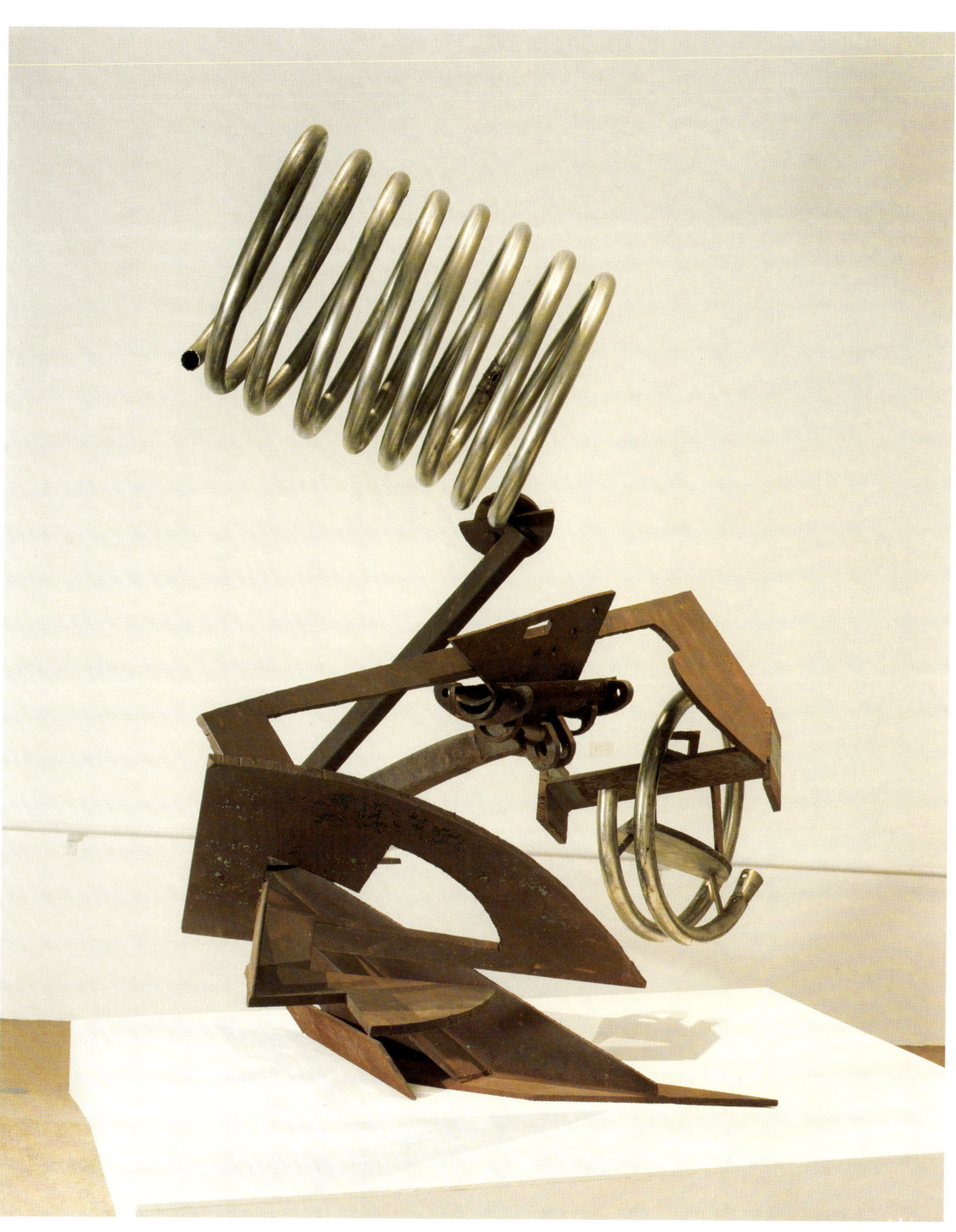

MARK DI SUVERO, ZAR, 1983

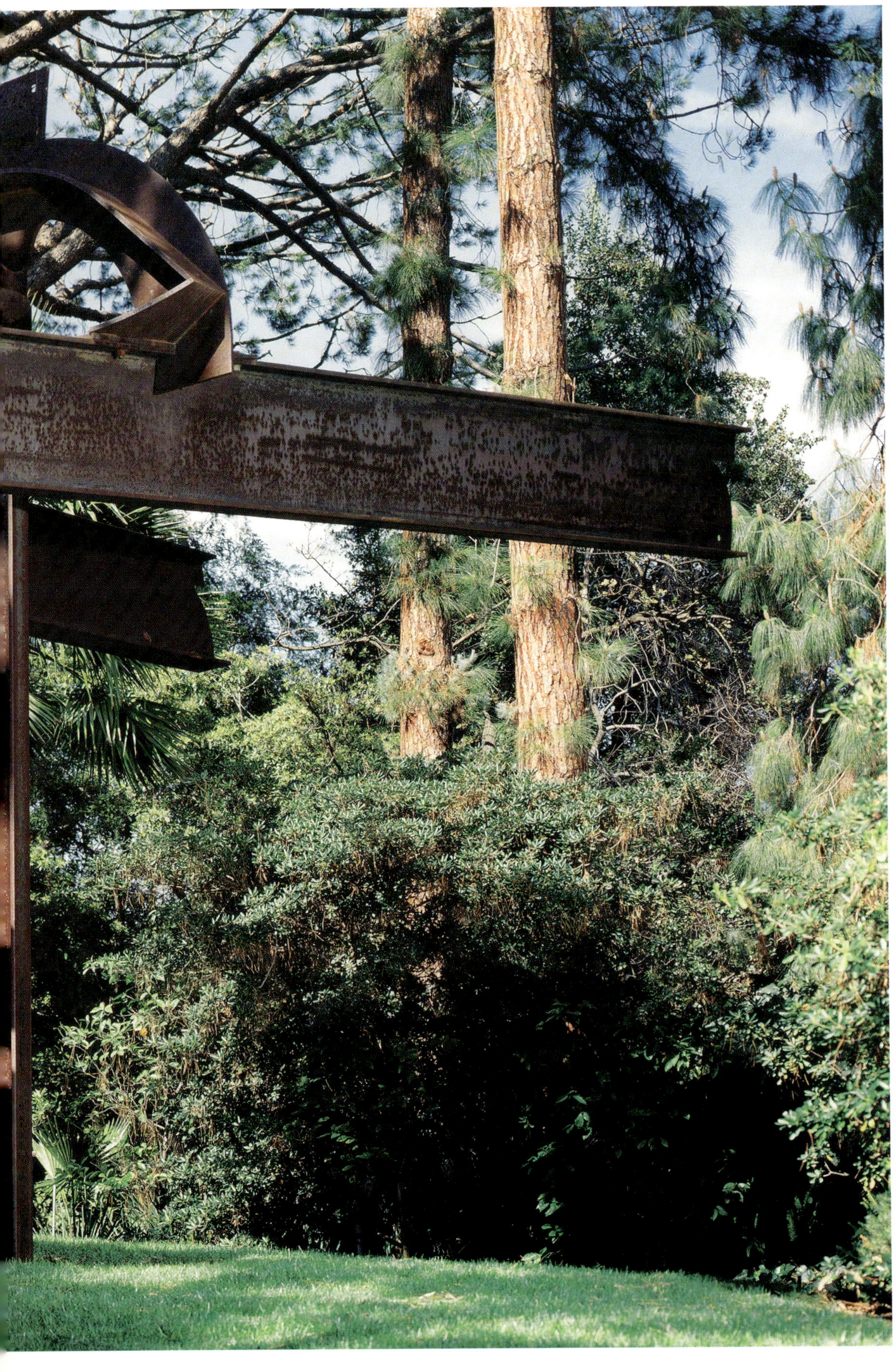

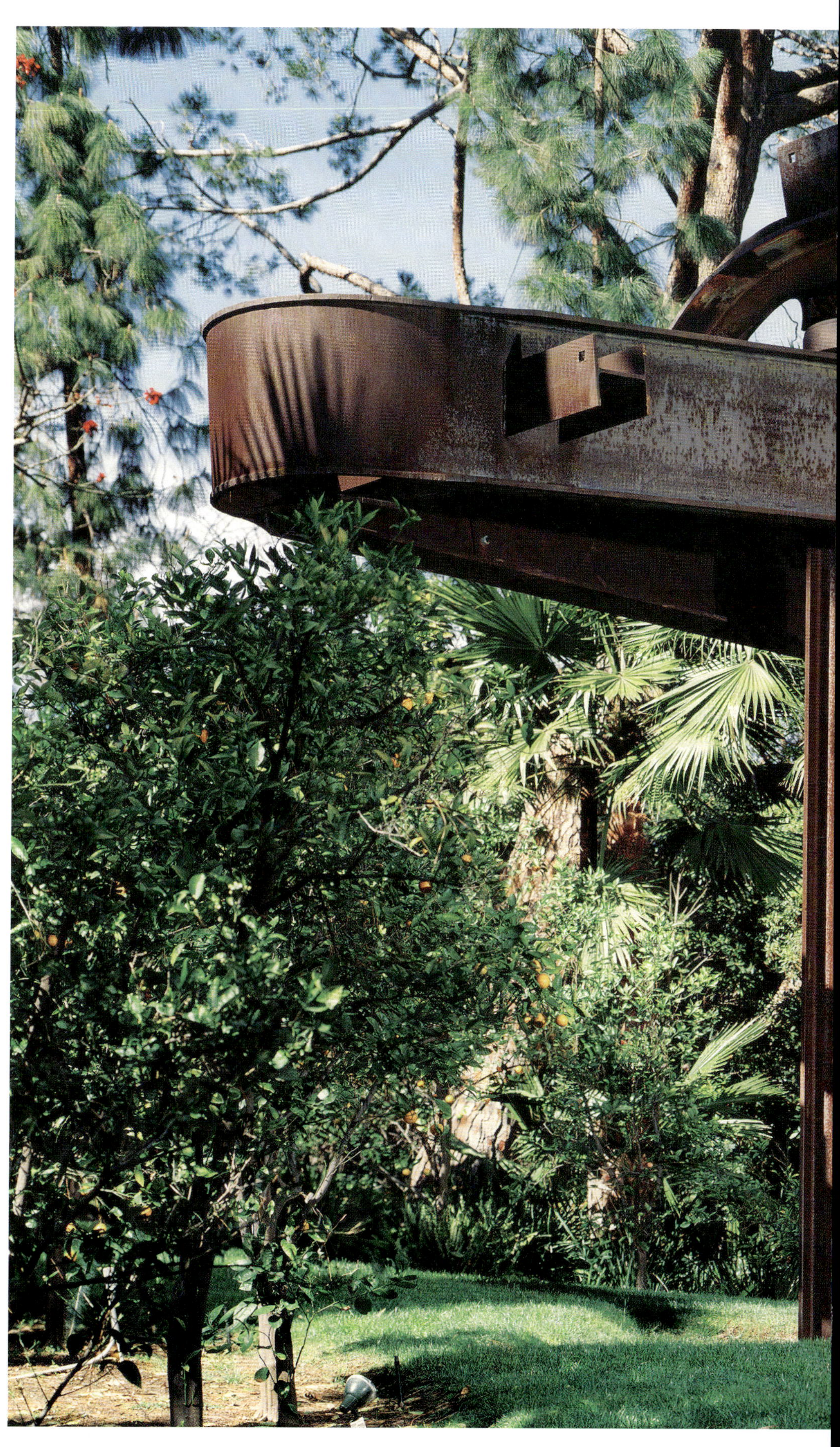

MARK DI SUVERO, MAHATMA, 1978-79

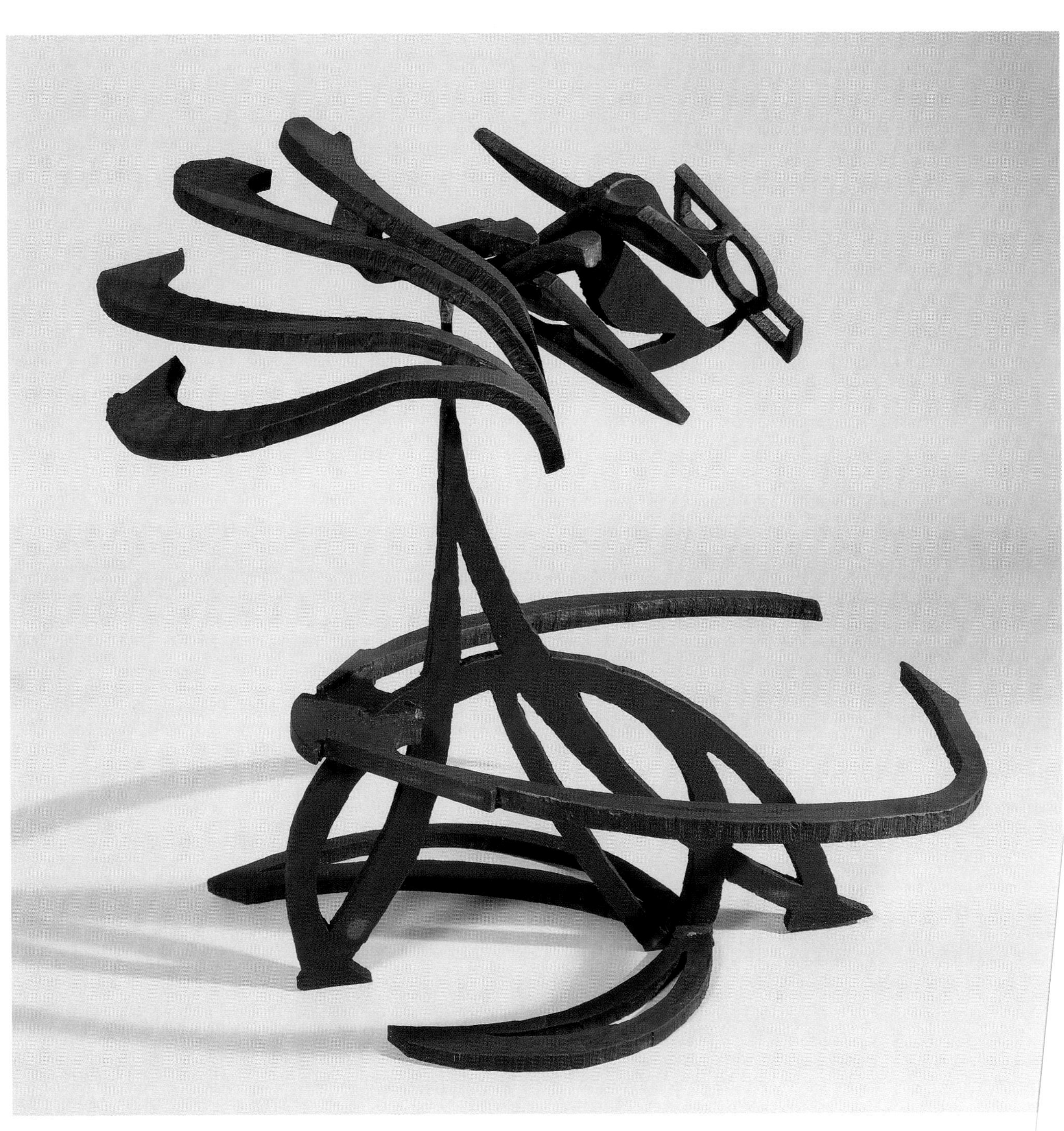

MARK DI SUVERO, UNTITLED, 1997

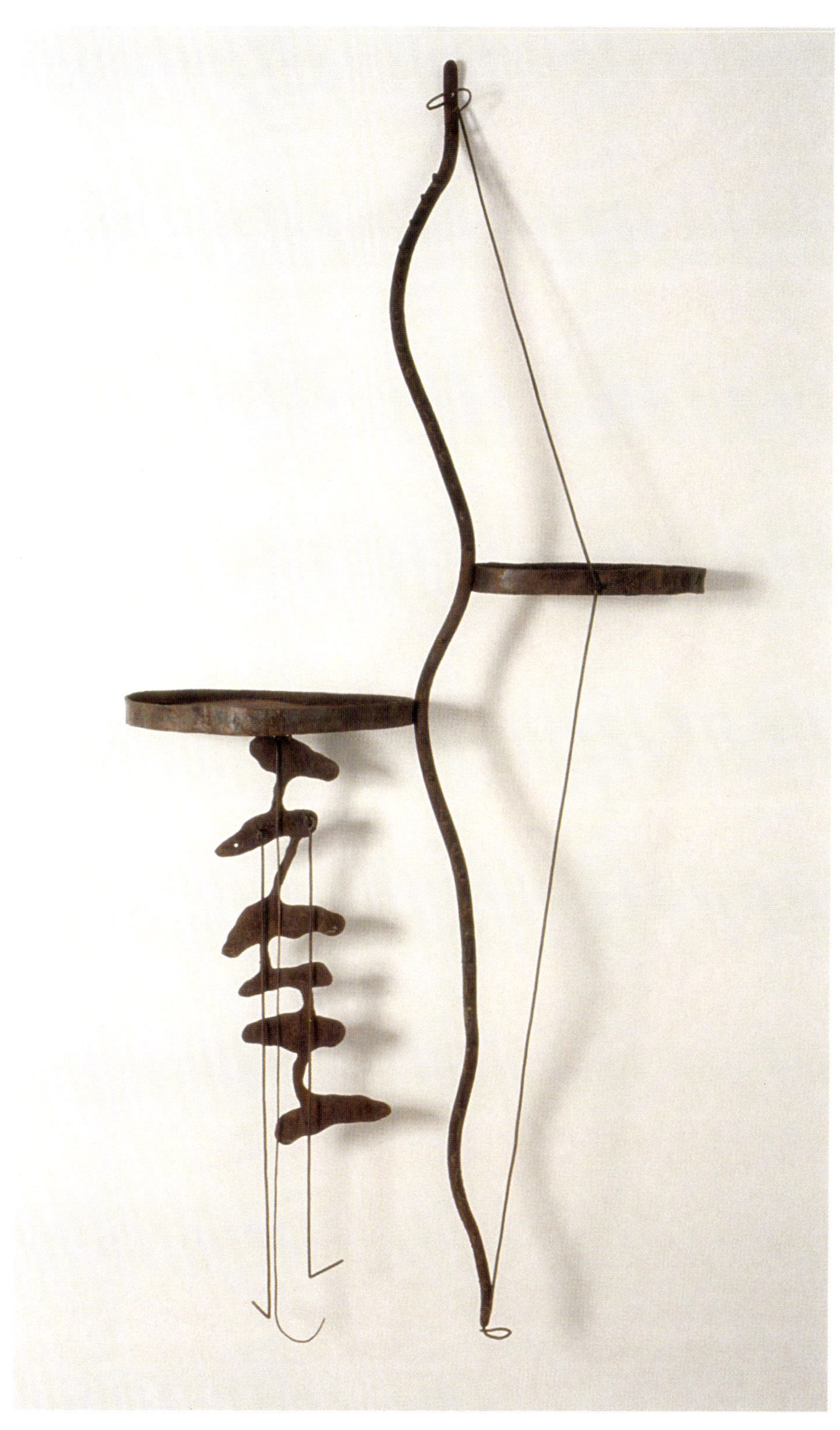

GEORGE DUDDING, THE TAYLOR'S SON'S GAME, 1990

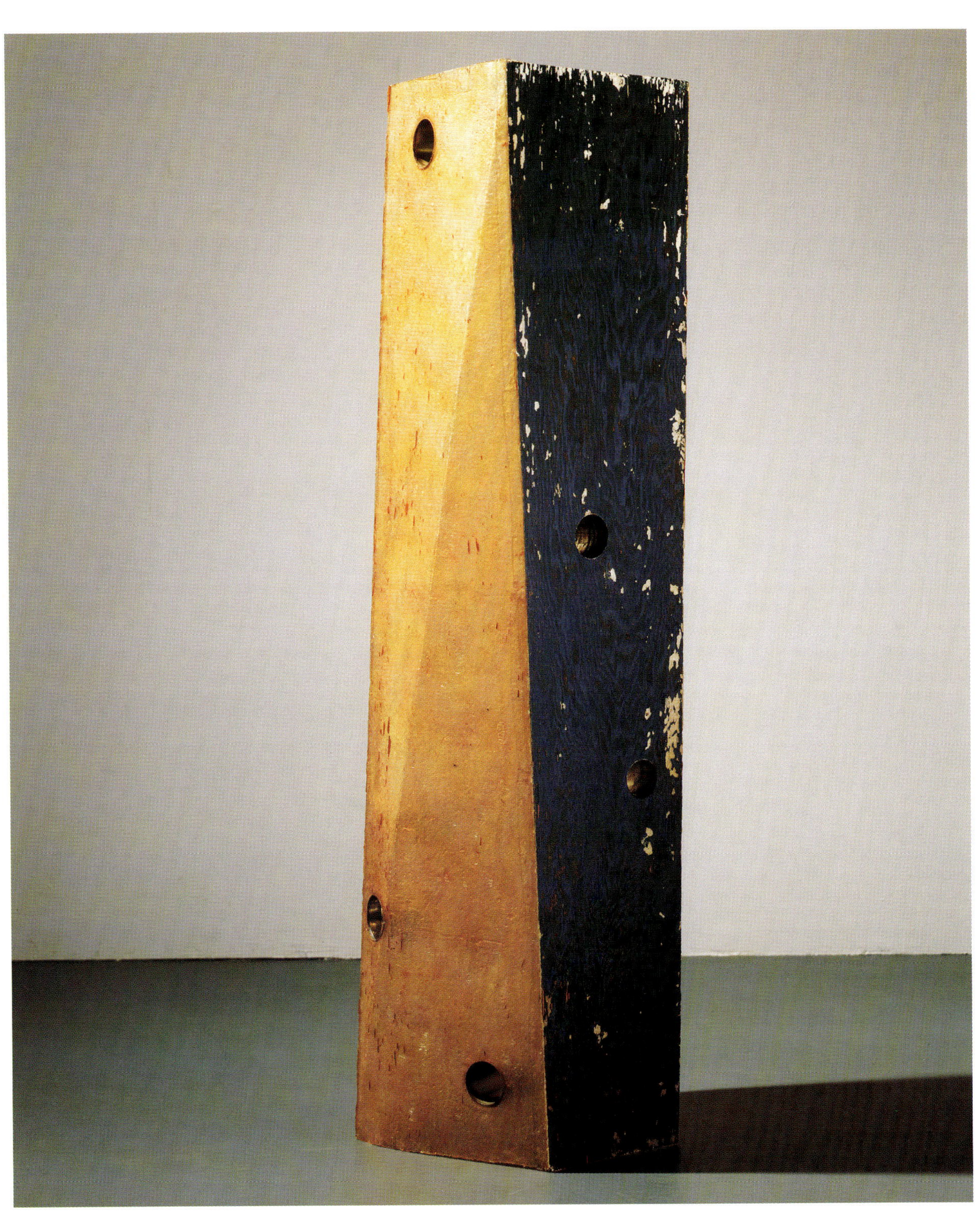

JOHN DUFF, RECIPROCATING COLUMN, 1982

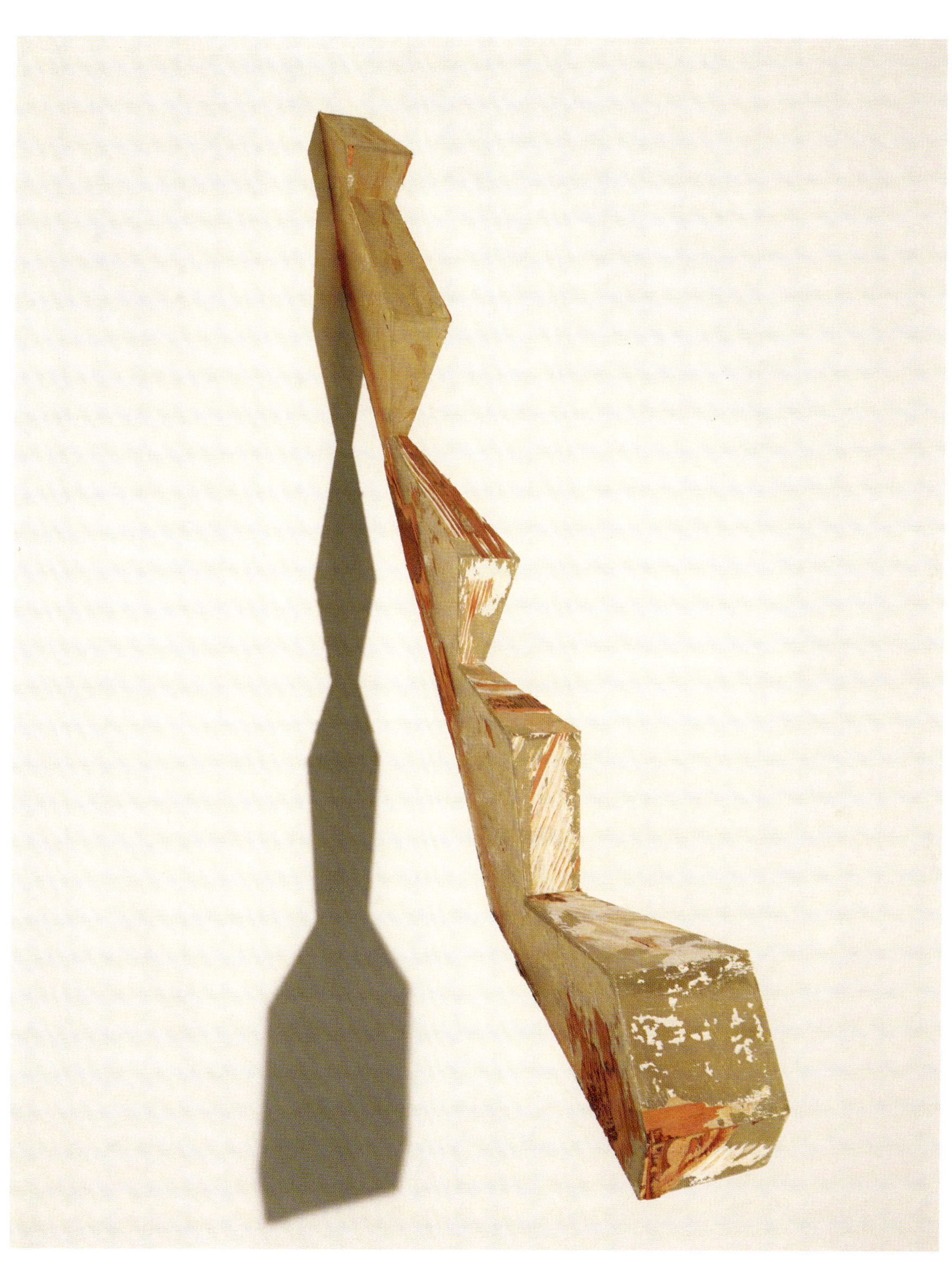

JOHN DUFF, WHITE SERRATED WEDGE, 1984

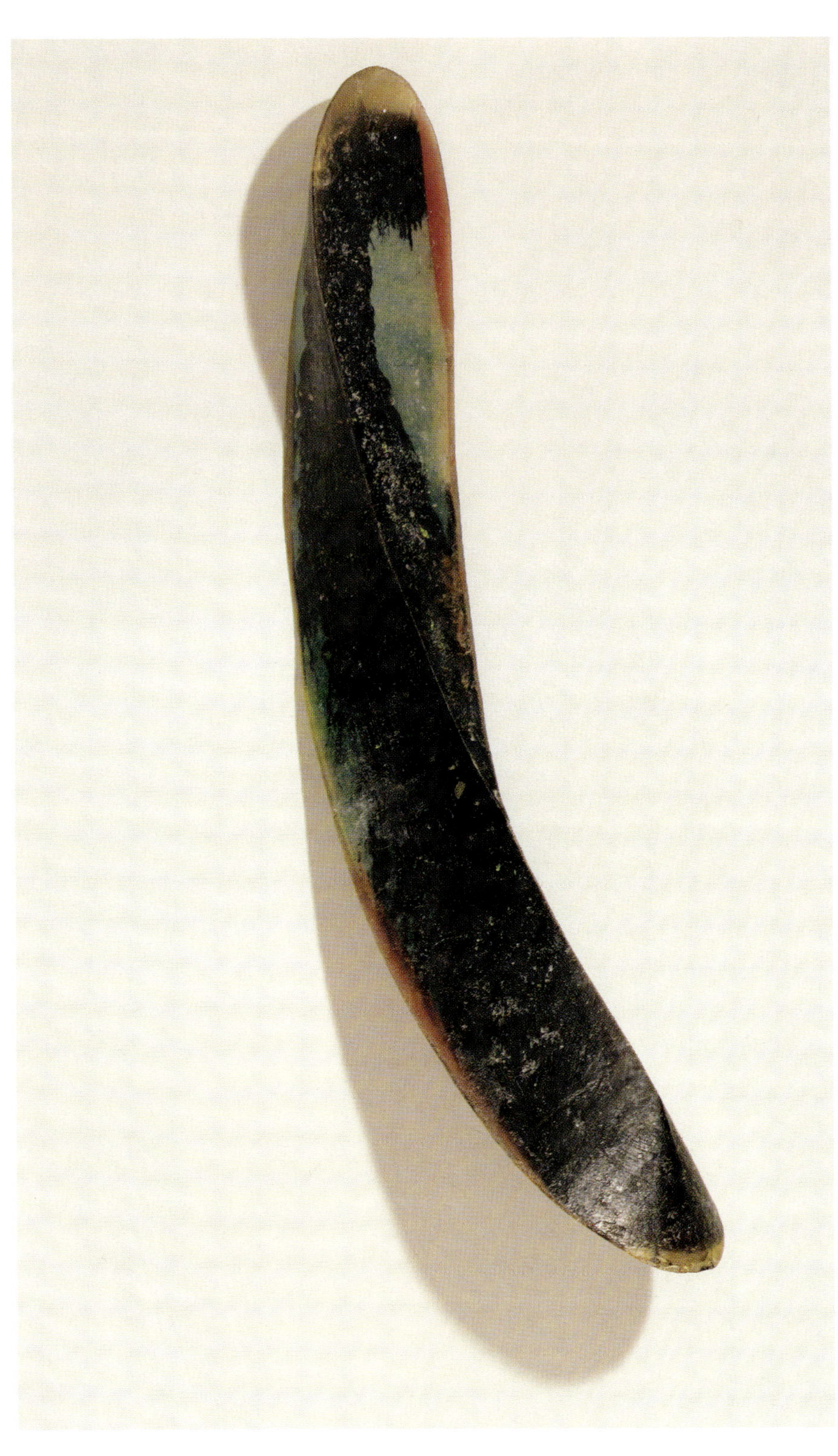

JOHN DUFF, PERNAMBUCO, 1985-86

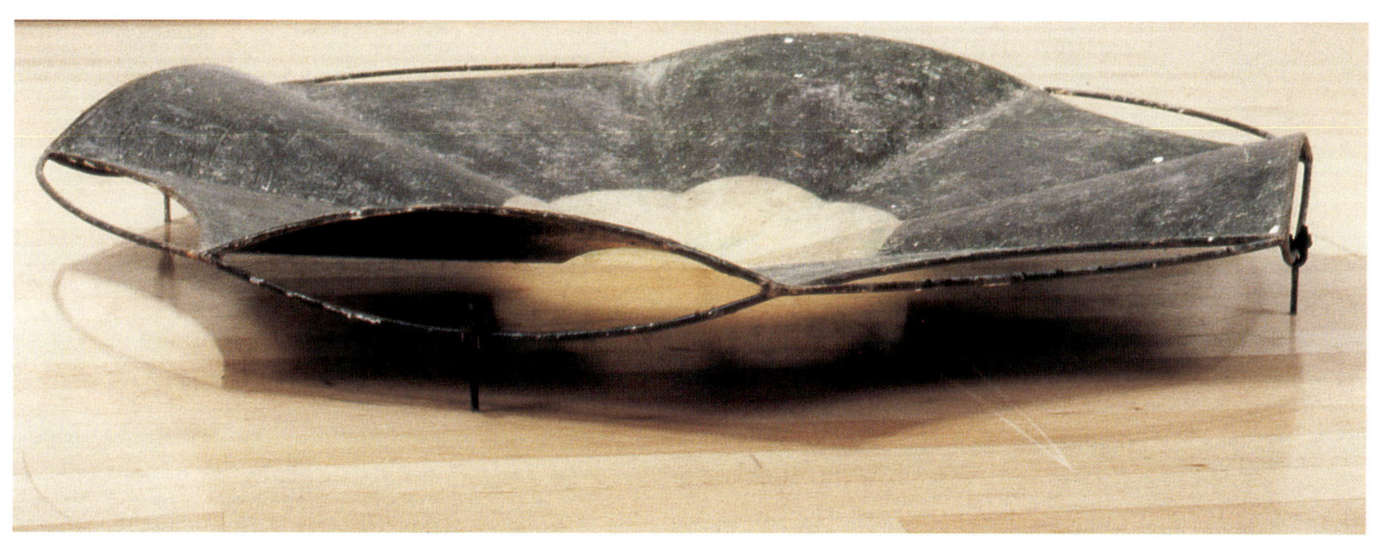

JOHN DUFF, BLACK FLOOR PIECE, 1992

JACOB EL HANANI, ASHSHUR, 1986

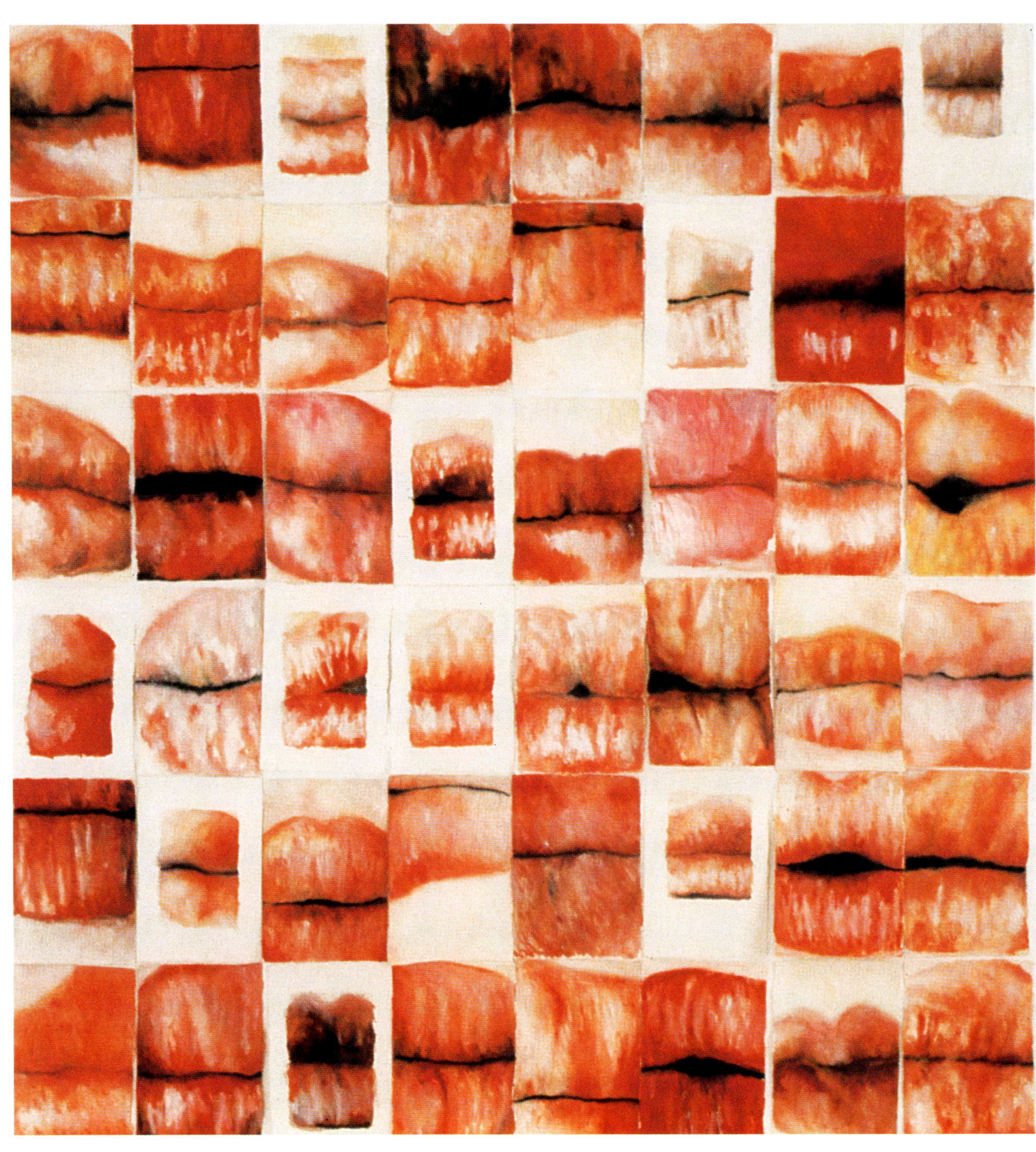

VALERIE FAVRE, LÈVRES, 1993

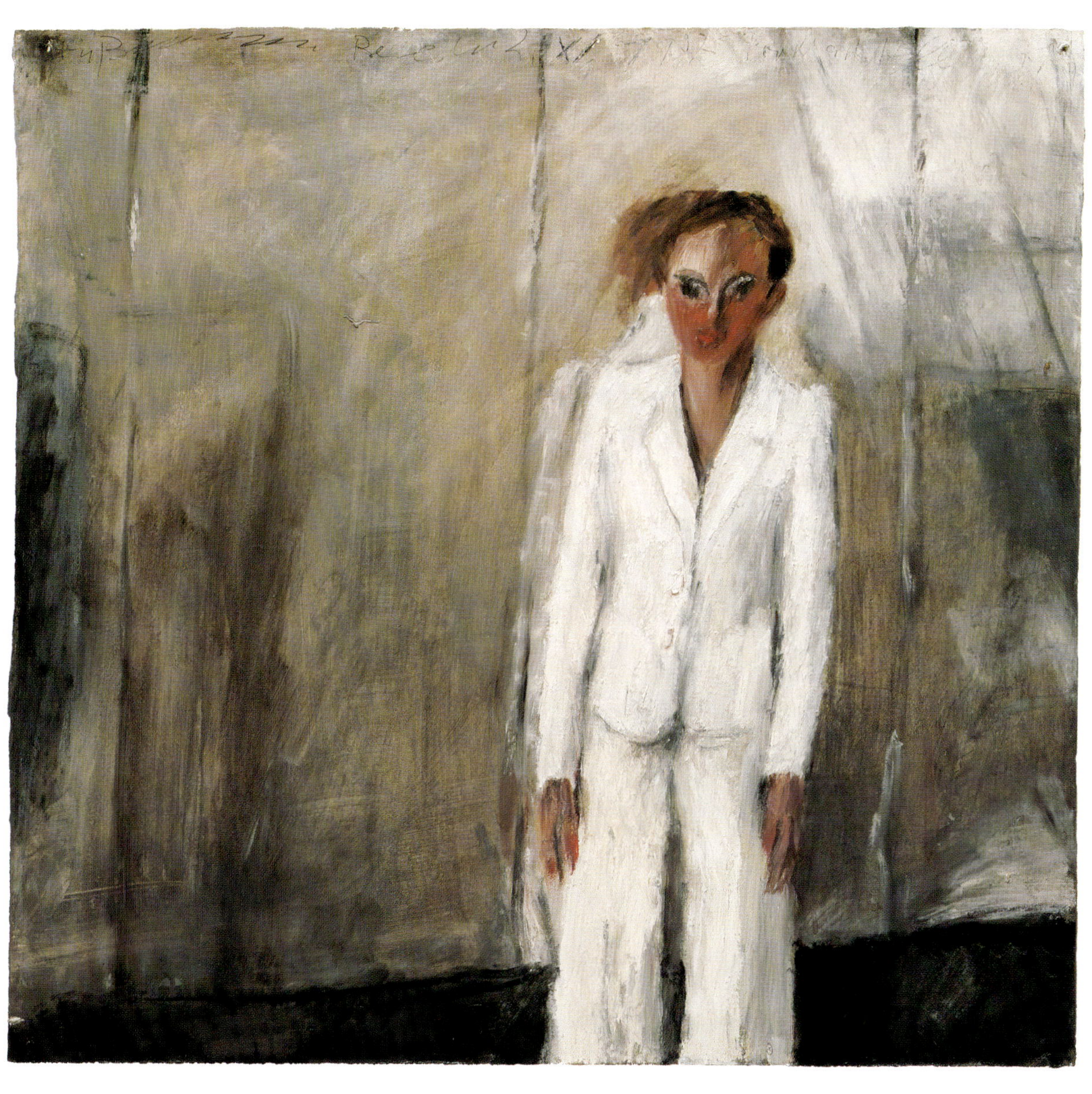

KLAUS FUSSMANN, HELLA K. IN WHITE BEFORE MIRROR, 1977

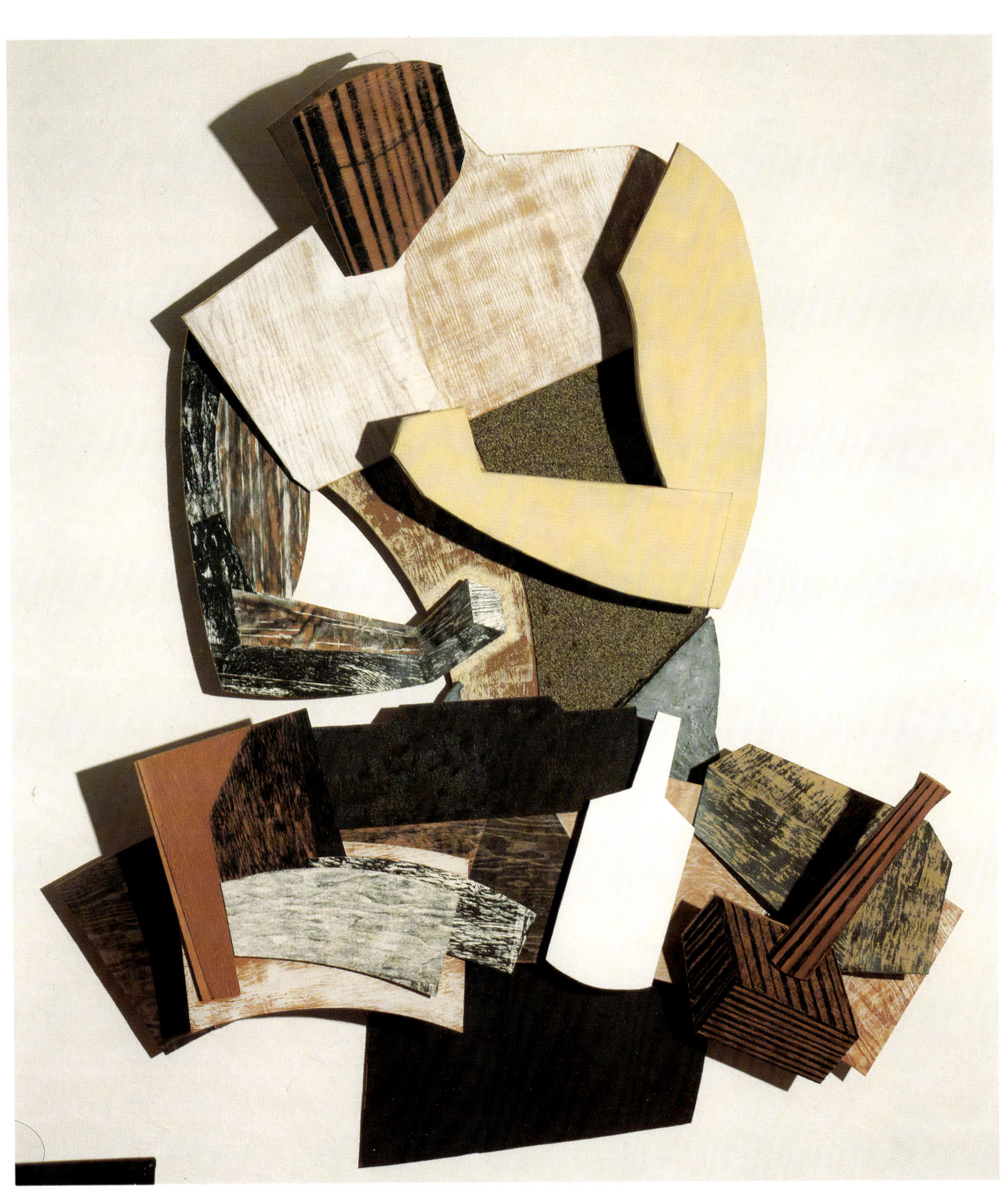

JILL GIEGERICH, UNTITLED (FIGURE WITH ARCH OF INDUSTRY), 1983

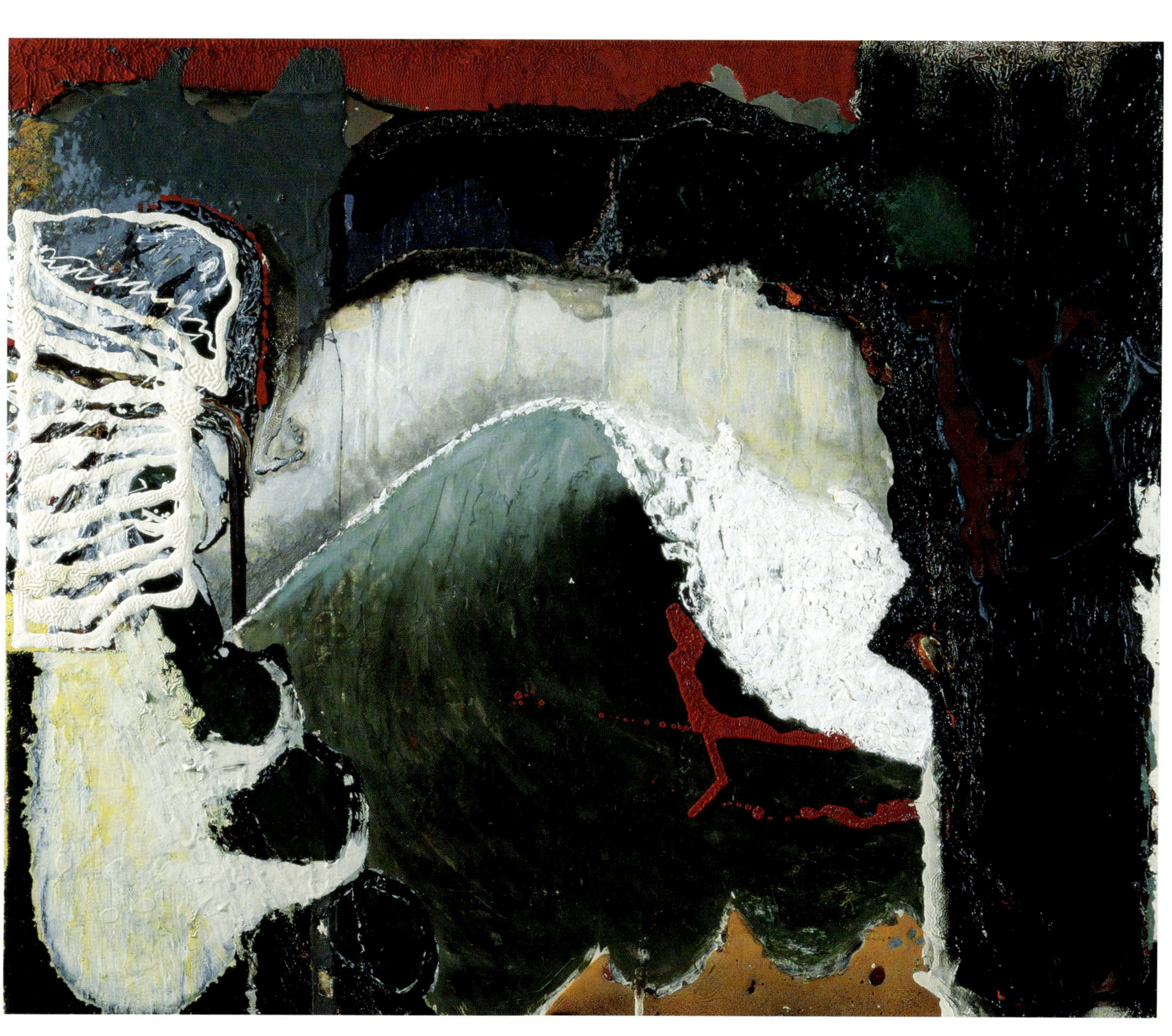

SPENCER GREGORY, UNDERNEATH, 1986-87

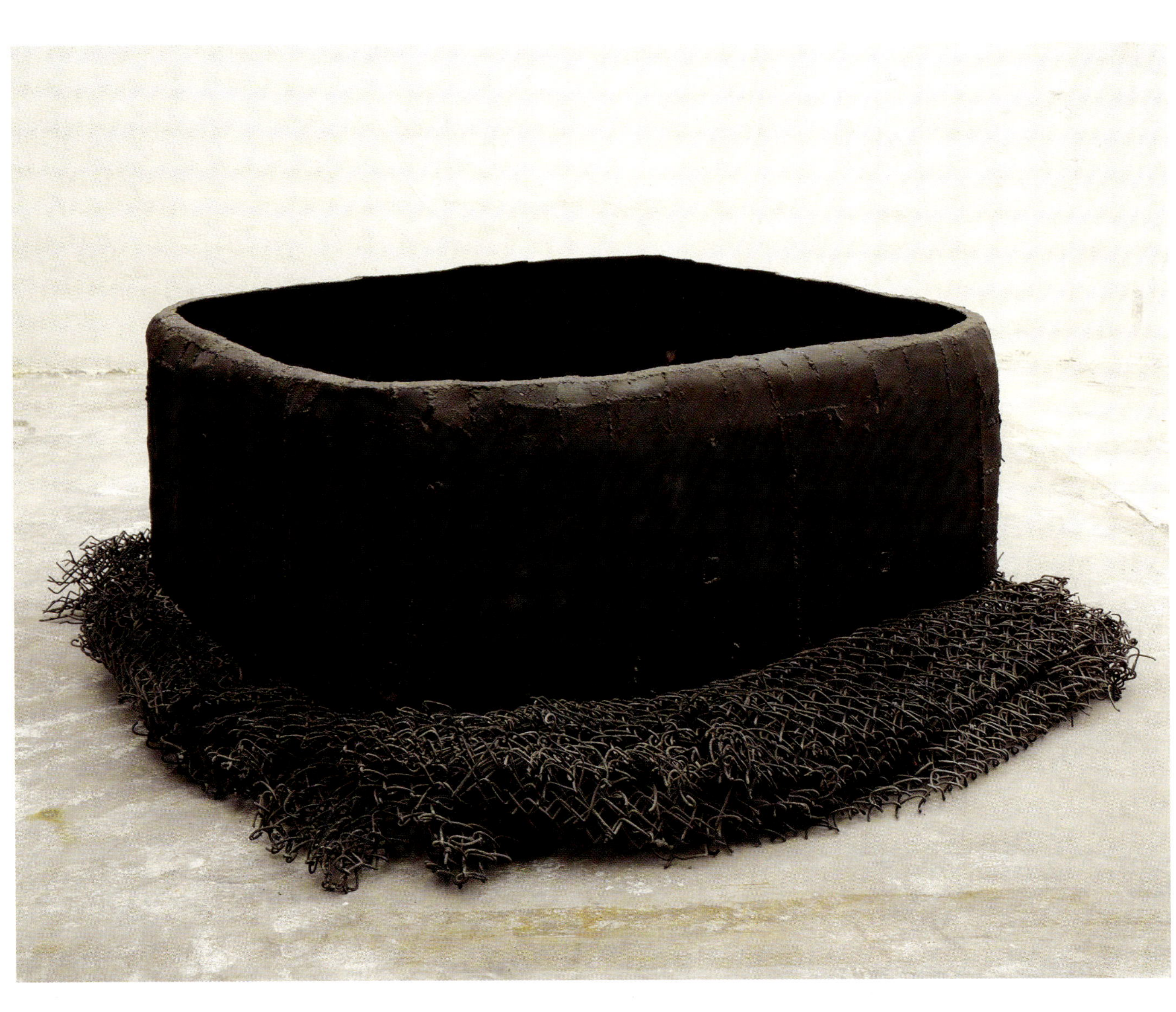

ROBERT GROSVENOR, UNTITLED, 1981-83

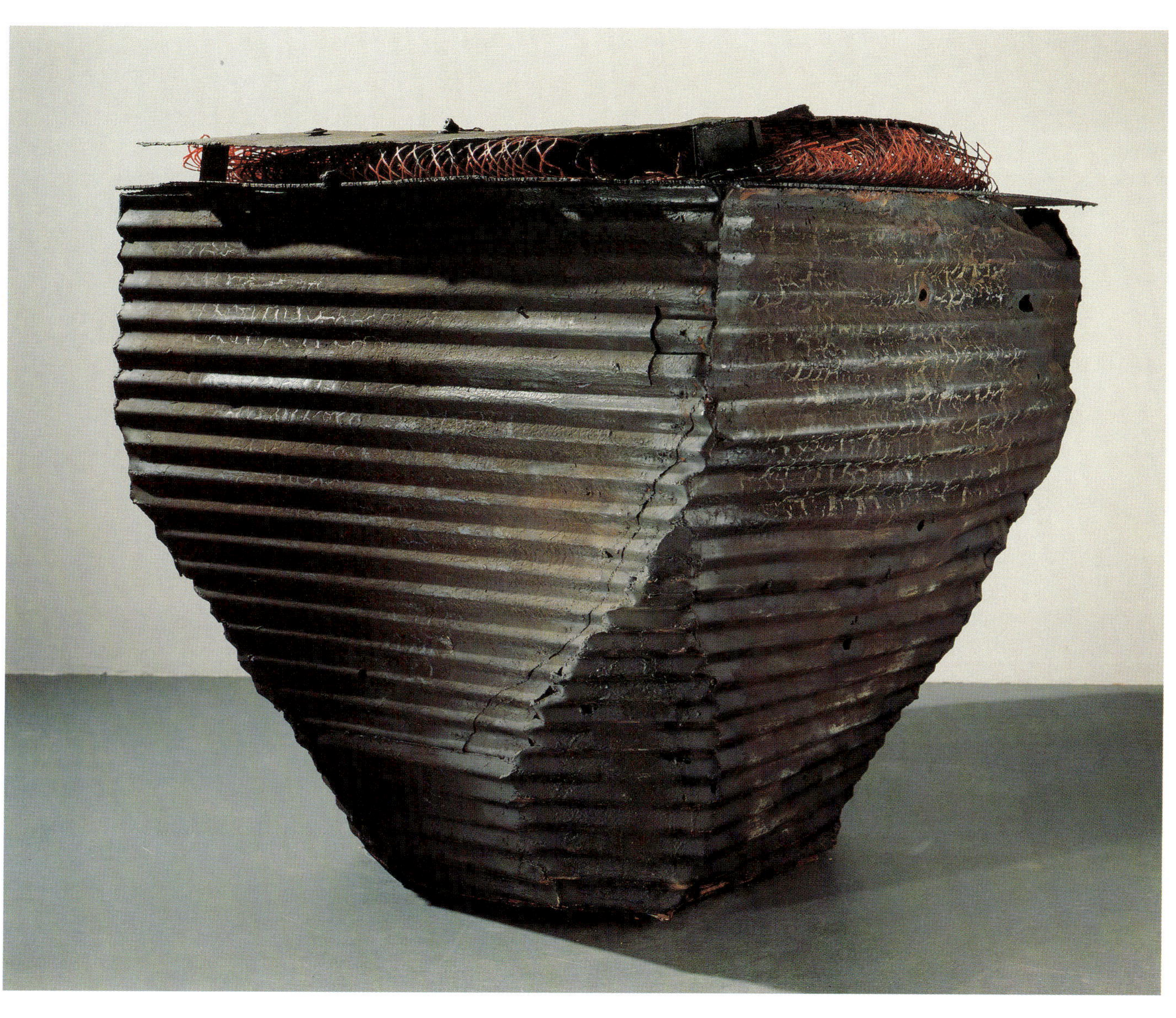

ROBERT GROSVENOR, UNTITLED, 1984-85

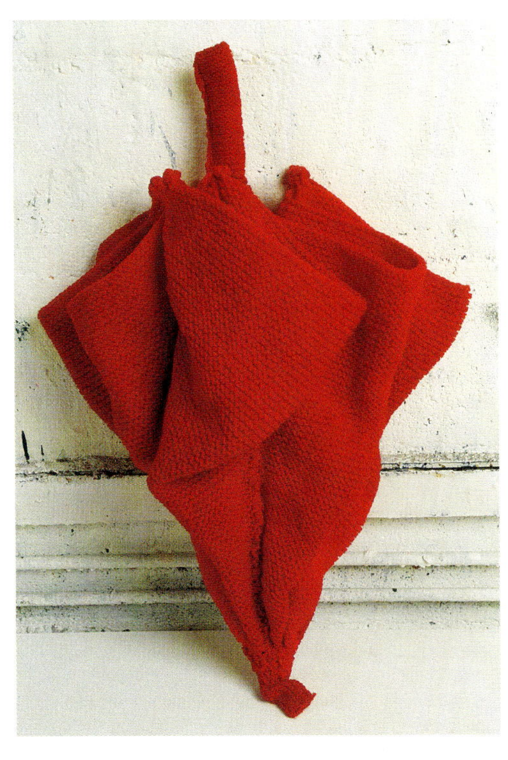

VALERIE FAVRE, PARAPLUIE, 1994

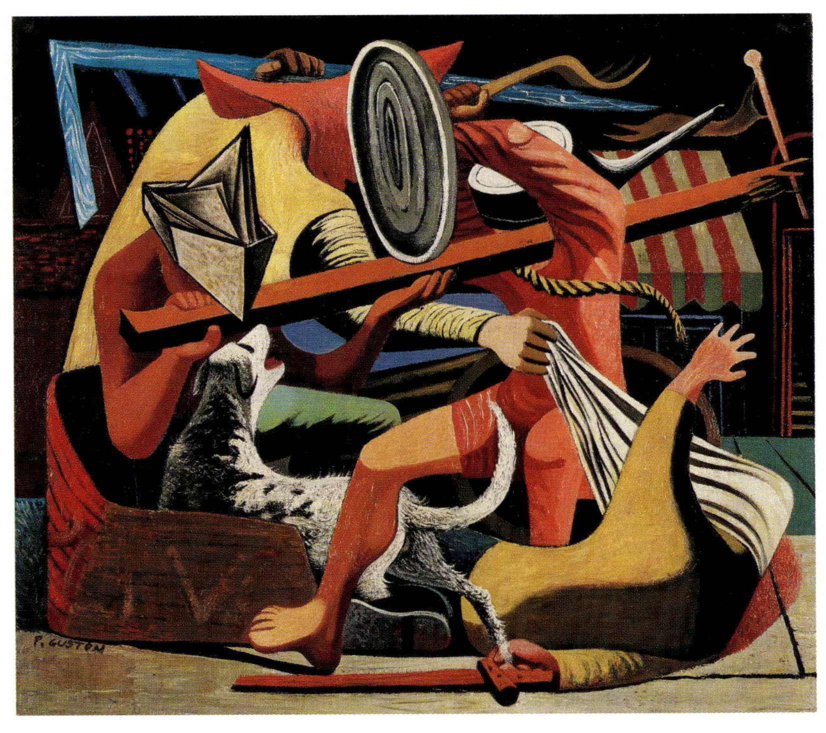

PHILIP GUSTON, GLADIATORS, 1938

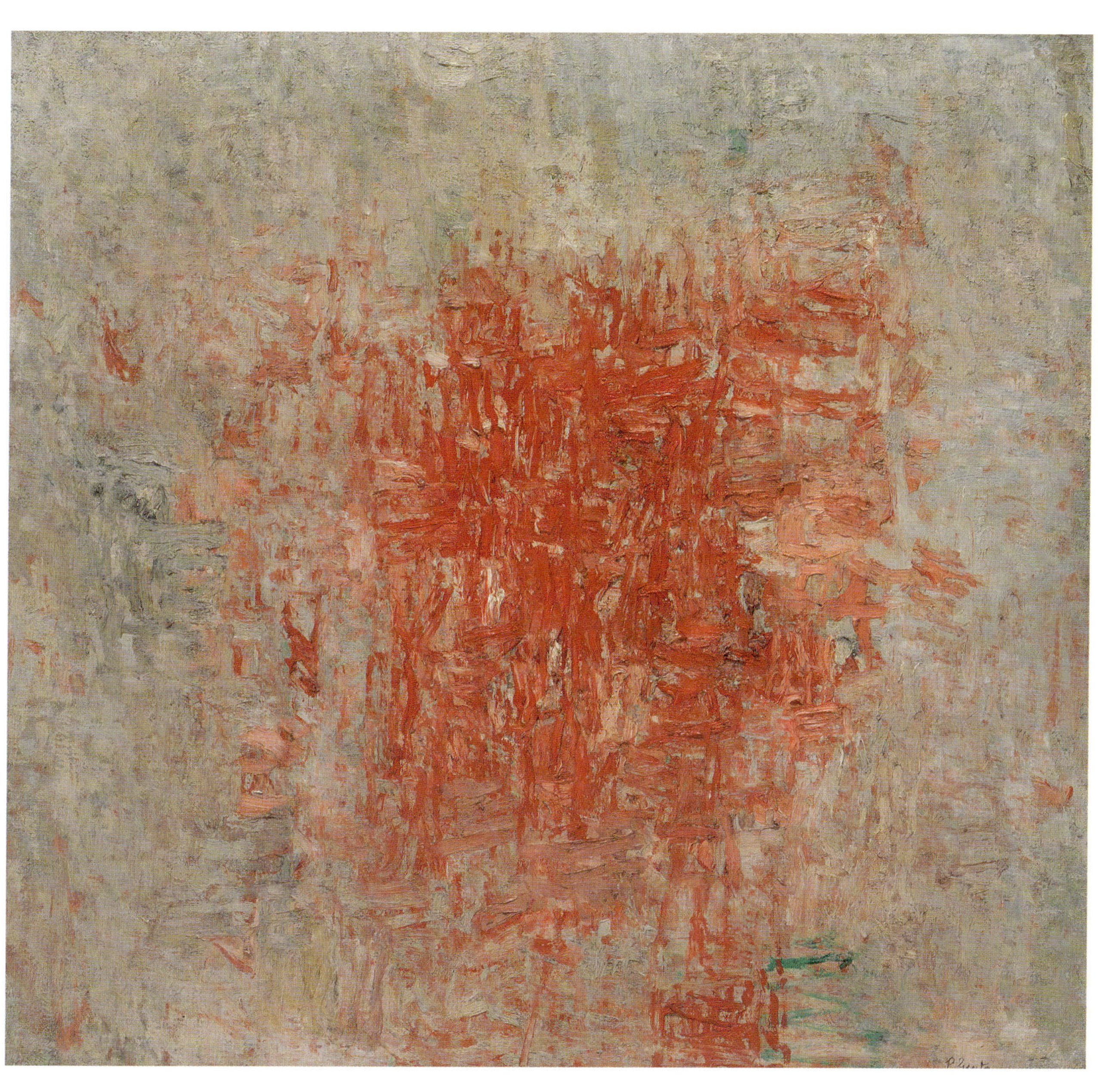

PHILIP GUSTON, ZONE, 1953-54

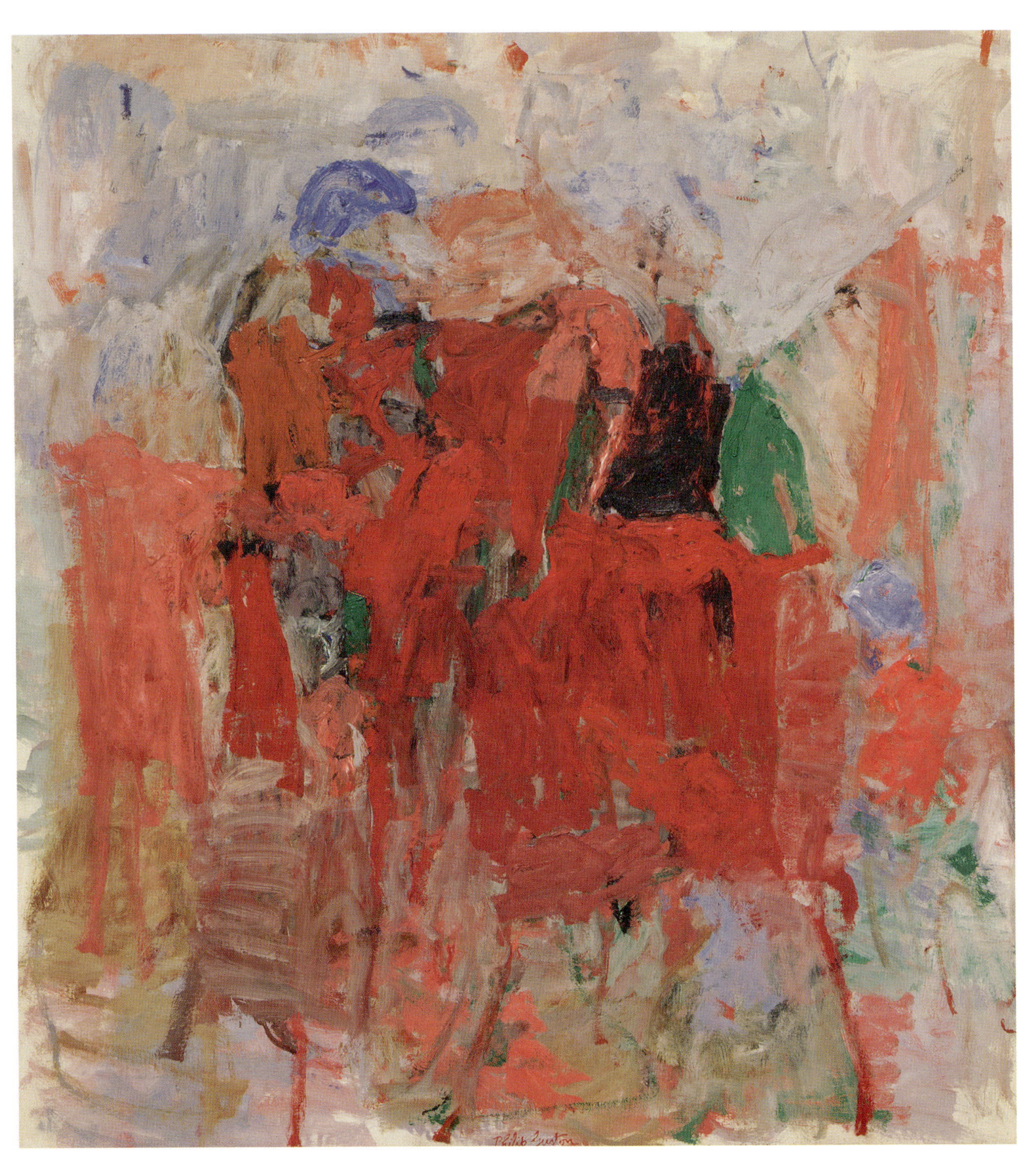

PHILIP GUSTON, THE MIRROR, 1957

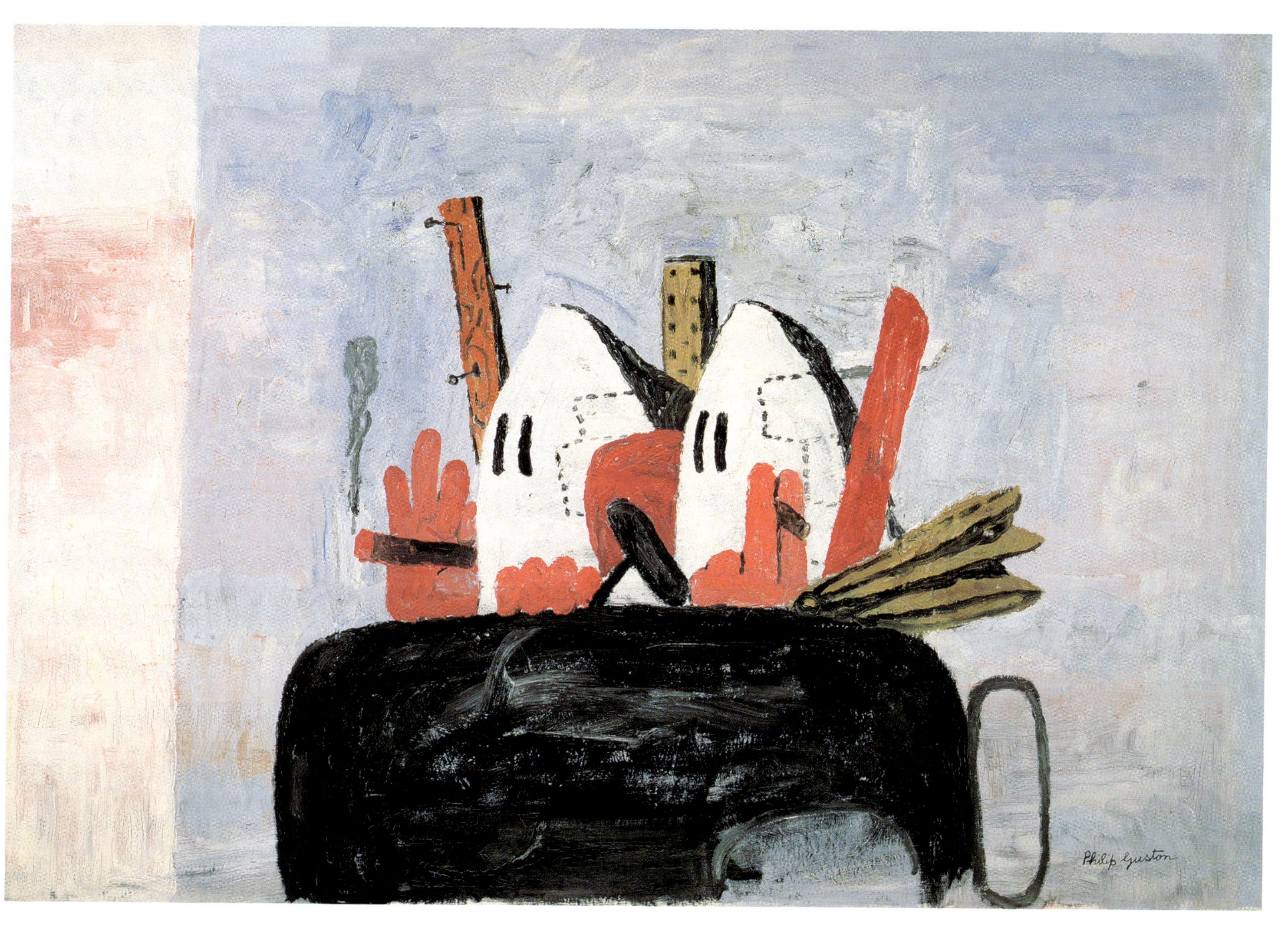

PHILIP GUSTON, EDGE OF TOWN, 1969

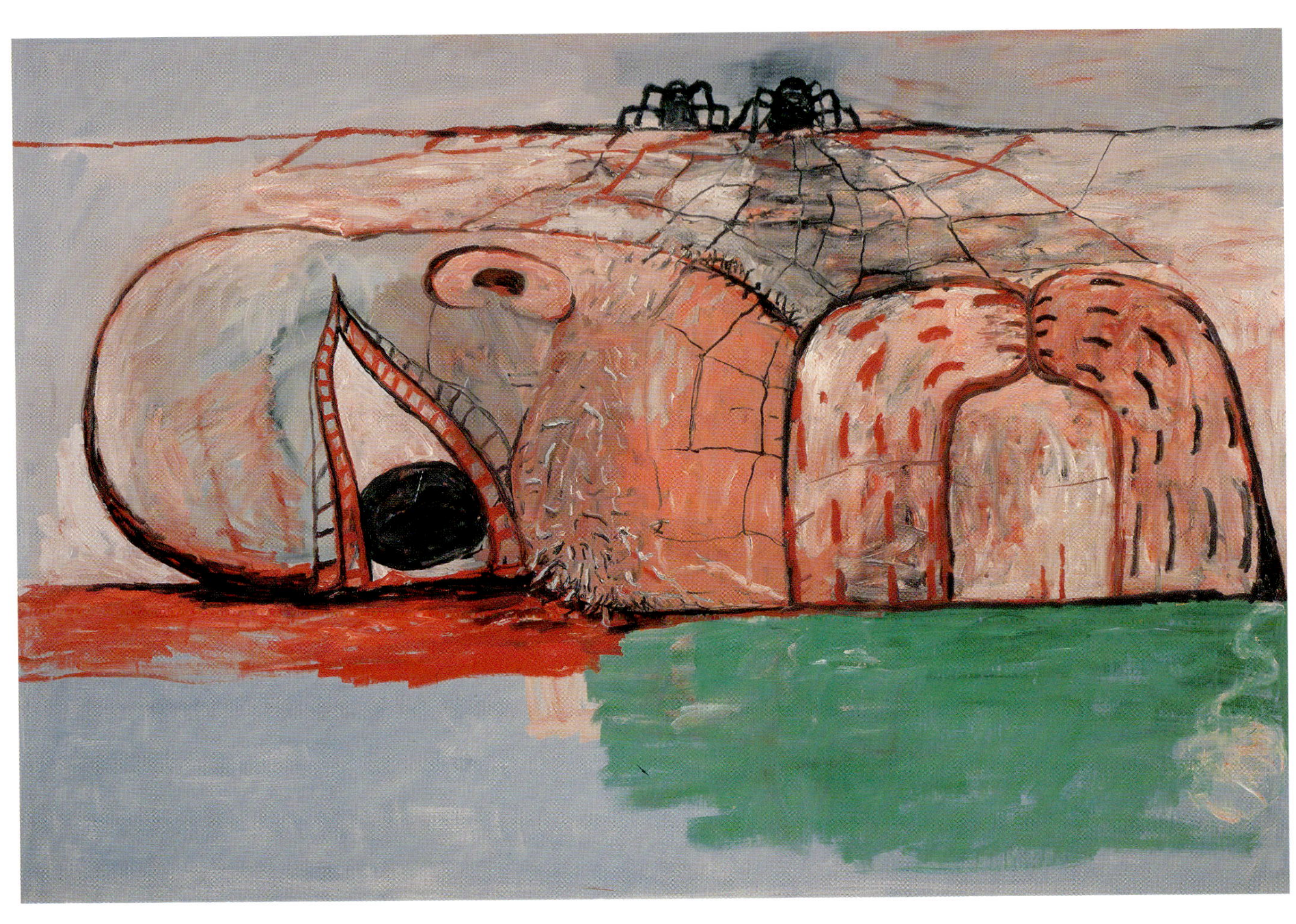

PHILIP GUSTON, WEB, 1975

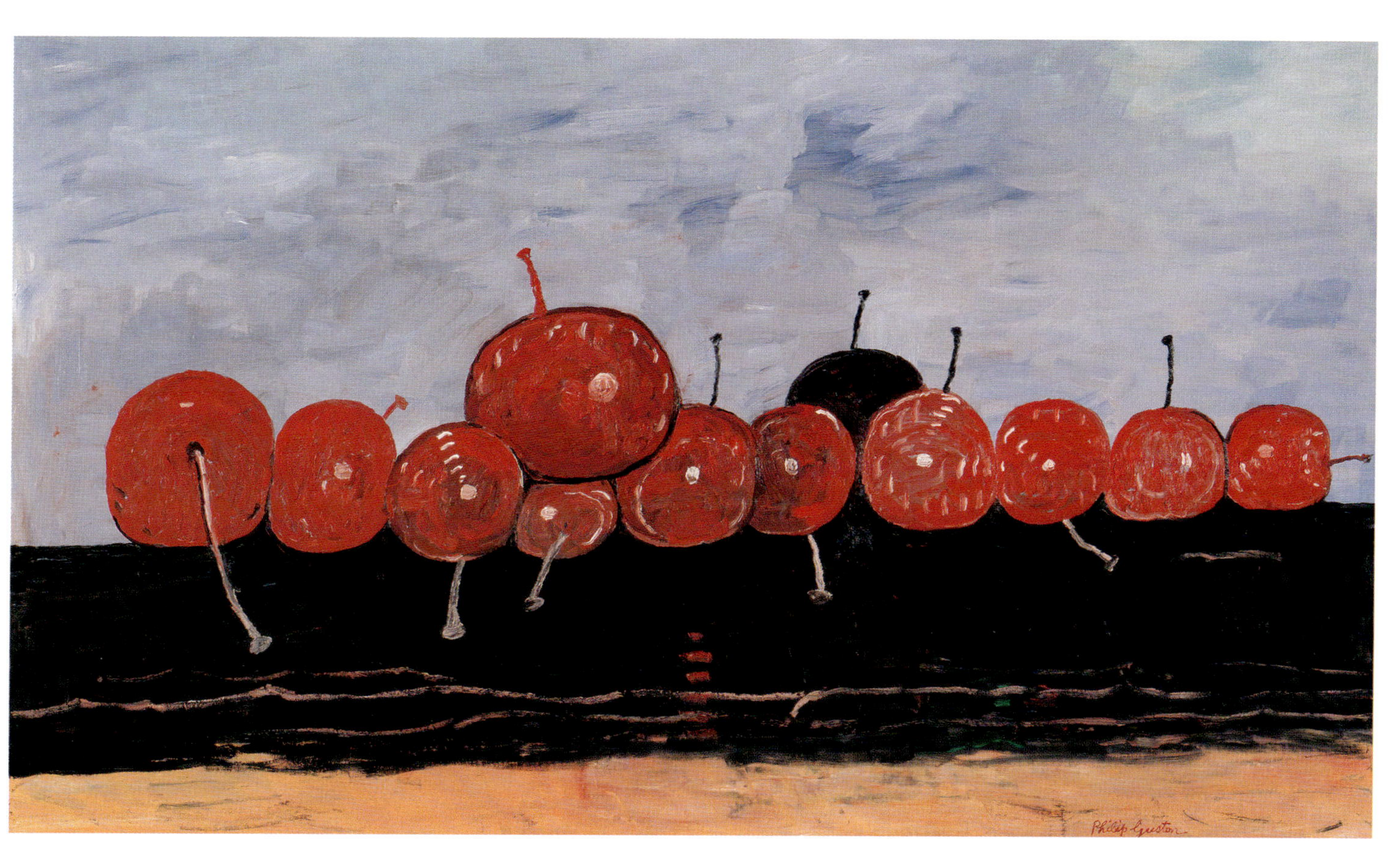

PHILIP GUSTON, CHERRIES, 1976

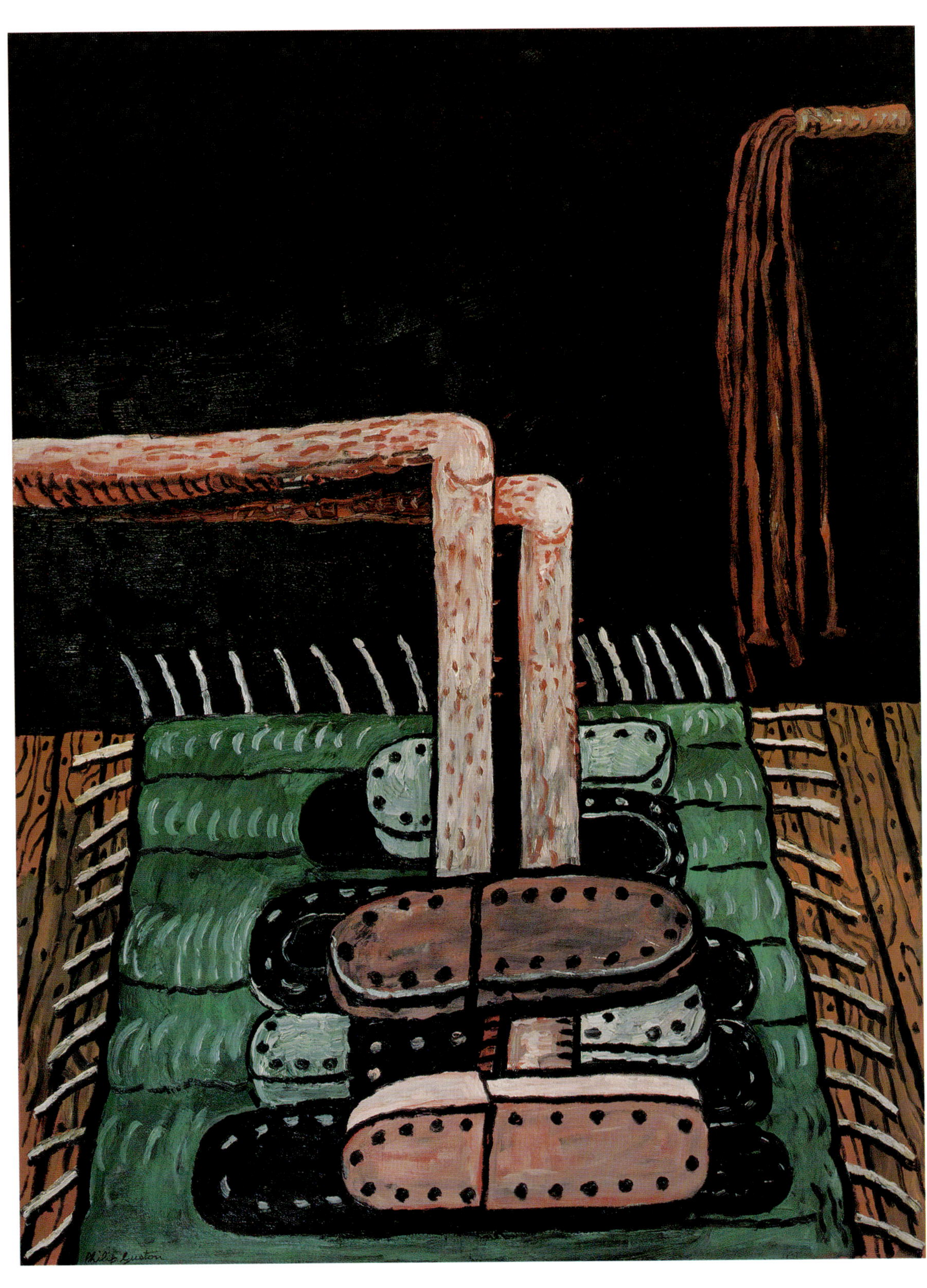

PHILIP GUSTON, GREEN RUG, 1976

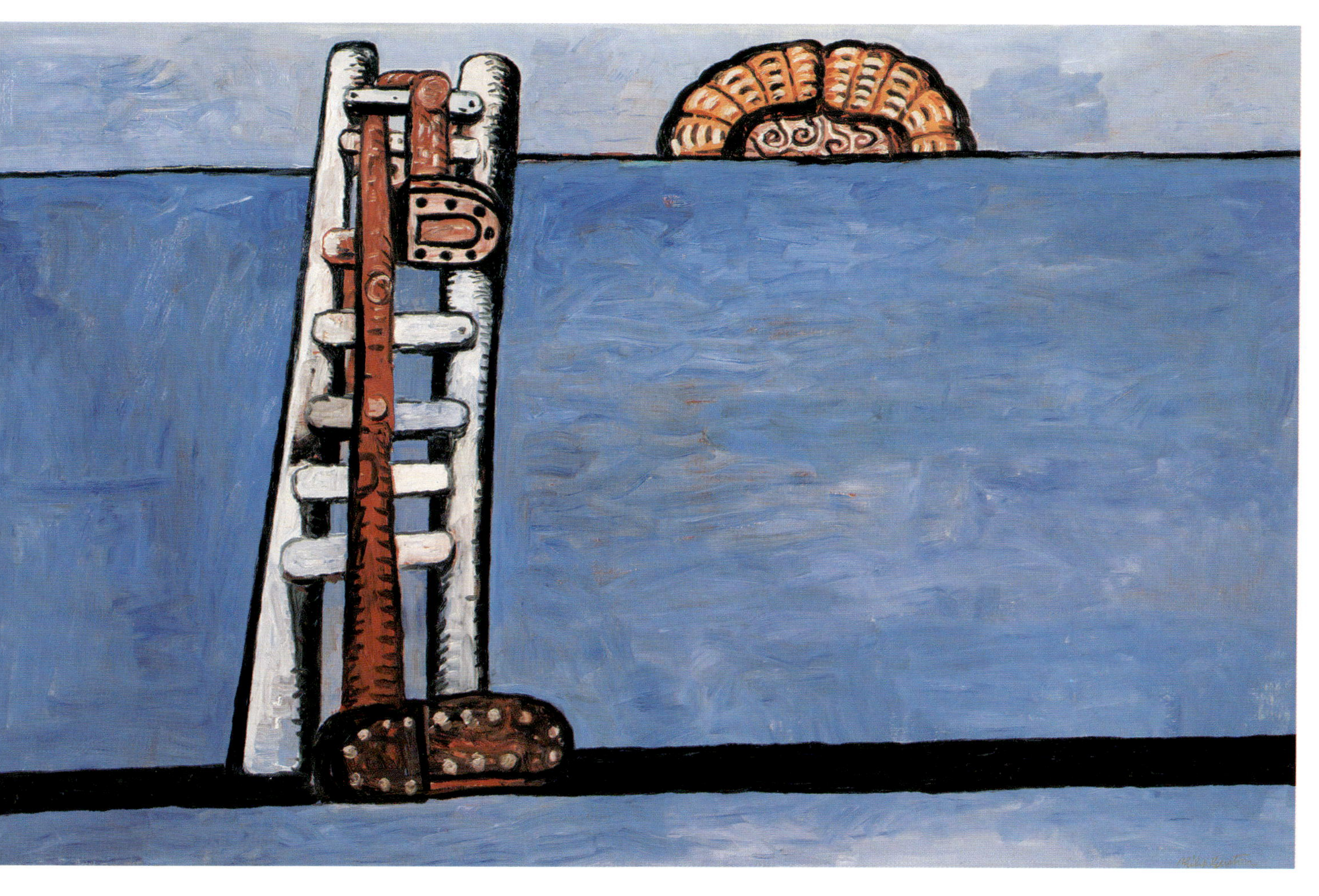

PHILIP GUSTON, LADDER, 1978

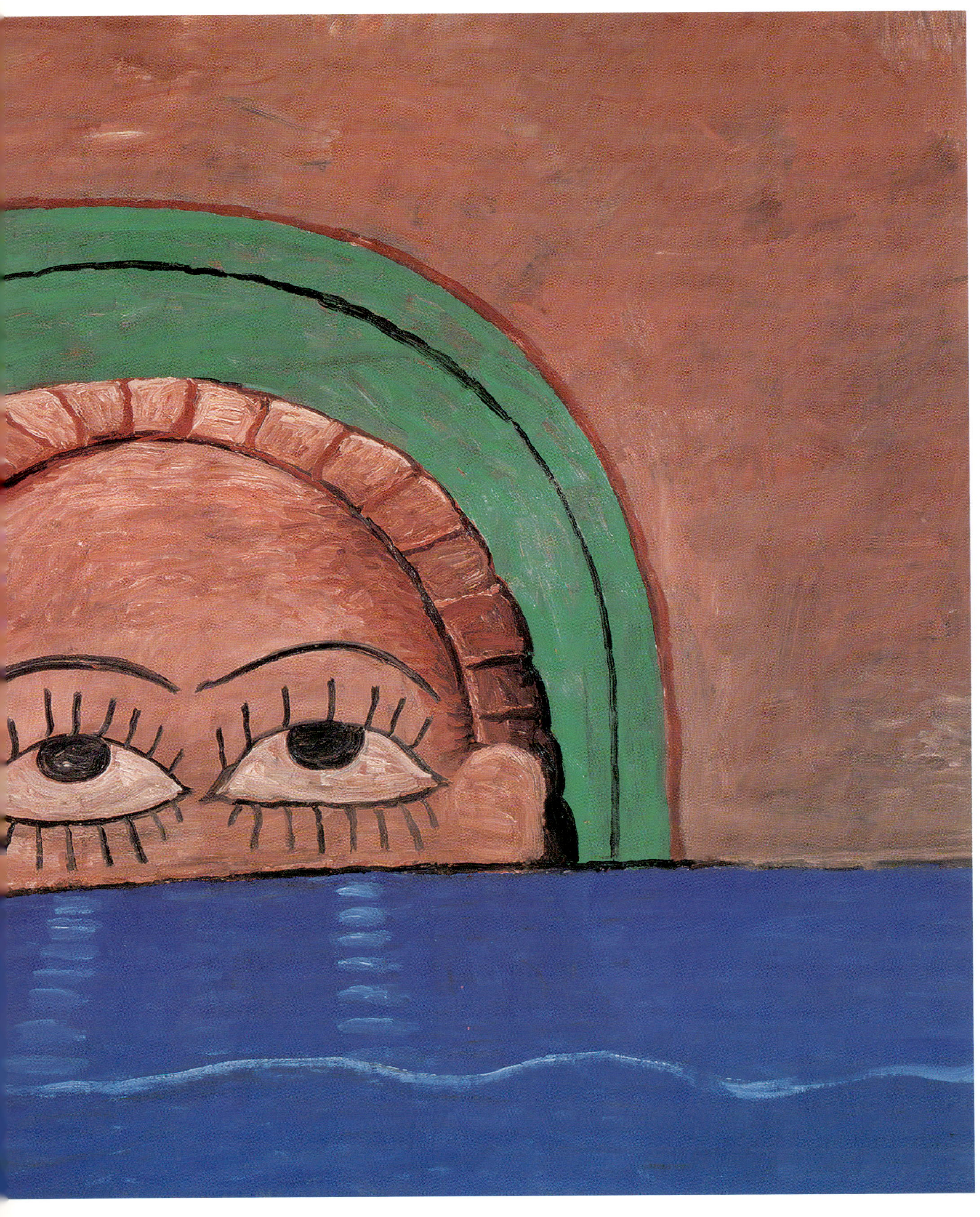

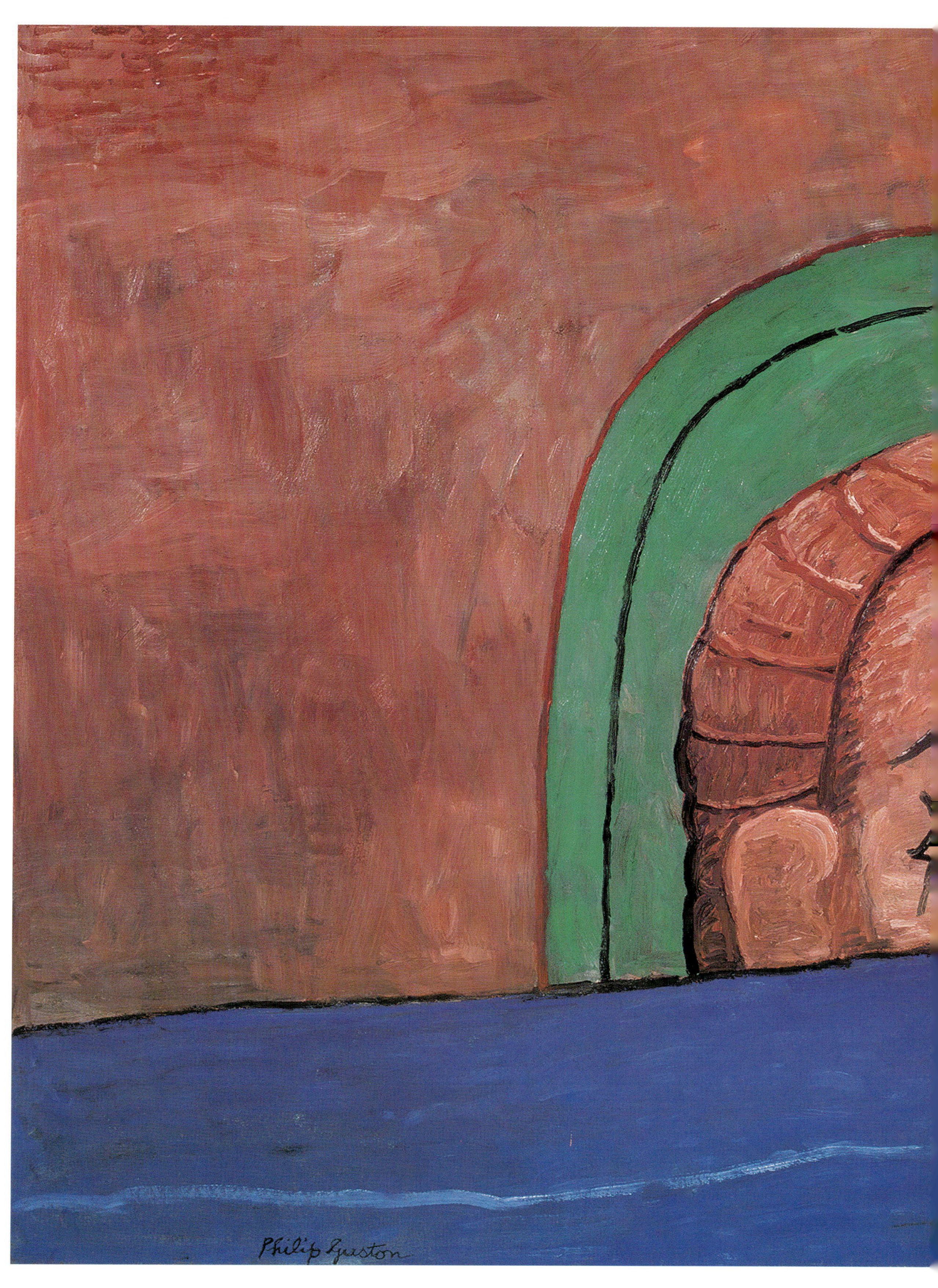

PHILIP GUSTON, SOURCE, 1976

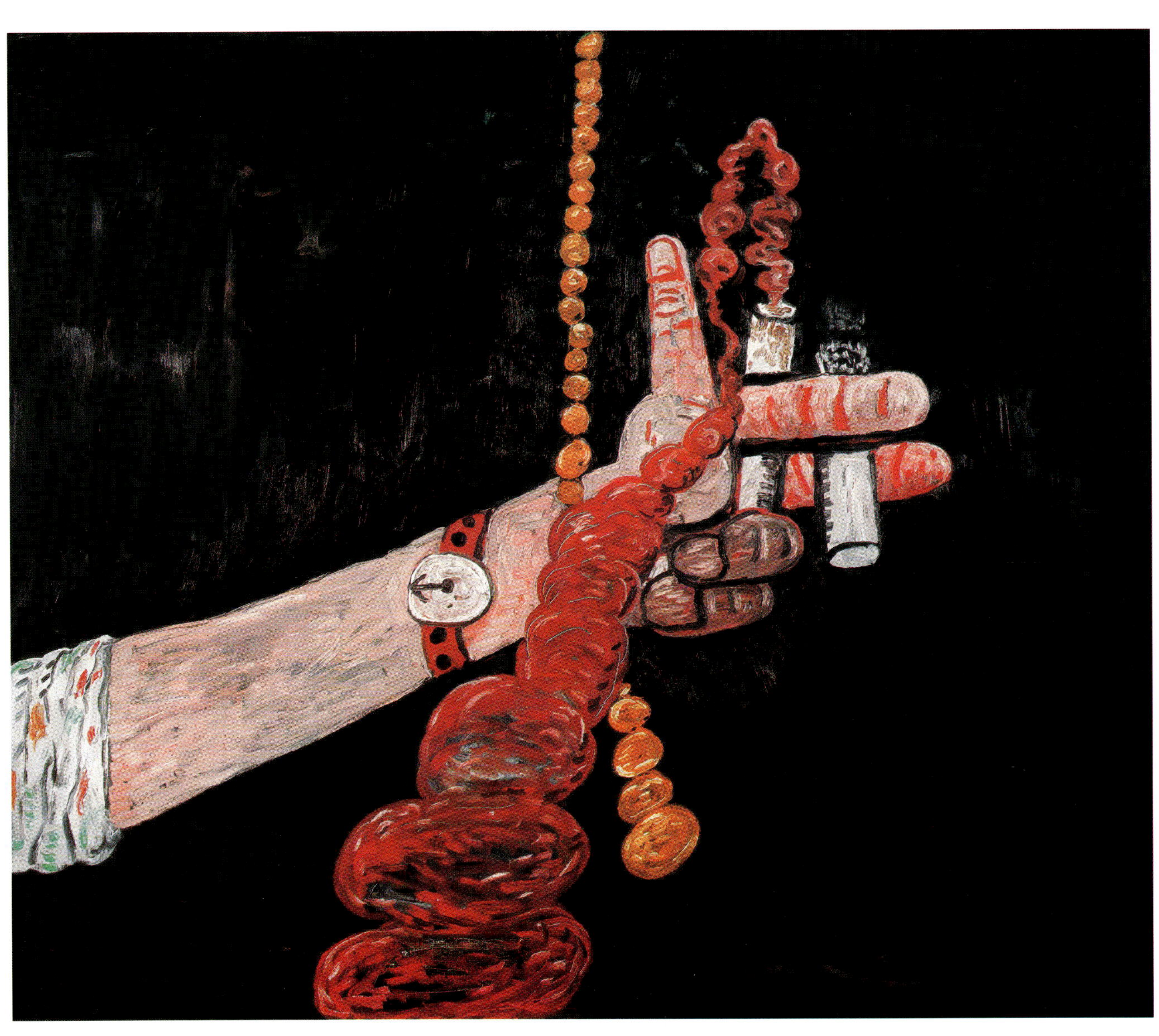

PHILIP GUSTON, TALKING, 1979

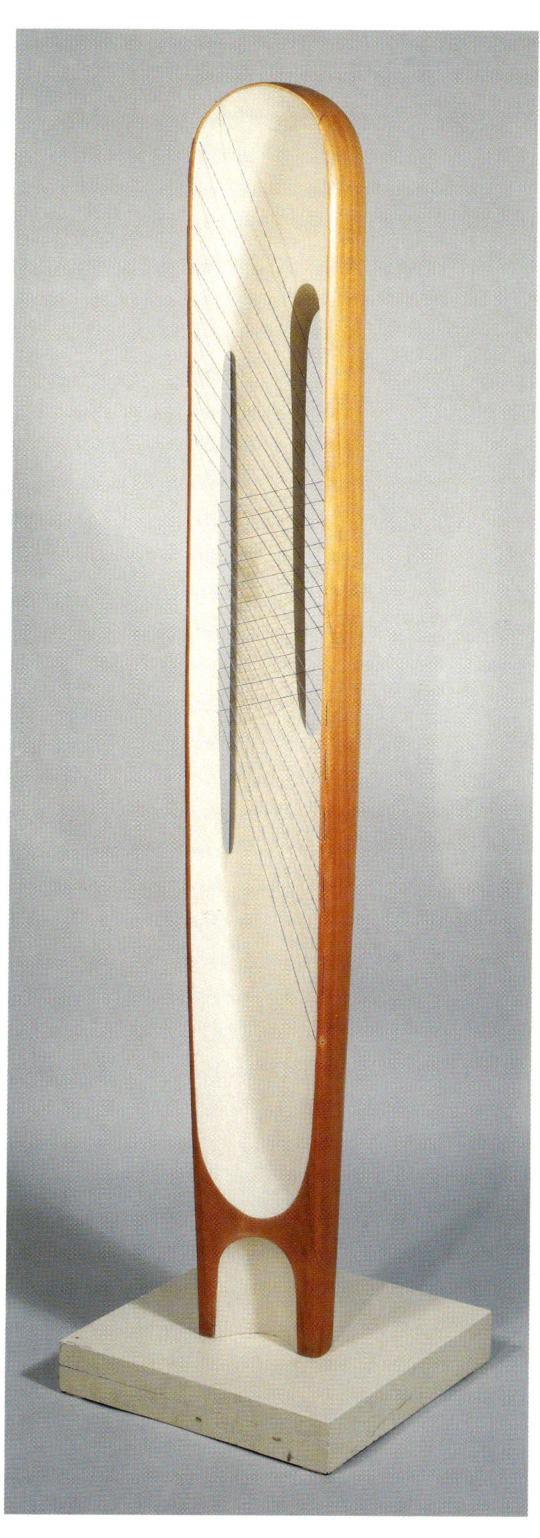

BARBARA HEPWORTH, FIGURE (ASCENDING FORM), 1956

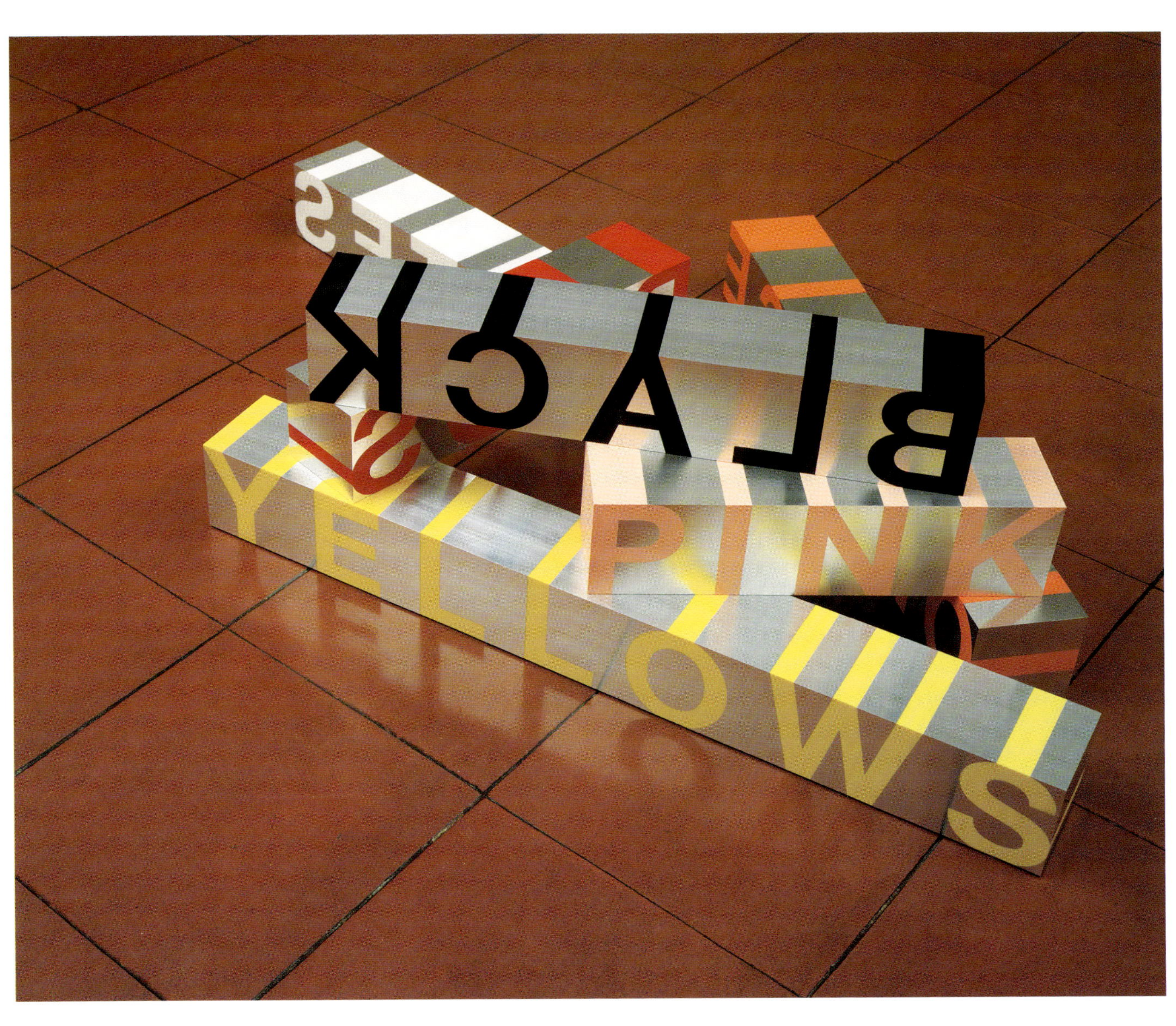

RONI HORN, STEVENS' BOUQUET, 1991

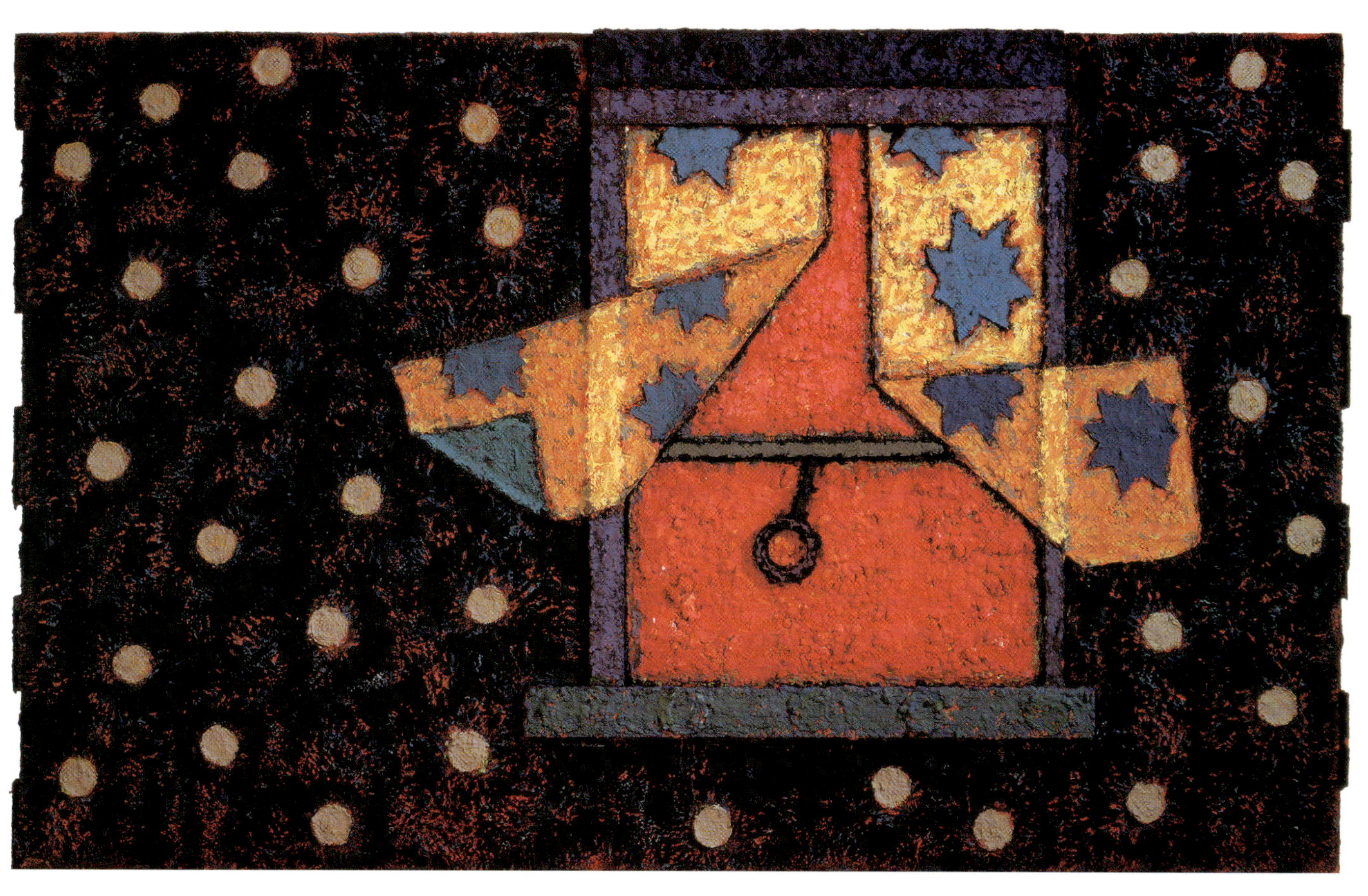

RALPH HUMPHREY, STORM FIELD, 1981-82

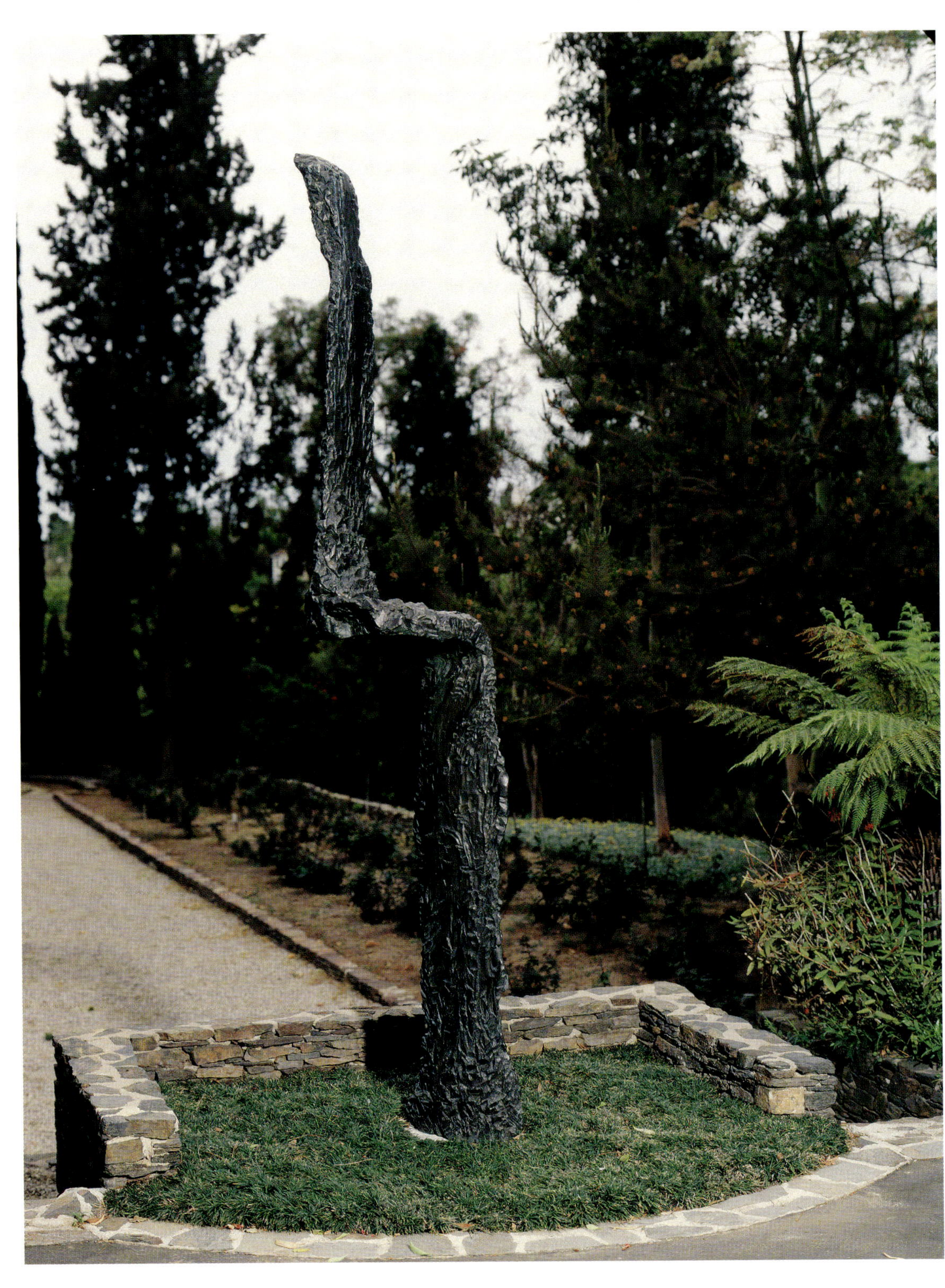

BRYAN HUNT, BIG TWIST, 1978

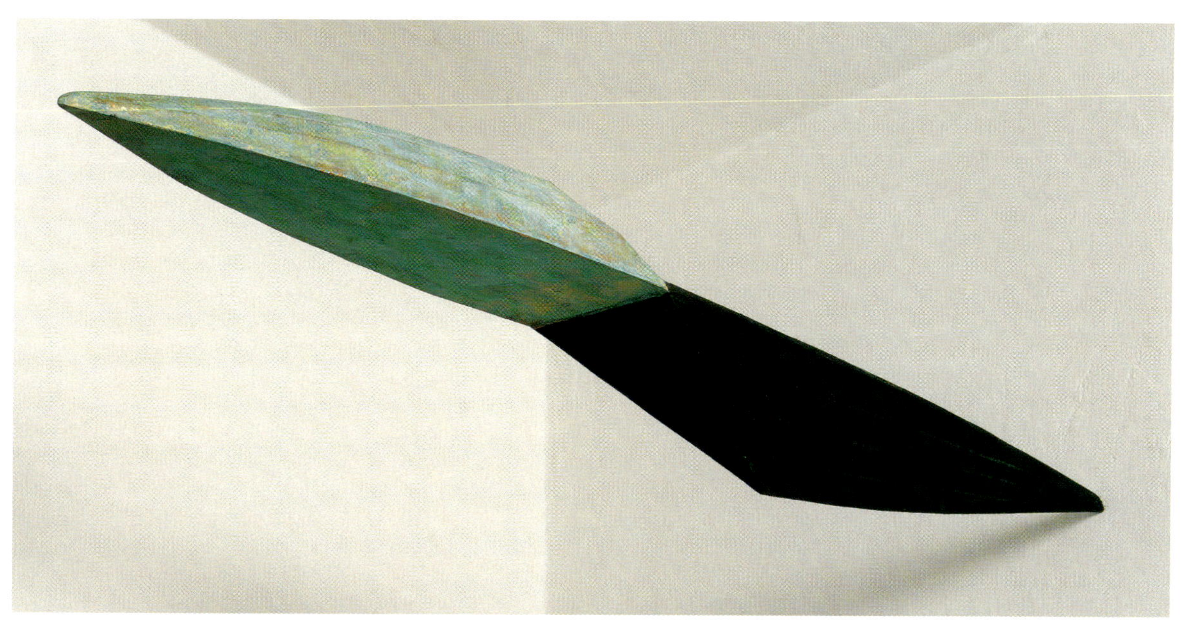

BRYAN HUNT, UNTITLED, 1981

DENZIL HURLEY, UNTITLED, 1984-86

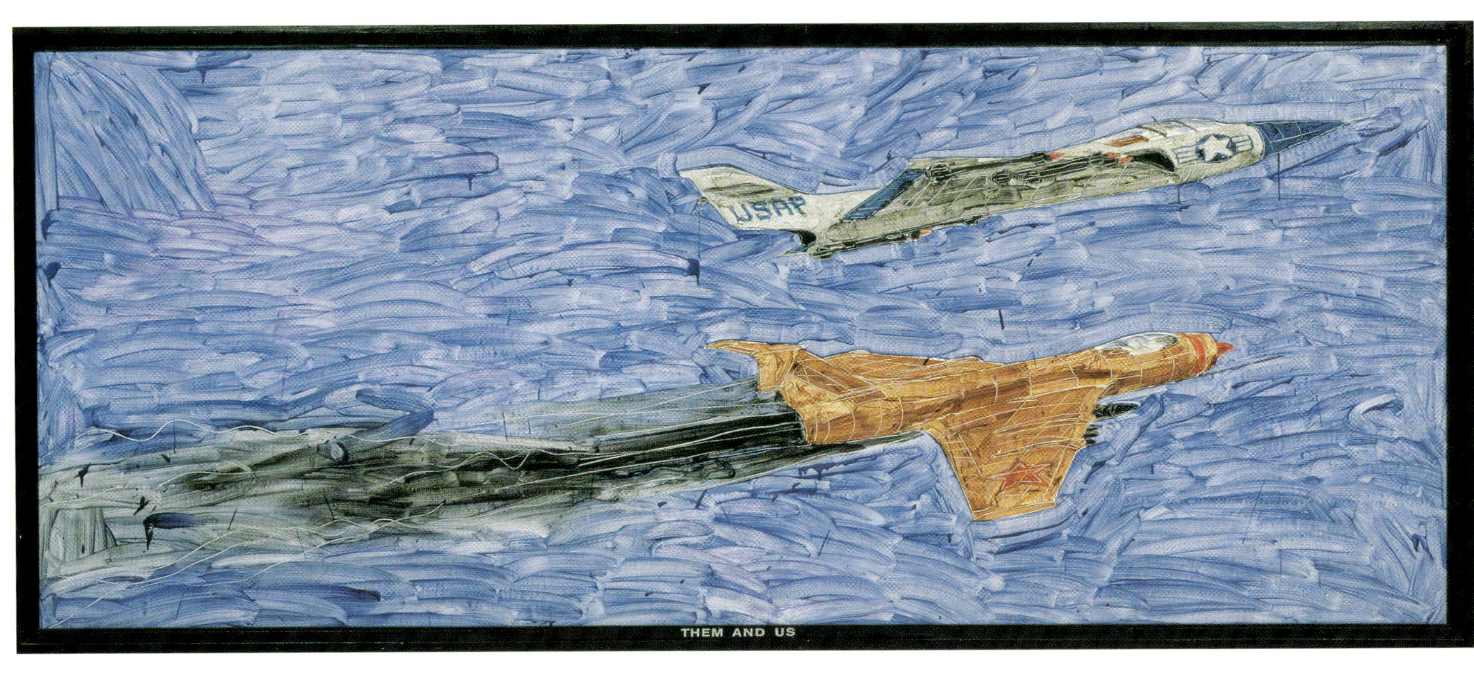

NEIL JENNEY, THEM AND US, 1969

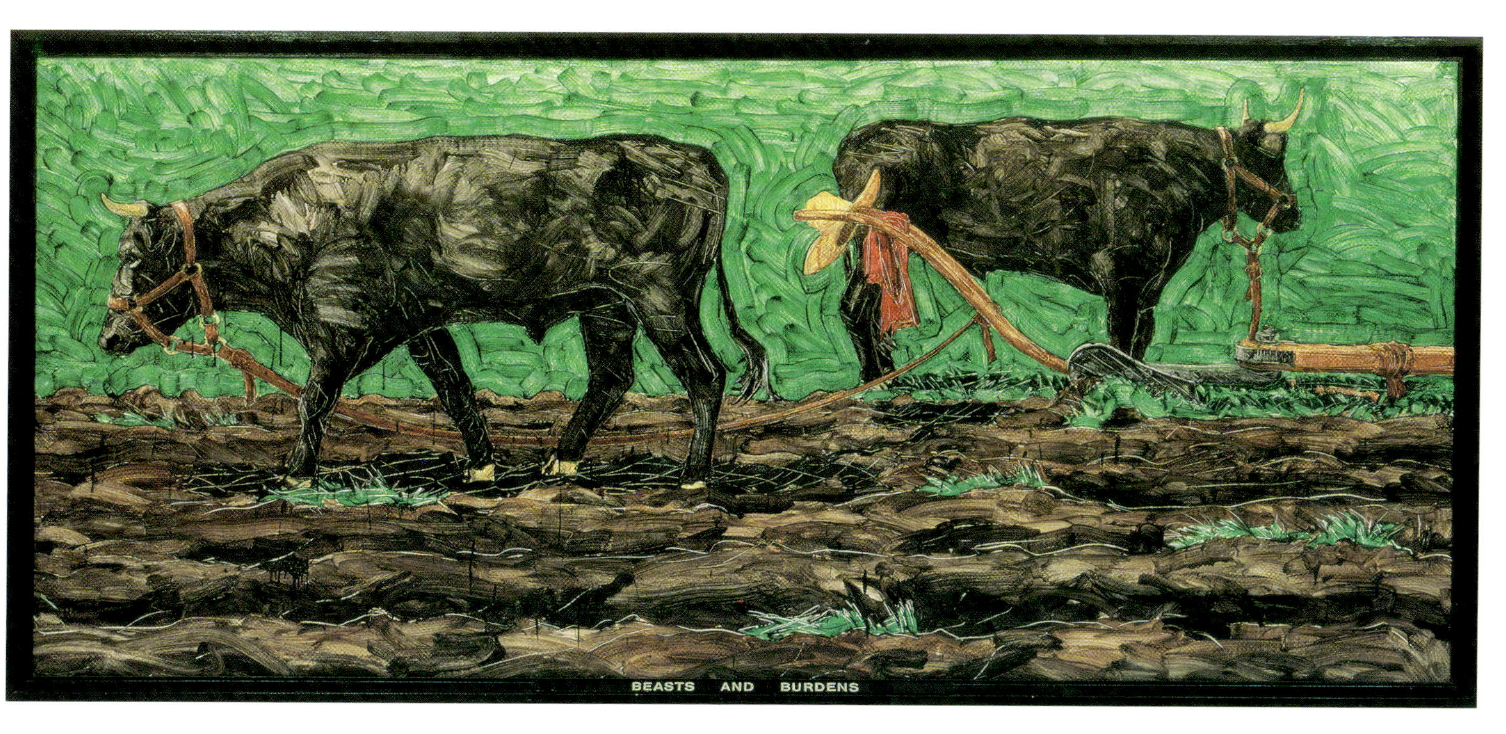

NEIL JENNEY, BEASTS AND BURDENS, 1970

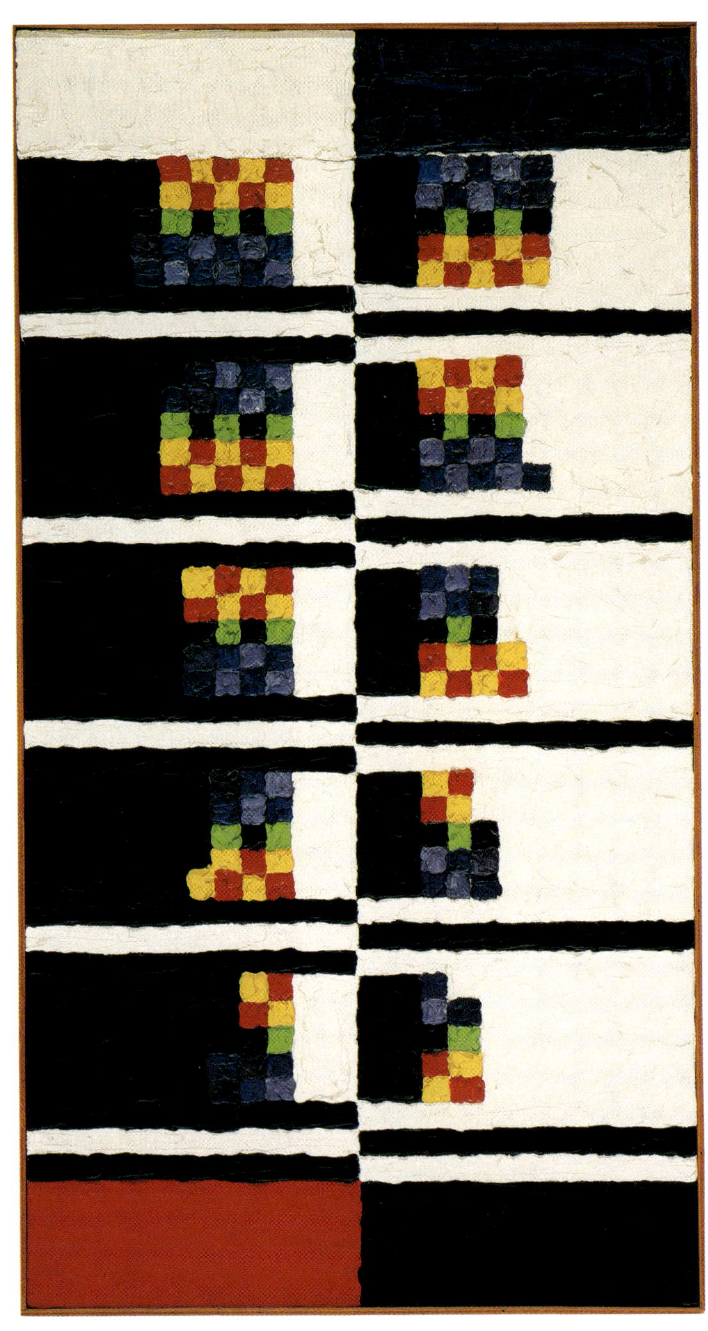

ALFRED JENSEN, INTERVAL IN SIX SCALES, 1963

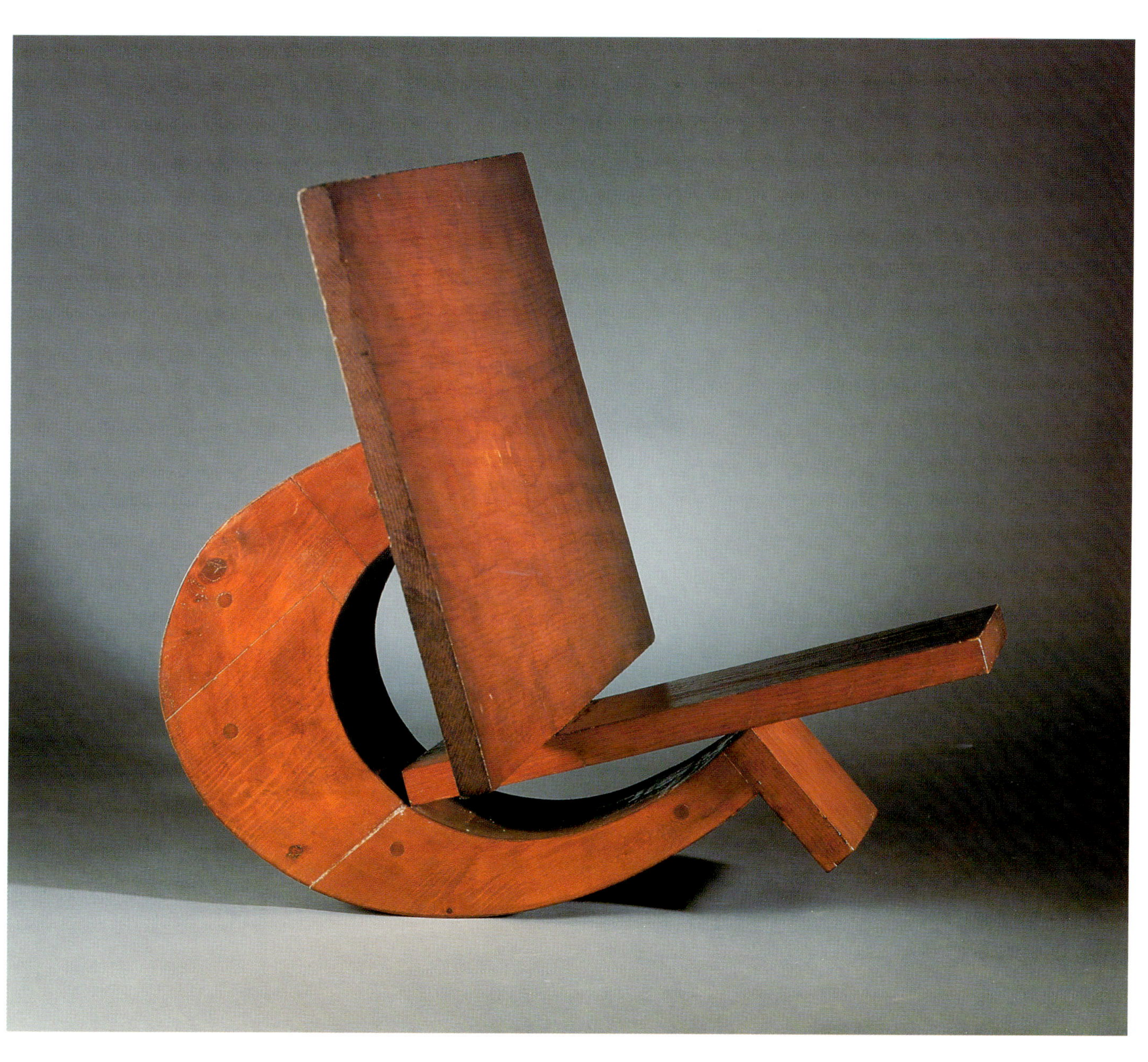

GABRIEL KOHN, VENTURA III, 1965

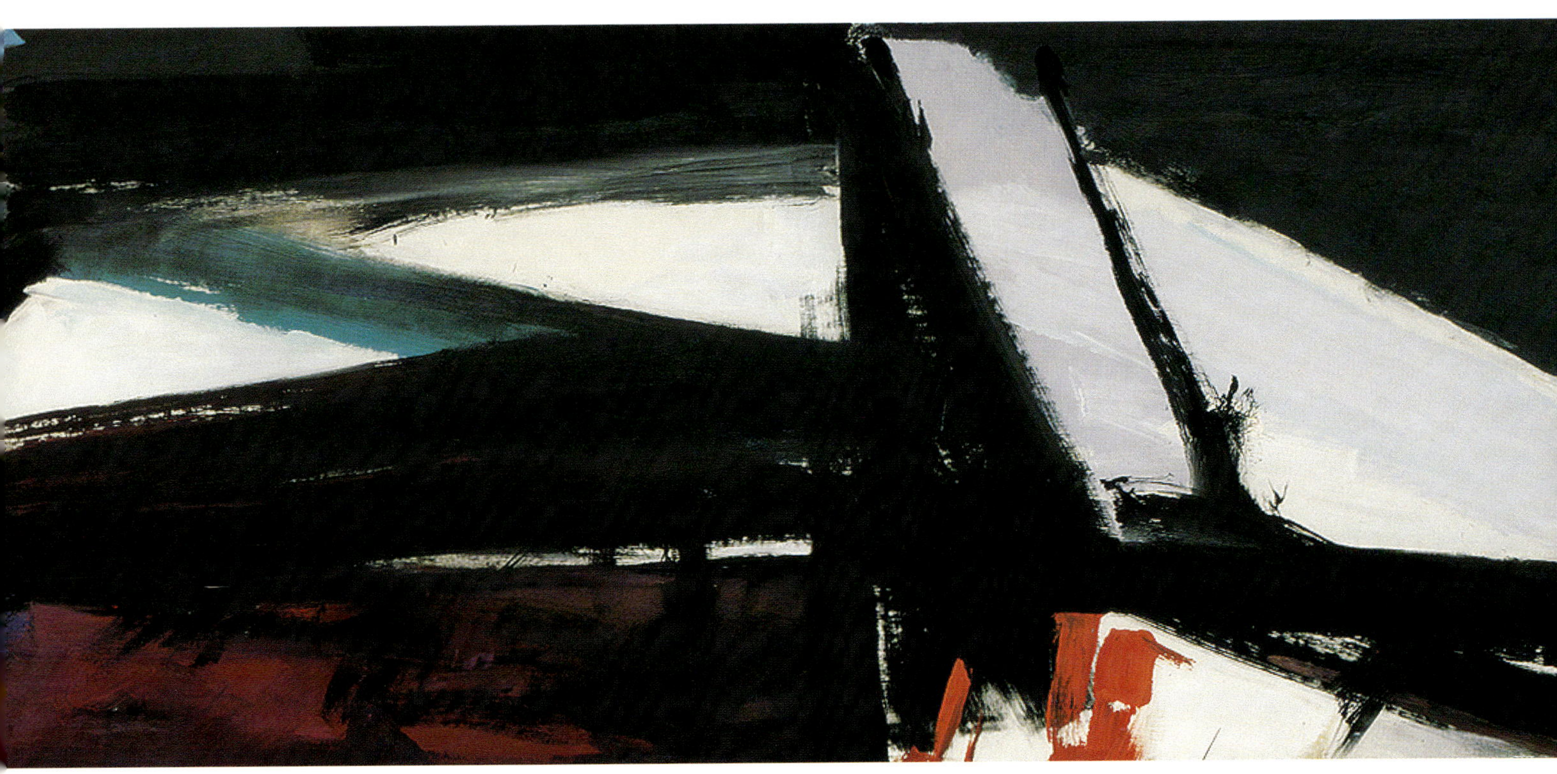

FRANZ KLINE, WASHINGTON WALL, 1959

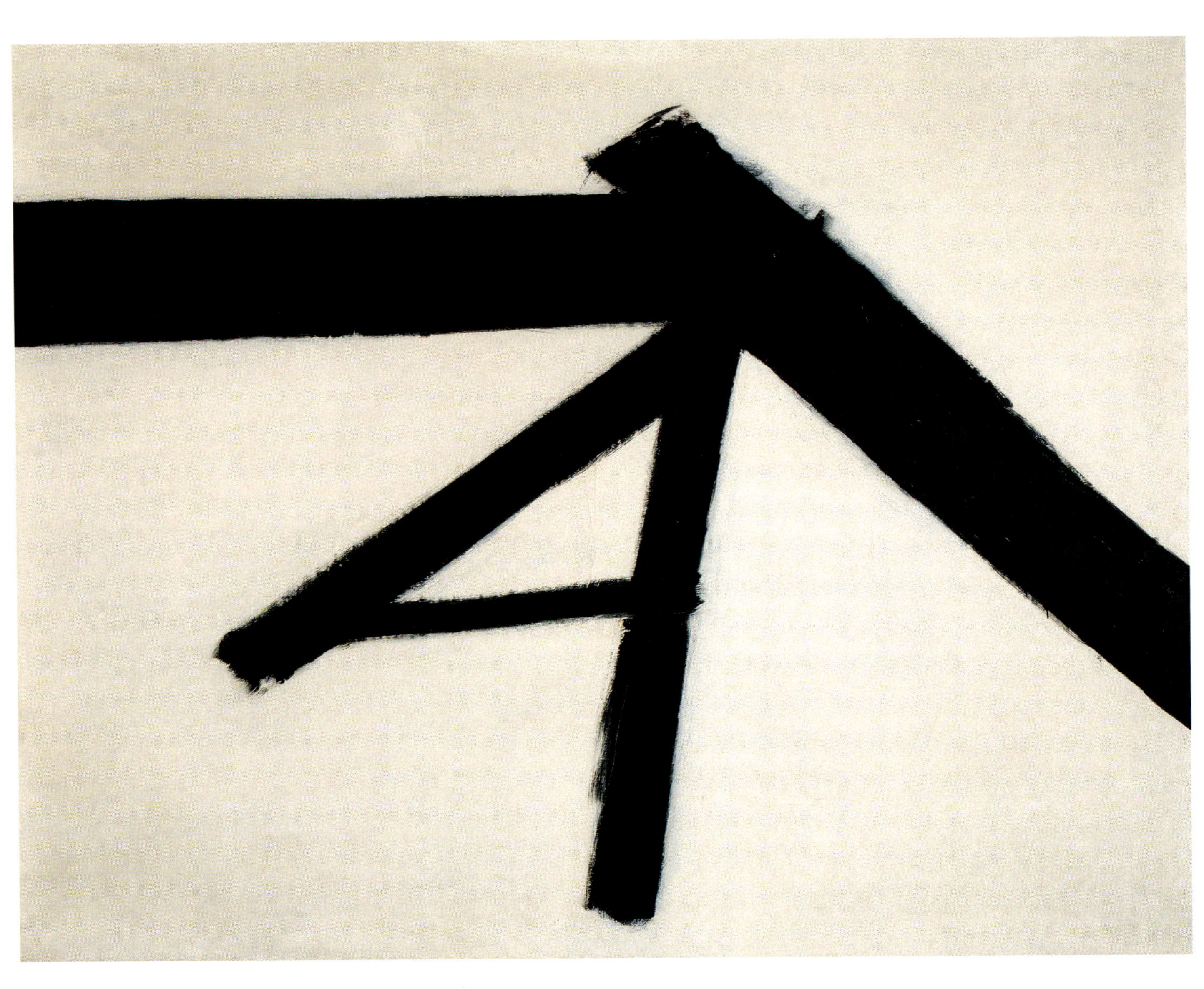

FRANZ KLINE, LUZERNE, 1956

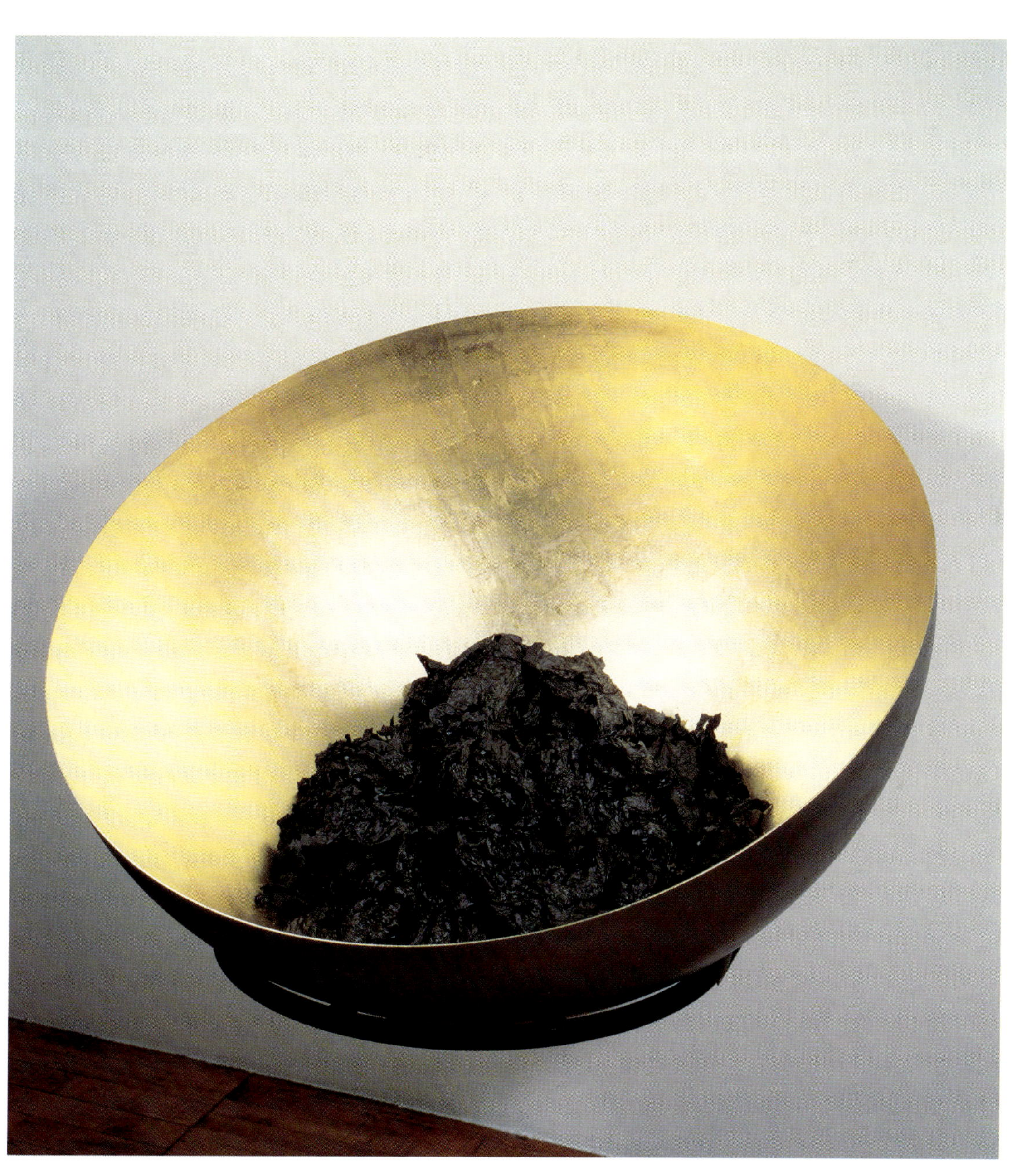

KRISTIN JONES AND ANDREW GINZEL, CINIS, 1989

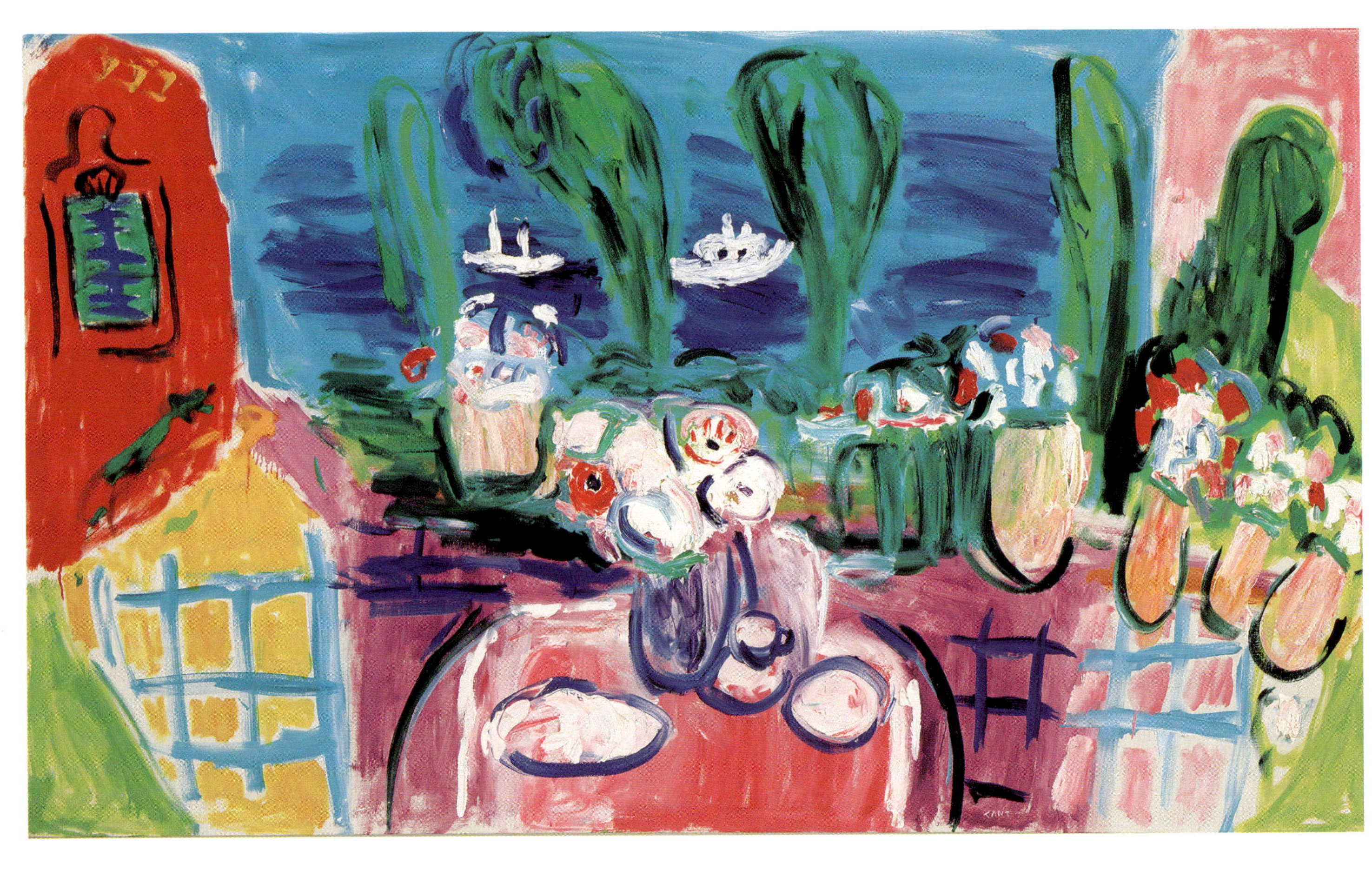

BOB KANE, TERRACE POSITANO, 1983

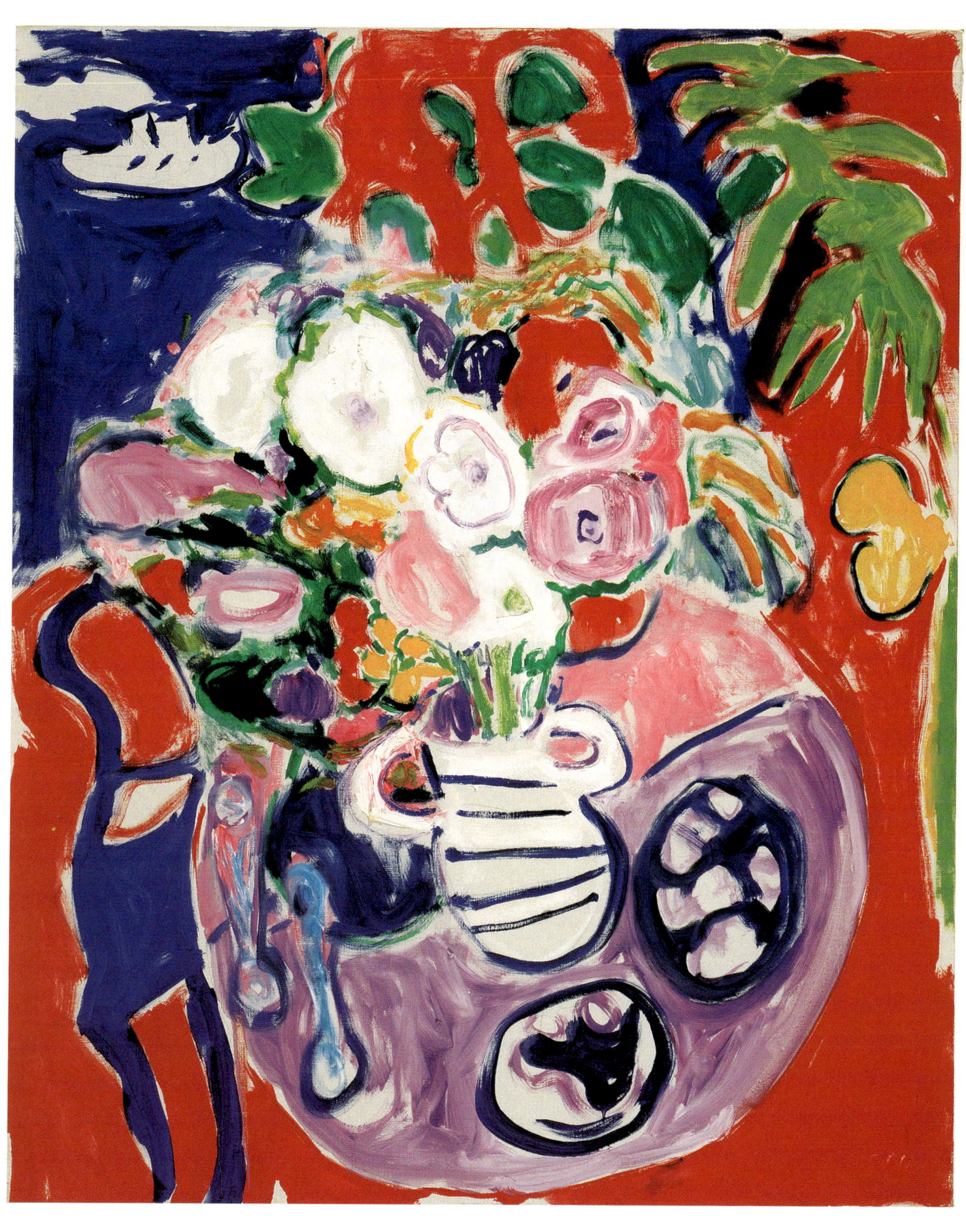

BOB KANE, UNTITLED, 1985

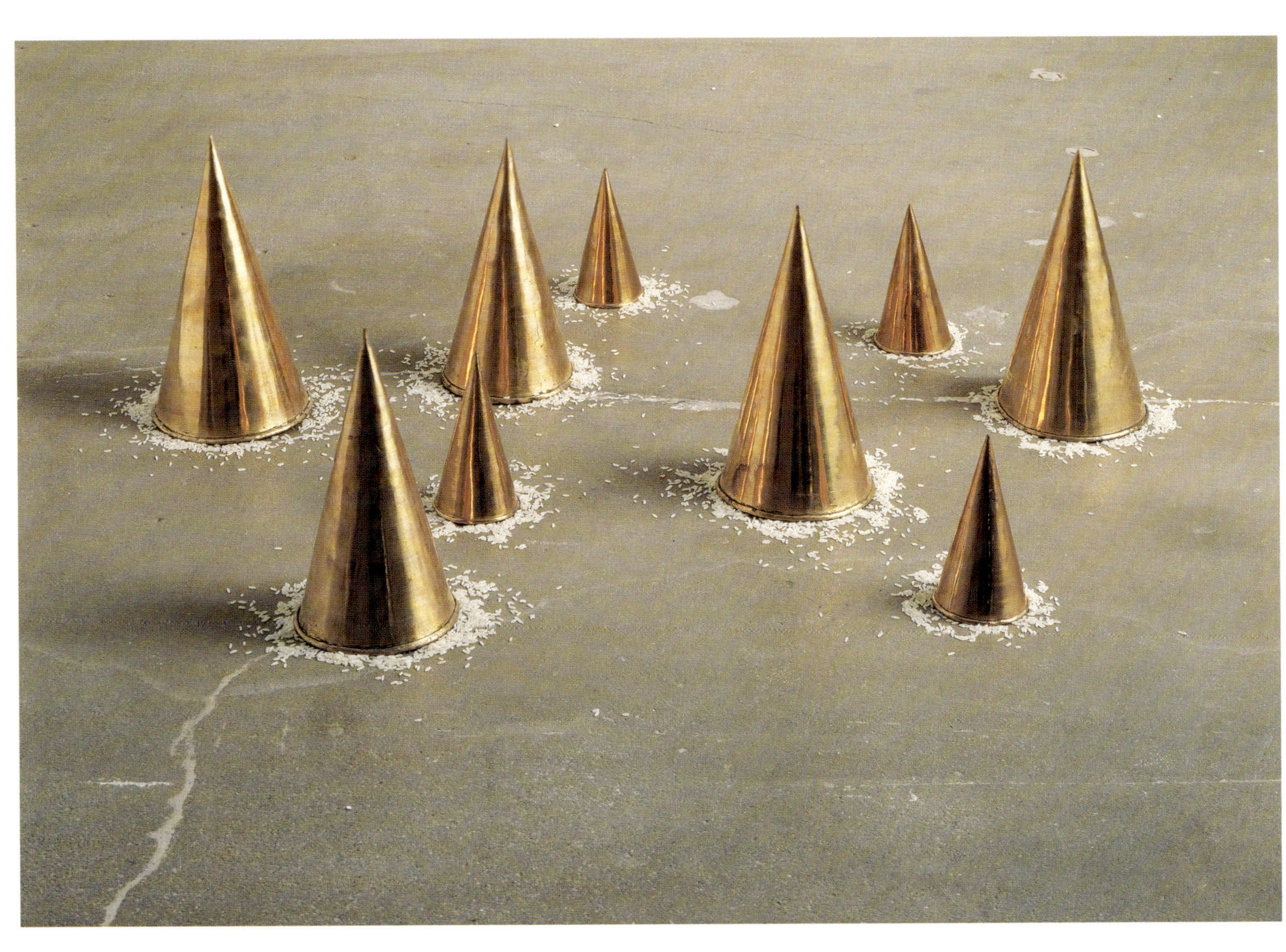

WOLFGANG LAIB, UNTITLED, 1983

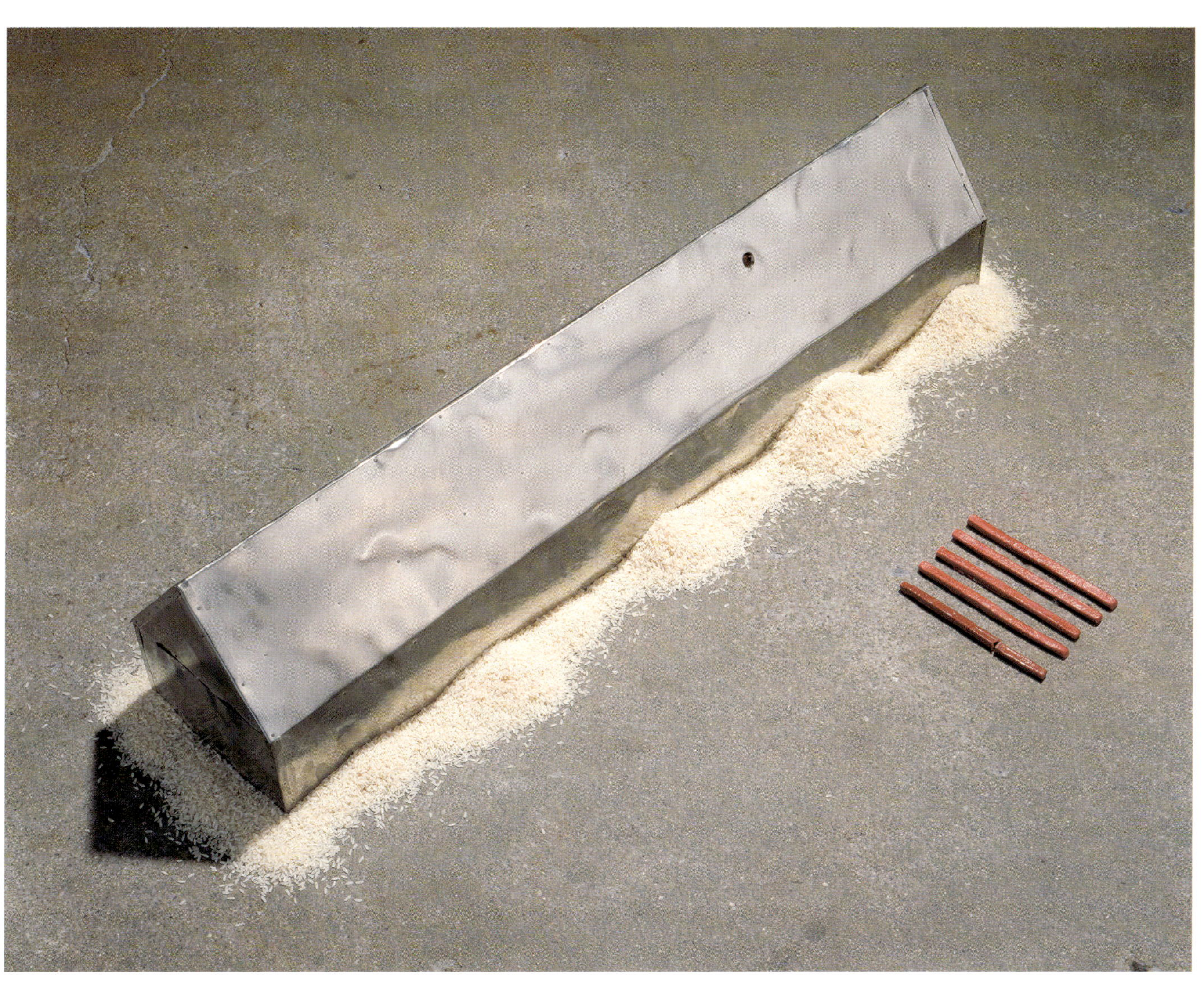

WOLFGANG LAIB, RICE HOUSE, 1986

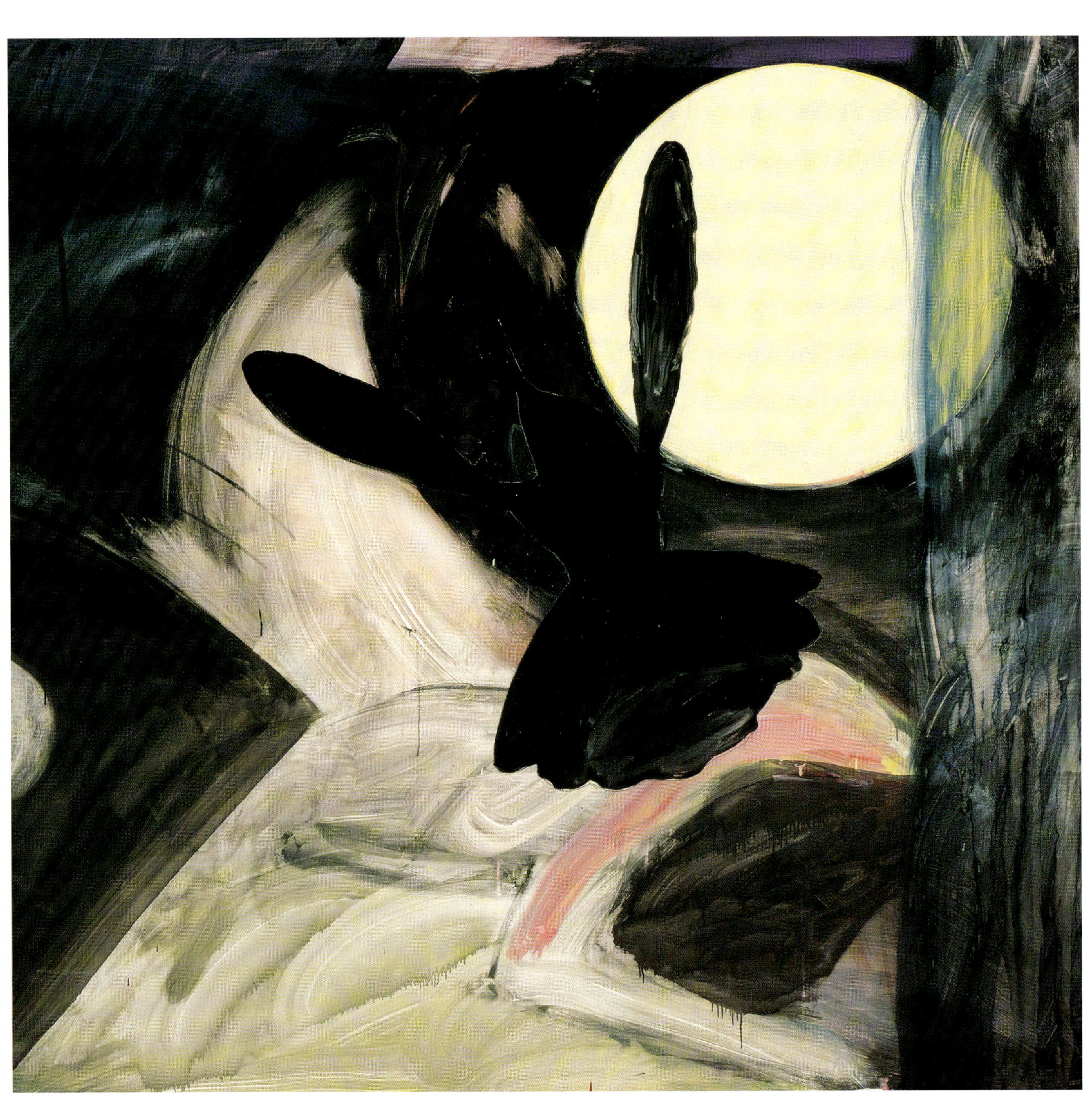

LOIS LANE, UNTITLED (BIRD, FULL MOON), 1985

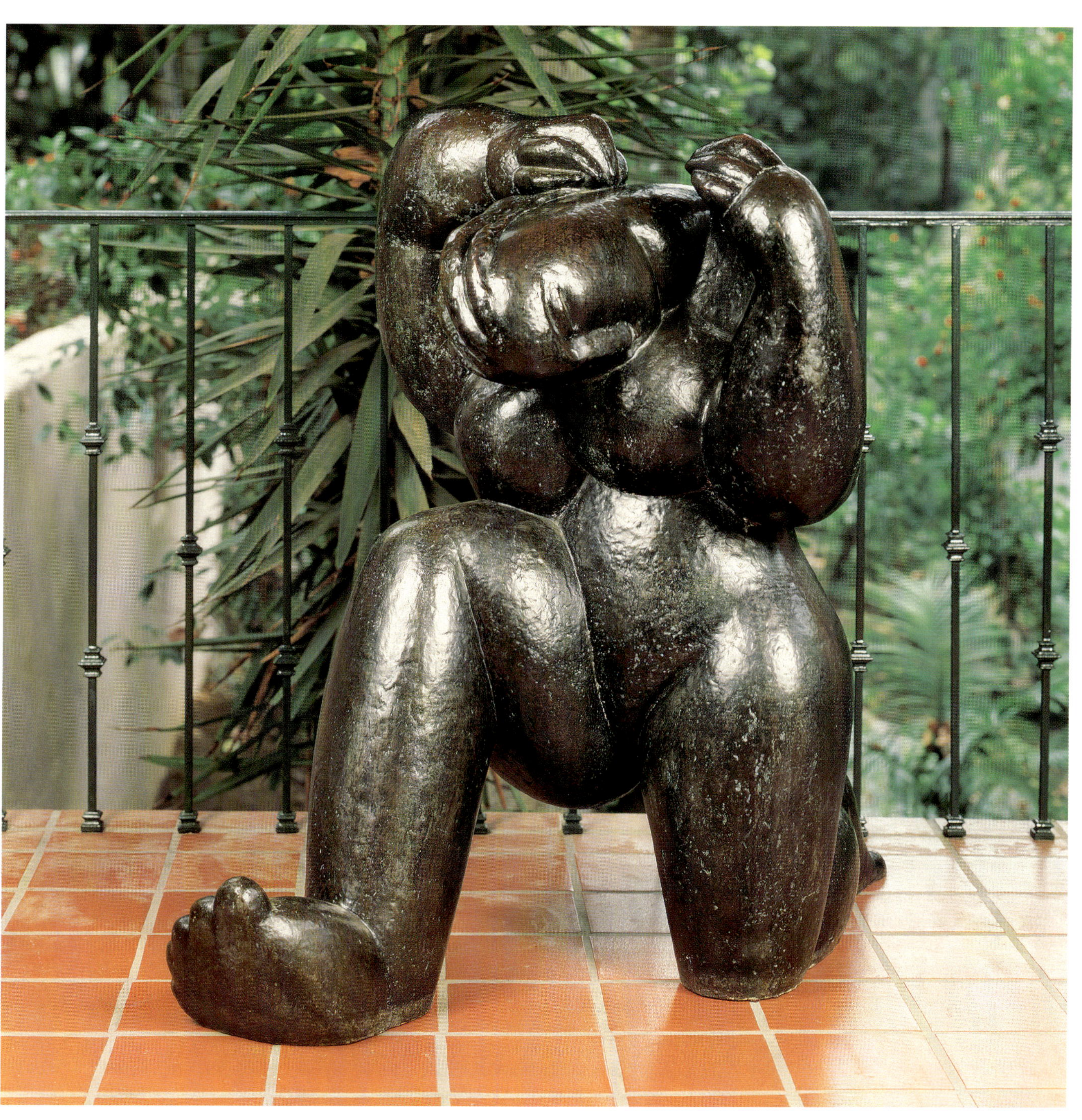

HENRI LAURENS, LE MATIN, 1944

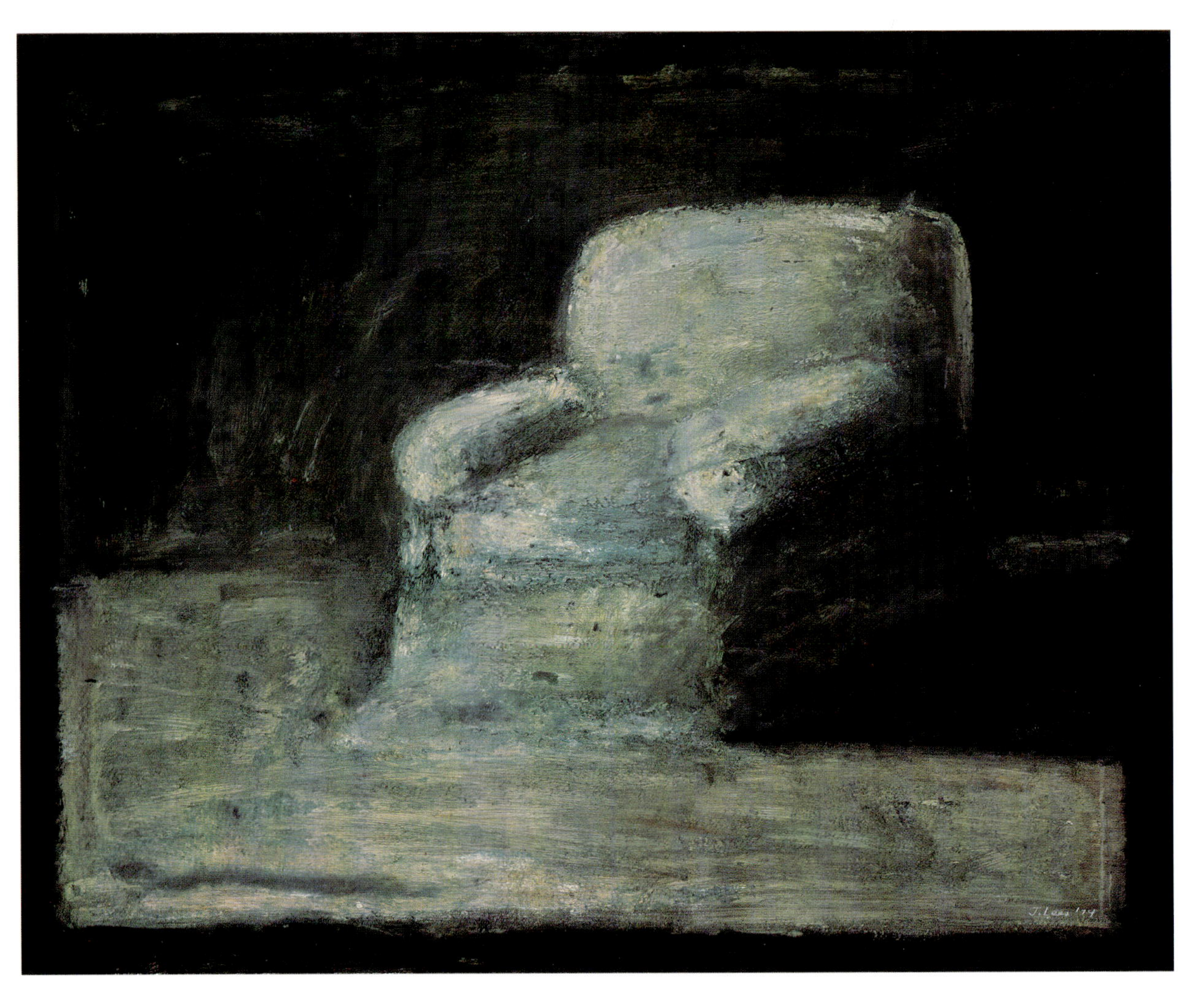

JOHN LEES, ARMCHAIR, 1974

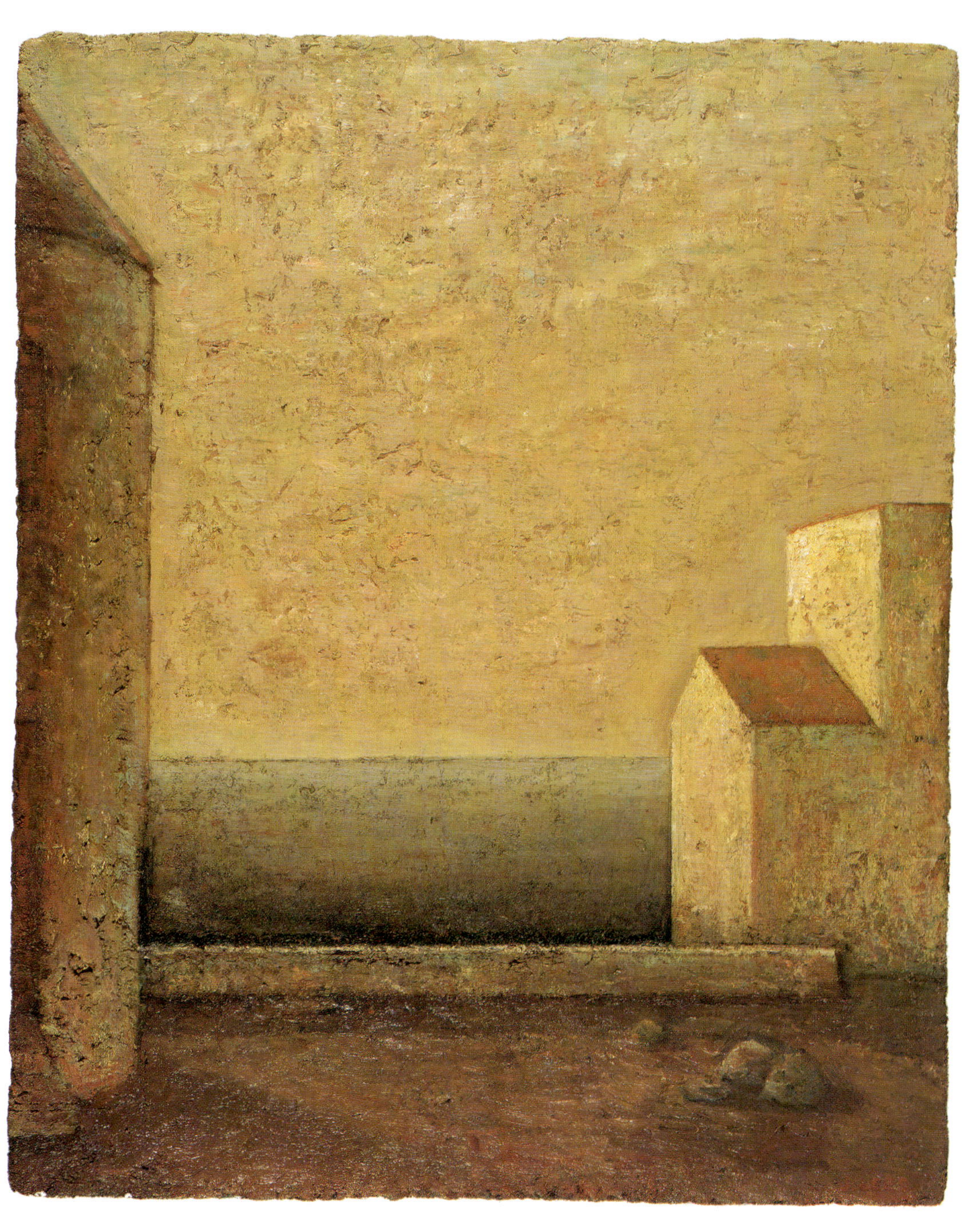

JOHN LEES, LANDSCAPE 1975-1982, 1975-82

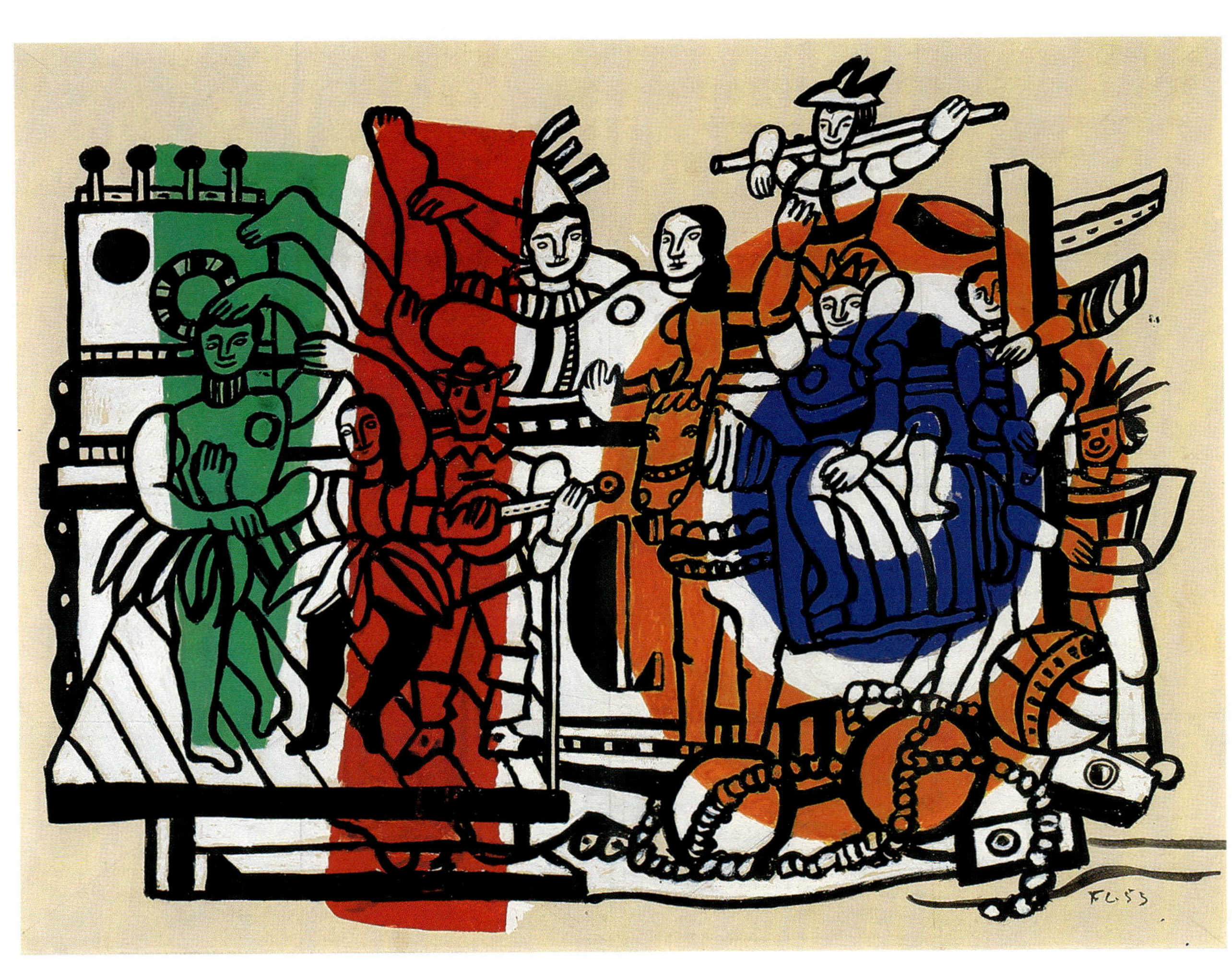

FERNAND LÉGER, STUDY FOR "THE GREAT PARADE," 1953

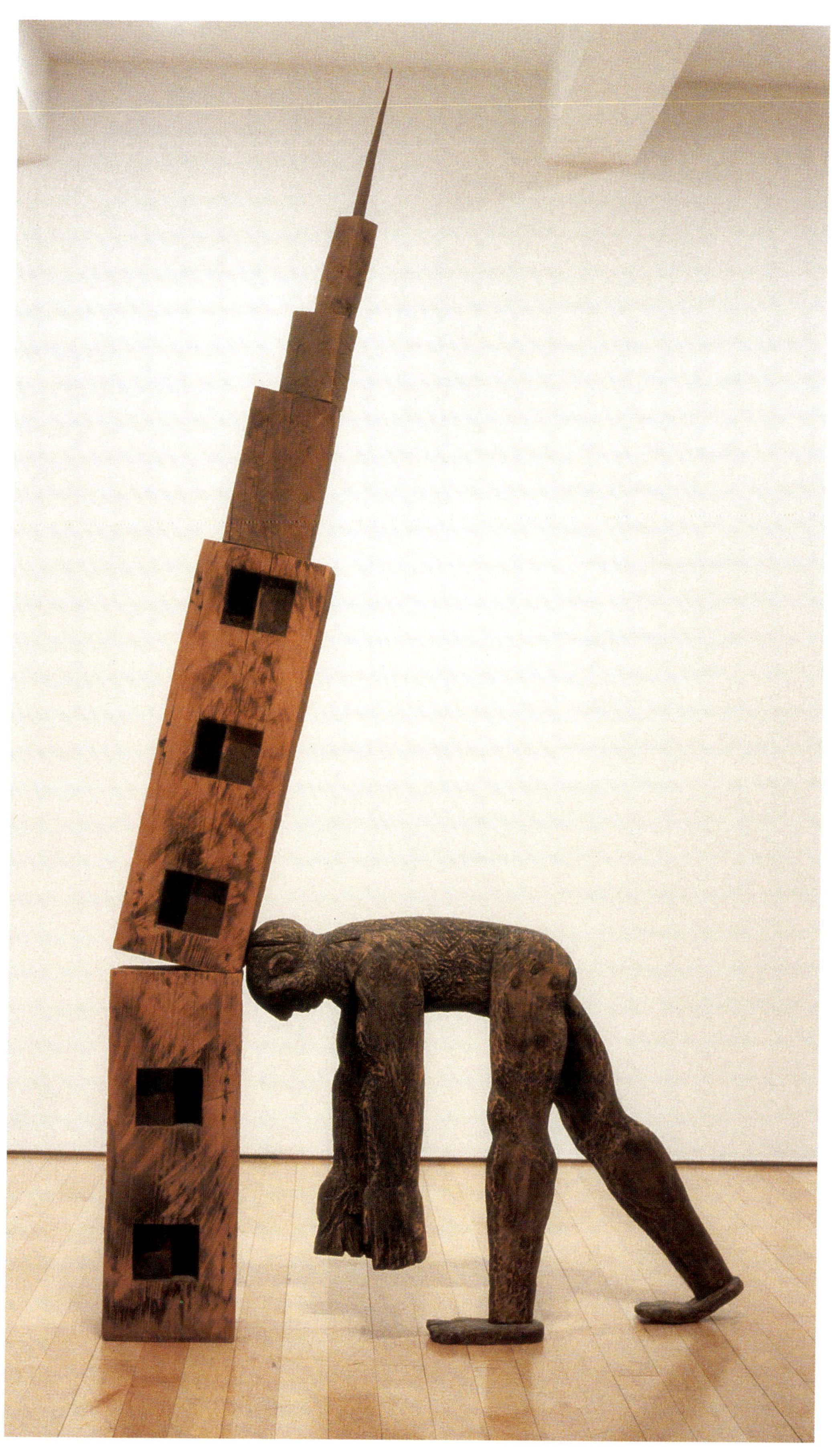

LEONID LERMAN, DAY OF SORROW, 1987

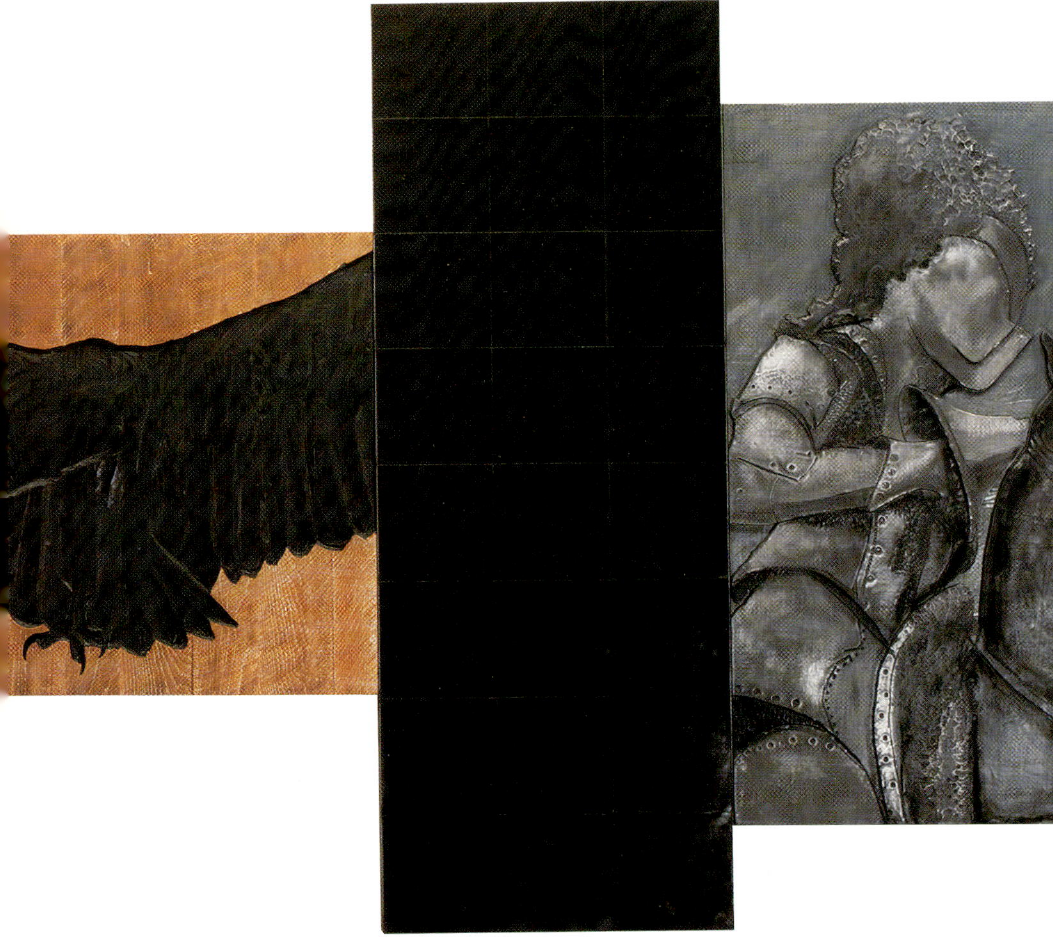
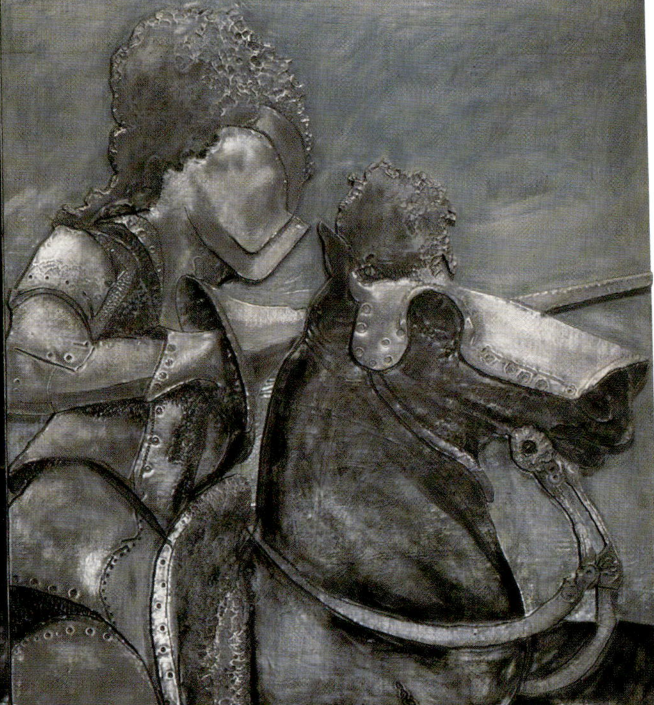
Courtesy of the Artist and Metro Pictures

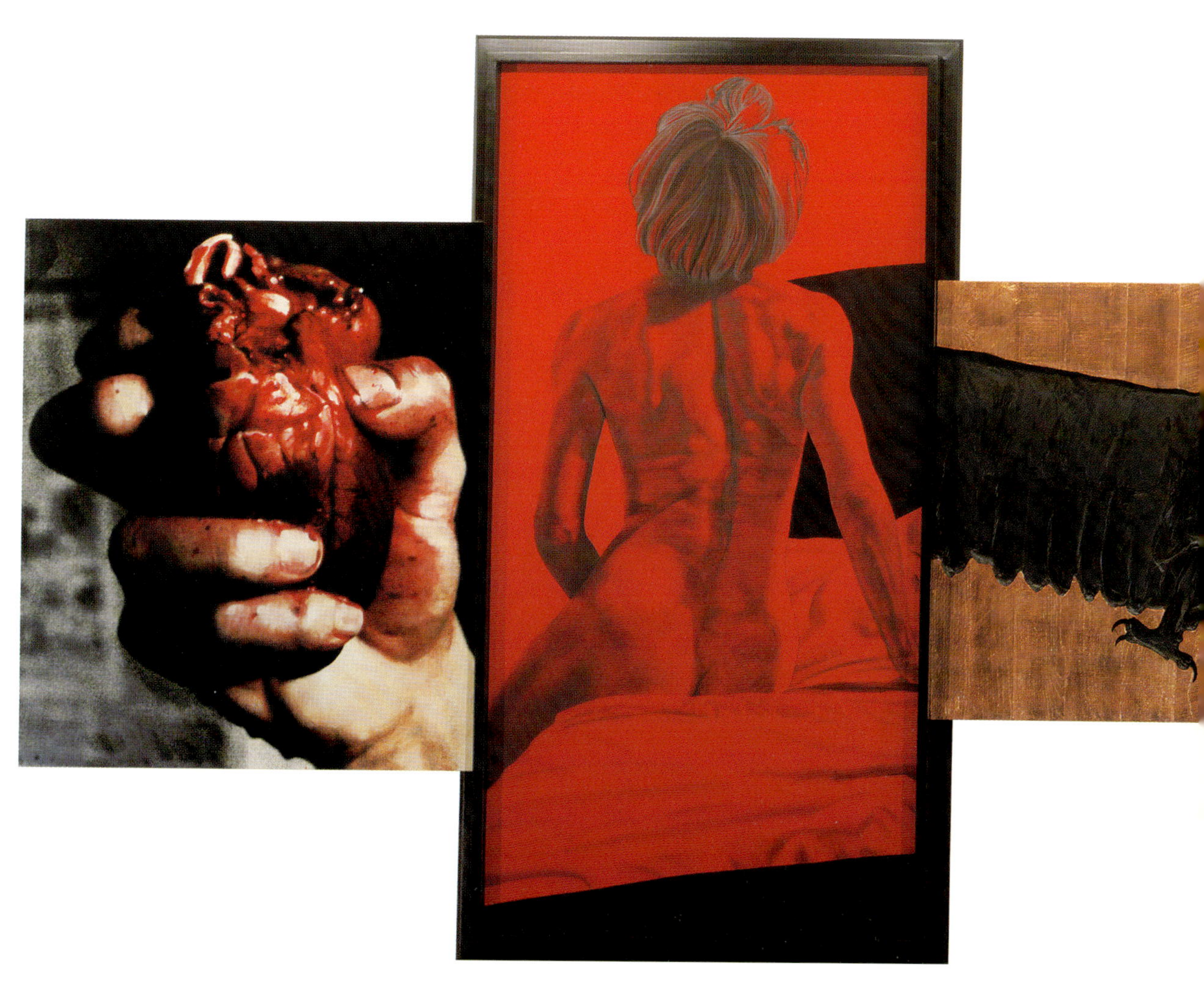

ROBERT LONGO, STILL, 1984

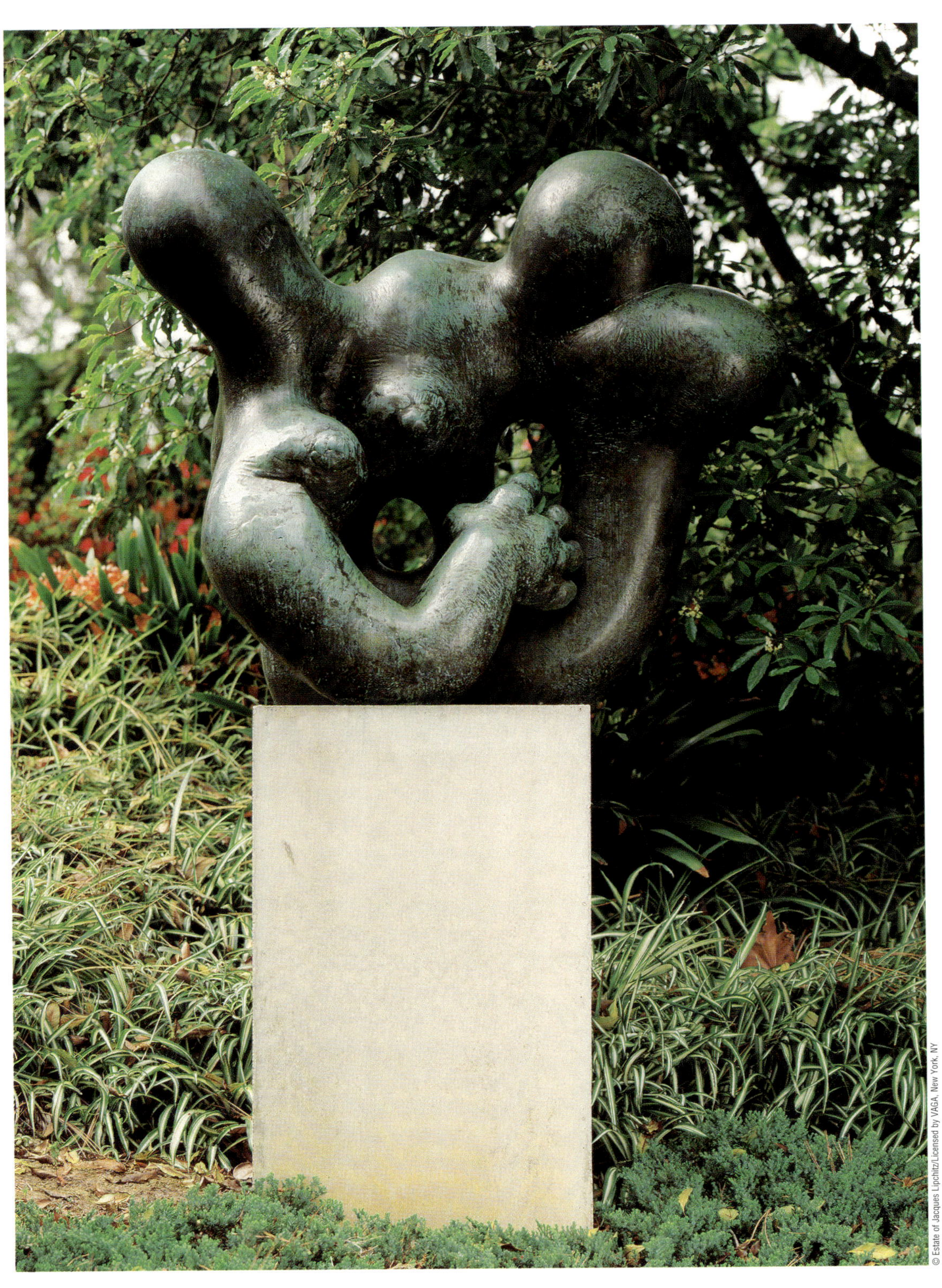

JACQUES LIPCHITZ, BENEDICTION I, 1942

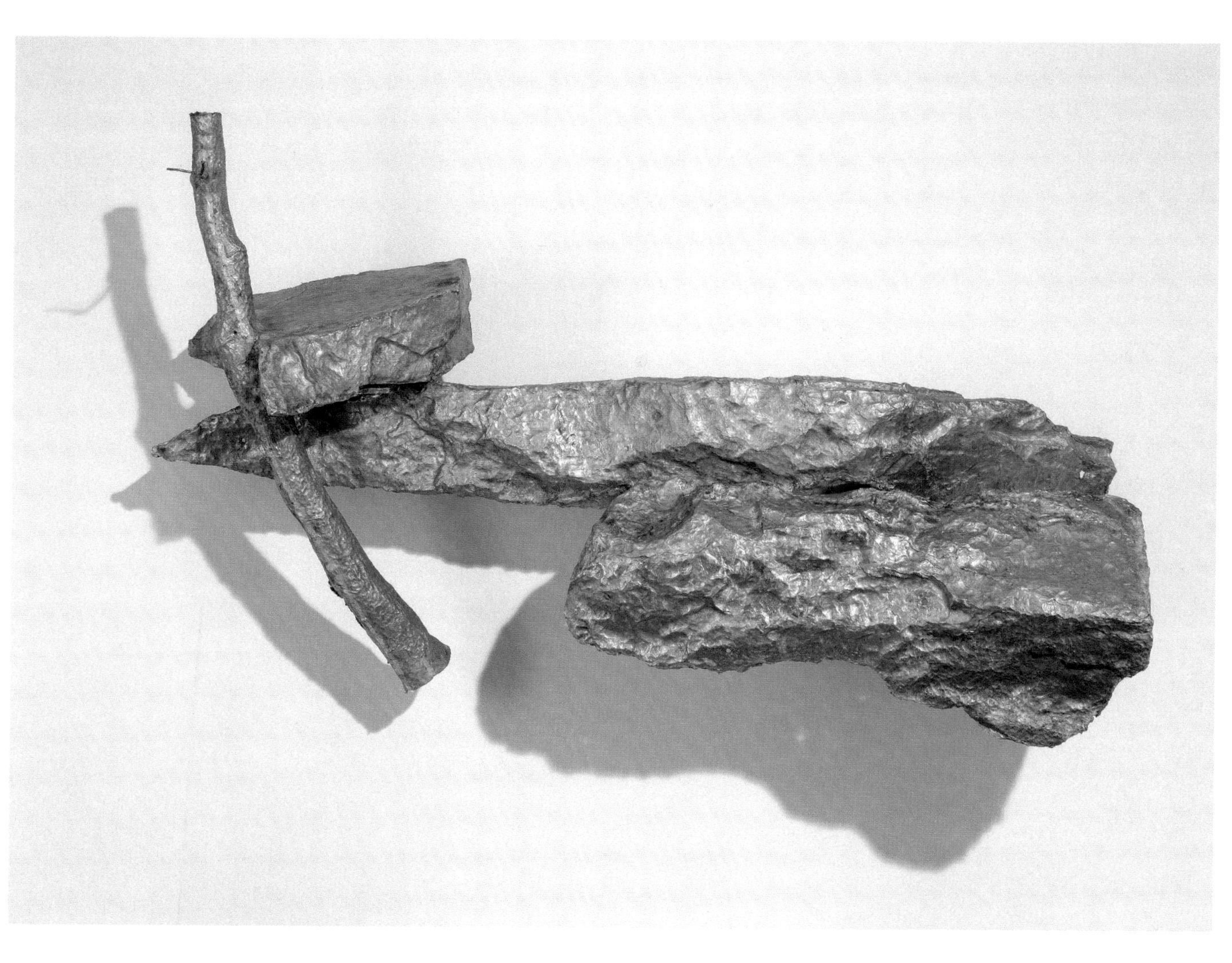

ROBERT LOBE, CULVER'S GAP, 1982

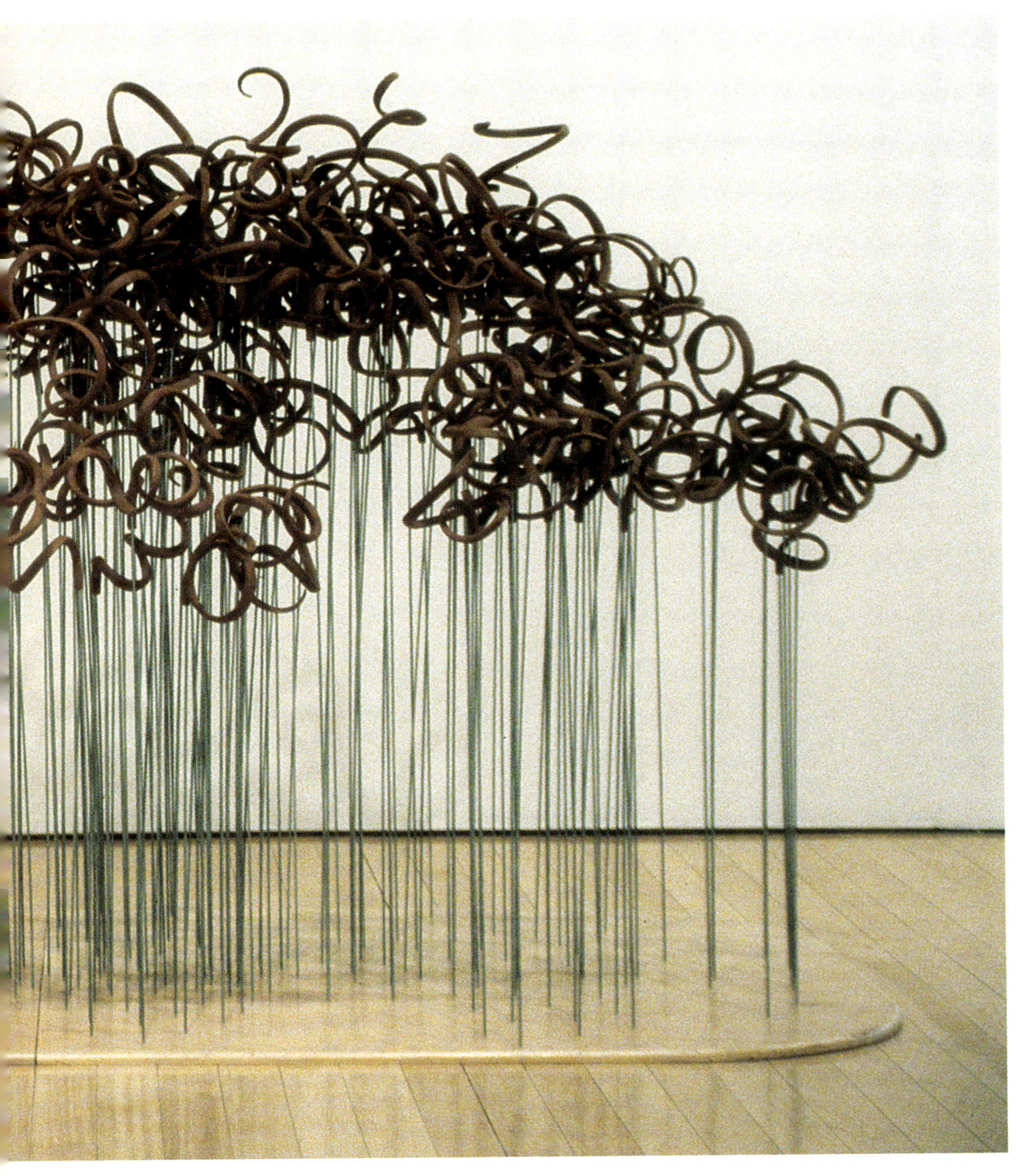

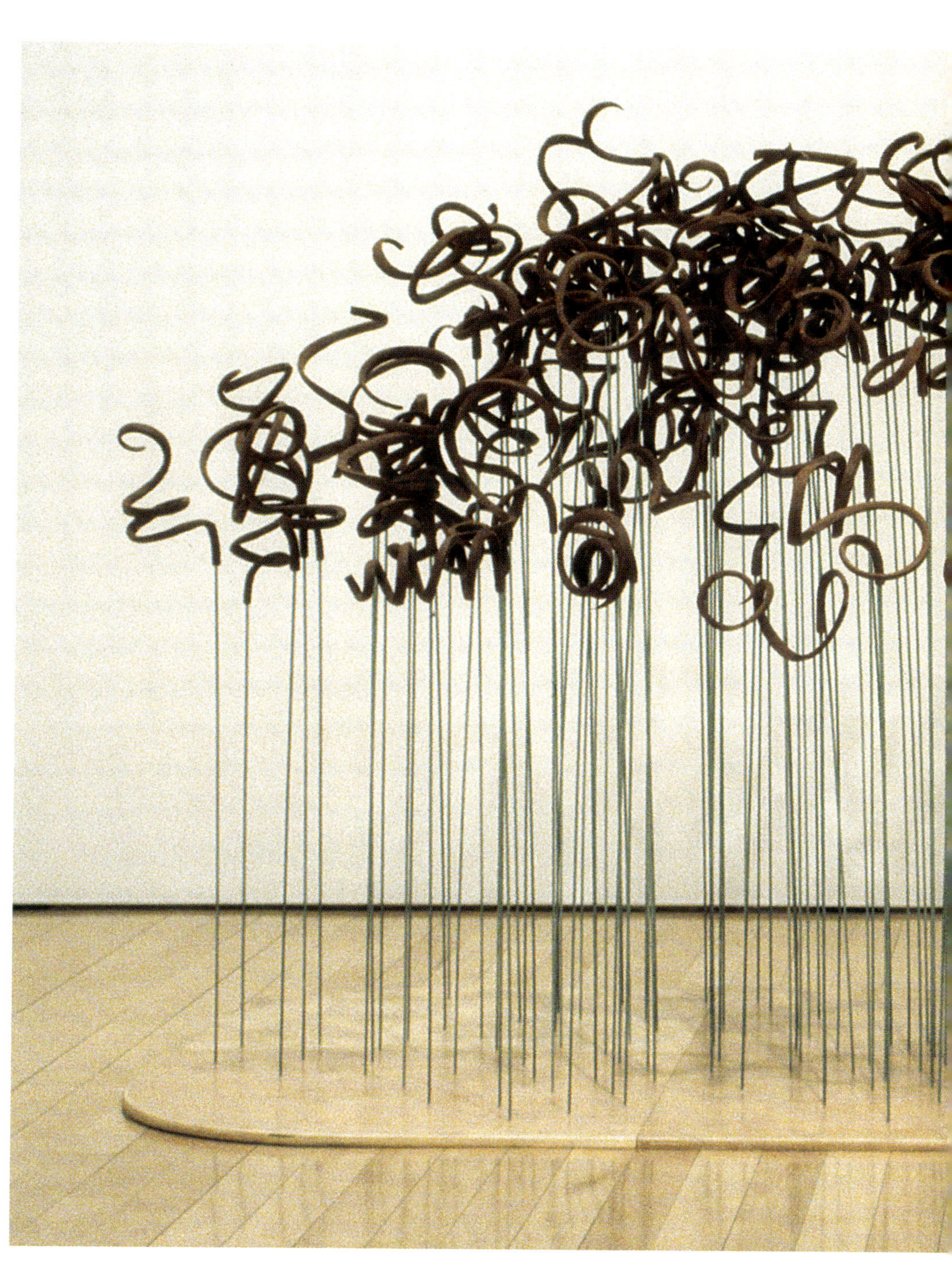

LOREN MADSEN, KNOTS, 1988-94

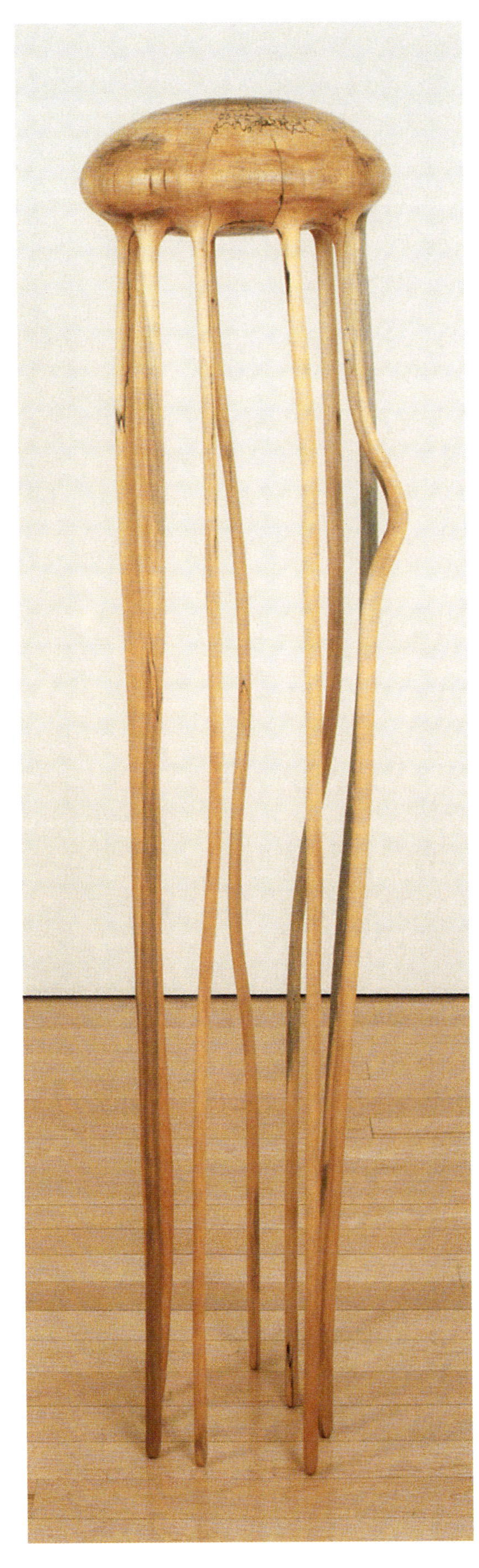

LOREN MADSEN, UNTITLED (NUMBER FOUR), 1994

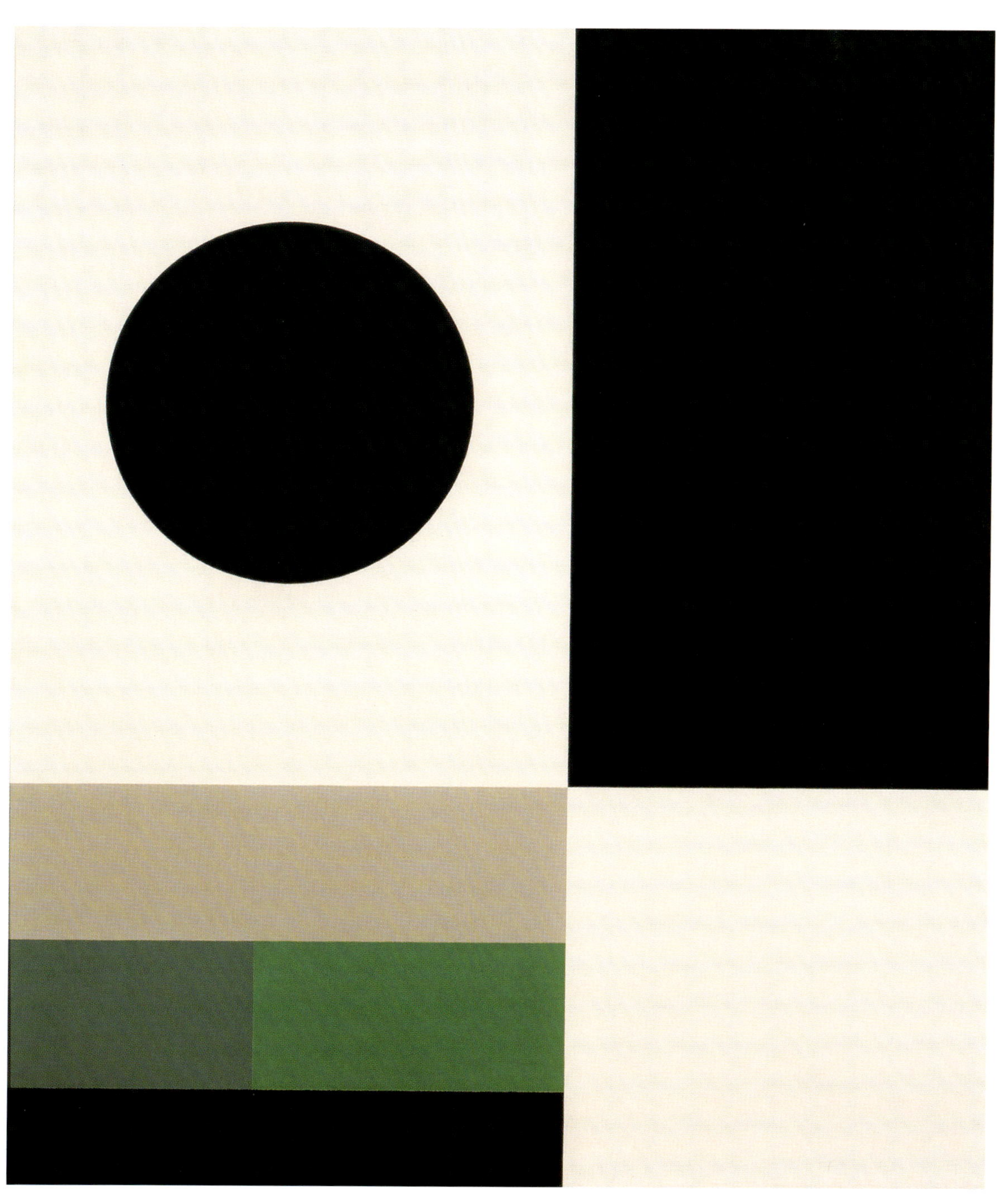

JOHN MCLAUGHLIN, UNTITLED, 1952

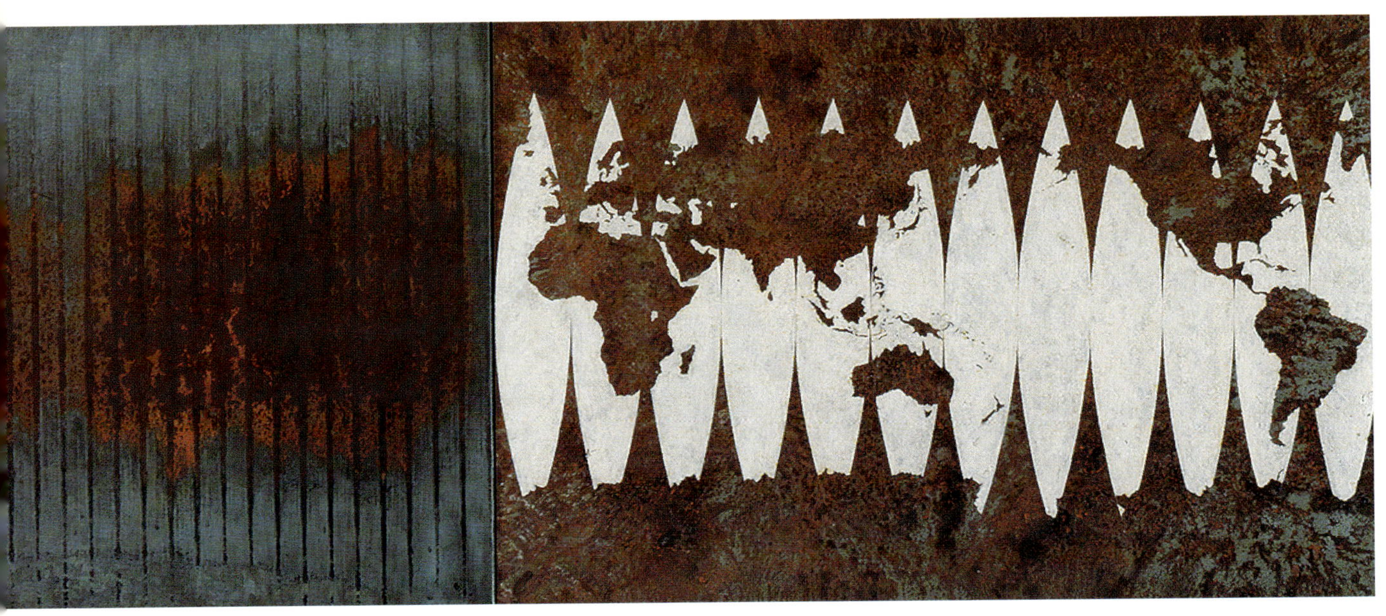

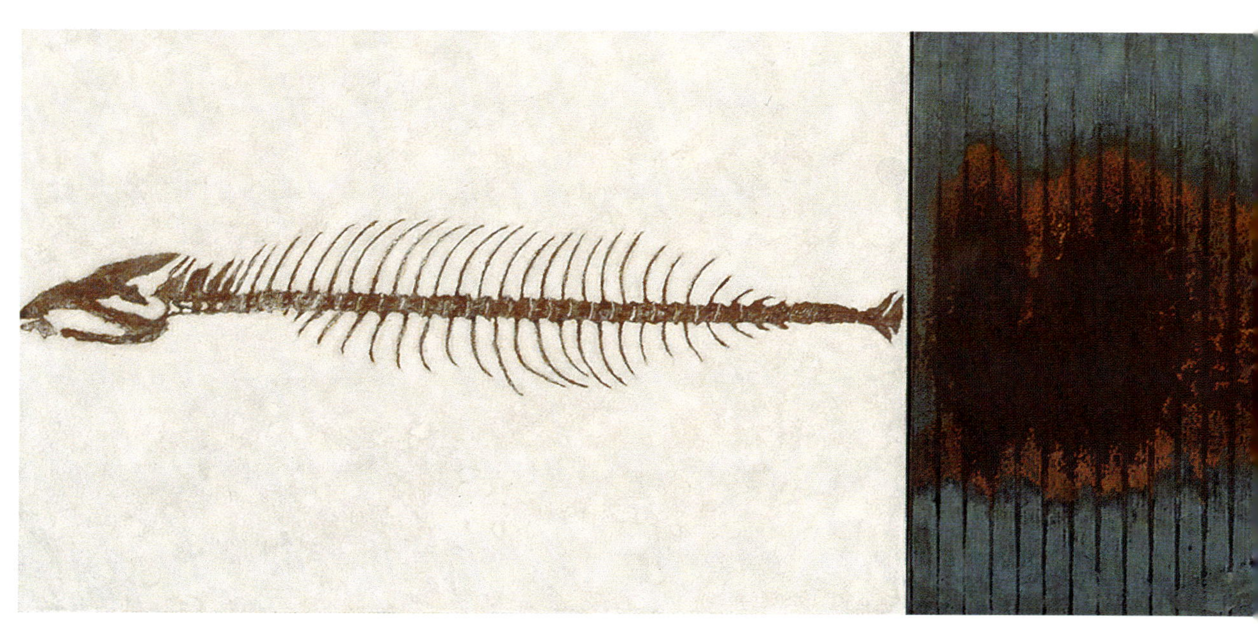

GREGORY MAHONEY, CIRCUMNAVIGATING TIME, 1991

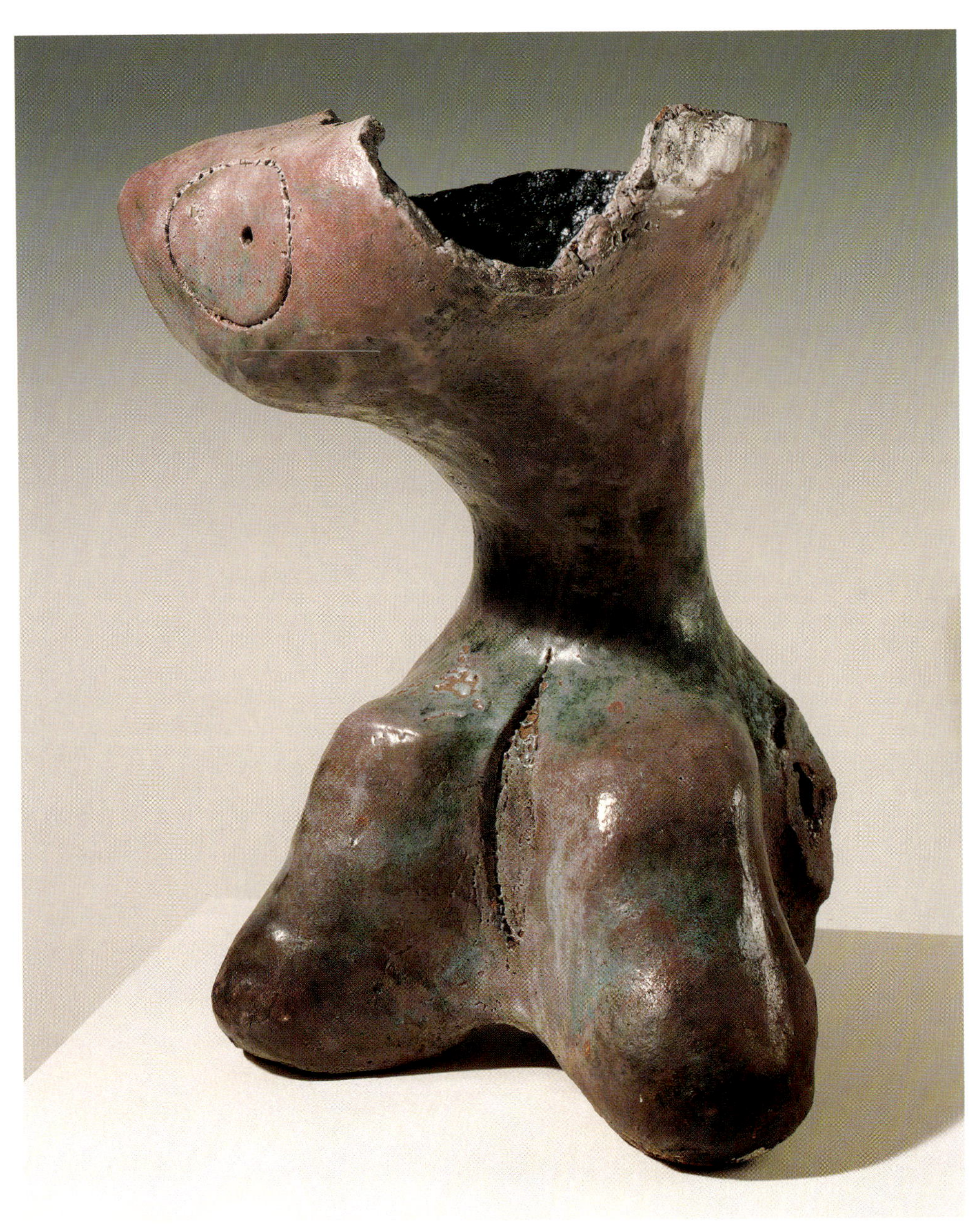

JOAN MIRÓ, FEMME VERTE, 1968

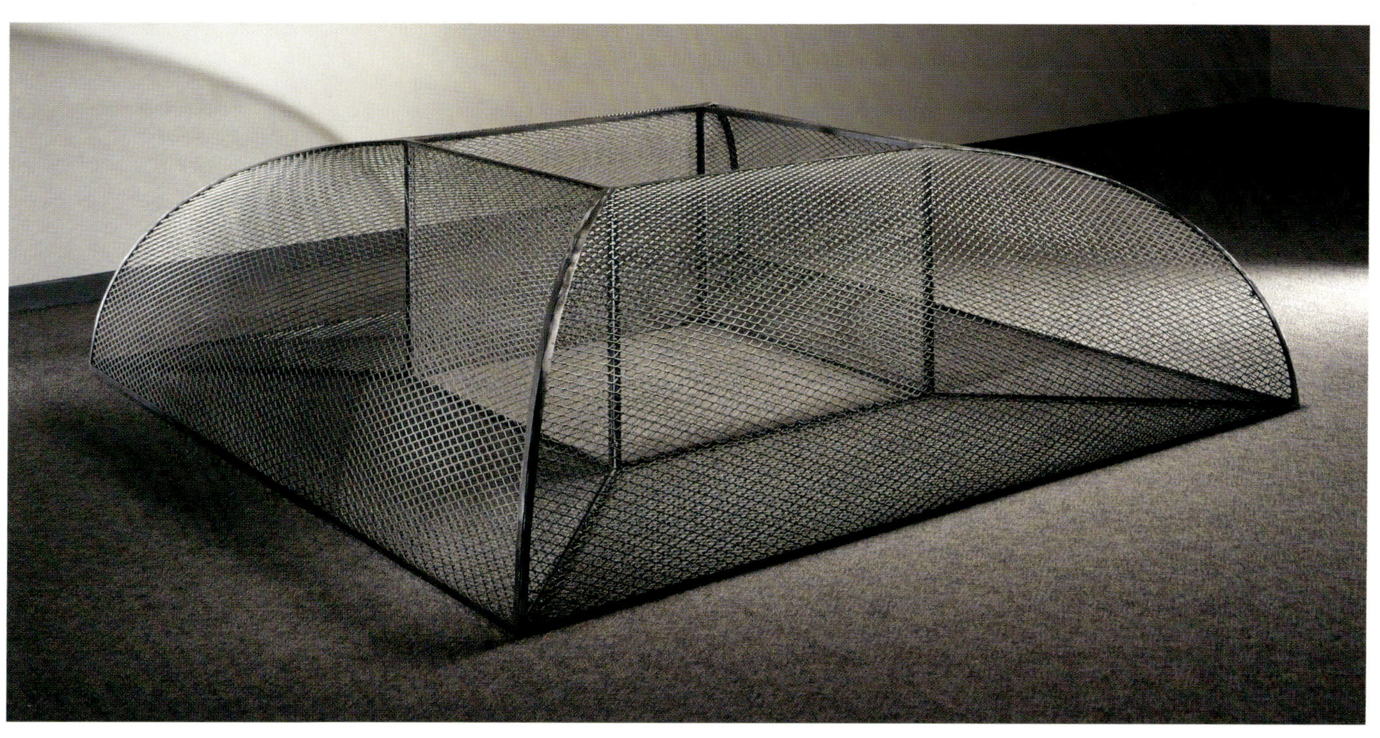

ROBERT MORRIS, UNTITLED, 1967-86

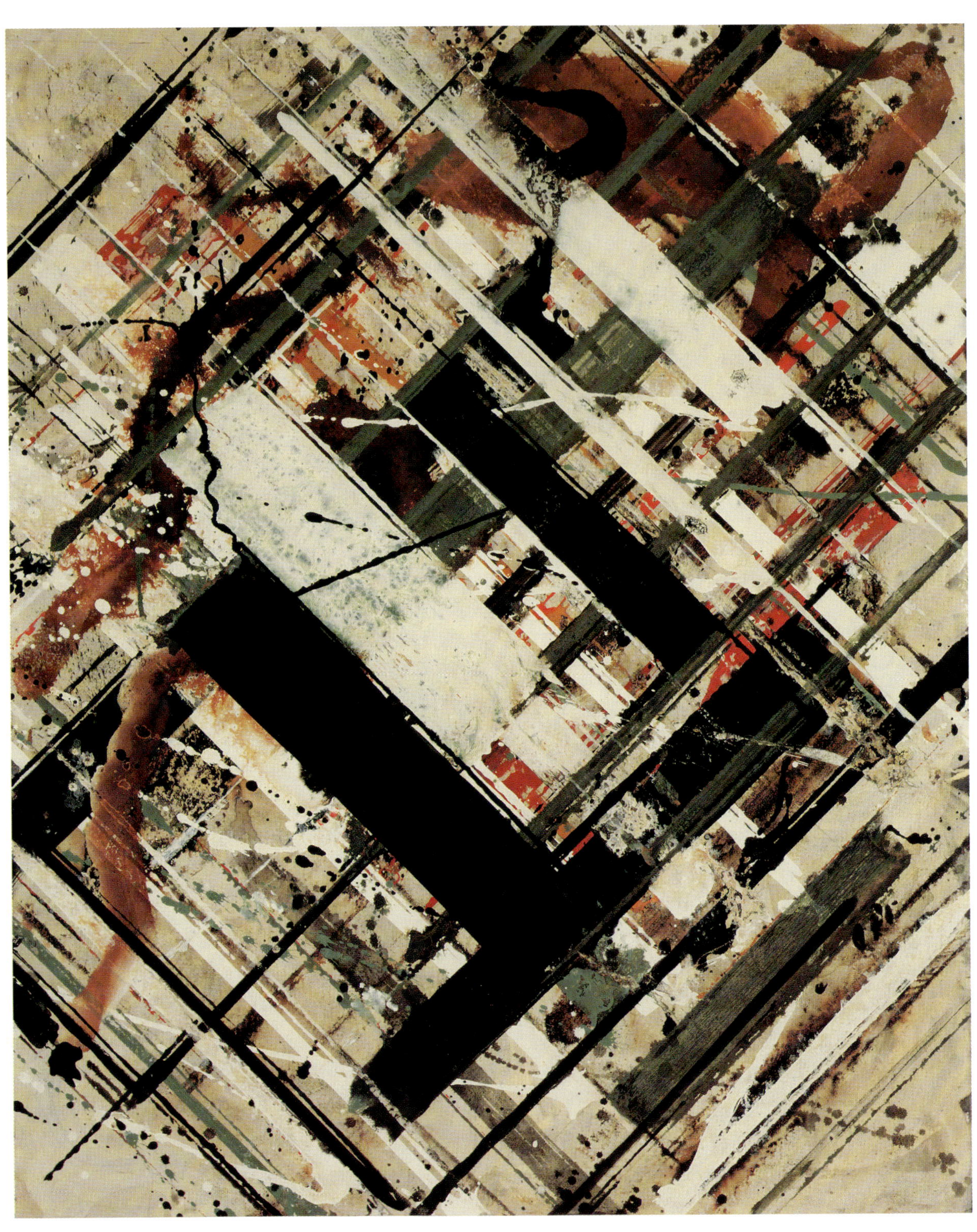

ED MOSES, UNTITLED (87.26), 1987

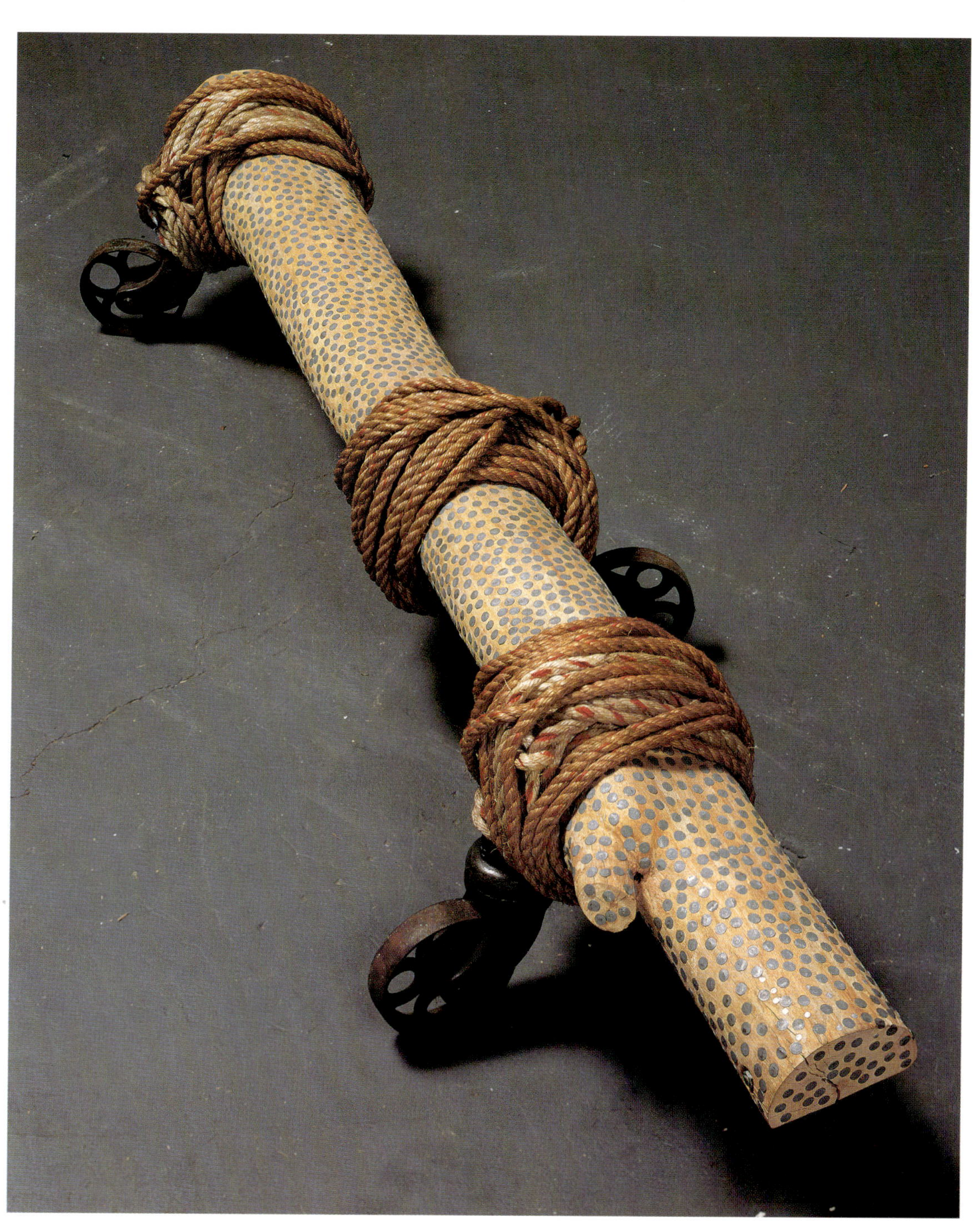

RON MURPHREE, UNTITLED, 1982

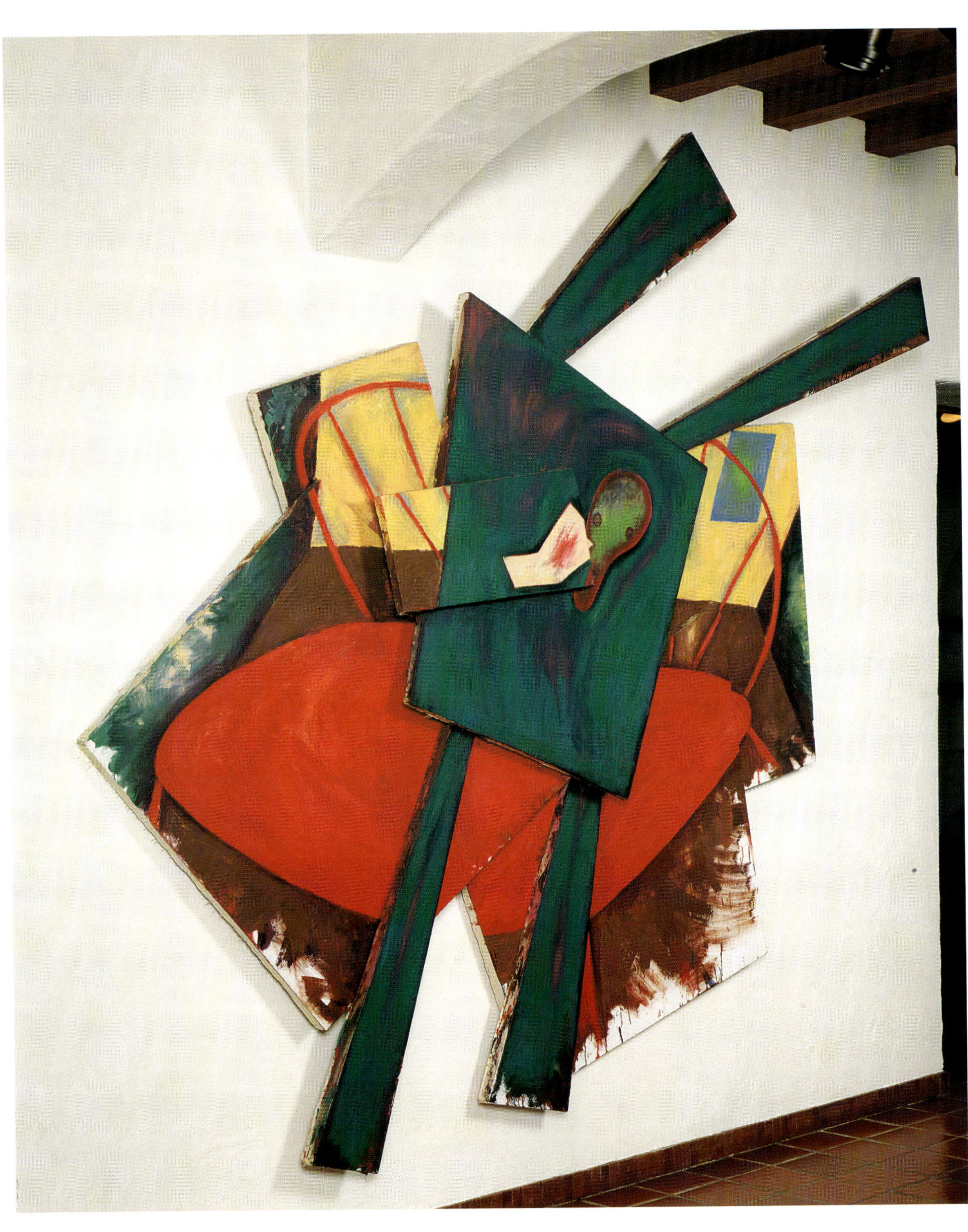

ELIZABETH MURRAY, MORE THAN YOU KNOW, 1983

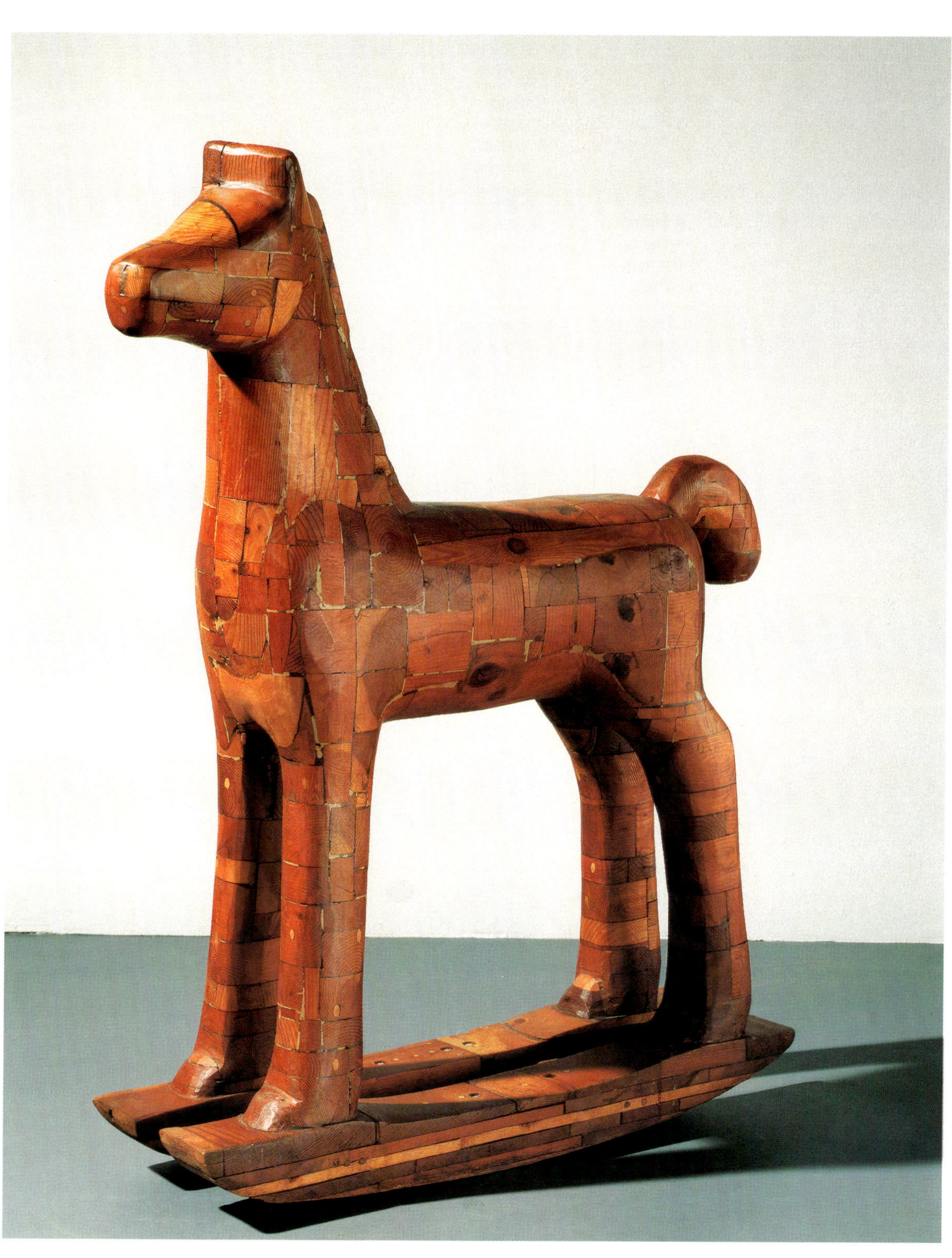

GWYNN MURRILL, ROCKING HORSE, 1970

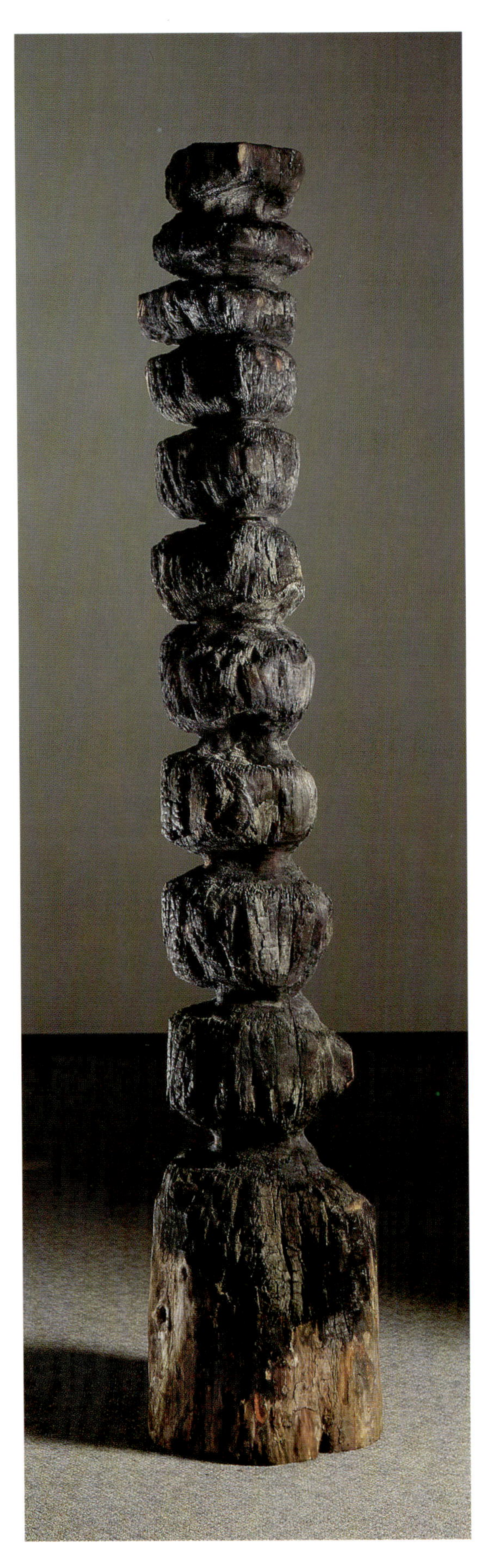

DAVID NASH, BLACK COLUMN, 1983

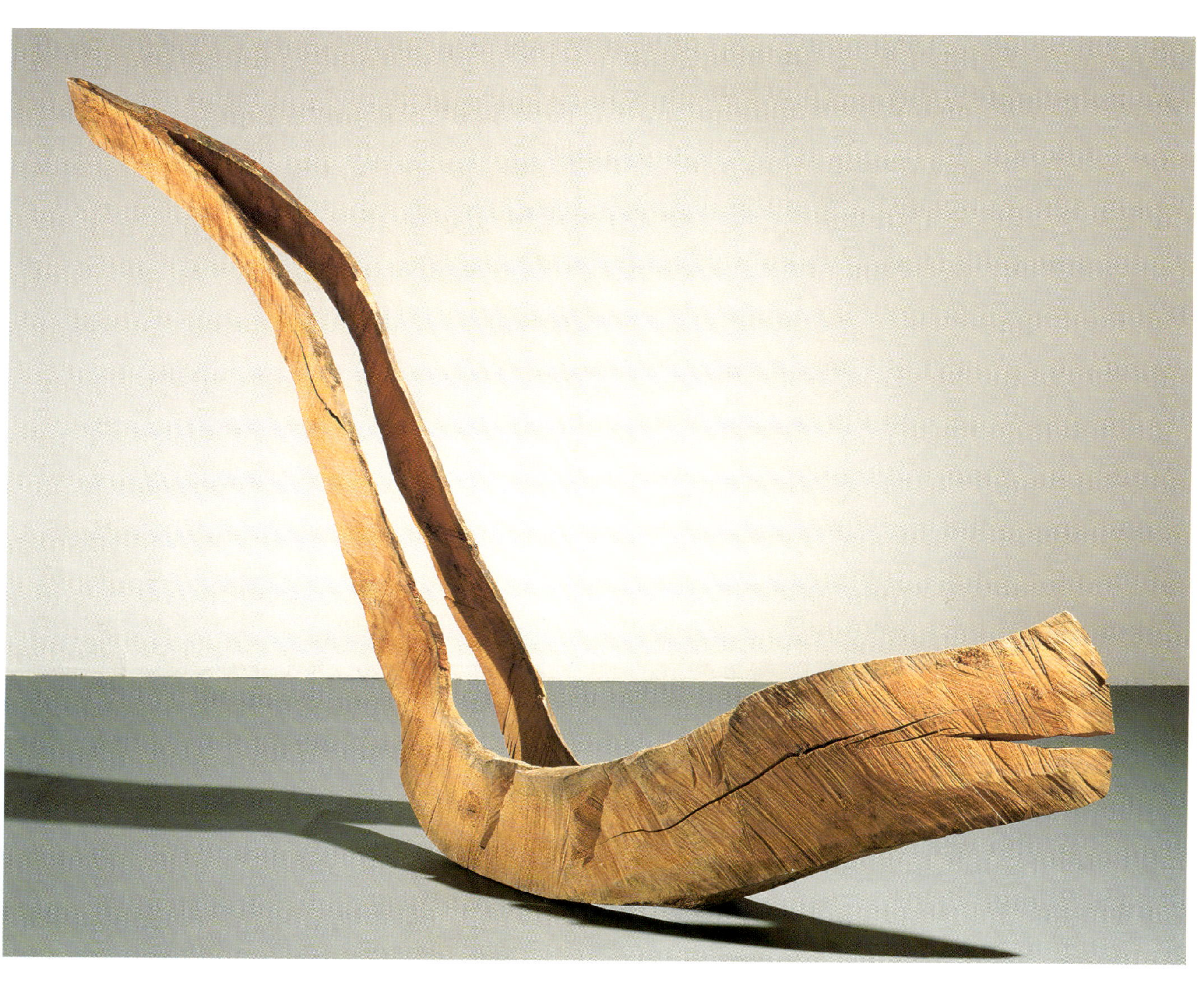

DAVID NASH, RISING BOAT, 1986

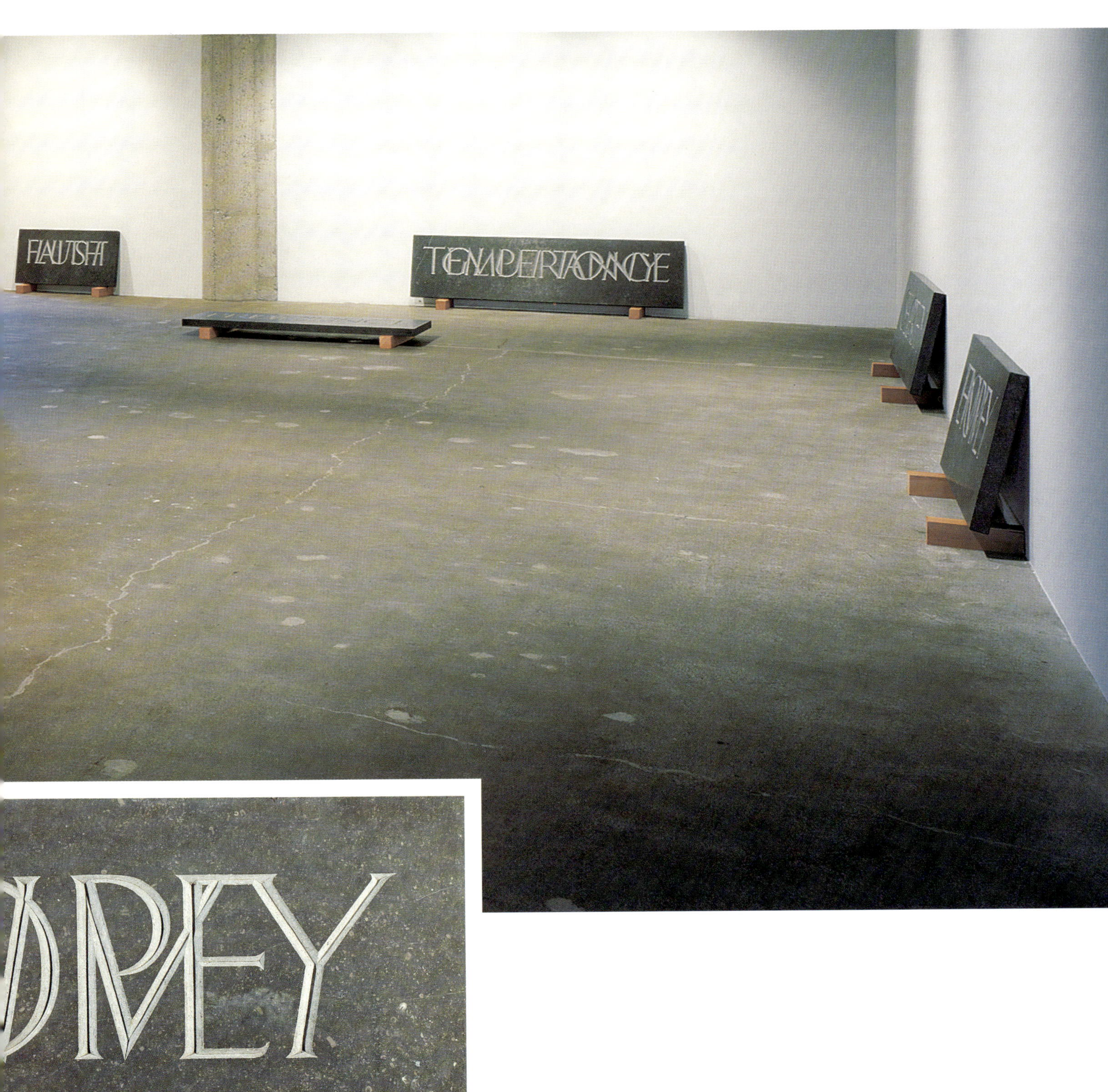

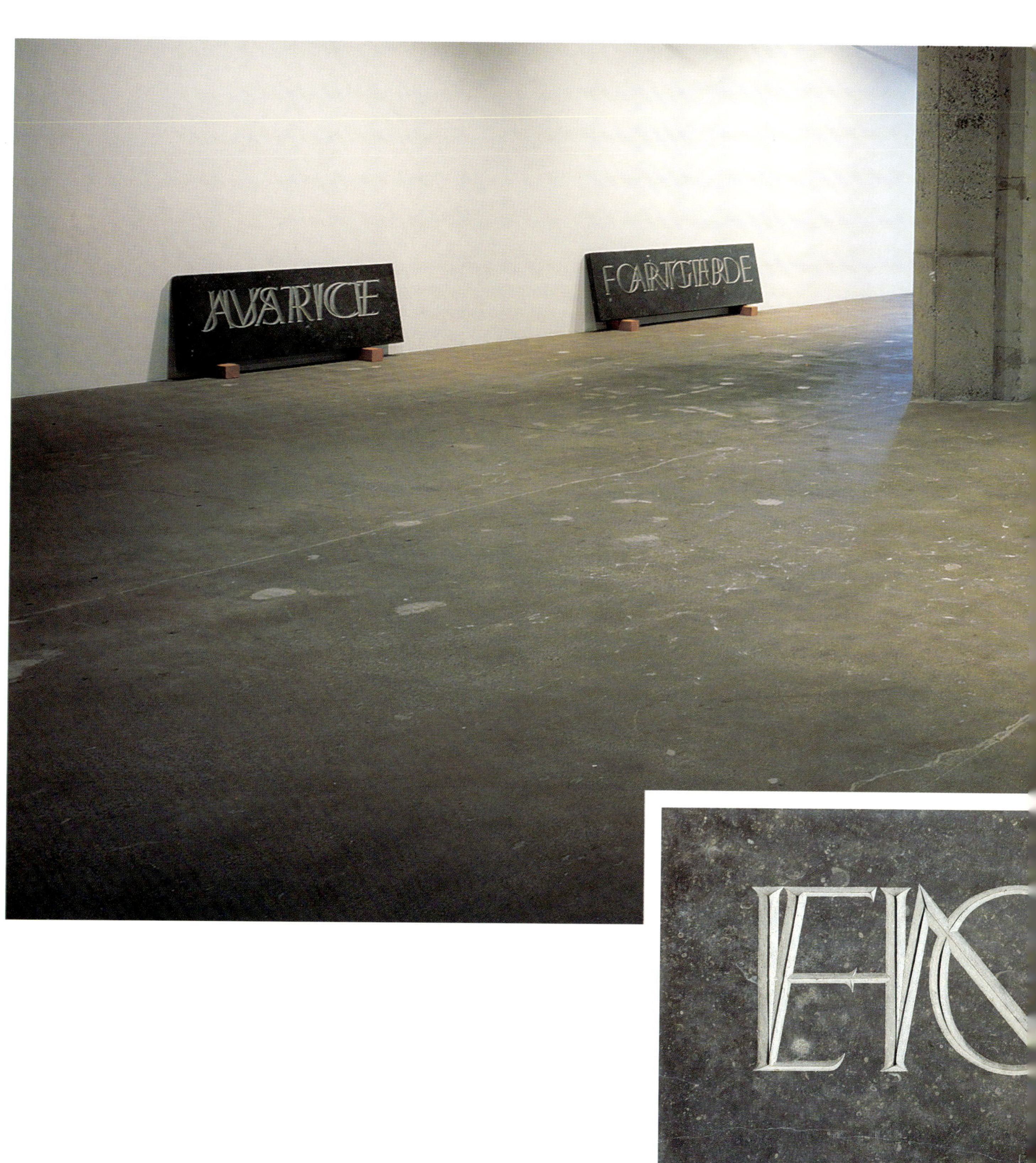

BRUCE NAUMAN, SEVEN VIRTUES AND SEVEN VICES, 1983-84, (INSTALLATION AND DETAIL)

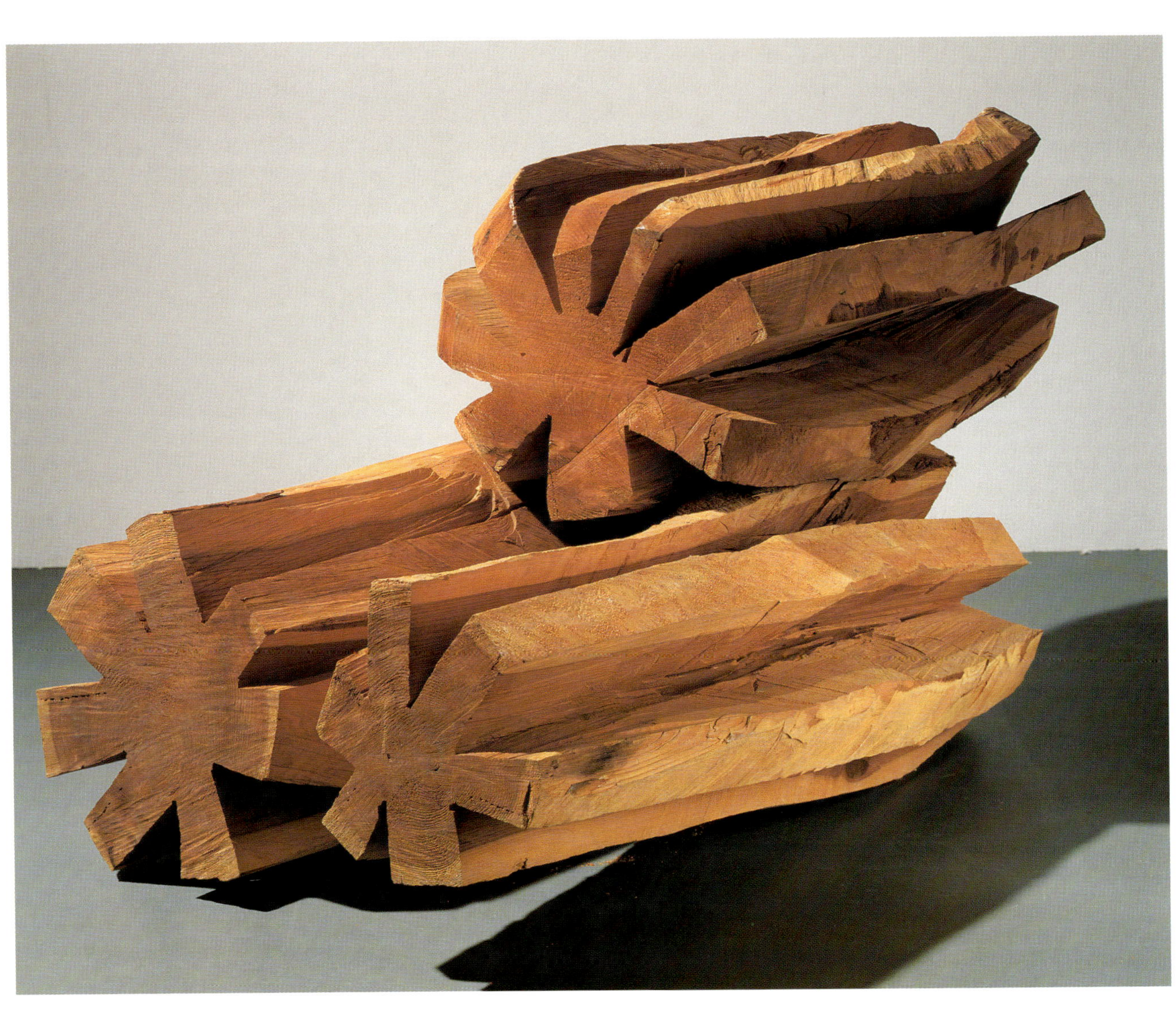

DAVID NASH, THREE COGS, 1987

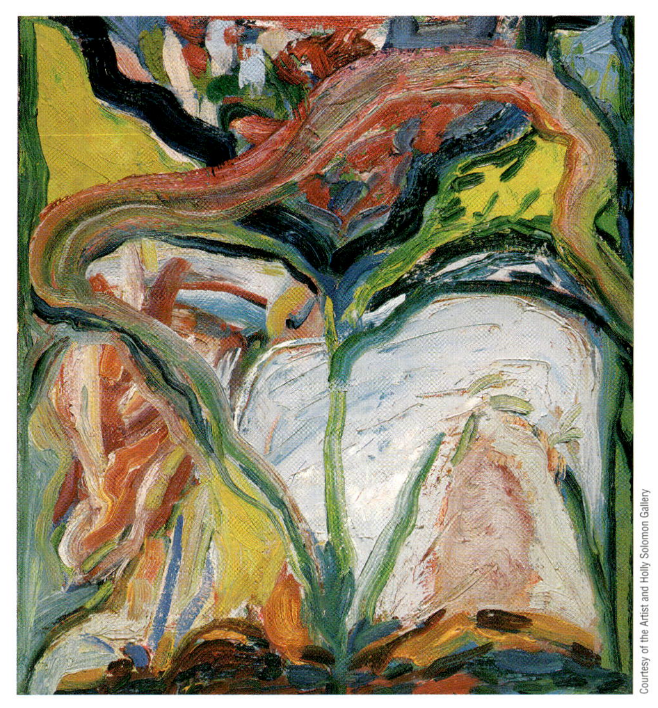

Courtesy of the Artist and Holly Solomon Gallery

MELISSA MEYER, OPHELIA, 1985

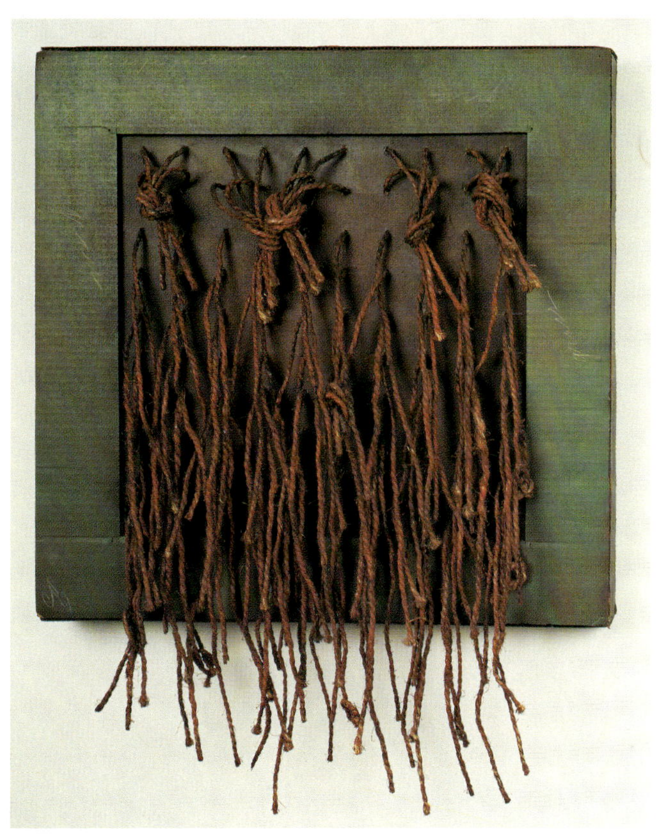

CLAES OLDENBURG, MODEL: ROPE GARDEN, 1969

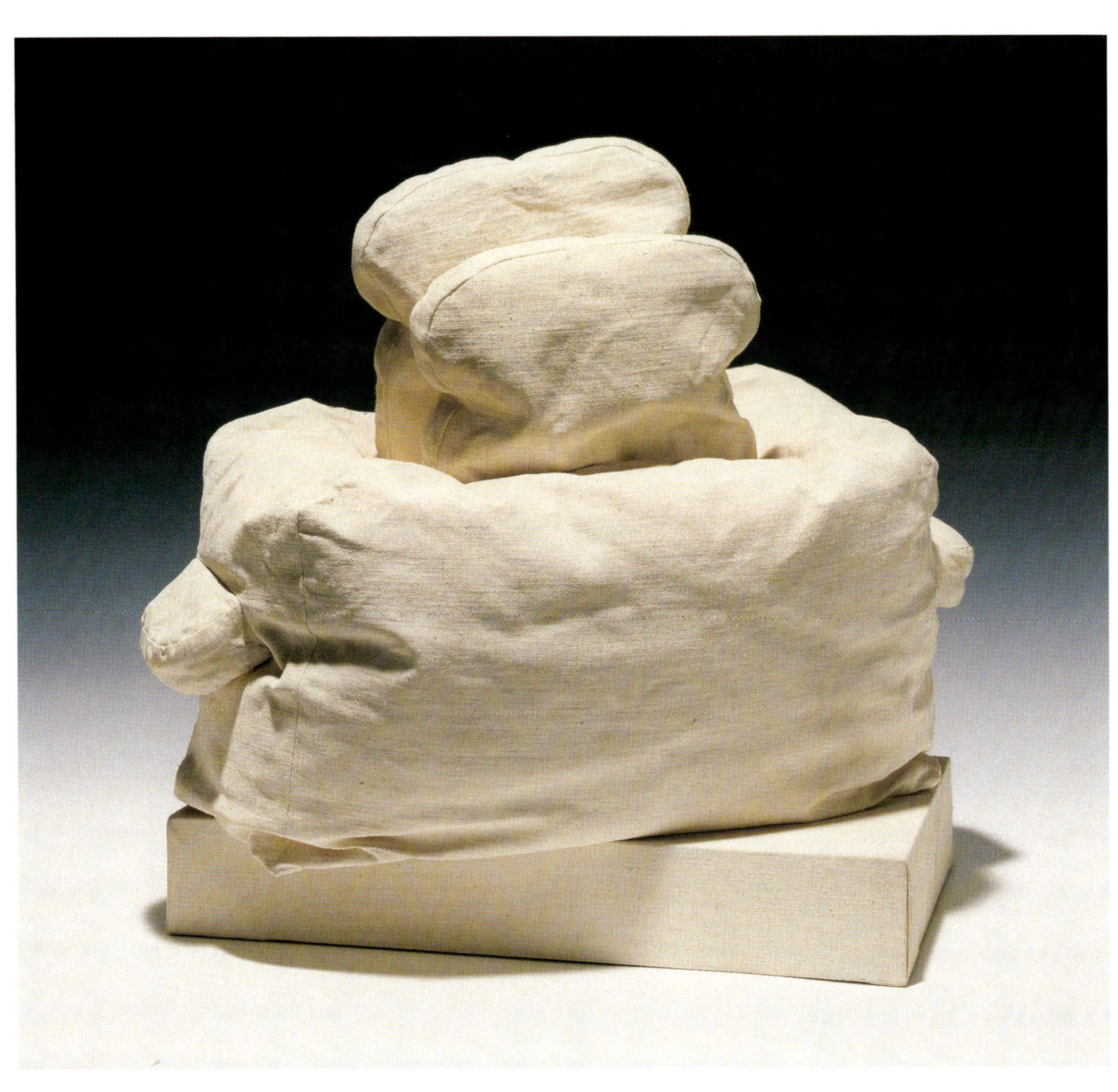

CLAES OLDENBURG, SOFT TOASTER- "GHOST VERSION" #3, 1963-72

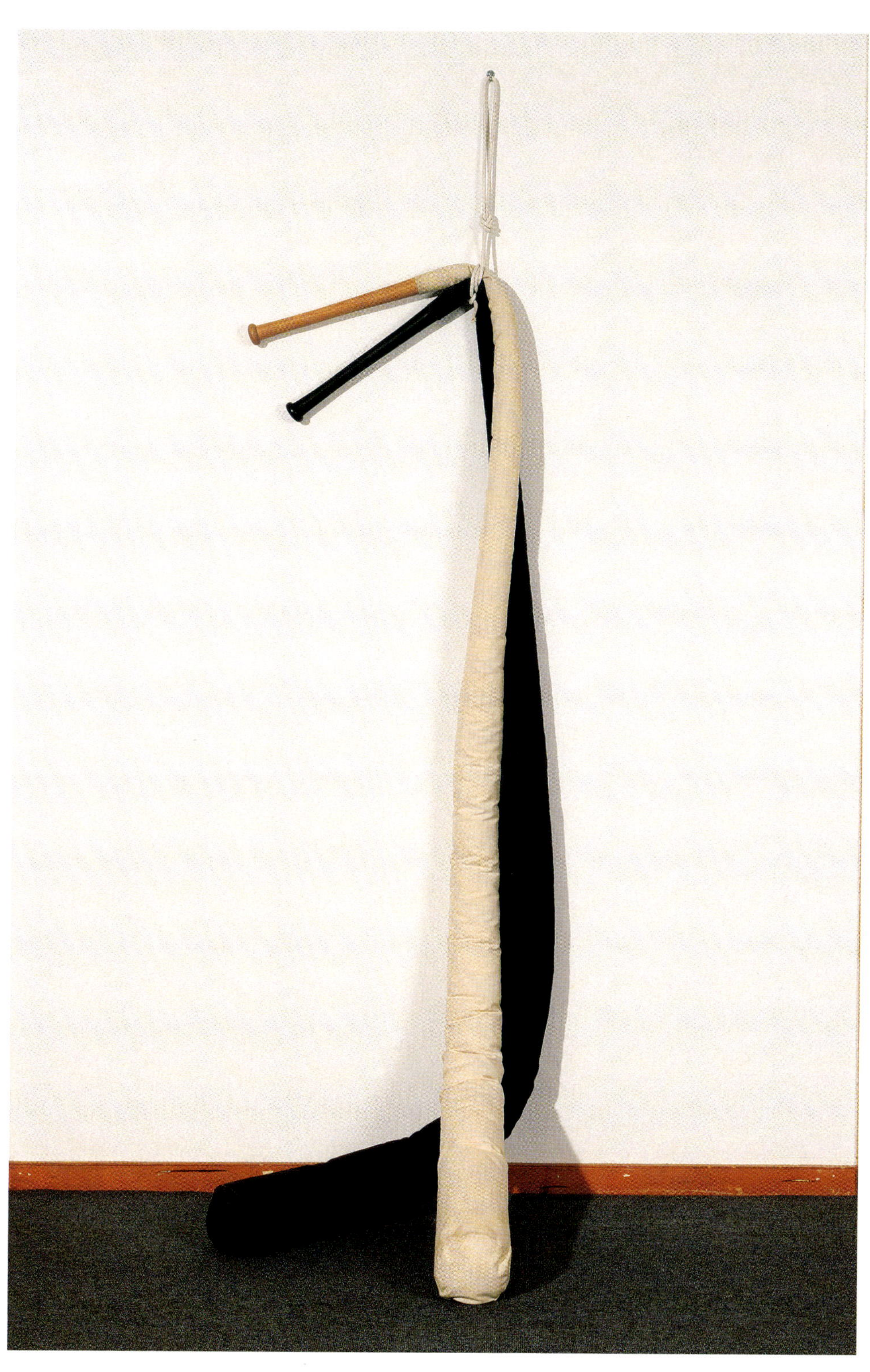

CLAES OLDENBURG, TWO BATS, BLACK AND WHITE, 1969-71

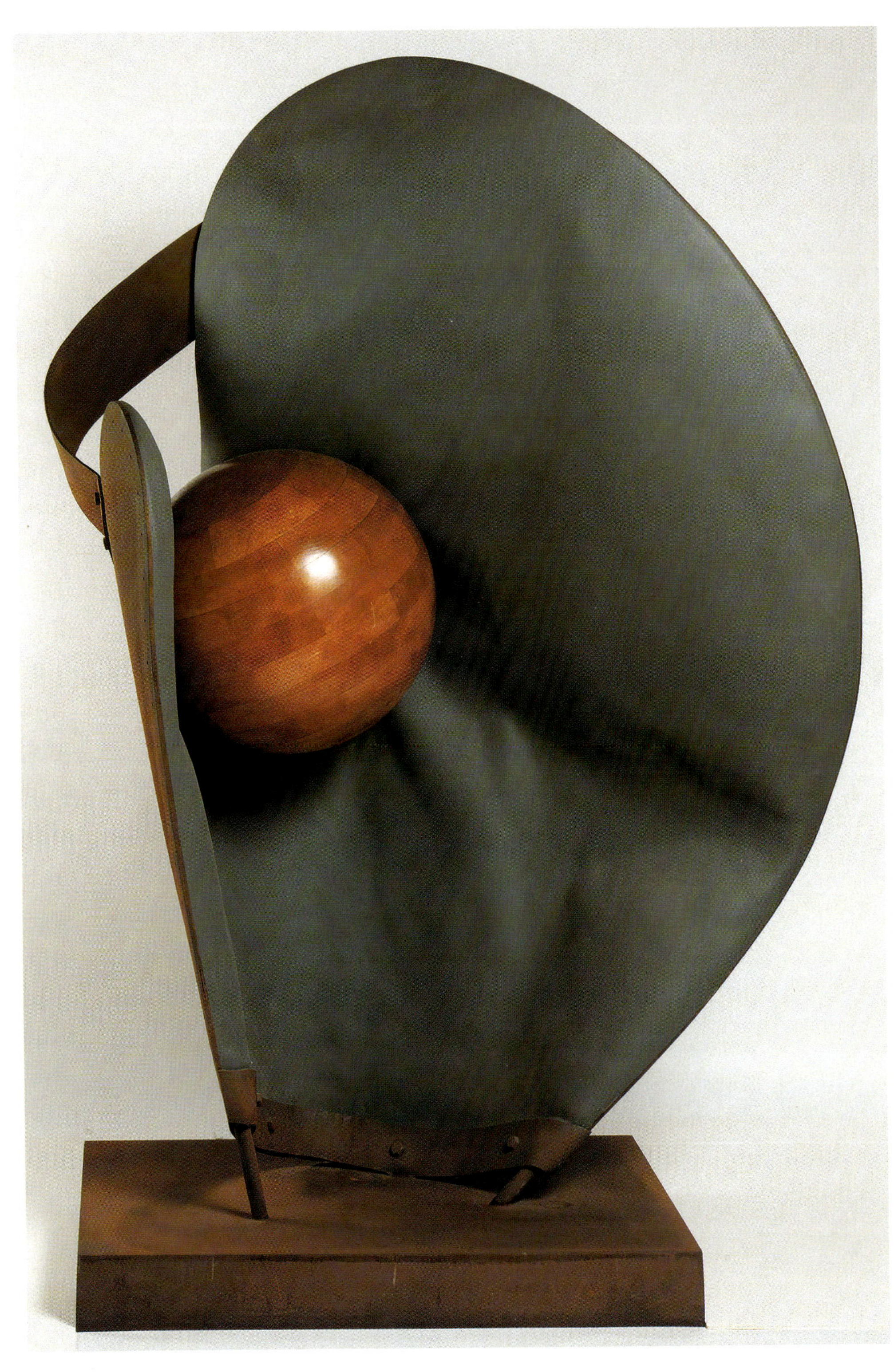

CLAES OLDENBURG, STANDING MITT WITH BALL, HALF SCALE, 6 FEET, 1974

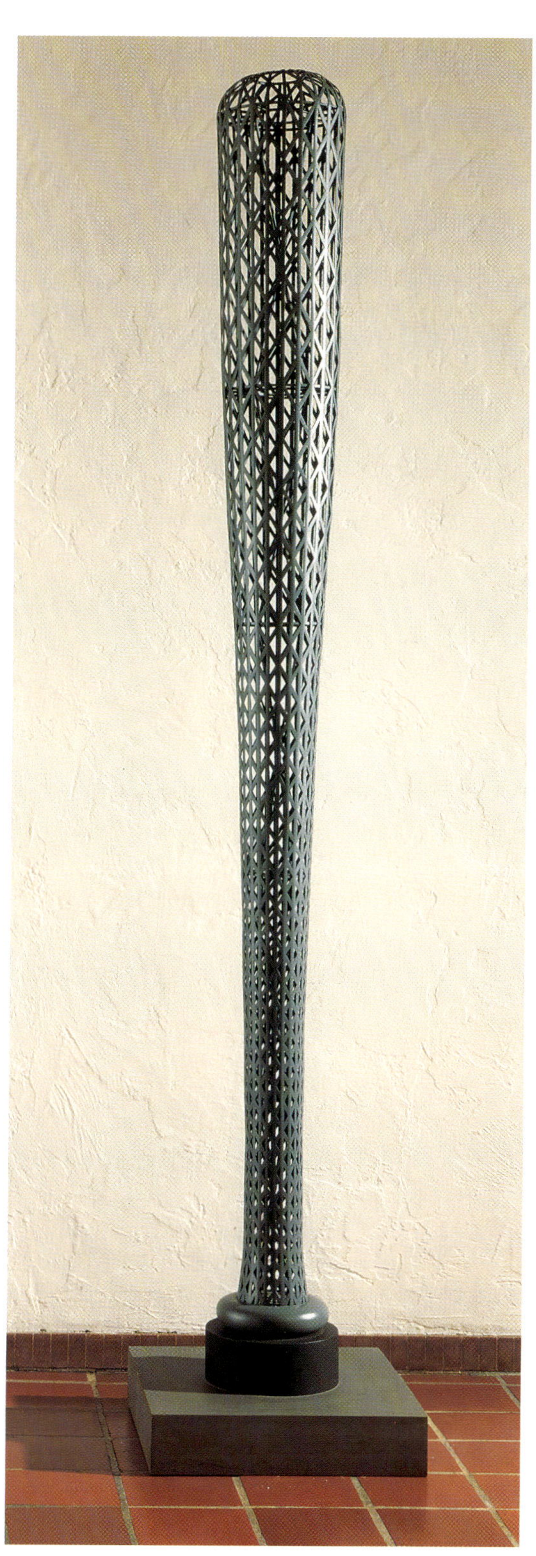

CLAES OLDENBURG, BATCOLUMN MODEL, 1980

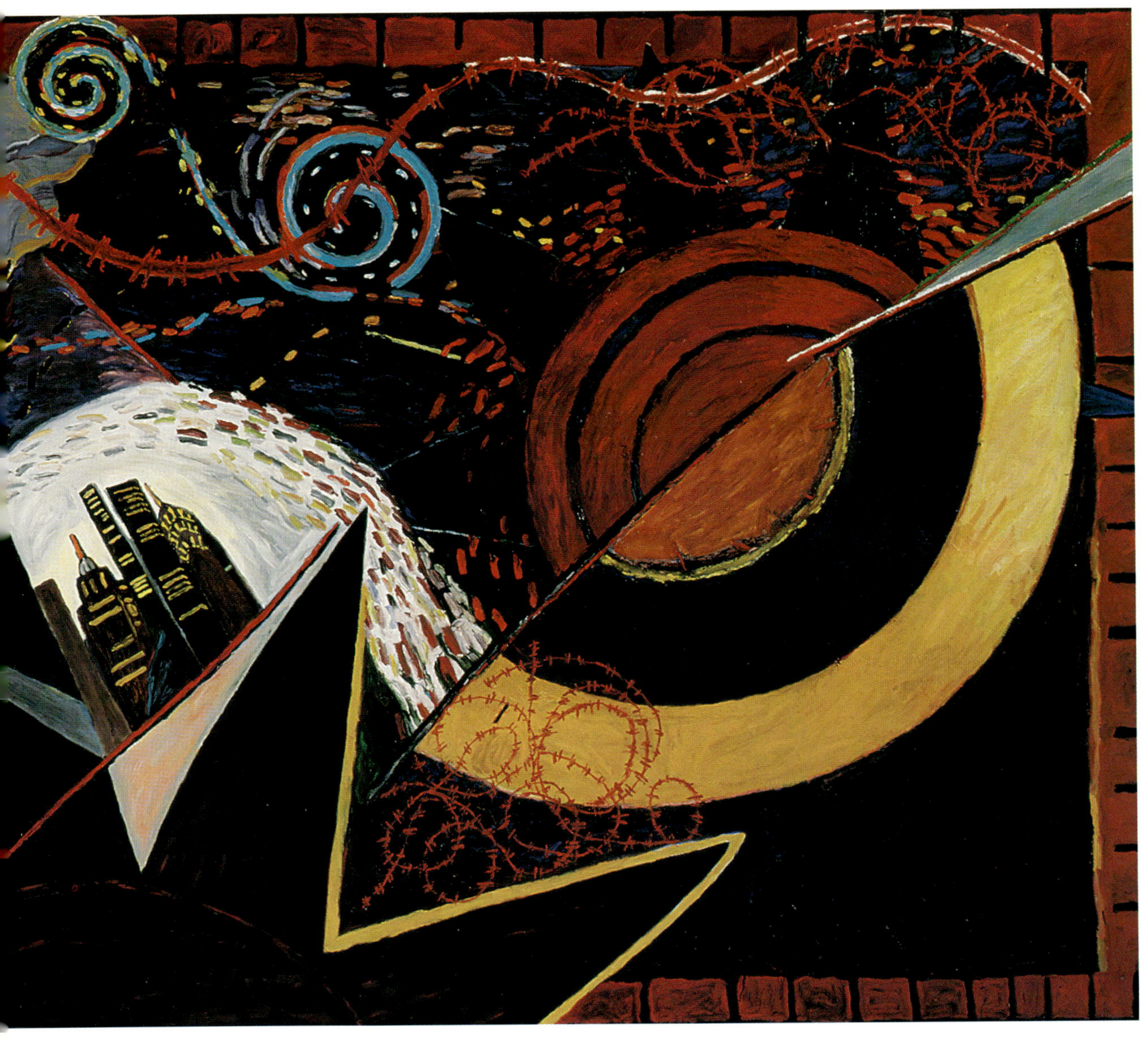

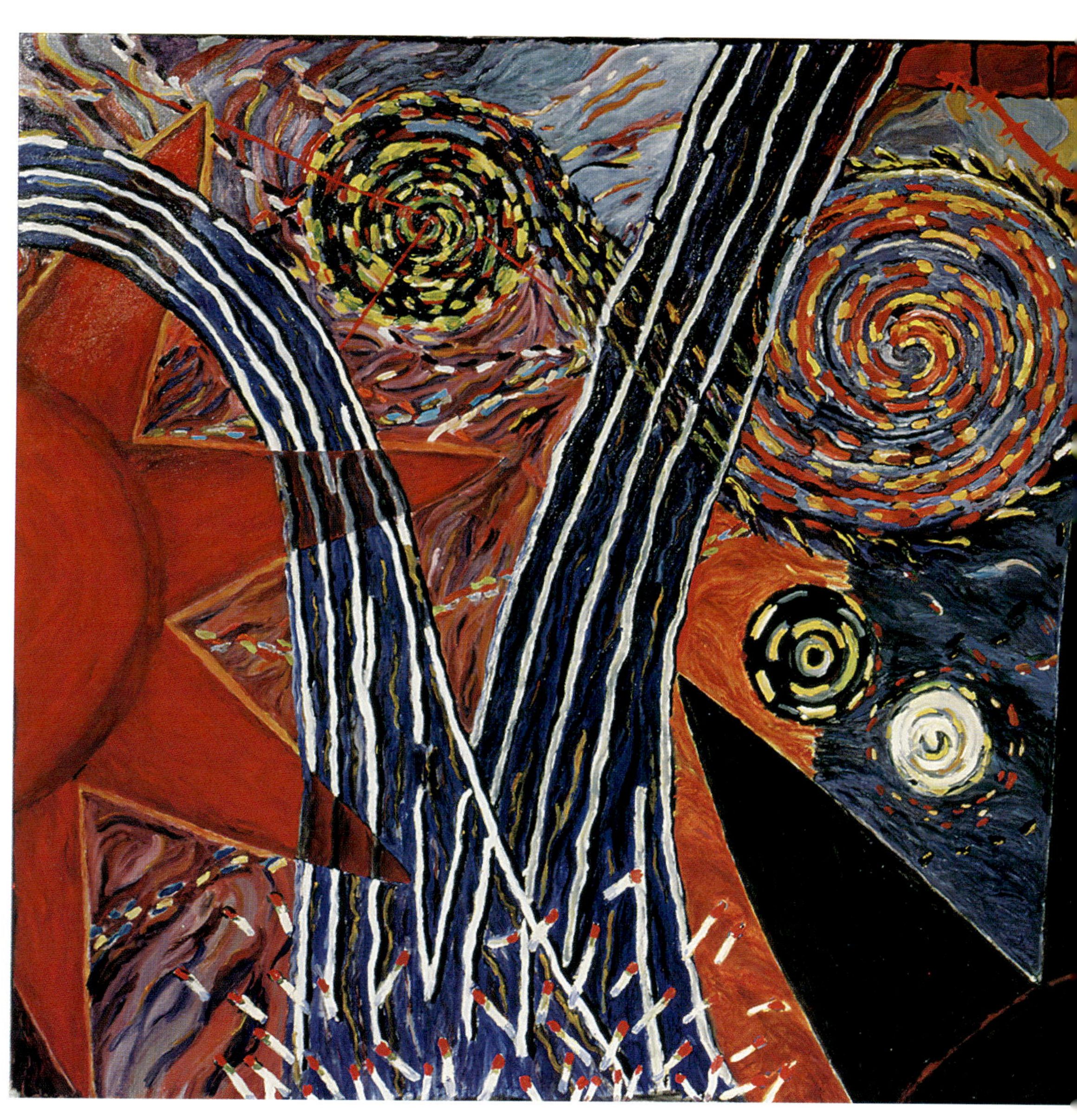

KATHERINE PORTER, THE CITY AT NIGHT, 1983

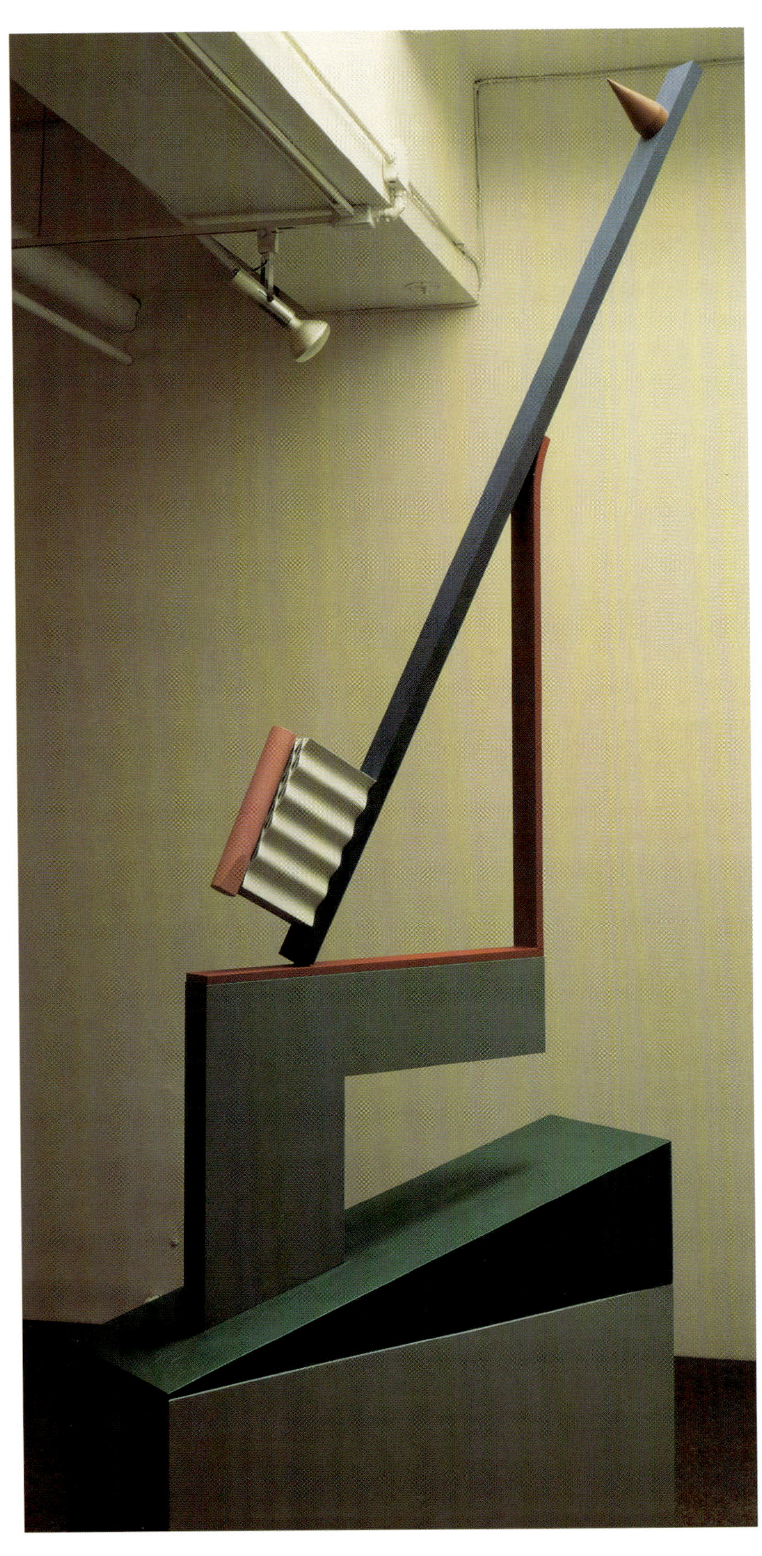

CLAES OLDENBURG, CROSS SECTION (SLICE THROUGH) OF A TOOTHBRUSH WITH PASTE, IN A CUP, ON A SINK: PORTRAIT OF COOSJE'S THINKING (MODEL), 1982

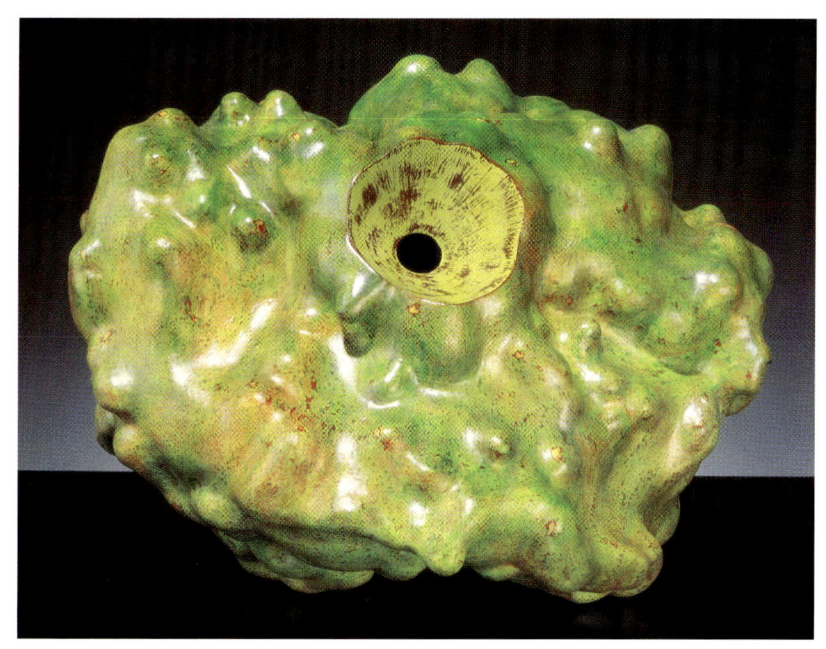

KENNETH PRICE, PHOBIA (CHARTREUSE, GREEN), 1995

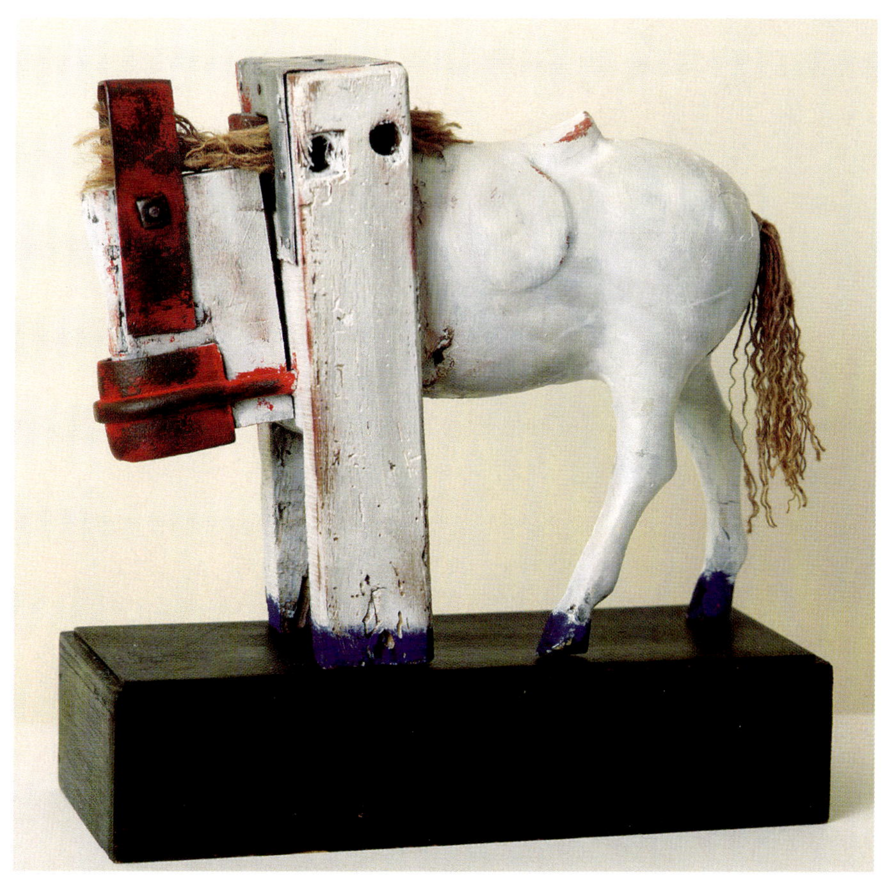

ALAIN PRILLARD, CHEVAL EVOLUTIF, 1990

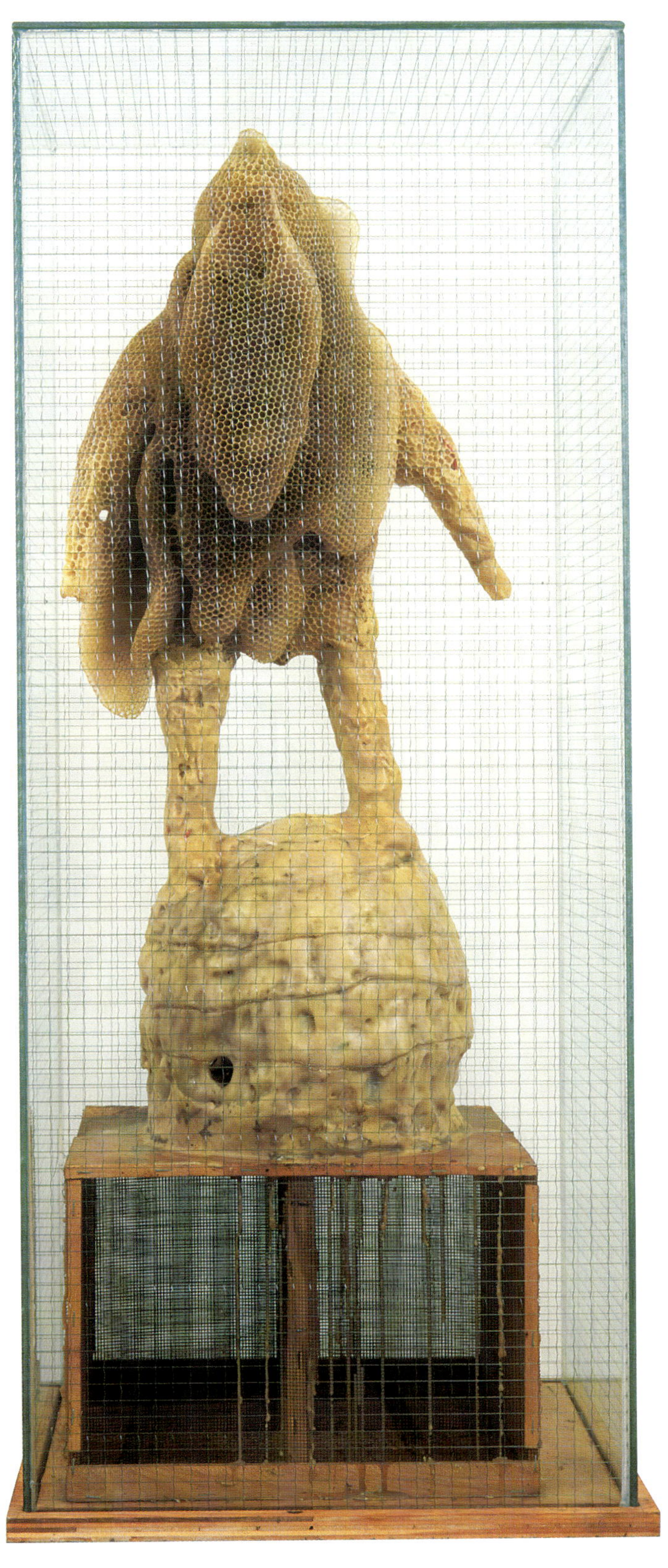

GARNETT PUETT, UNTITLED, 1985

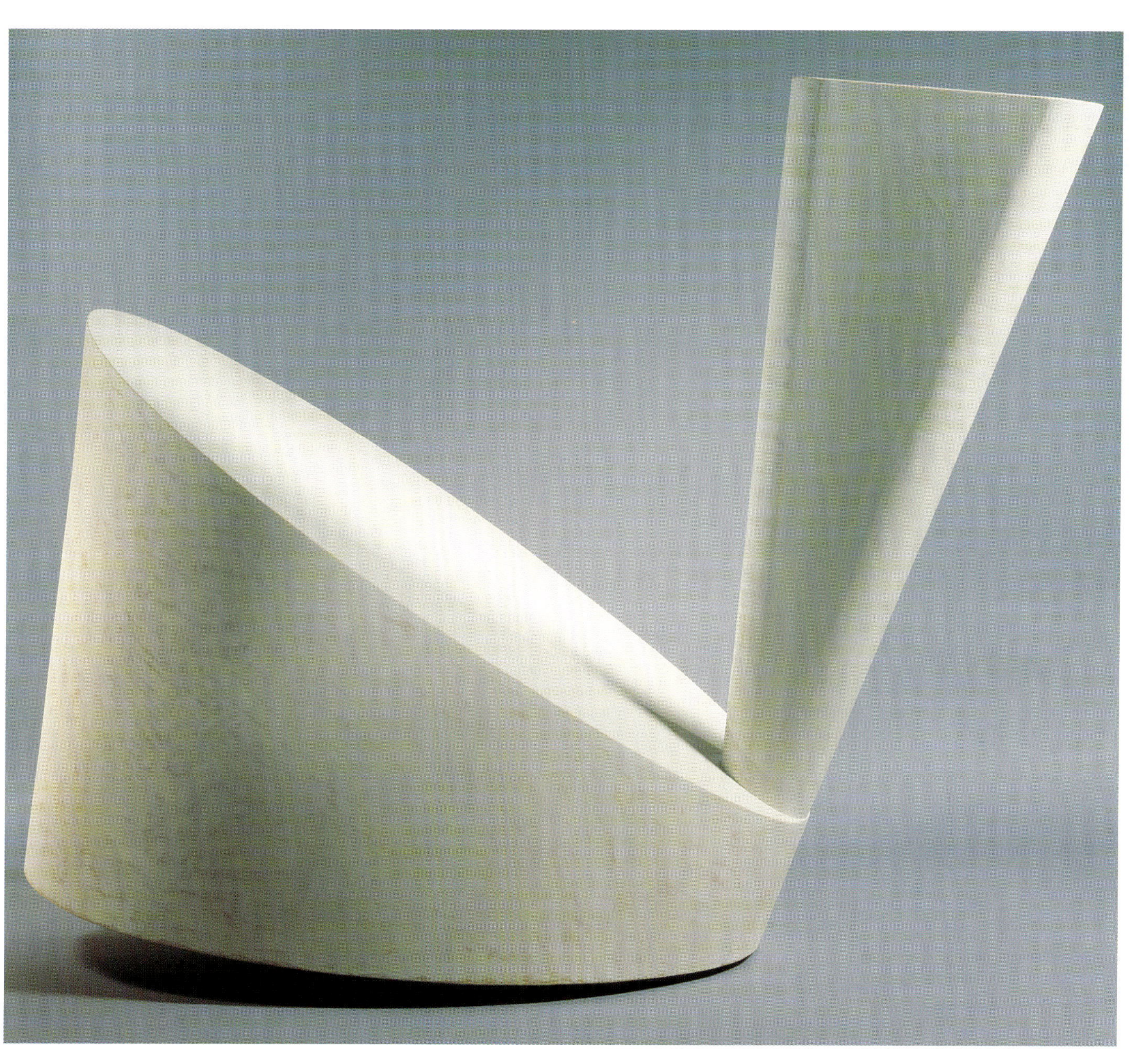

MARTIN PURYEAR, VERGE, 1987

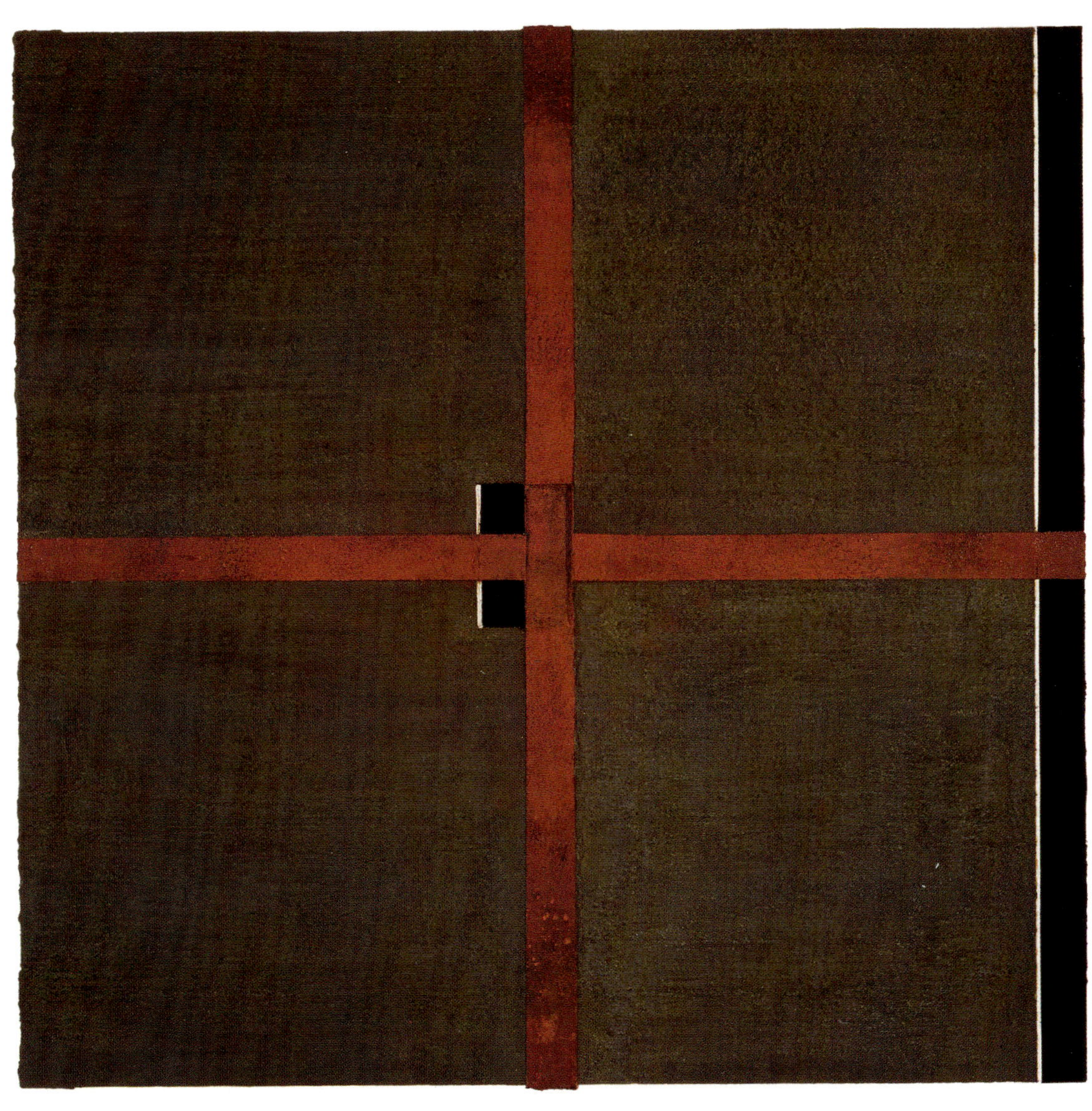

HARVEY QUAYTMAN, IVORY SLIVER, 1986

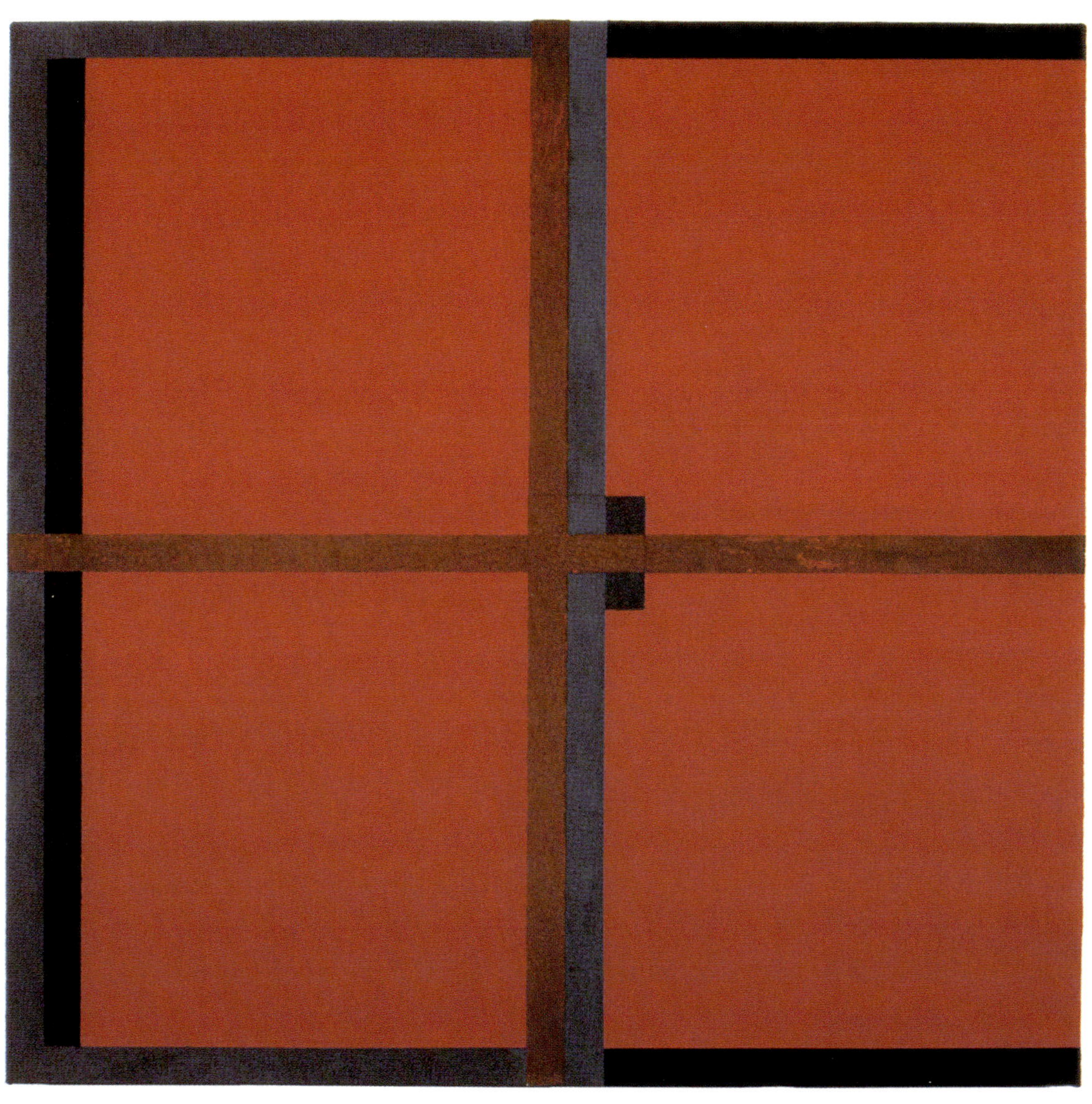

HARVEY QUAYTMAN, HERCULANEUM, 1992

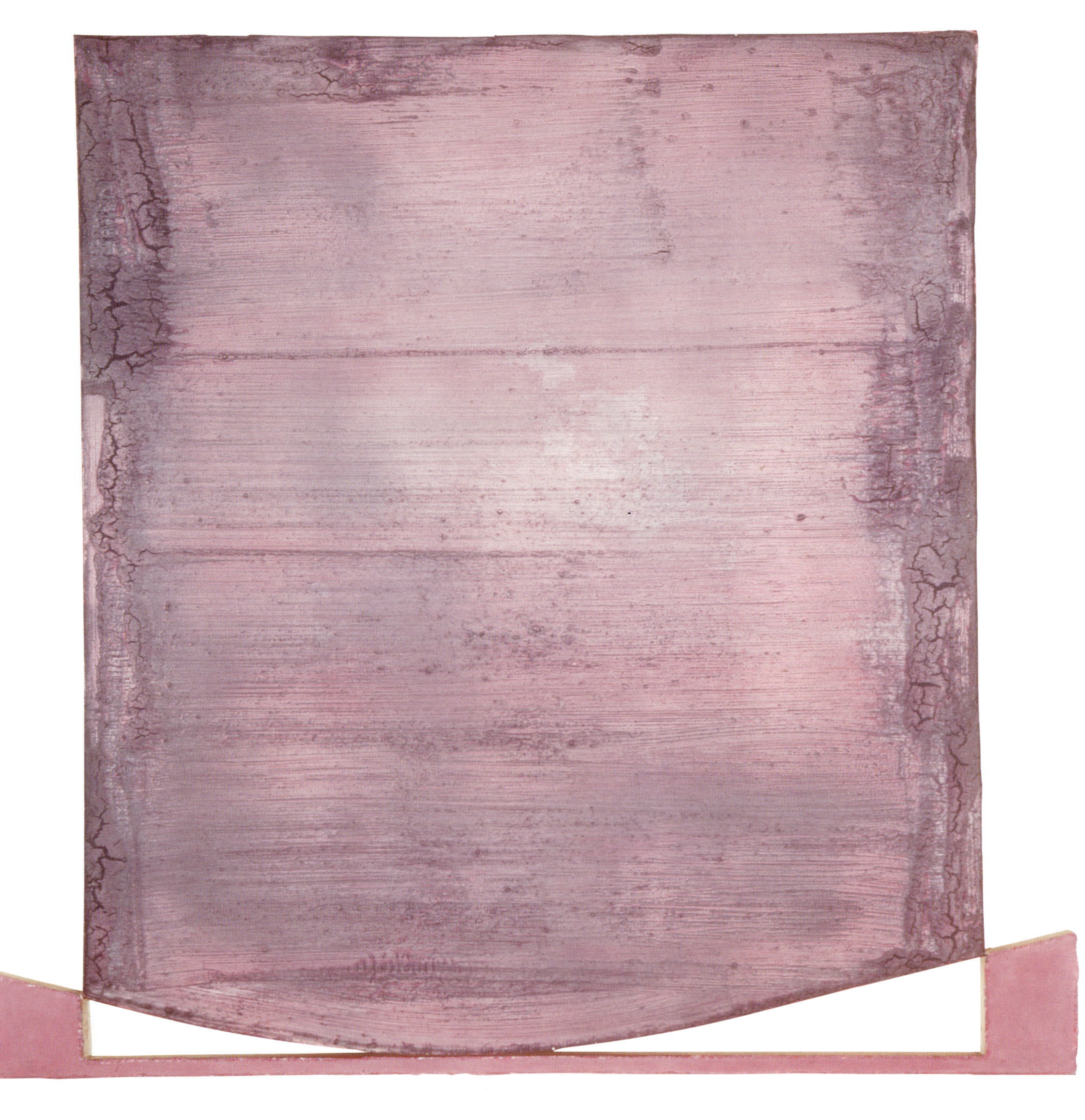

HARVEY QUAYTMAN, HARMONICA YP, 1972

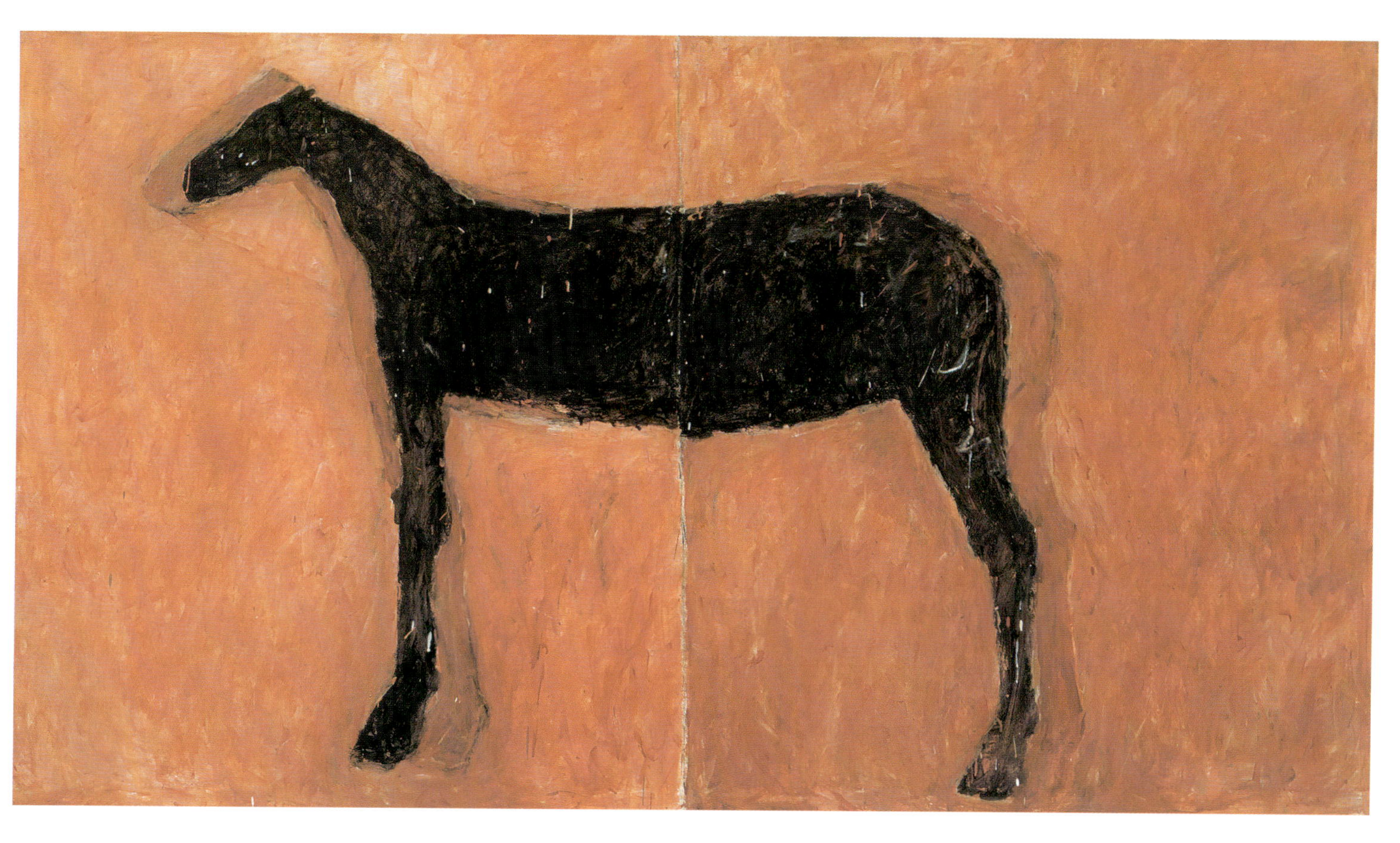

SUSAN ROTHENBERG, TRIPHAMMER BRIDGE, 1974

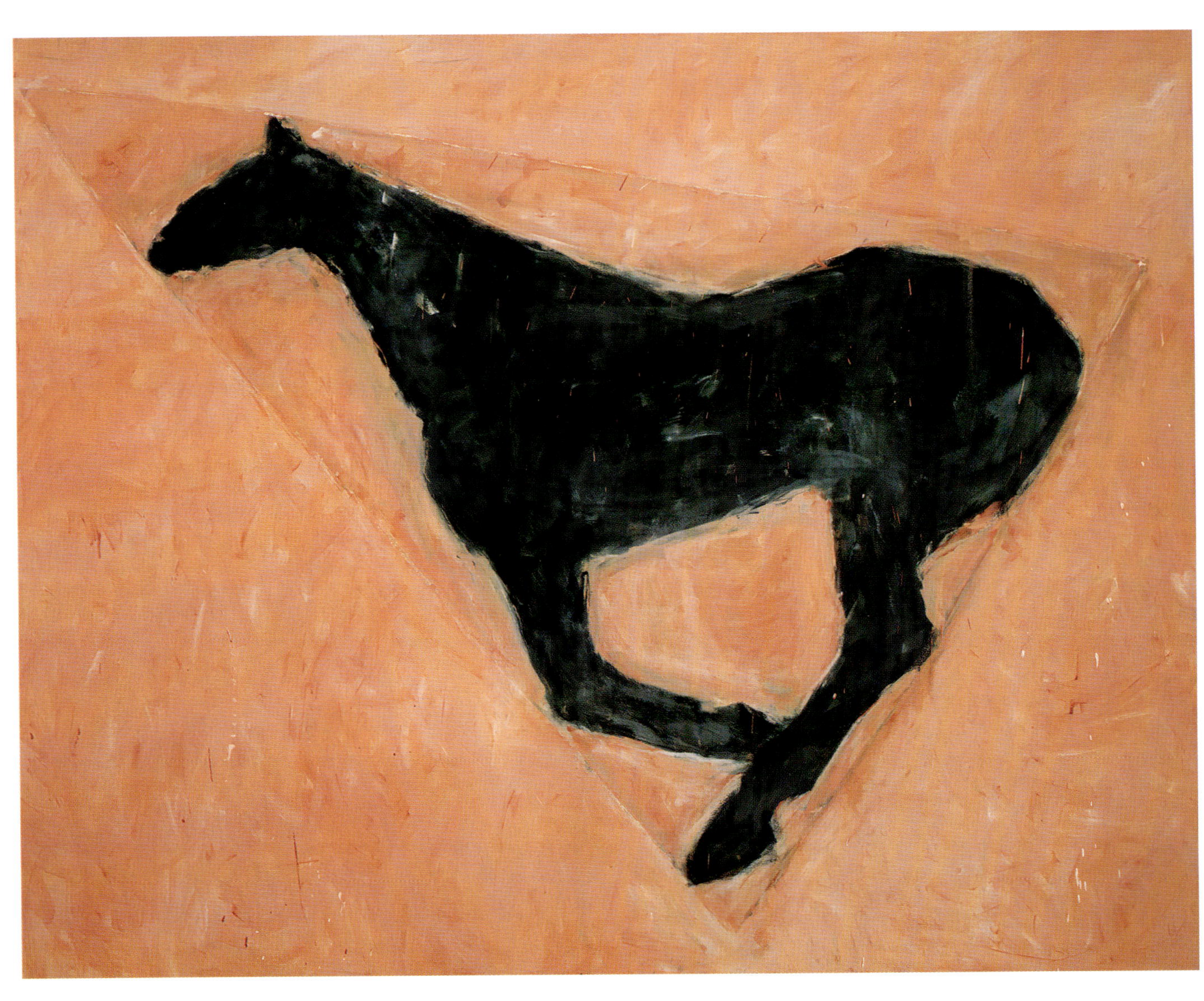

SUSAN ROTHENBERG, BLACK IN PLACE, 1976

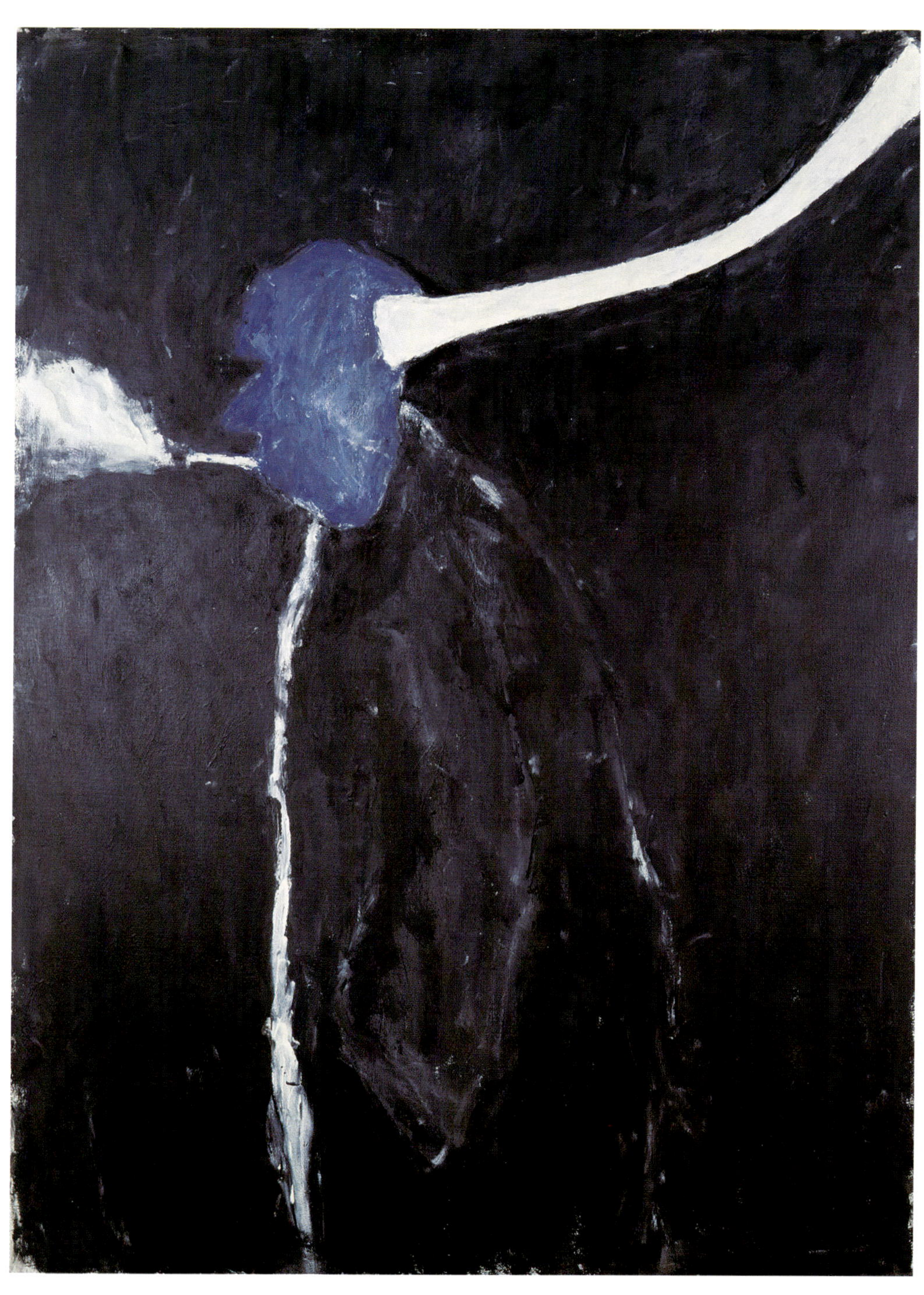

SUSAN ROTHENBERG, SMOKER, 1978-79

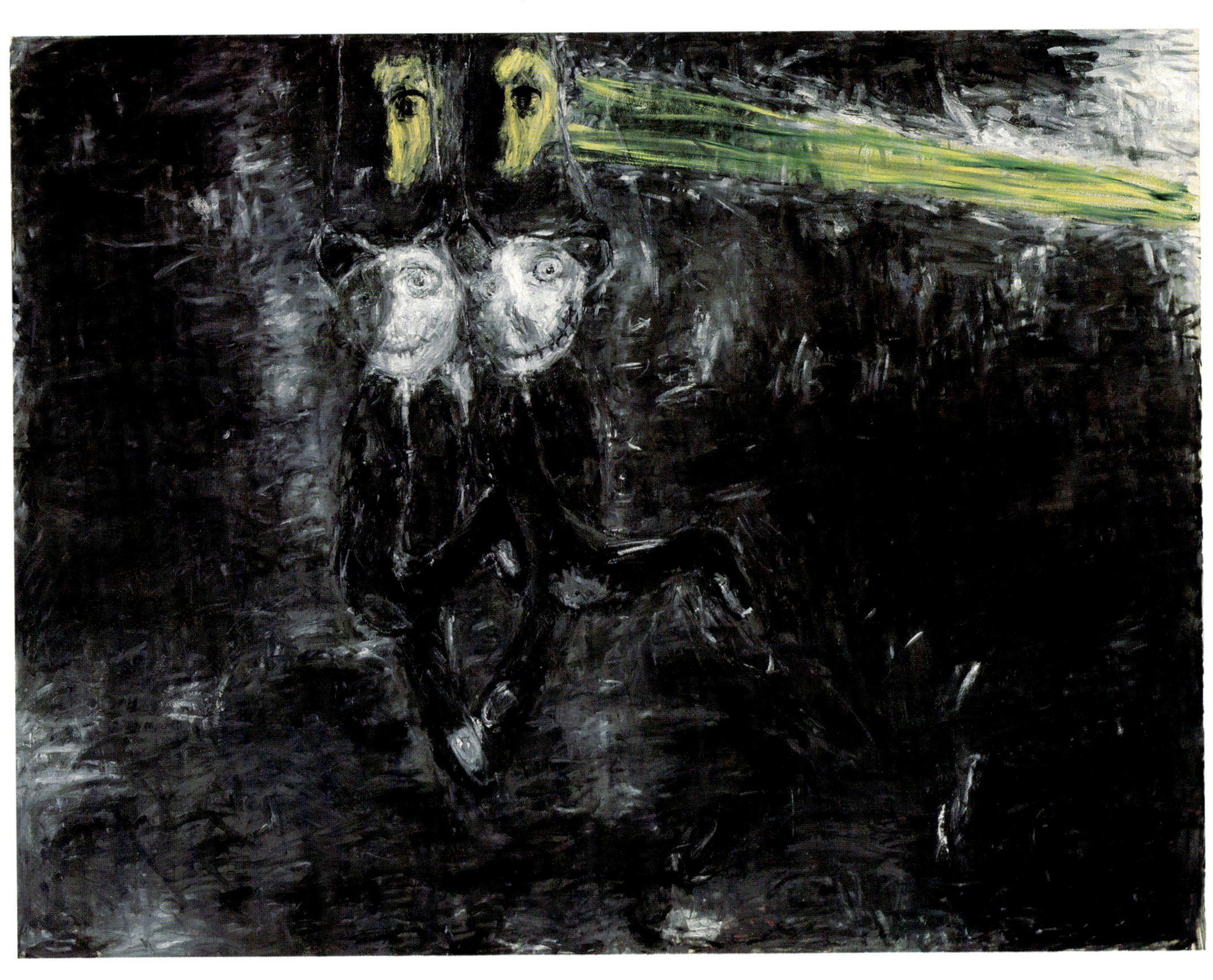

SUSAN ROTHENBERG, GREEN RAY, 1984

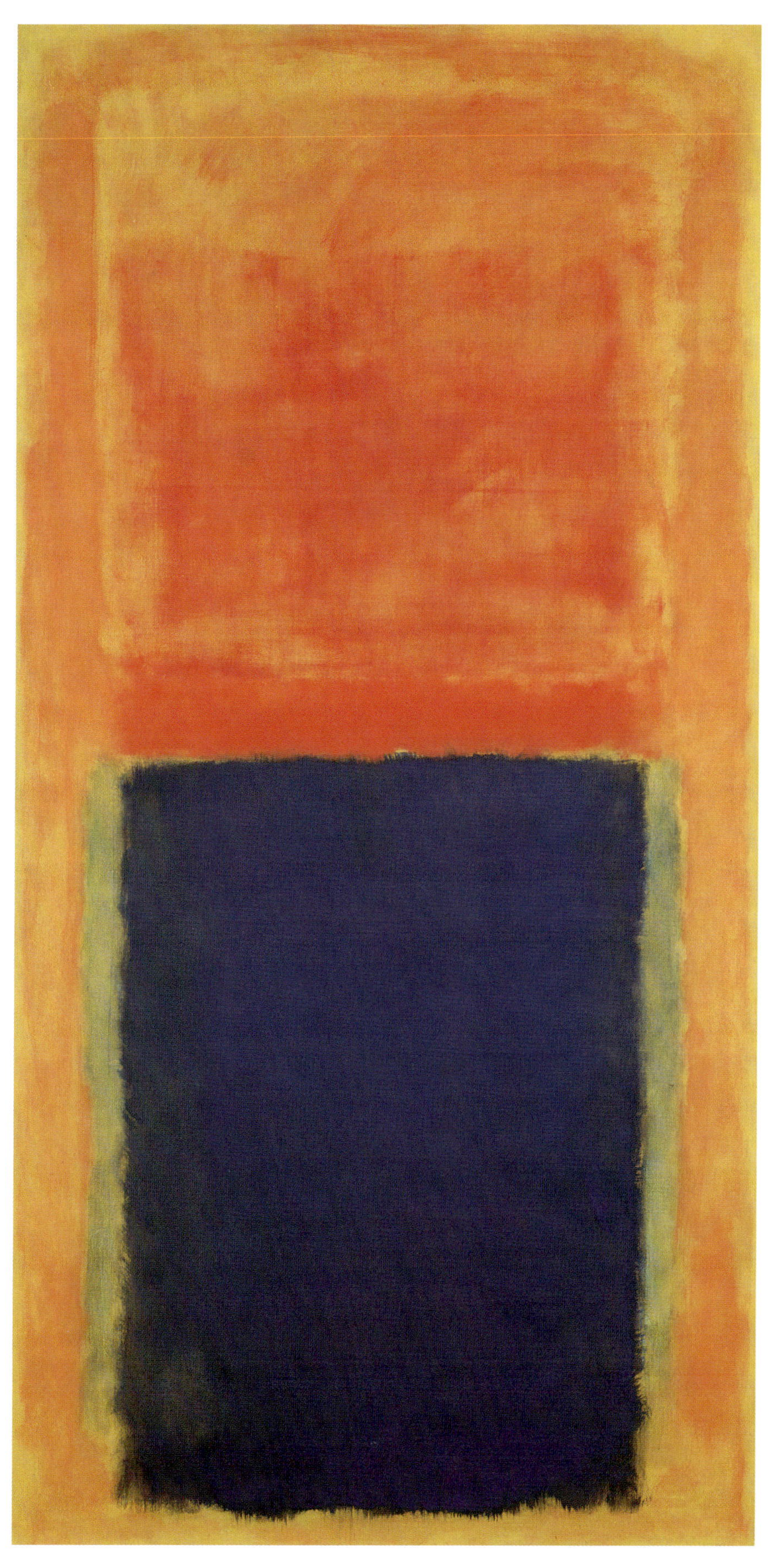

MARK ROTHKO, HOMAGE TO MATISSE, 1954

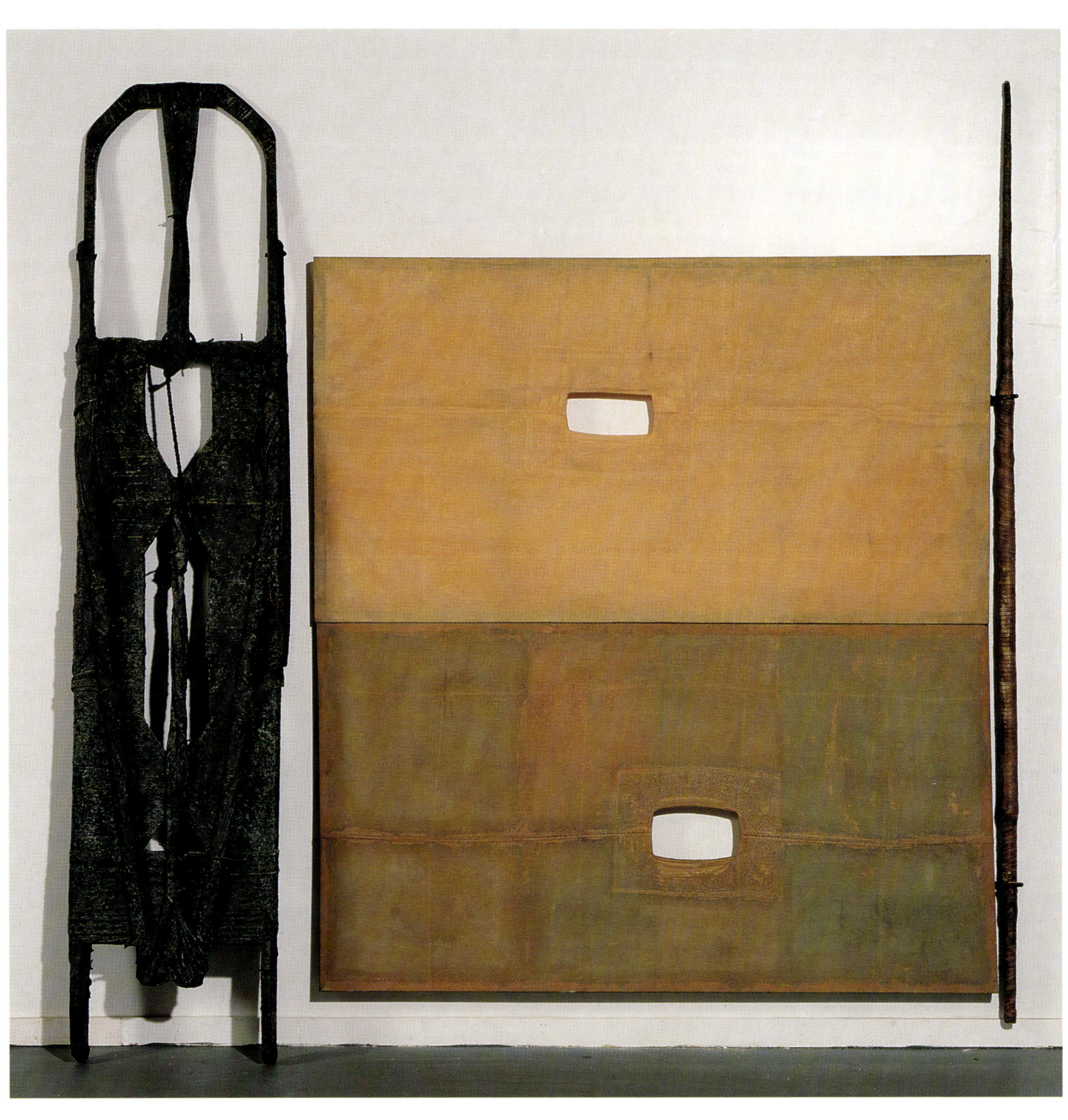

SAL SCARPITTA, GO-DEVIL SLED, 1976-77

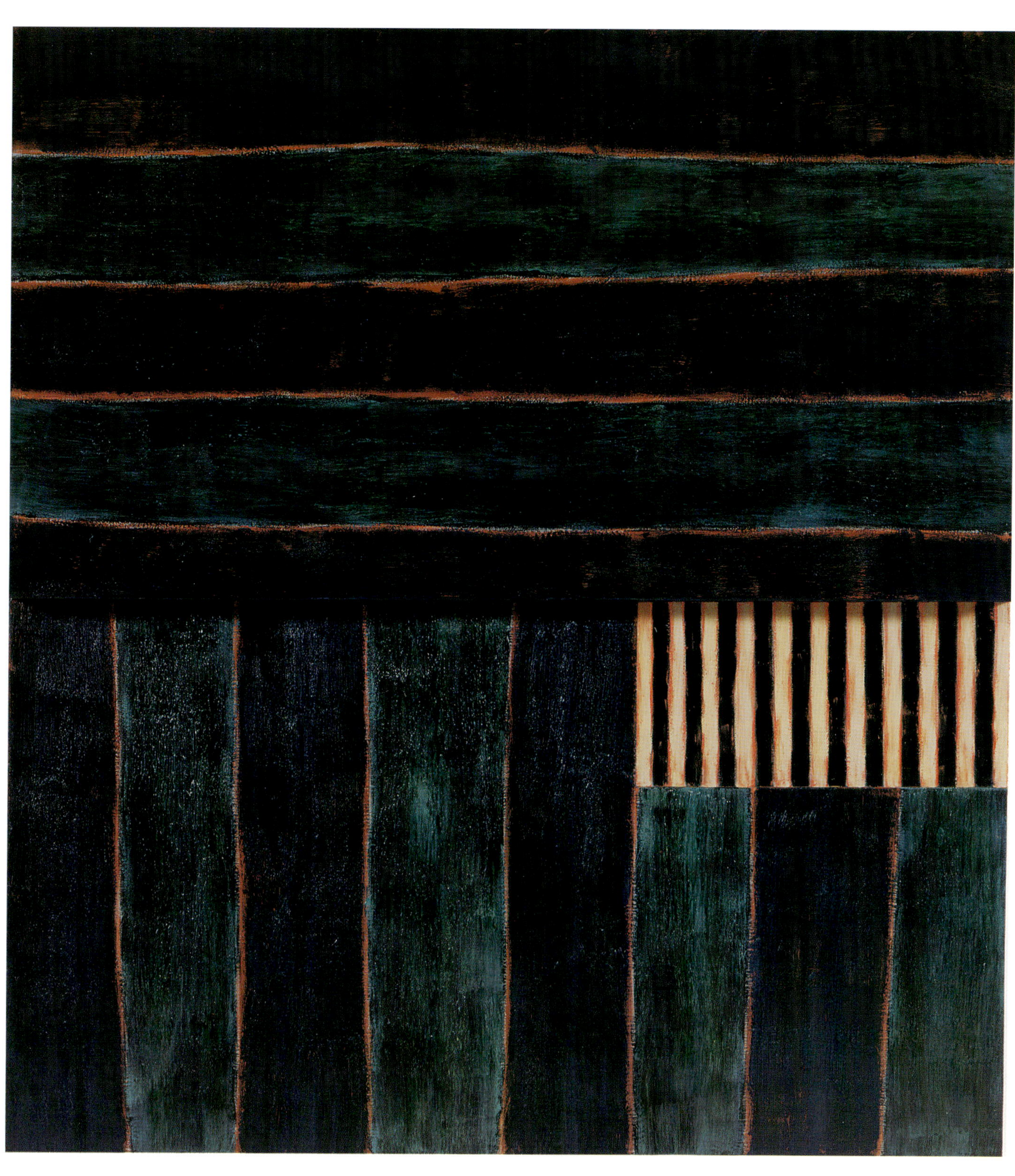

SEAN SCULLY, NARCISSUS, 1984

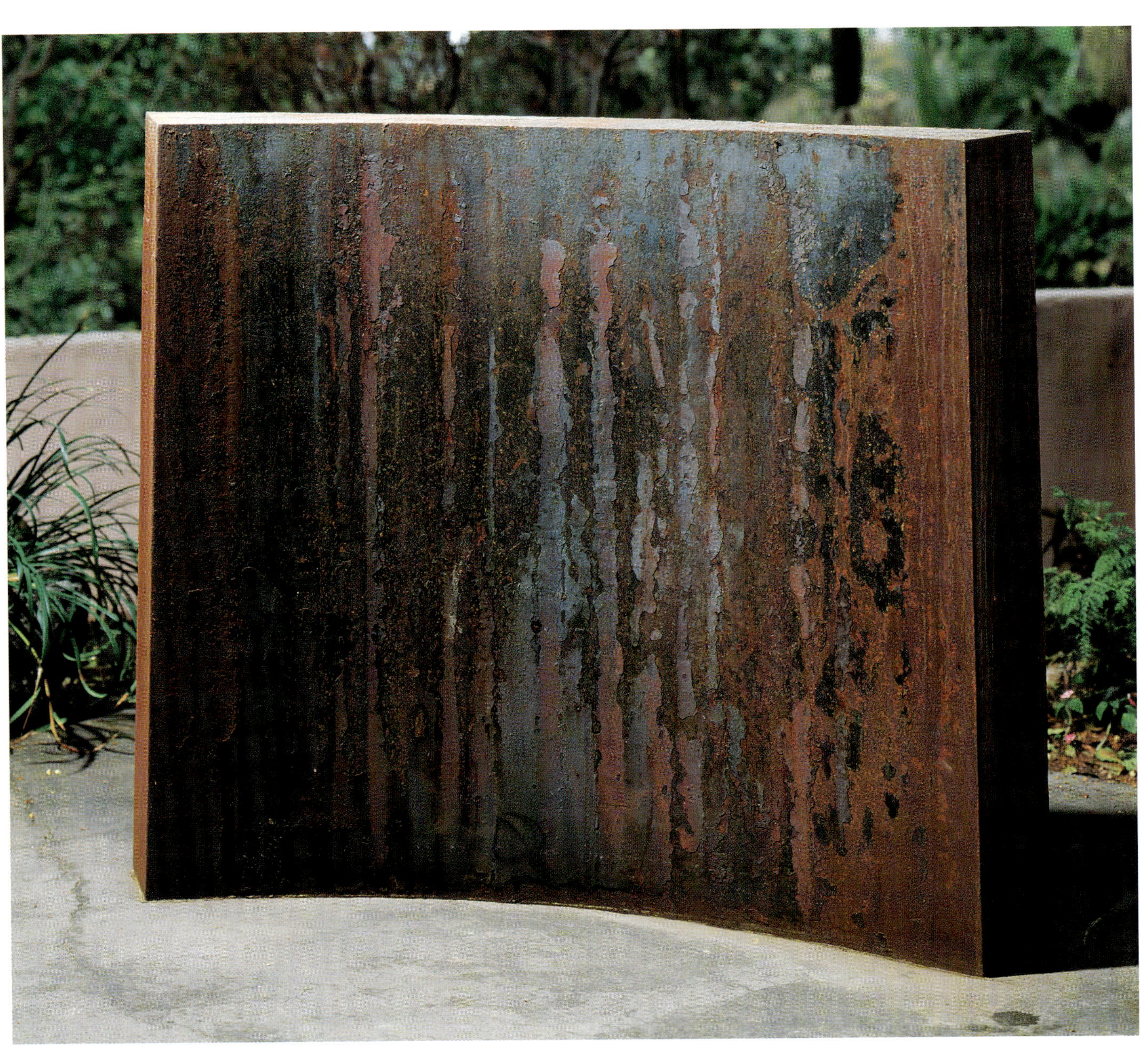

RICHARD SERRA, W.W.I., 1984

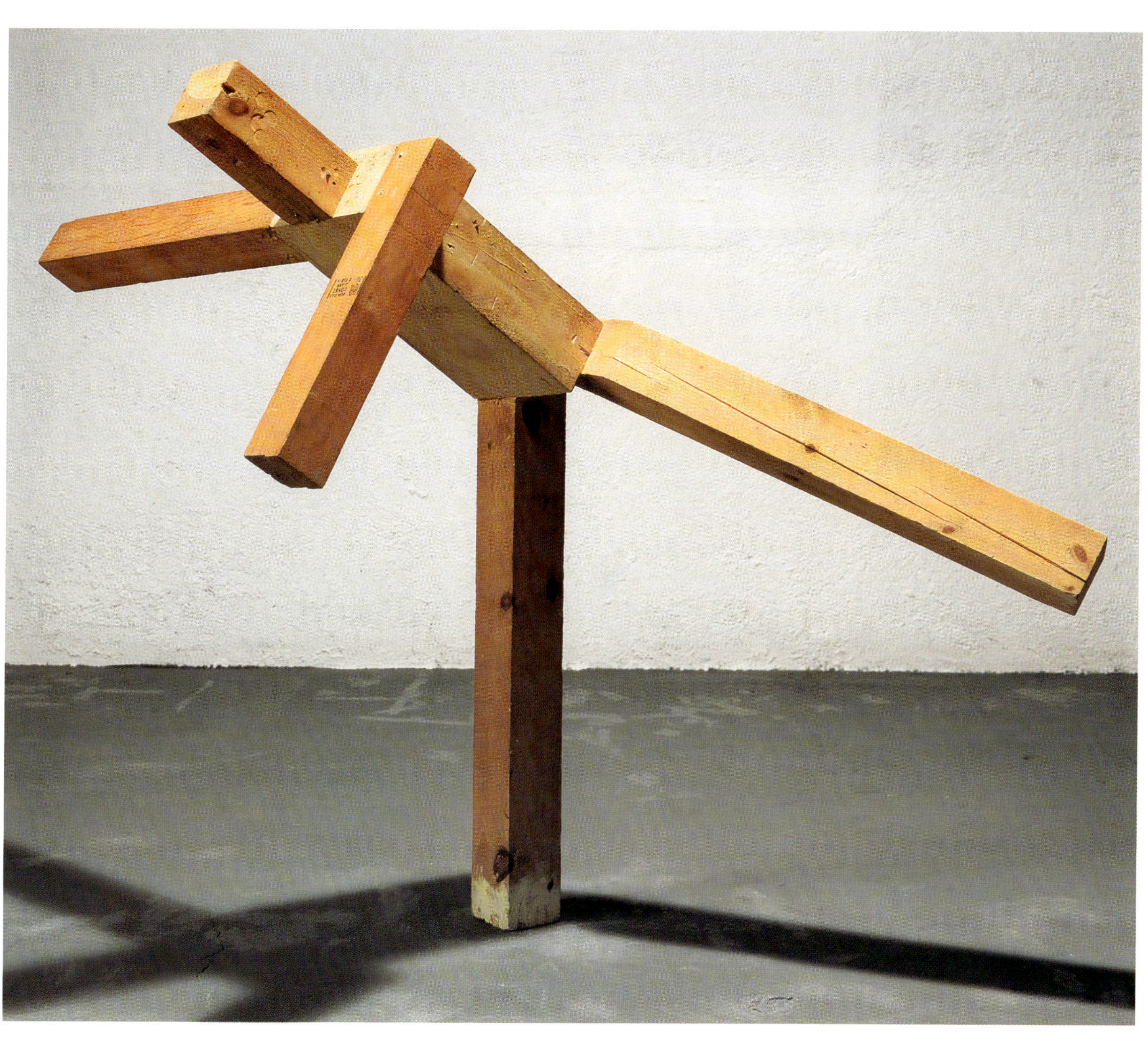

JOEL SHAPIRO, UNTITLED, 1980

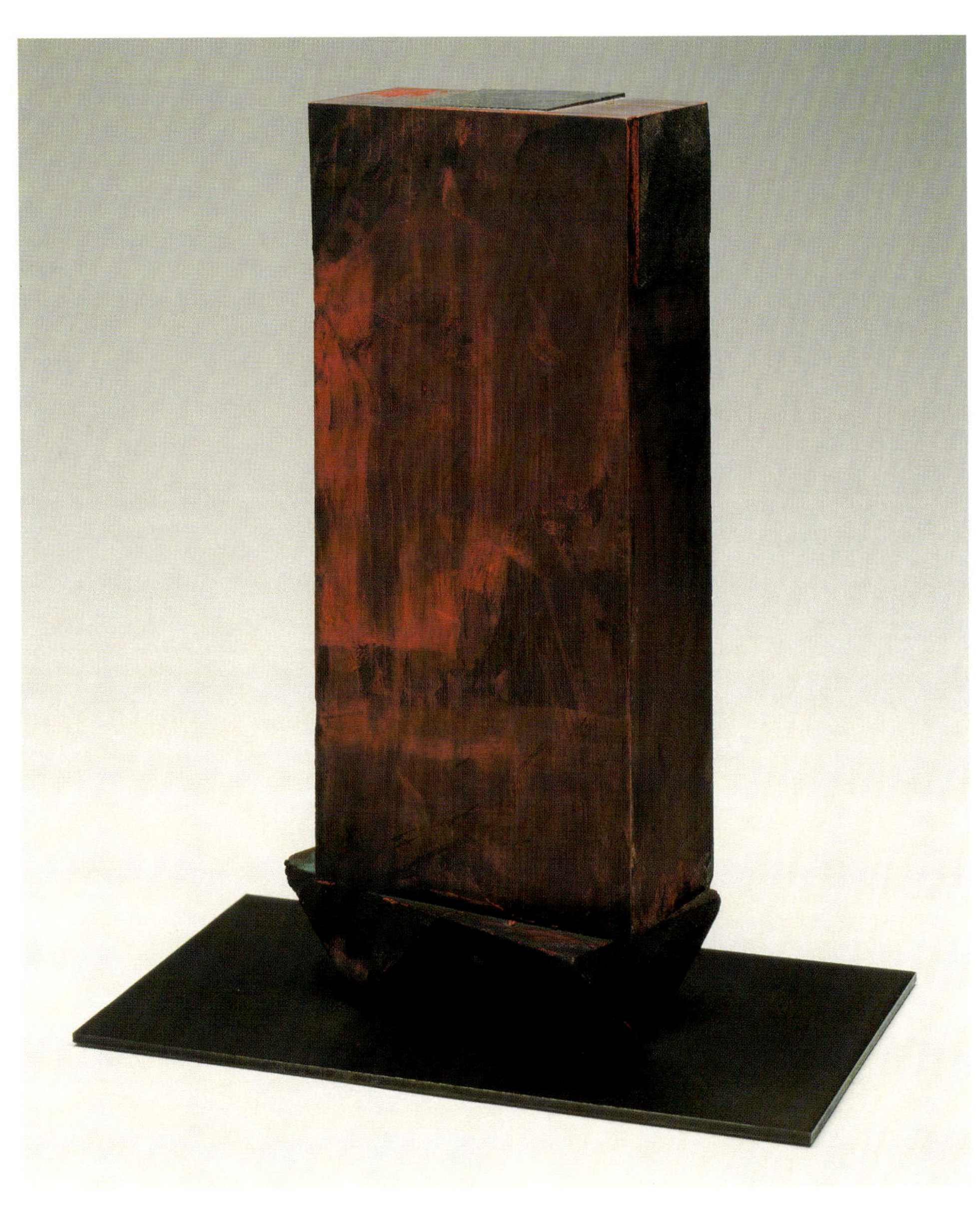

JOEL SHAPIRO, UNTITLED, 1980-81

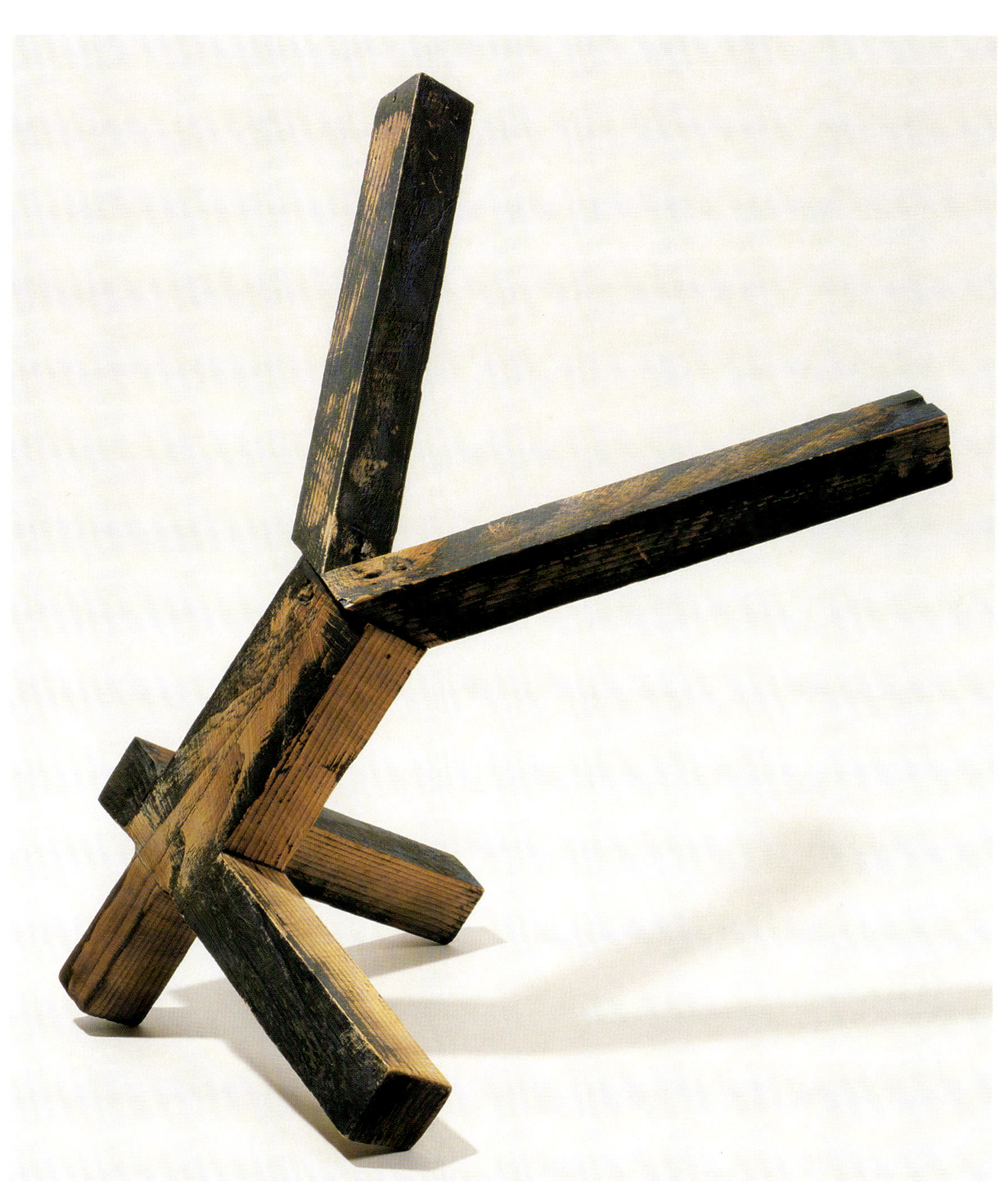

JOEL SHAPIRO, UNTITLED, 1980-82

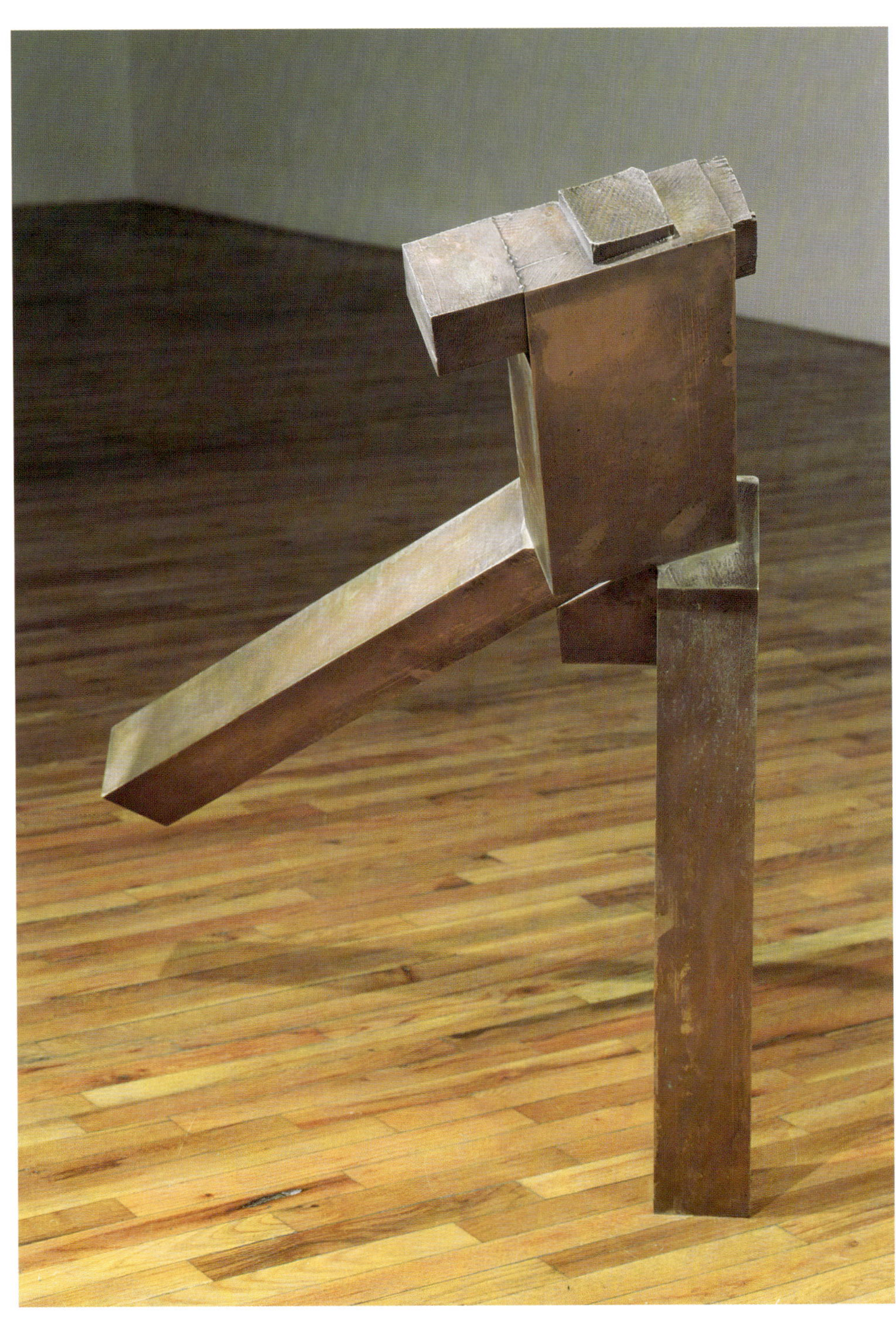

JOEL SHAPIRO, UNTITLED, 1982-83

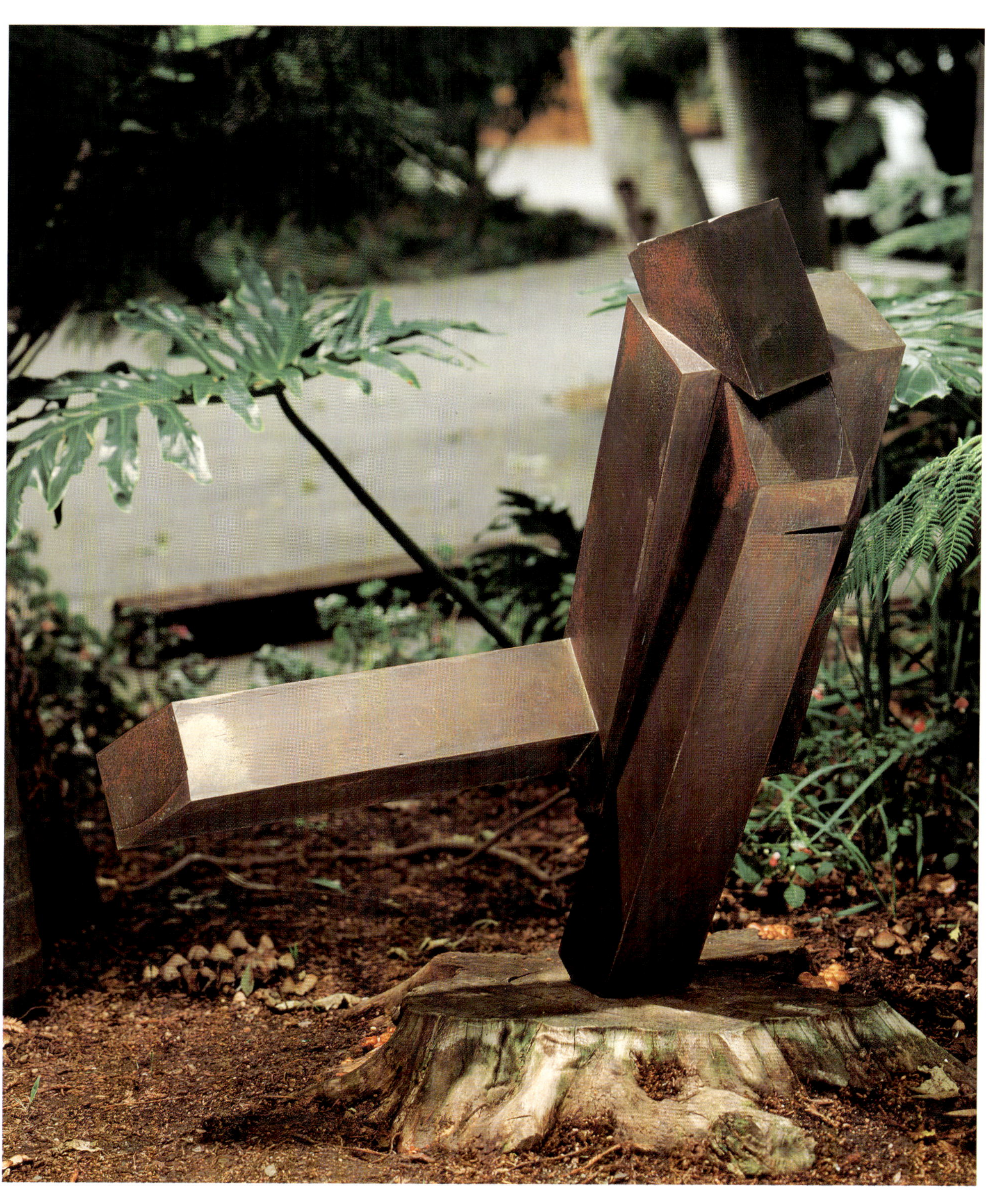

JOEL SHAPIRO, UNTITLED, 1982-84

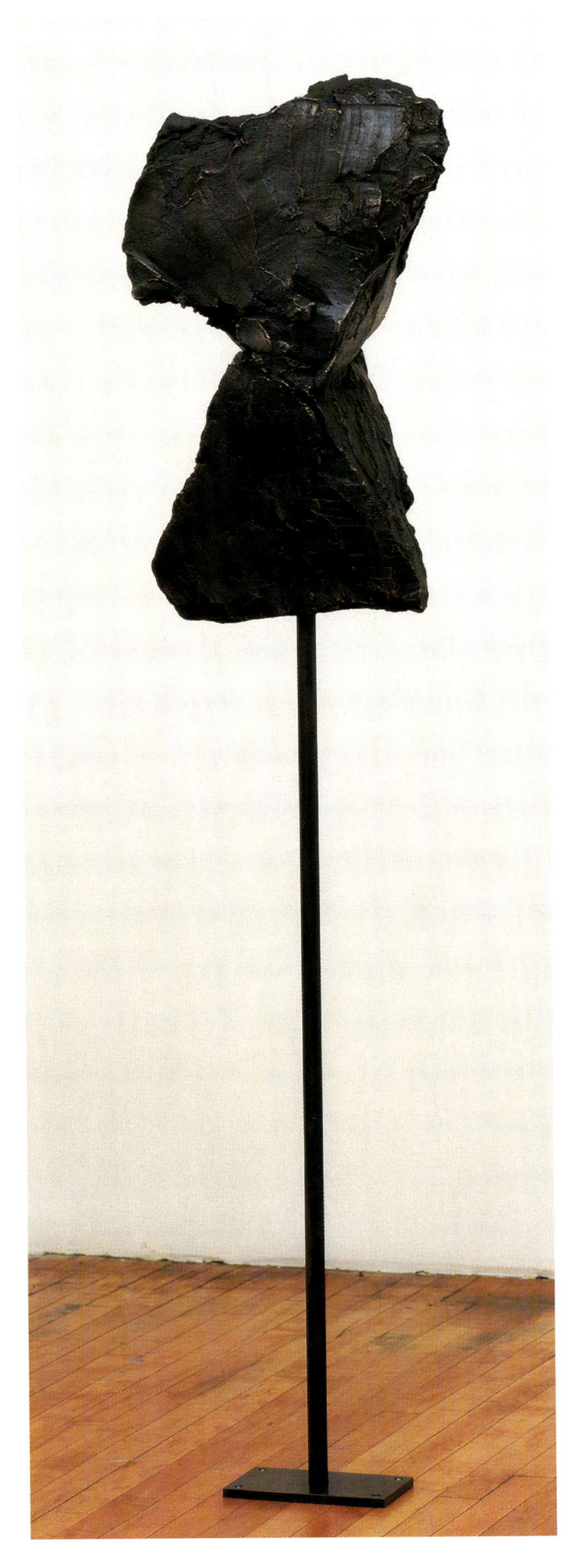

JOEL SHAPIRO, UNTITLED, 1987-88

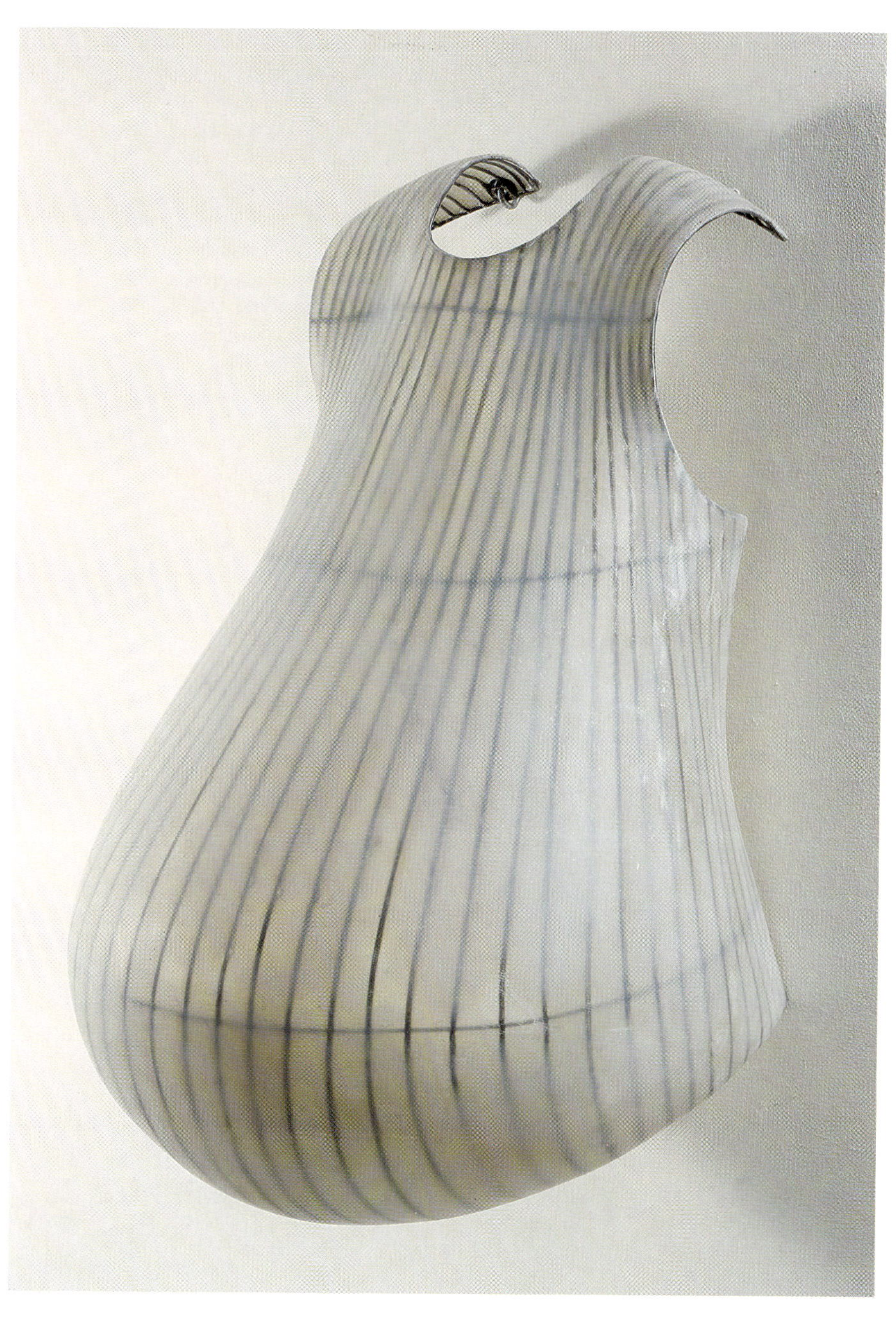

PETER SHELTON, CLEARBELLY, 1987

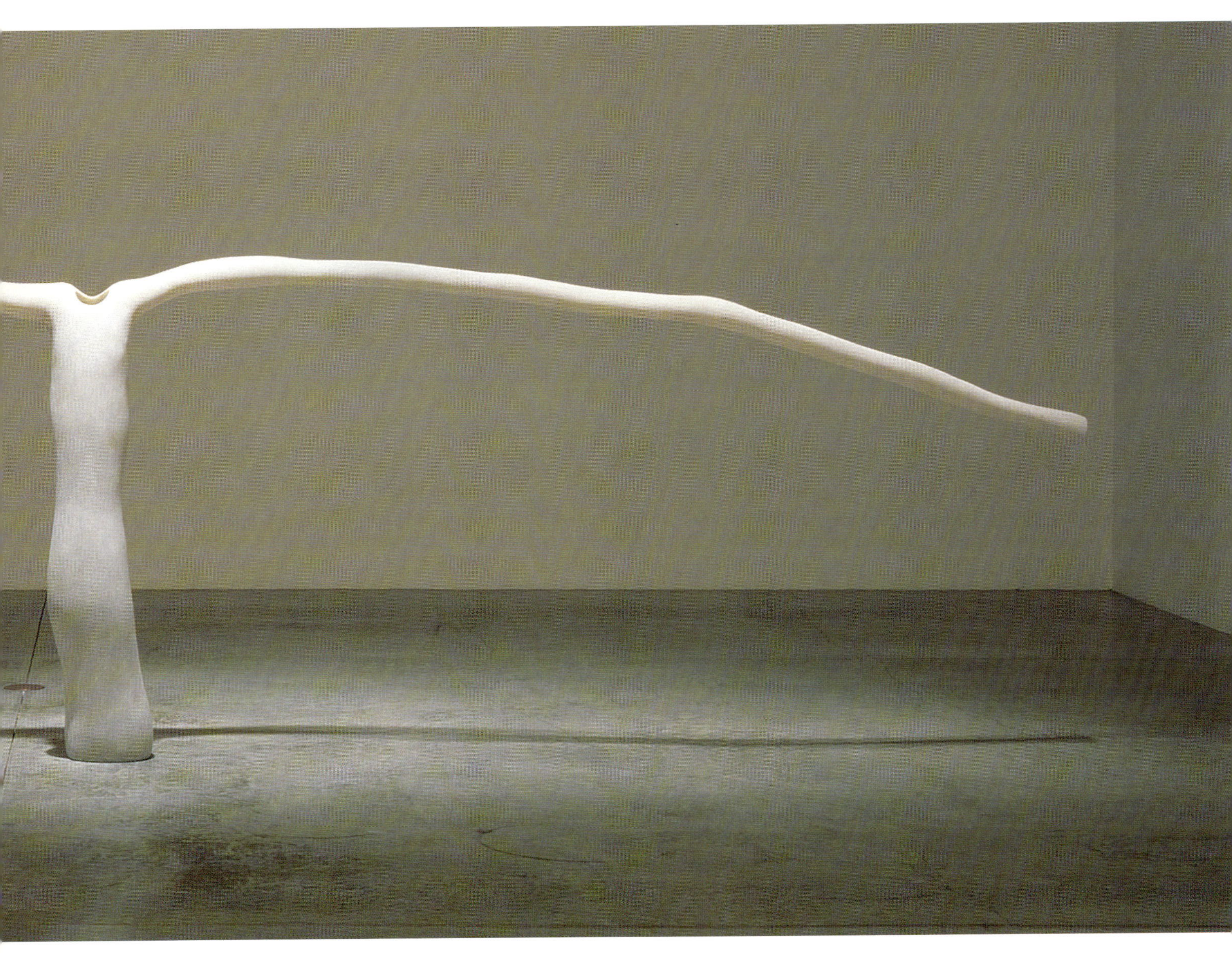

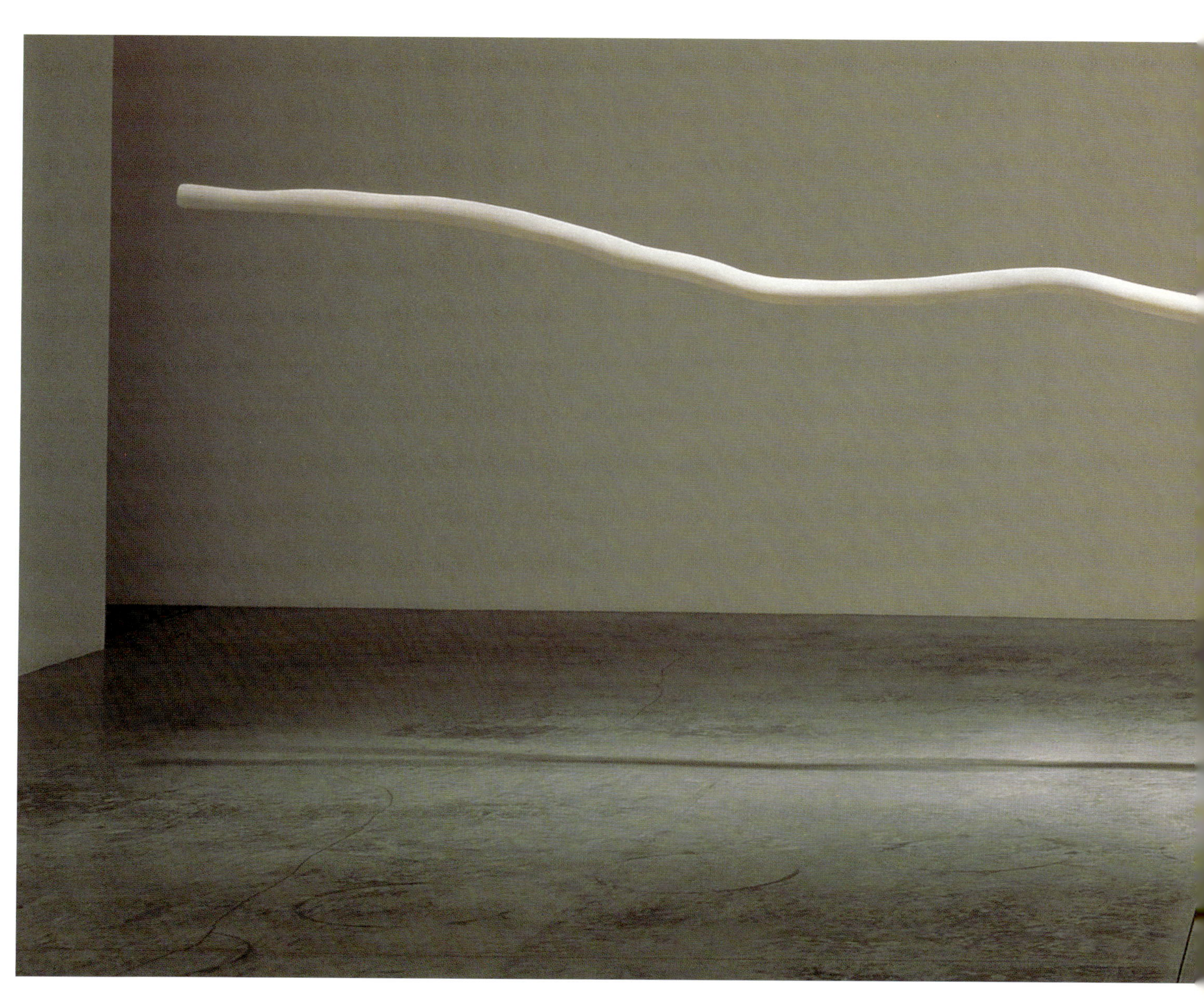

PETER SHELTON, ALLARMS, 1990-96

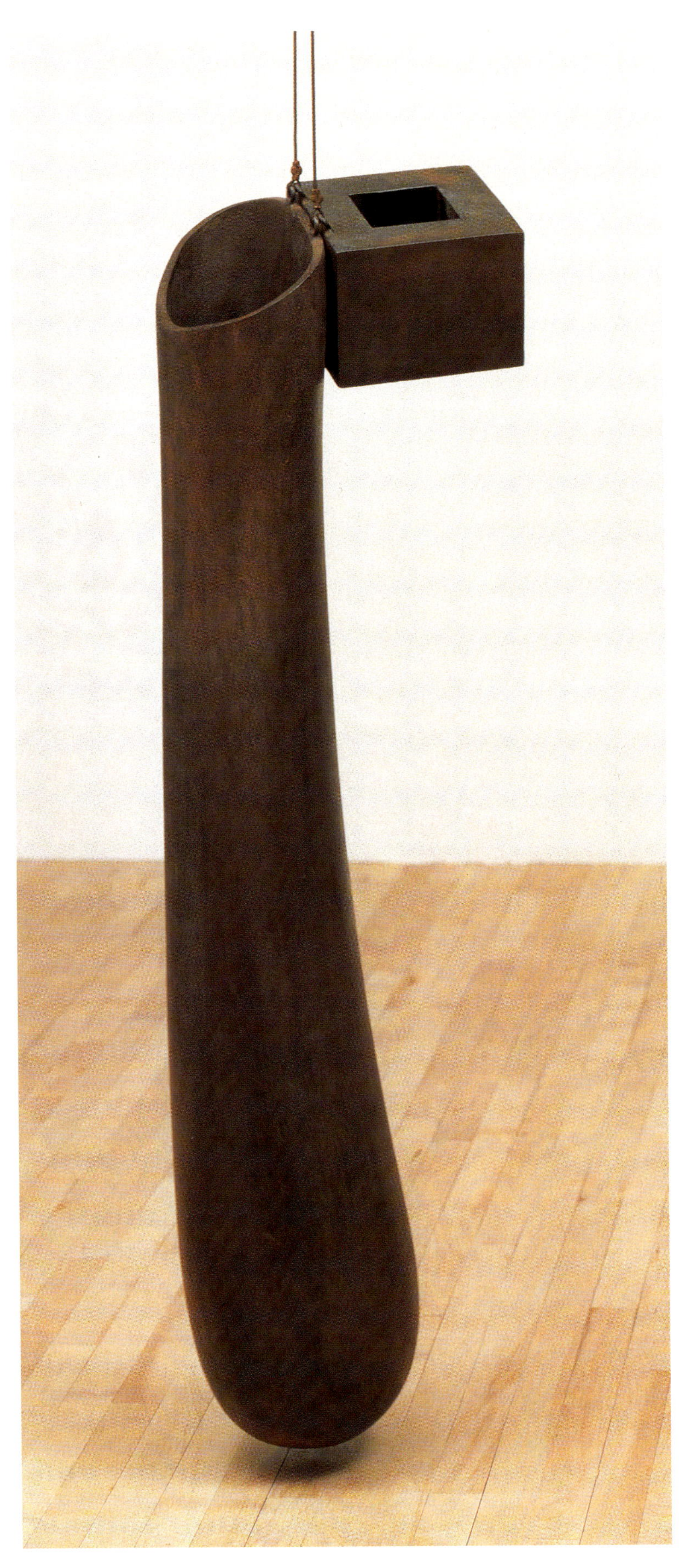

PETER SHELTON, BAGBOX, 1988-89

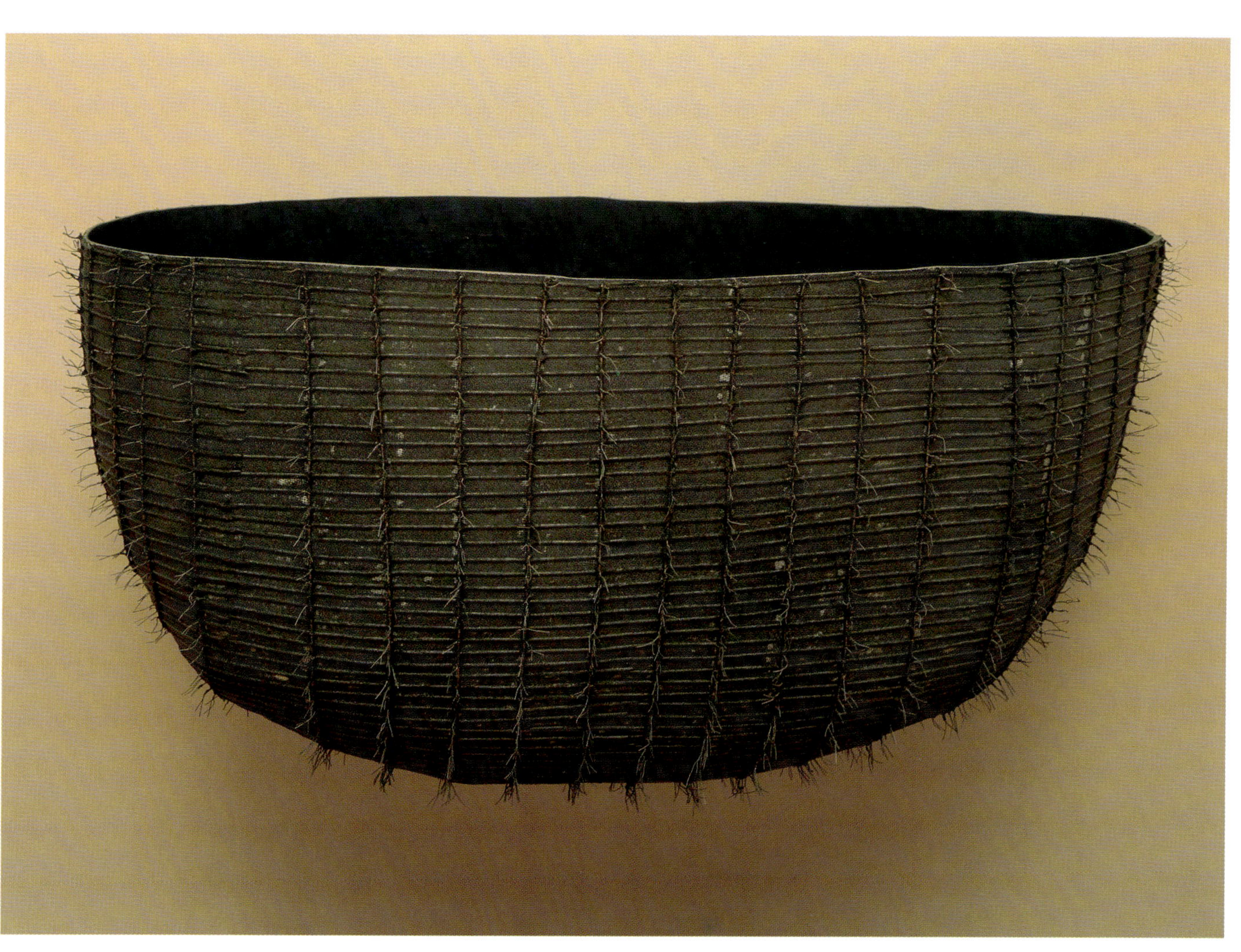

PETER SHELTON, BLUEPOOL, 1997

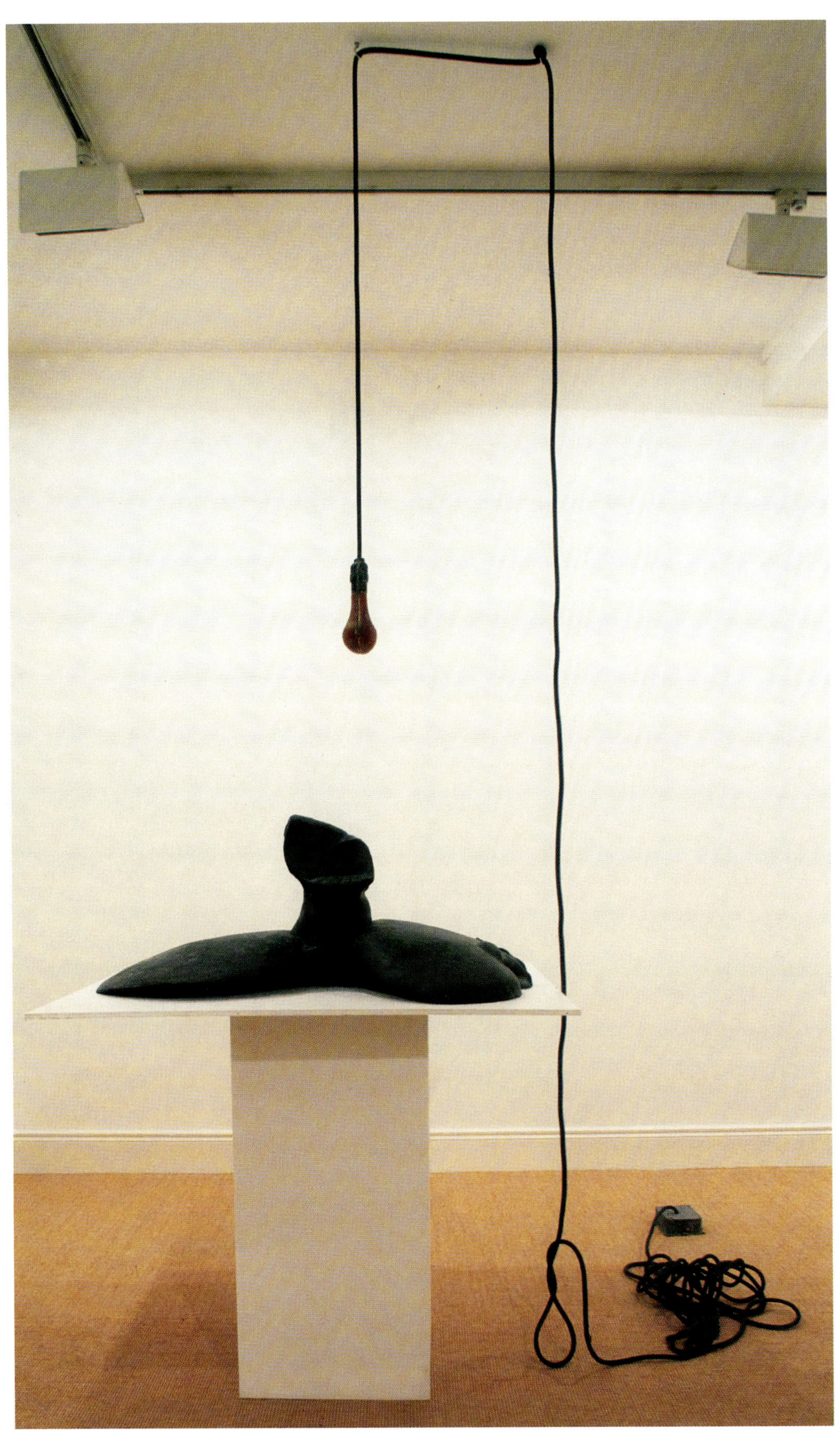

JEANNE SILVERTHORNE, UNTITLED, 1994

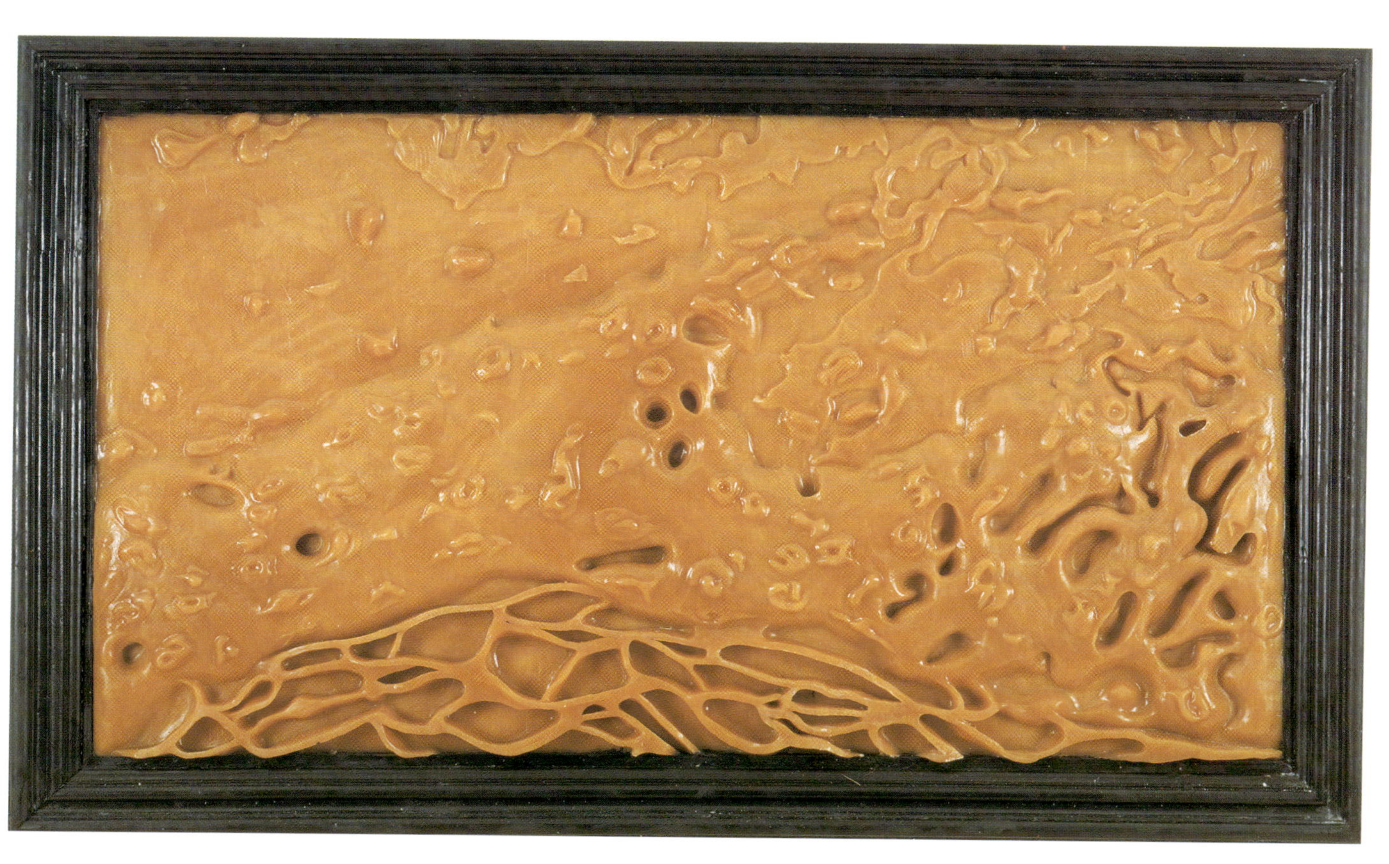

JEANNE SILVERTHORNE, CROSS SECTION, 1997

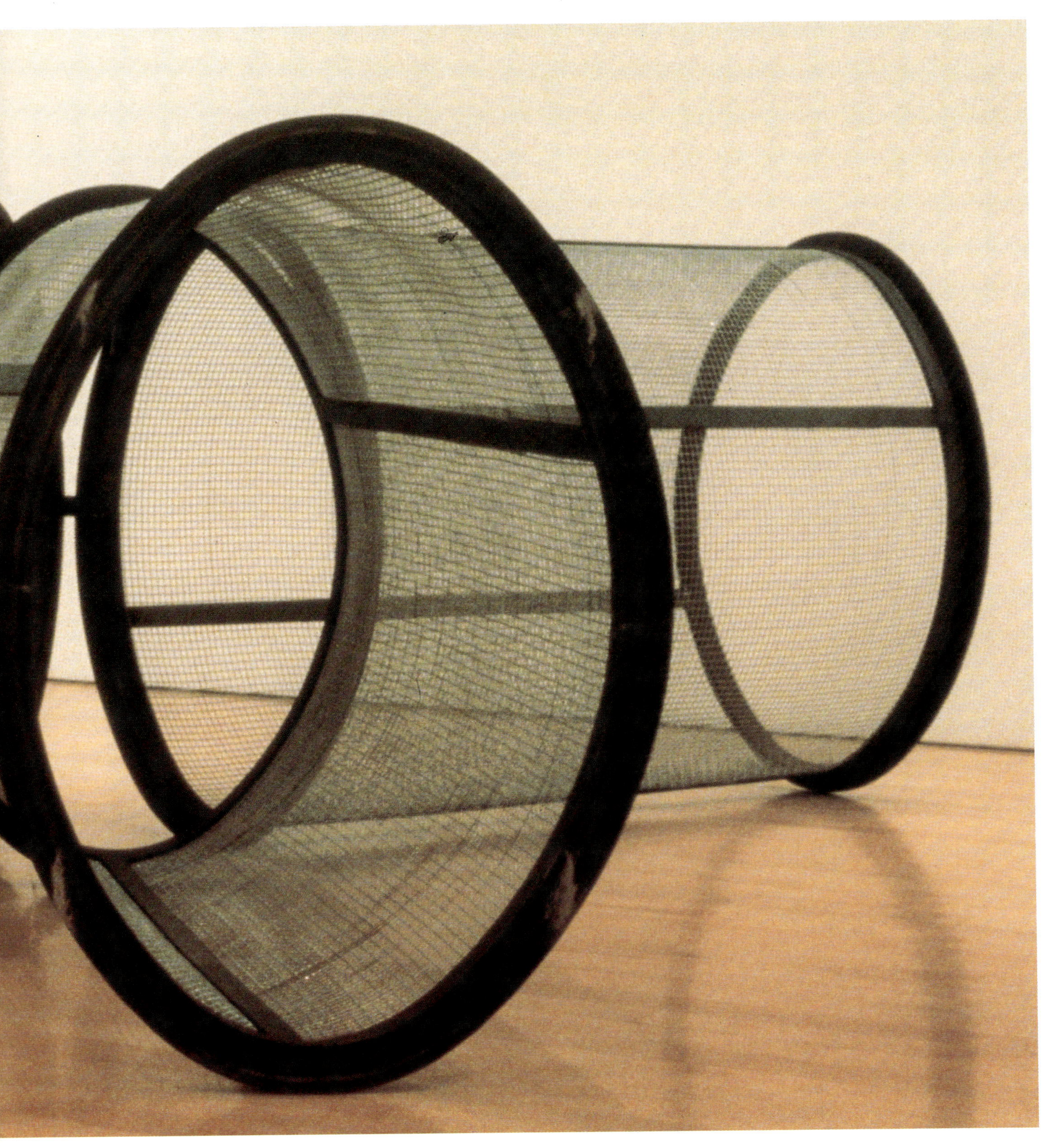

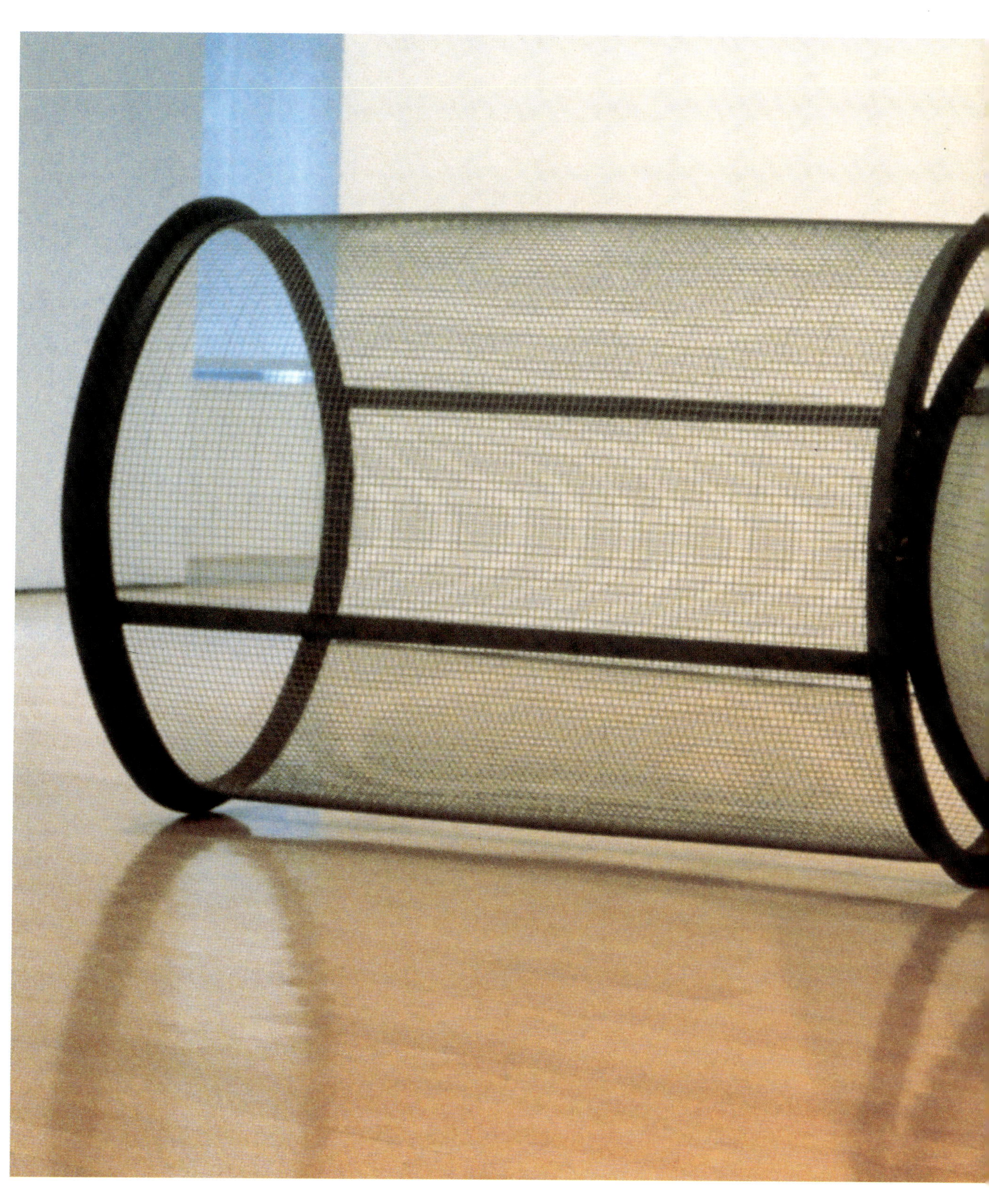

SUSANA SOLANO, ADJUSTMENT IN THE VOID NO. 2, 1996

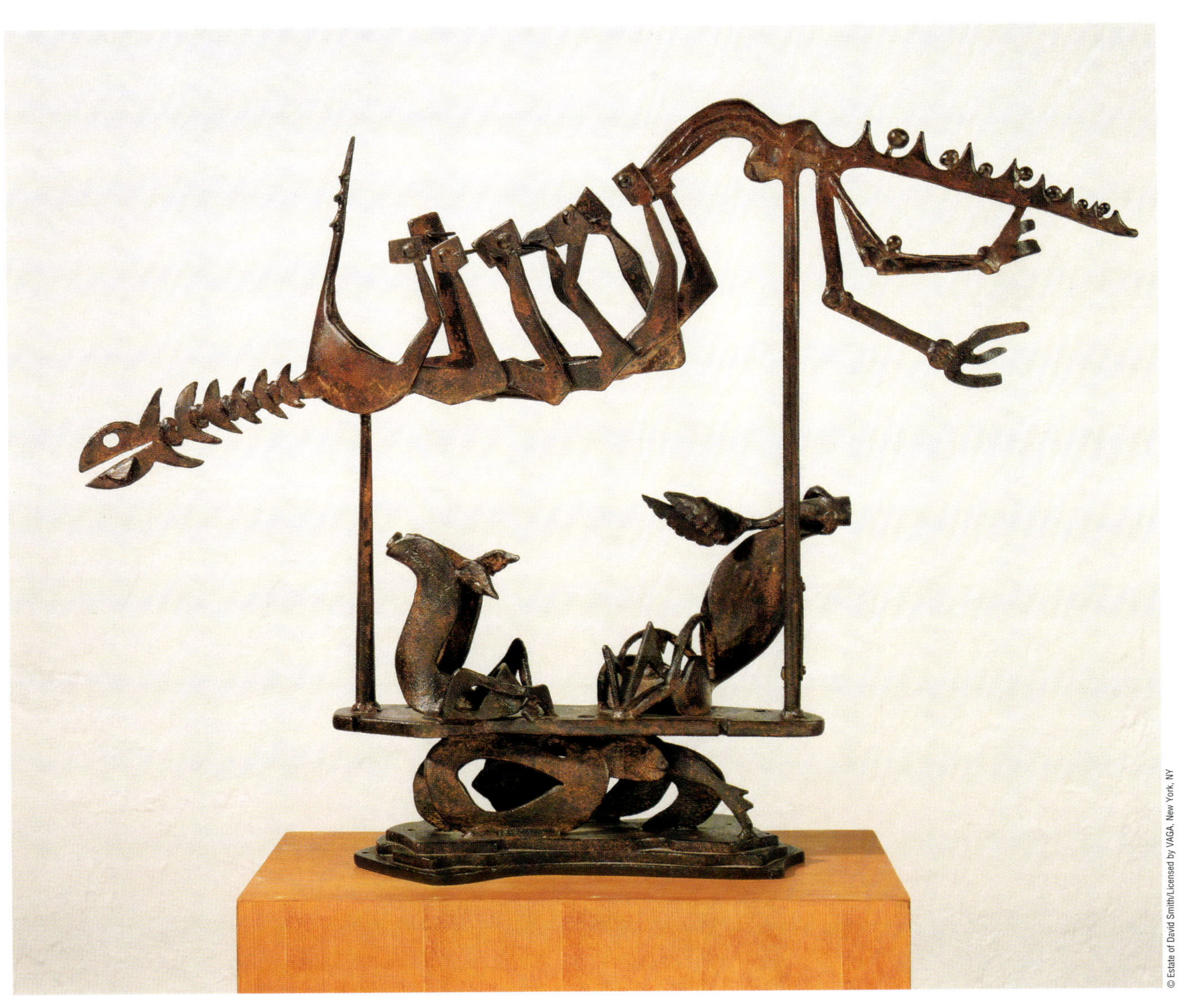

DAVID SMITH, JURASSIC BIRD, 1945

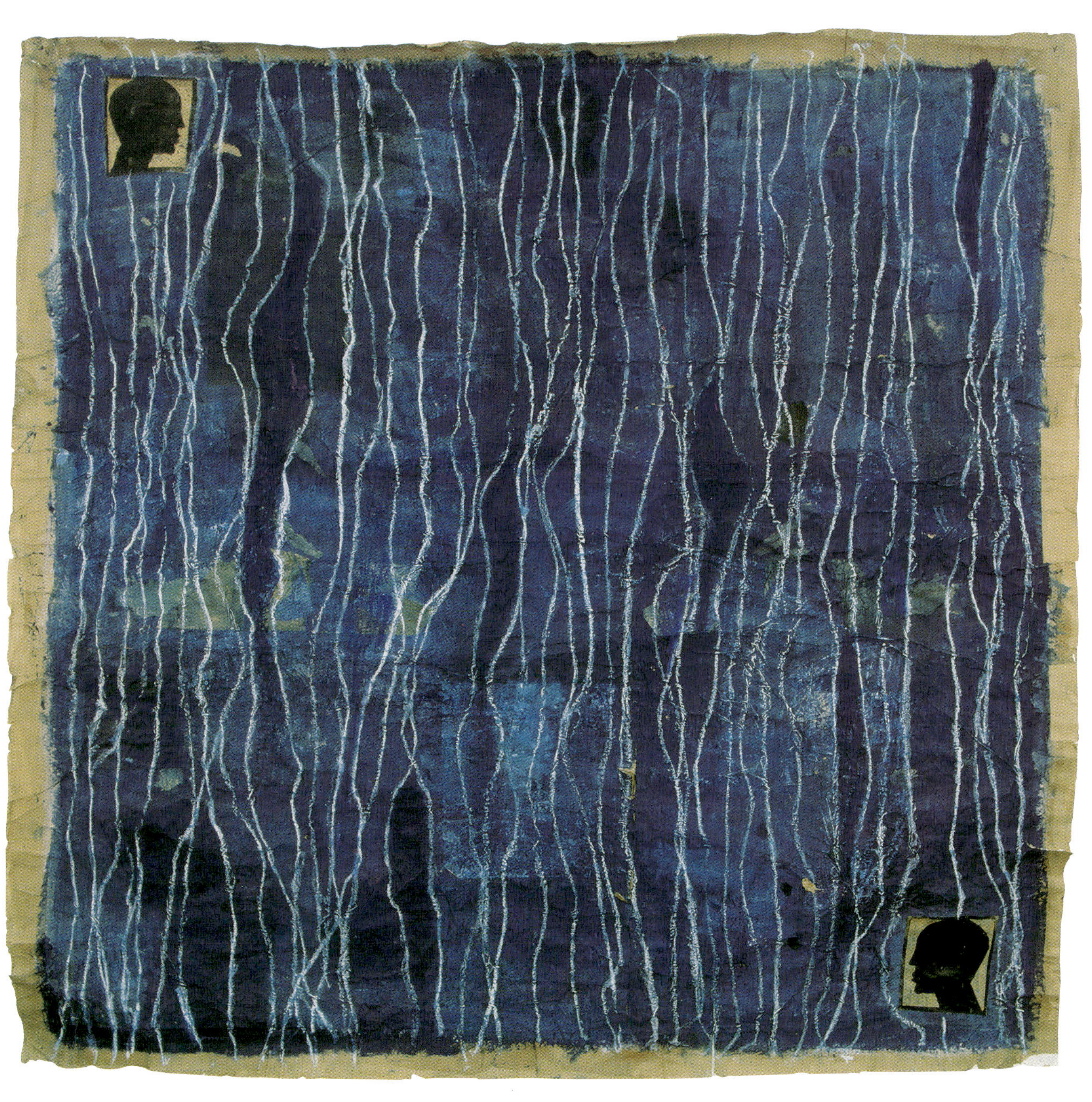

ROMAIN TAIEB, TÊTE DANS LE BLEU, 1993

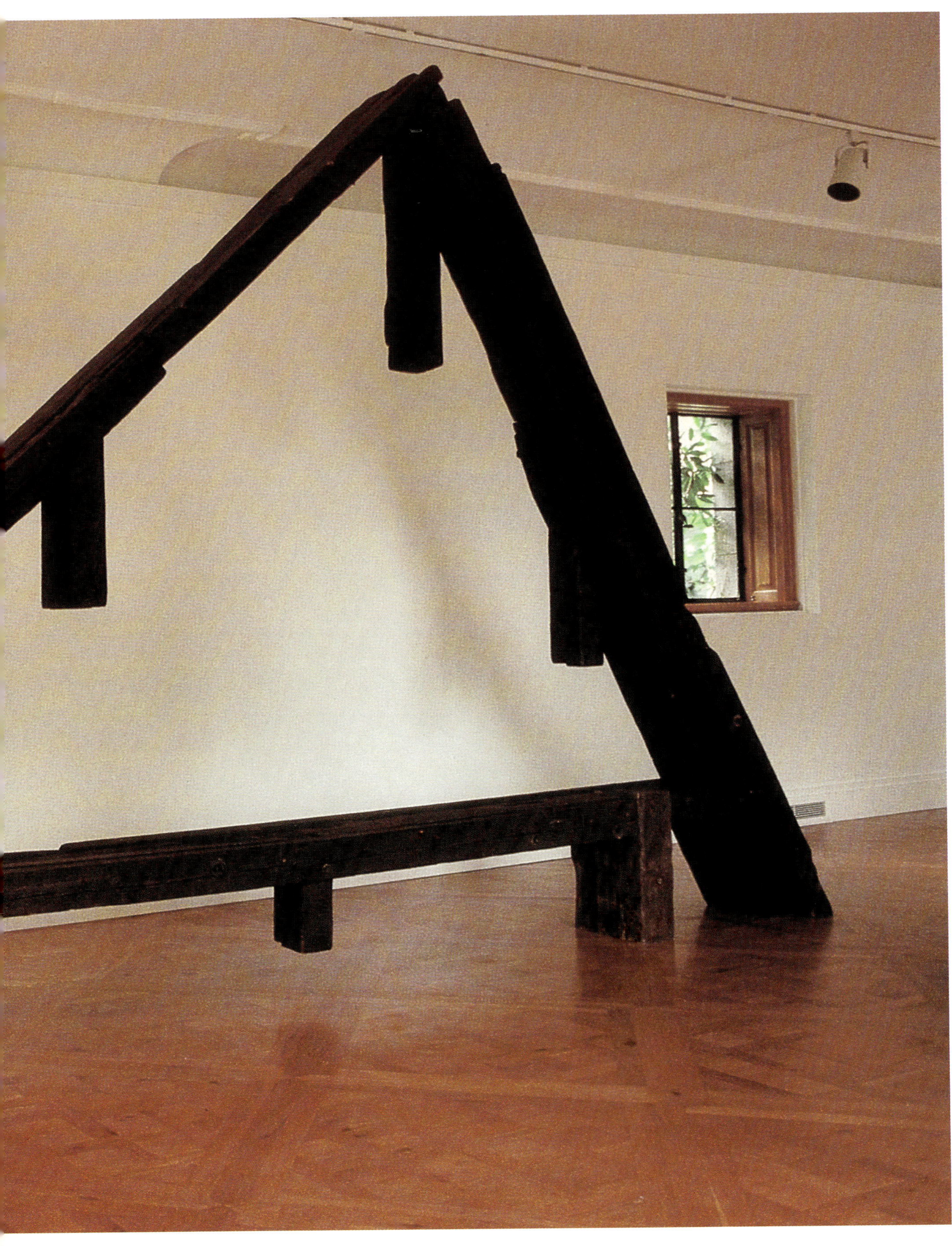

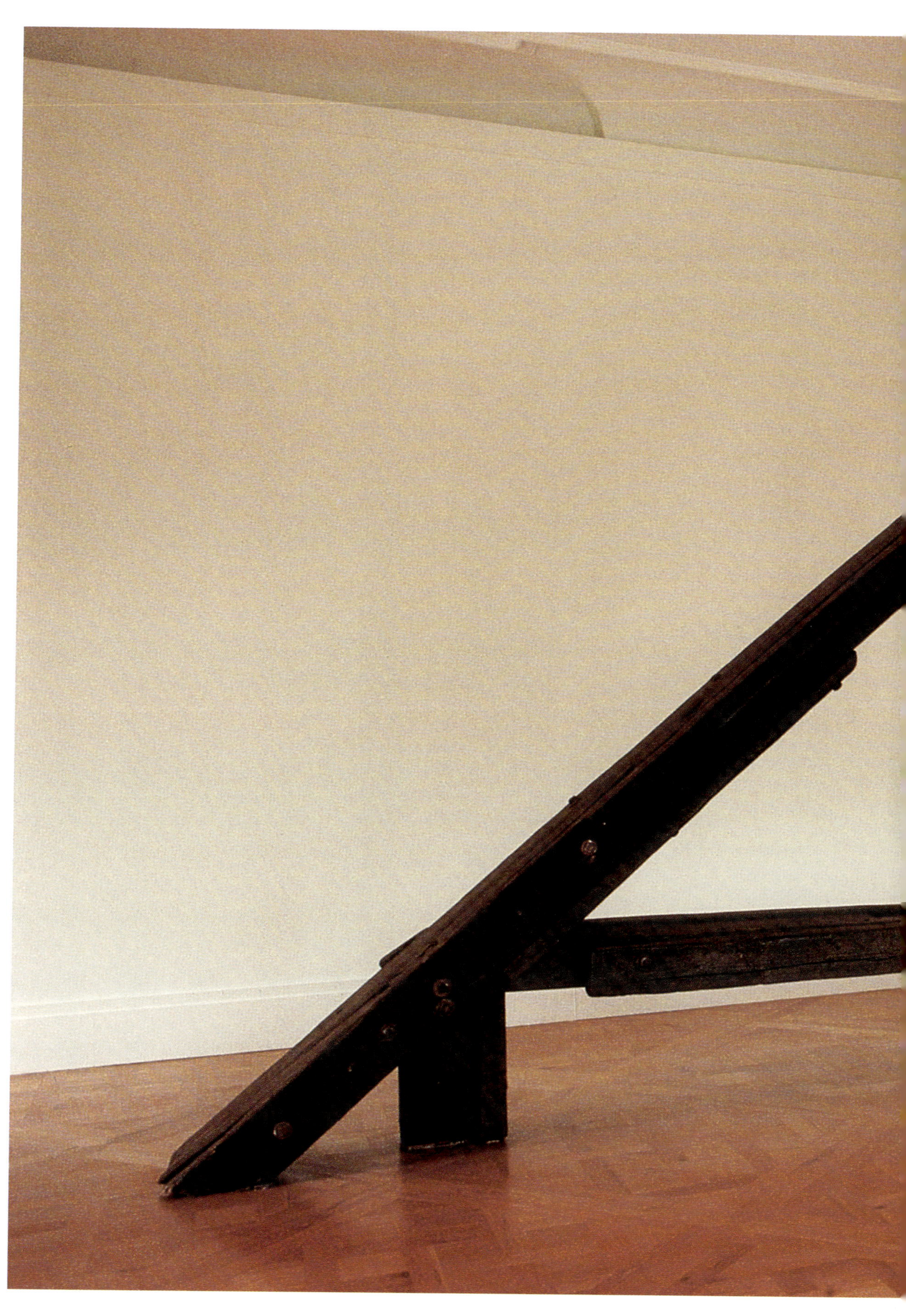

WILLIAM TUCKER, THE HOUSE OF THE HANGED MAN, 1981

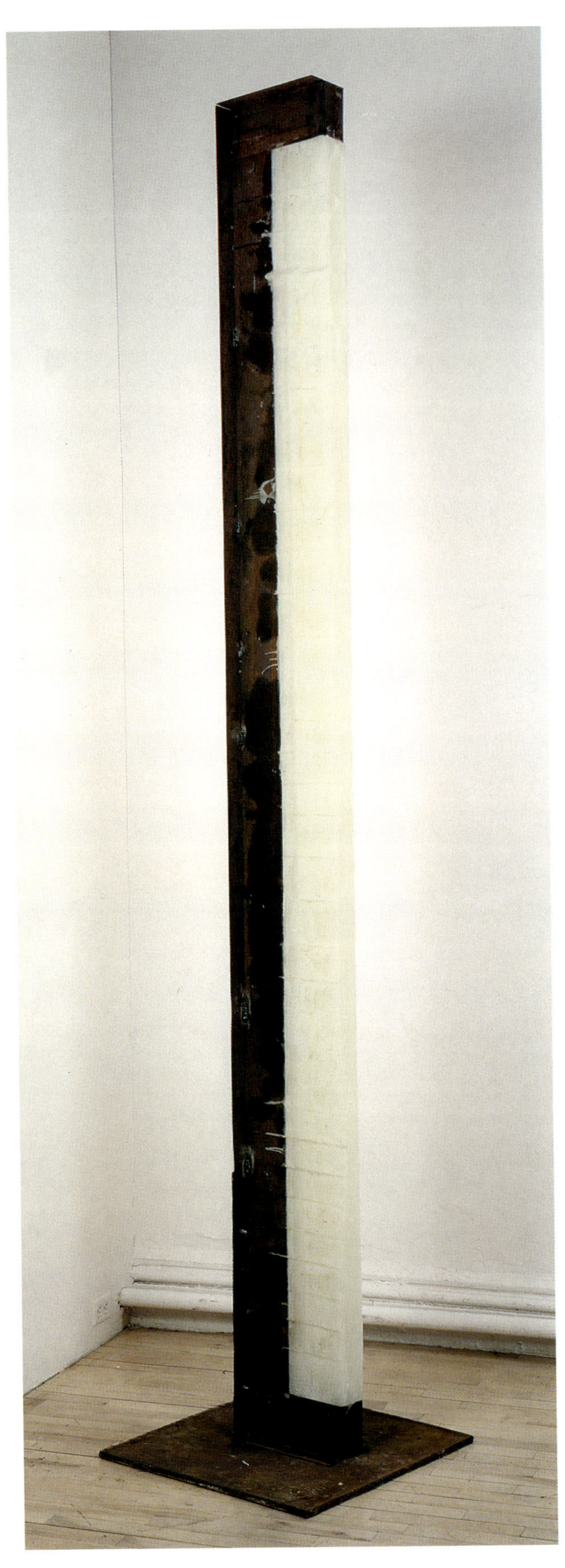

OSAMI TANAKA, UNTITLED V, 1986

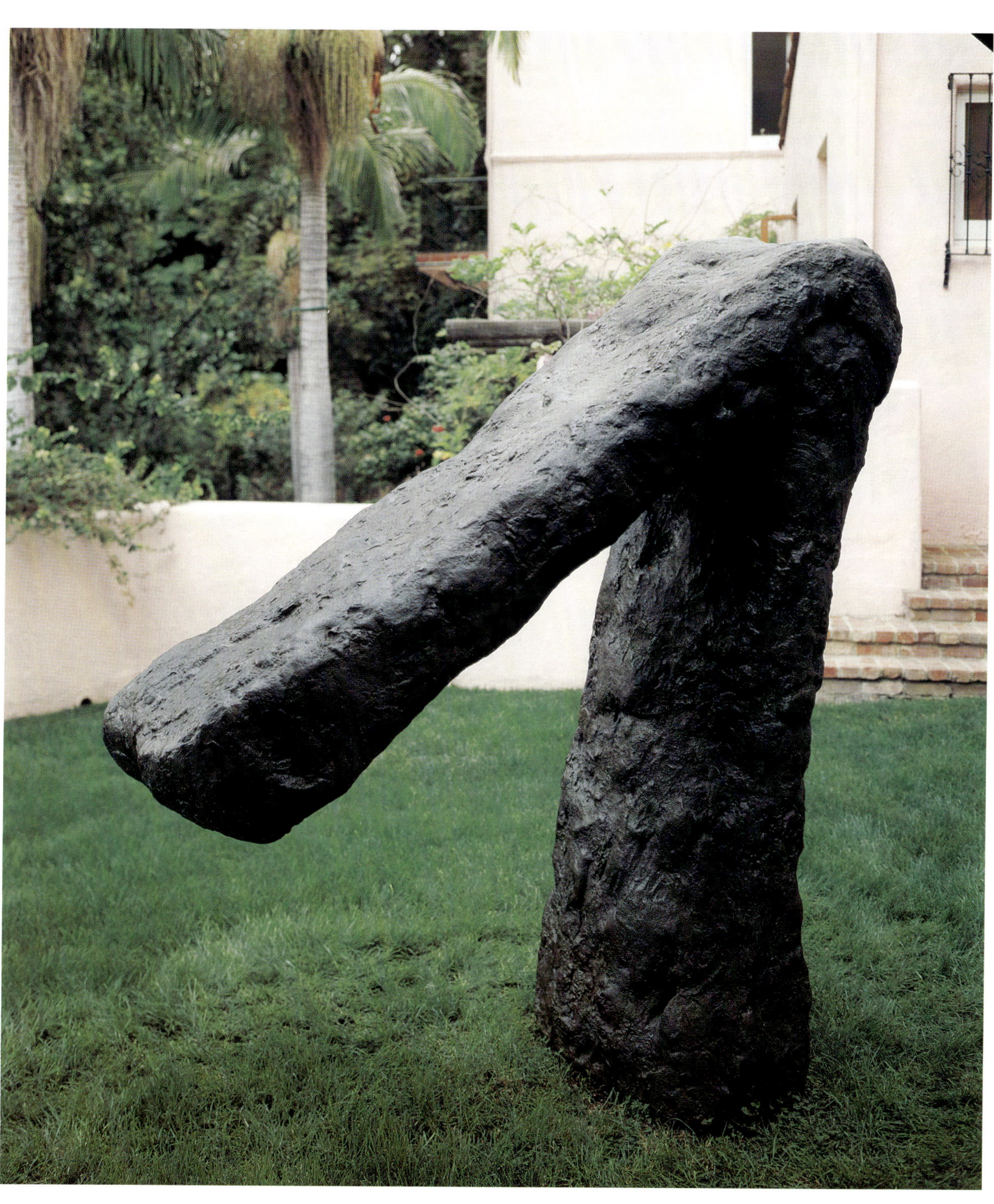

WILLIAM TUCKER, GYMNAST II, 1985

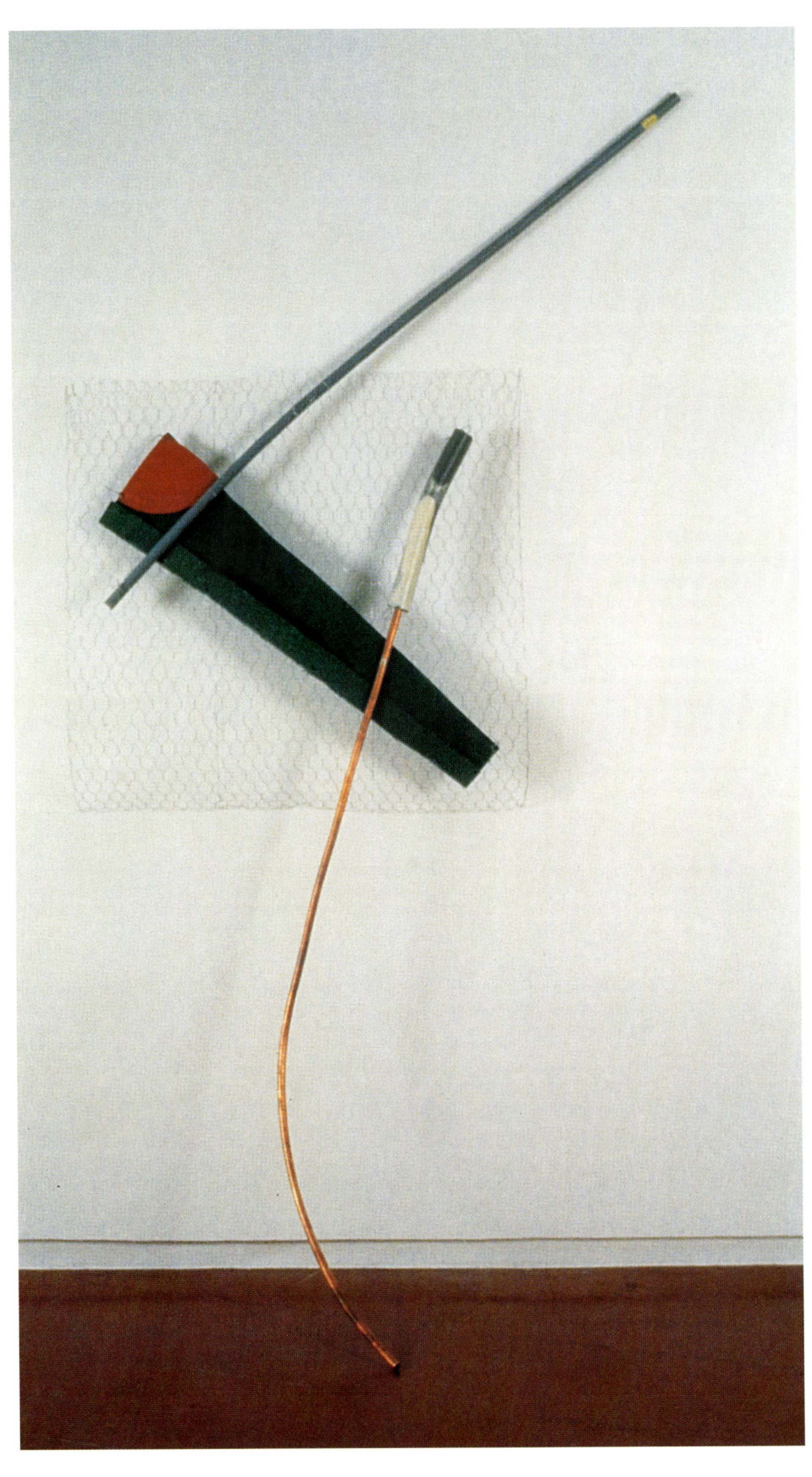

RICHARD TUTTLE, PEACE AND TIME (XII), 1993

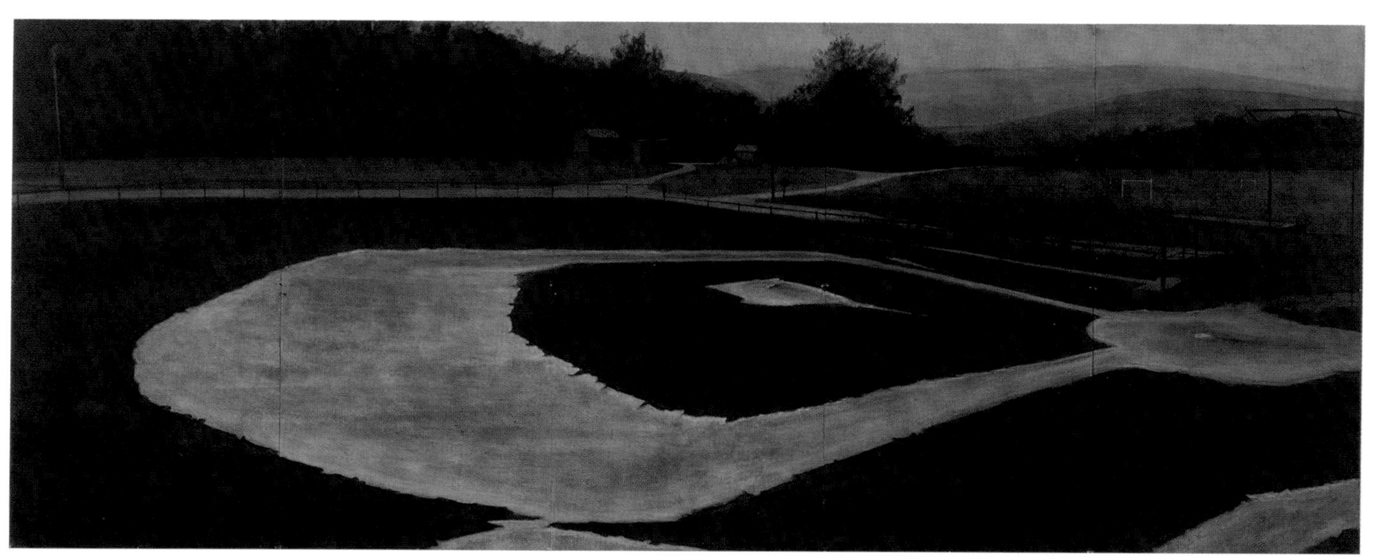

PETER WAITE, THE LITTLE LEAGUE FIELD, 1988

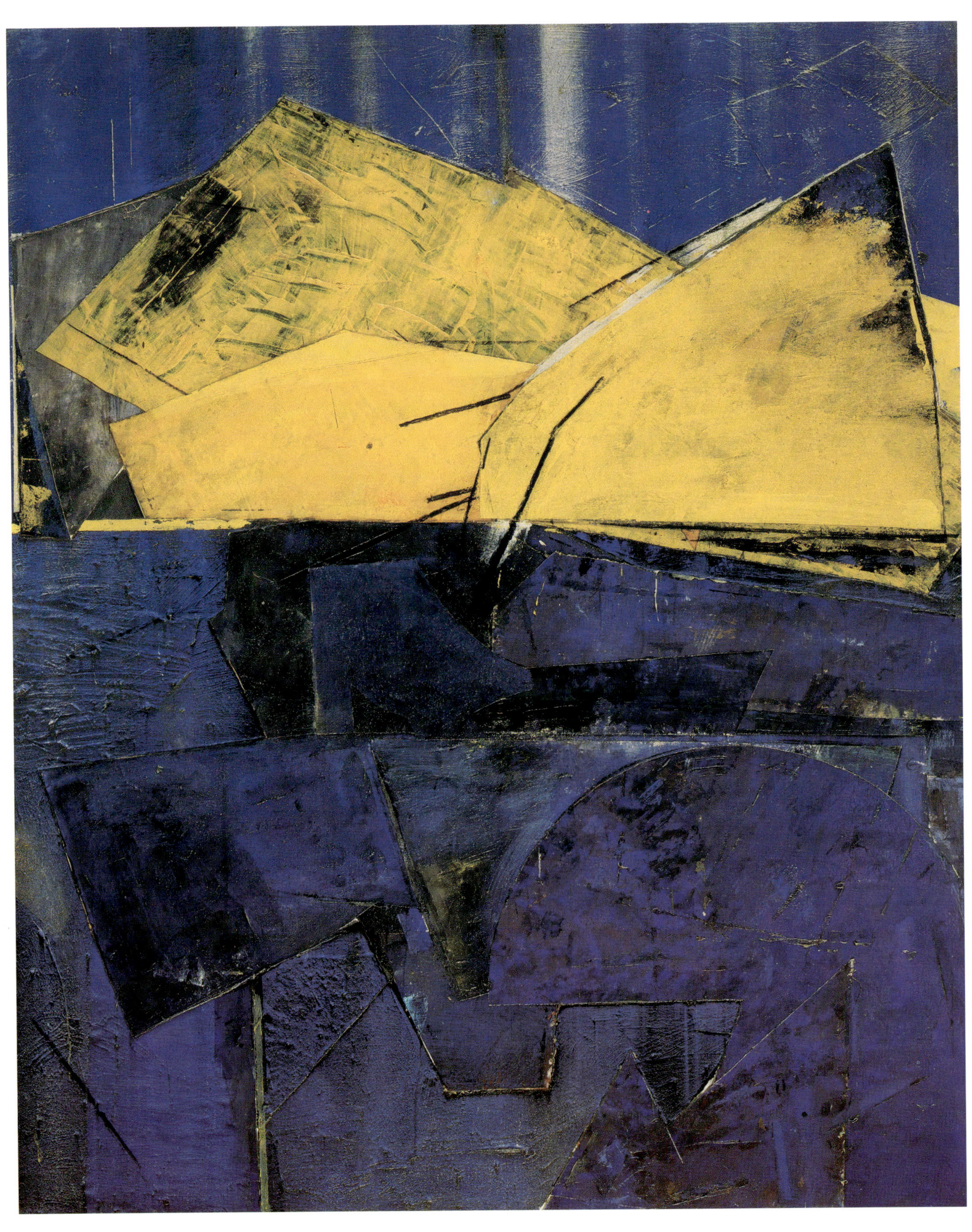

JOHN WALKER, A LETTER, 1976

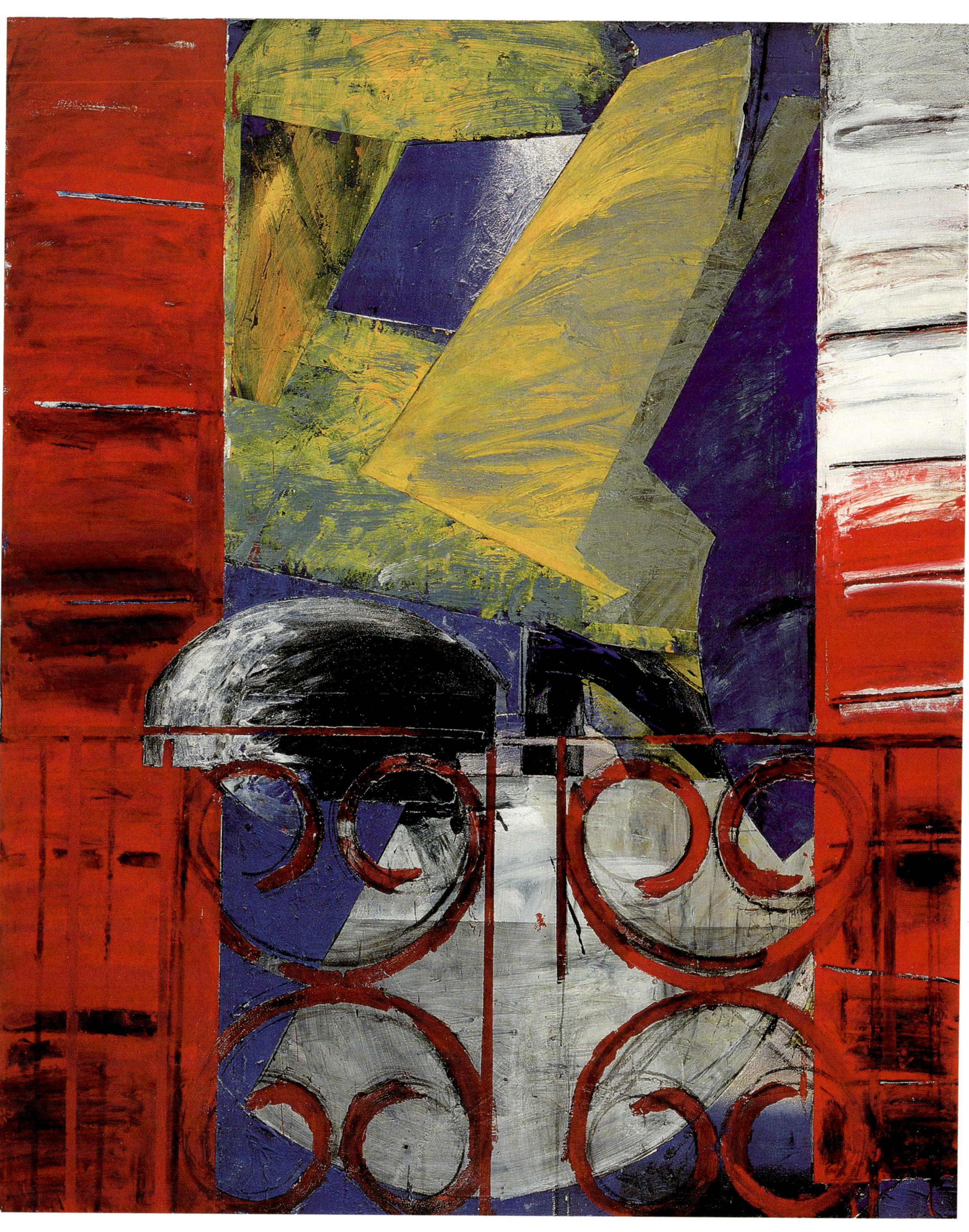

JOHN WALKER, NUMINOUS VII, 1978

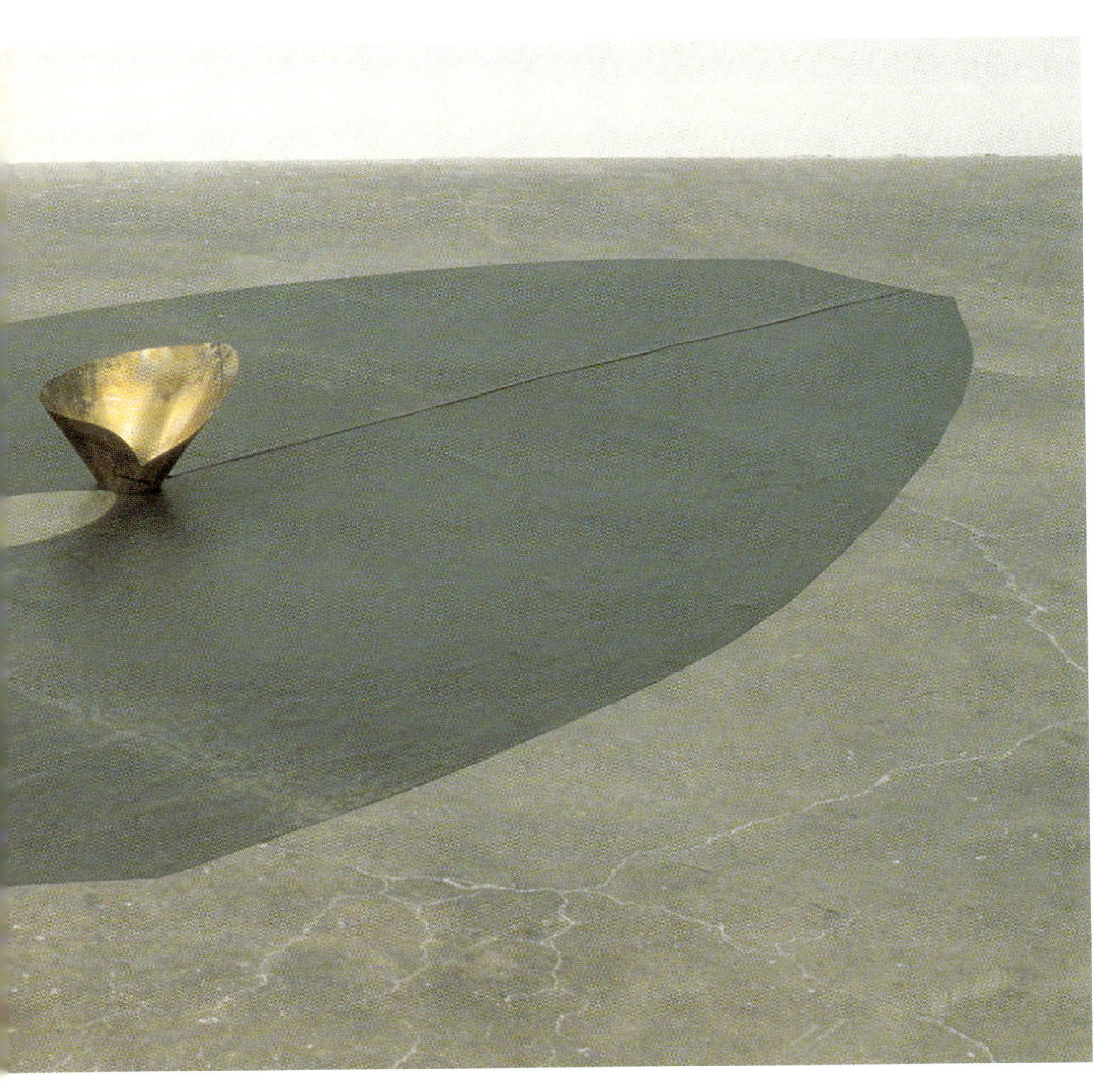

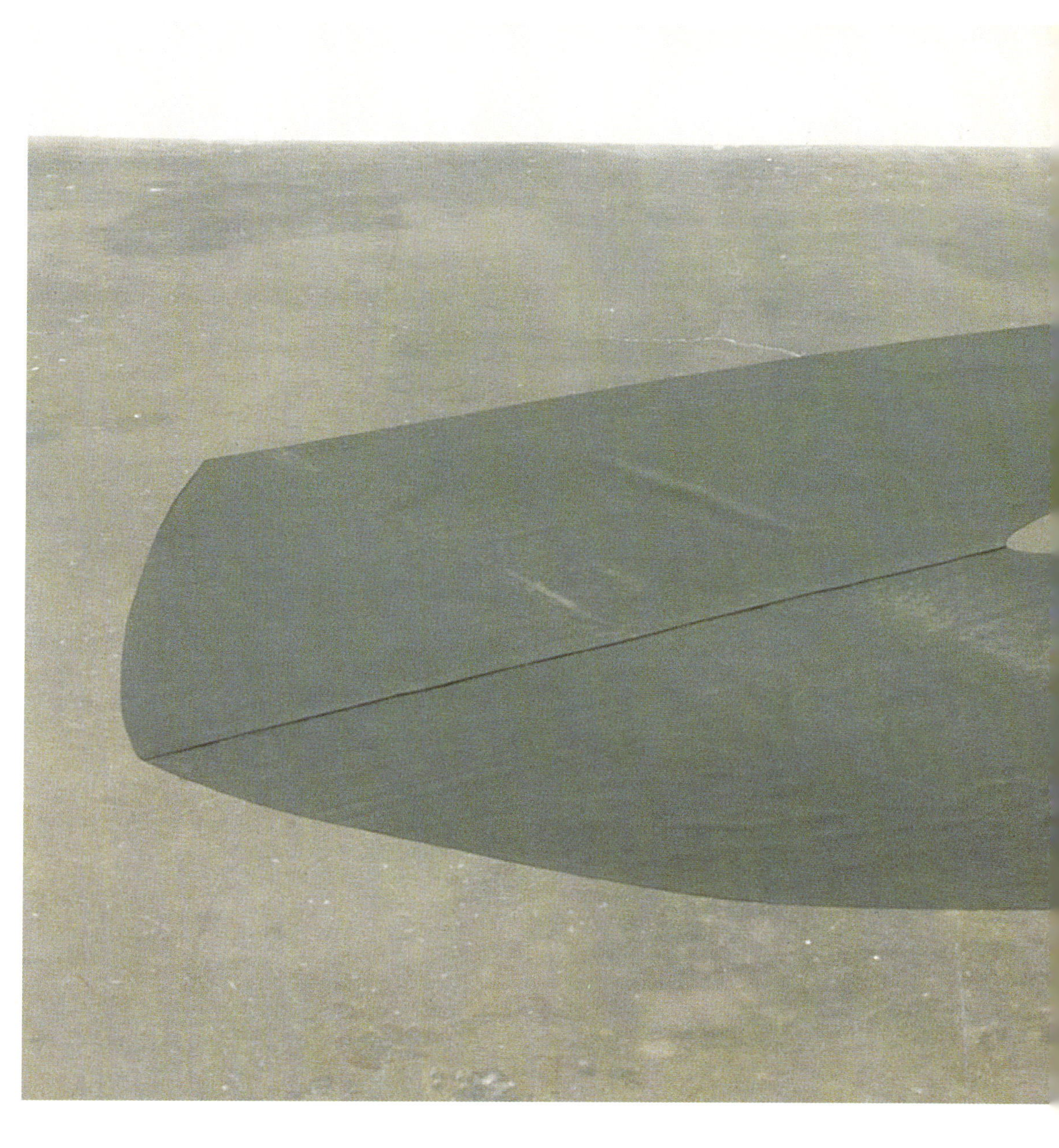

ALISON WILDING, CORE II, 1985

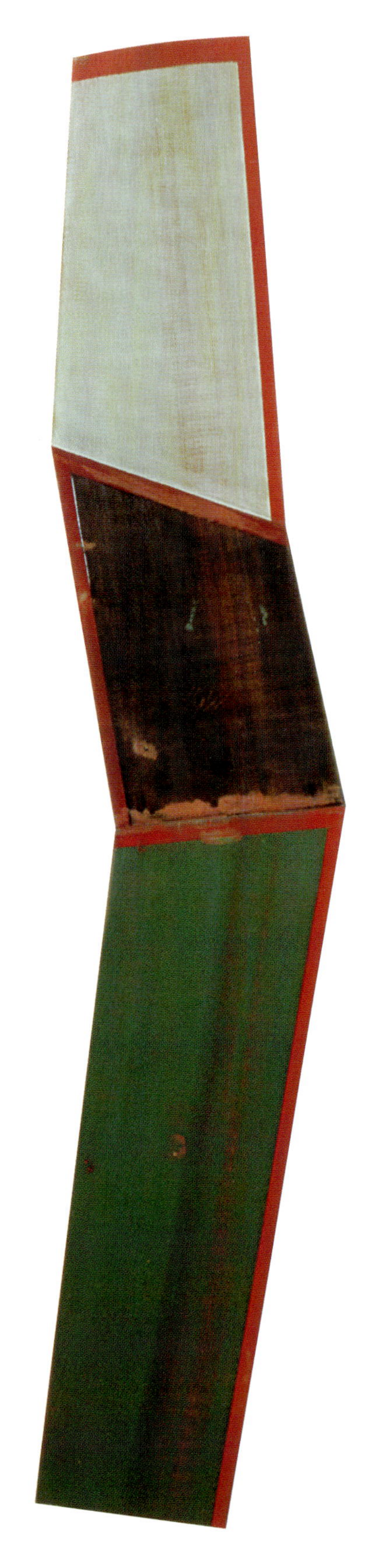

TAD WILEY, WAVE EATER, 1987

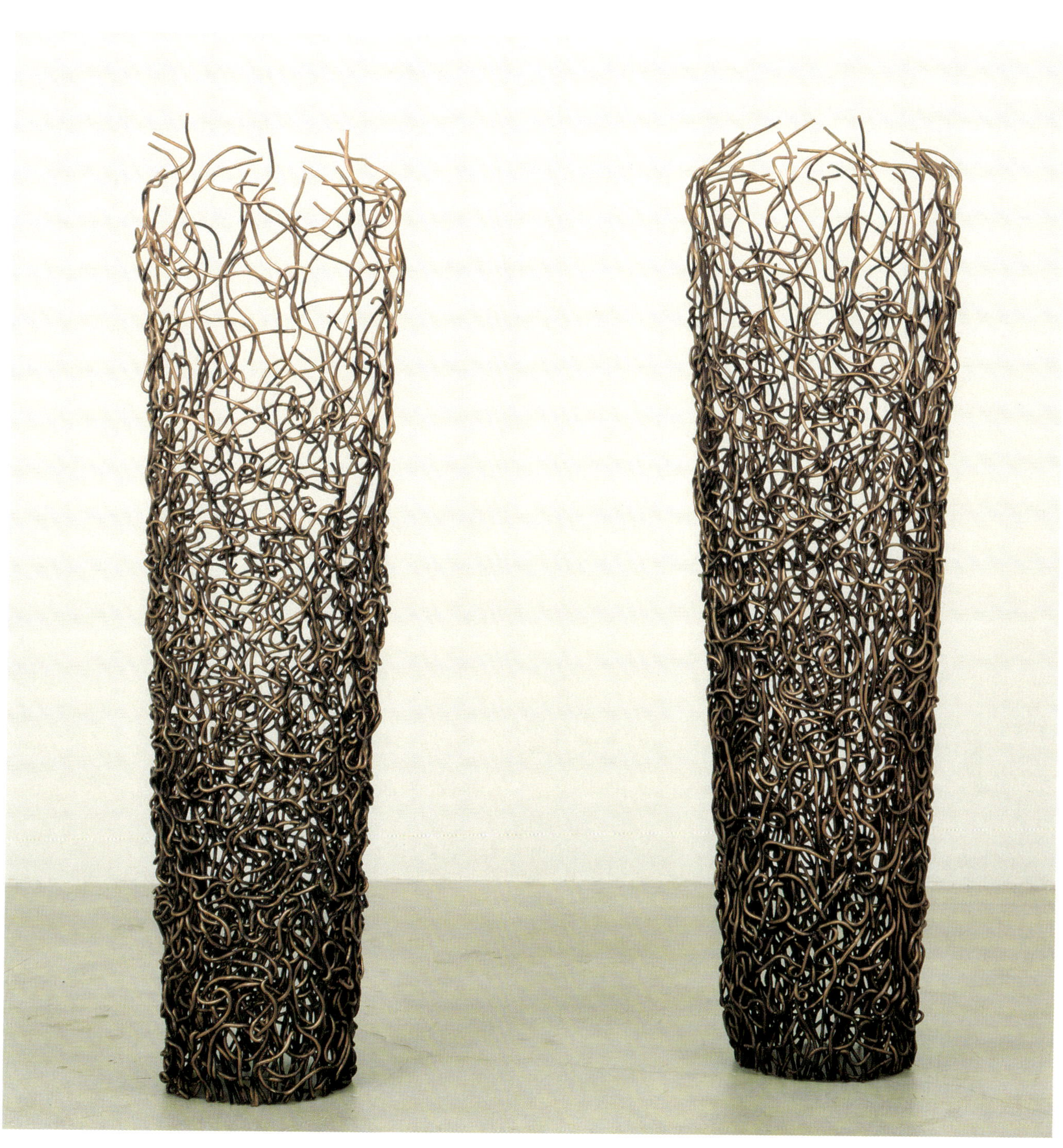

ALISON WILDING, BURNED, 1991-92

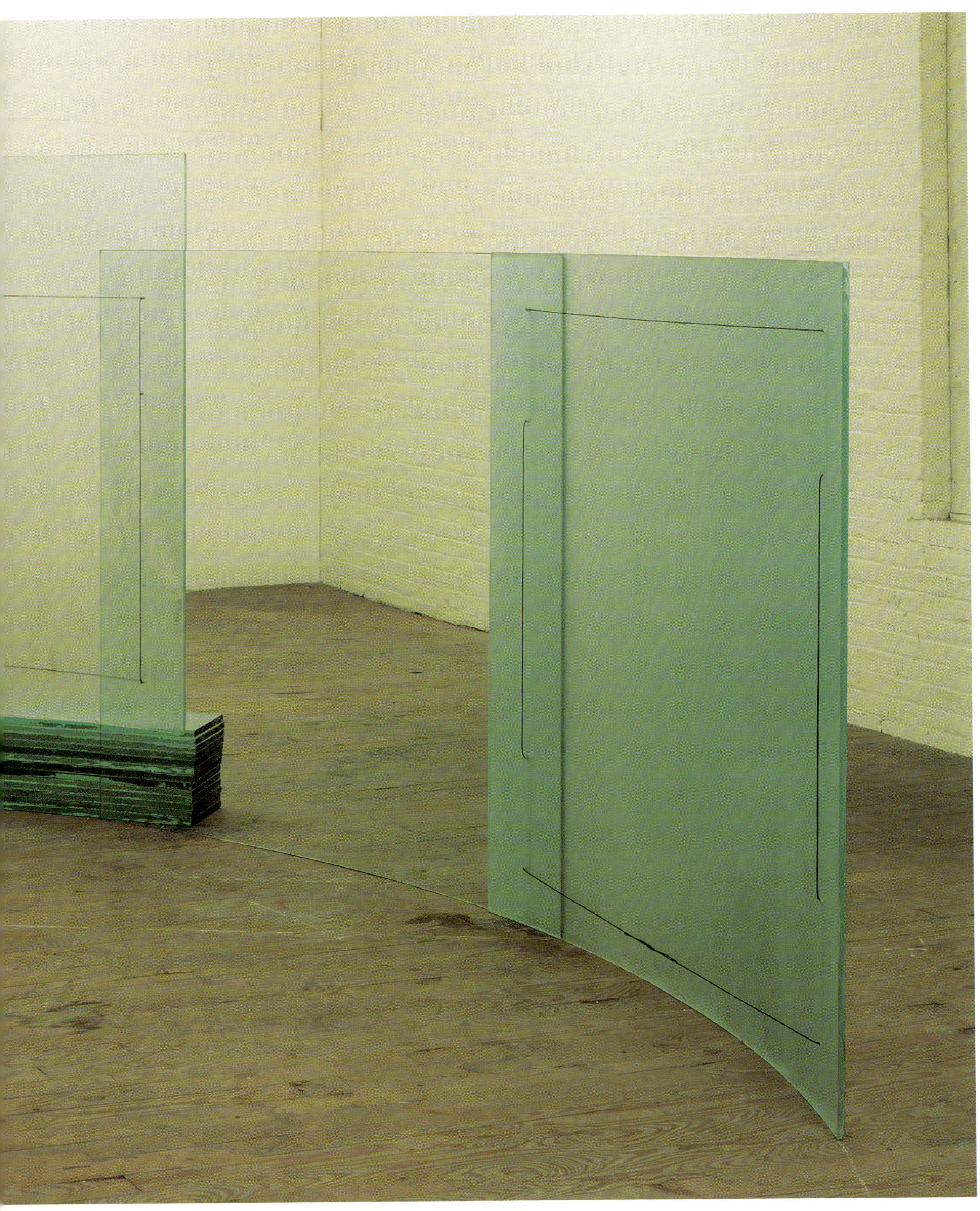

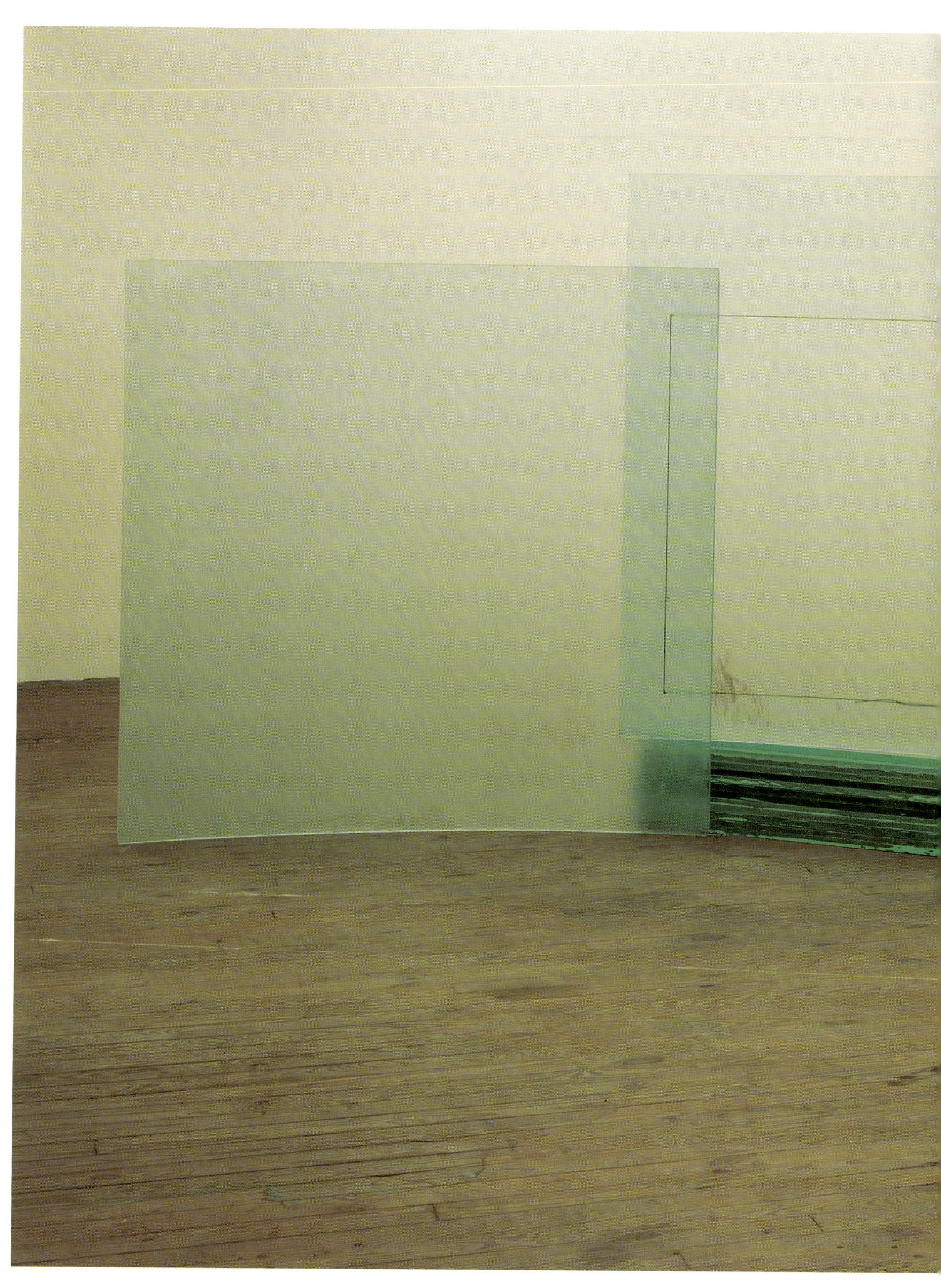

CHRISTOPHER WILMARTH, TINA TURNER, 1970-71

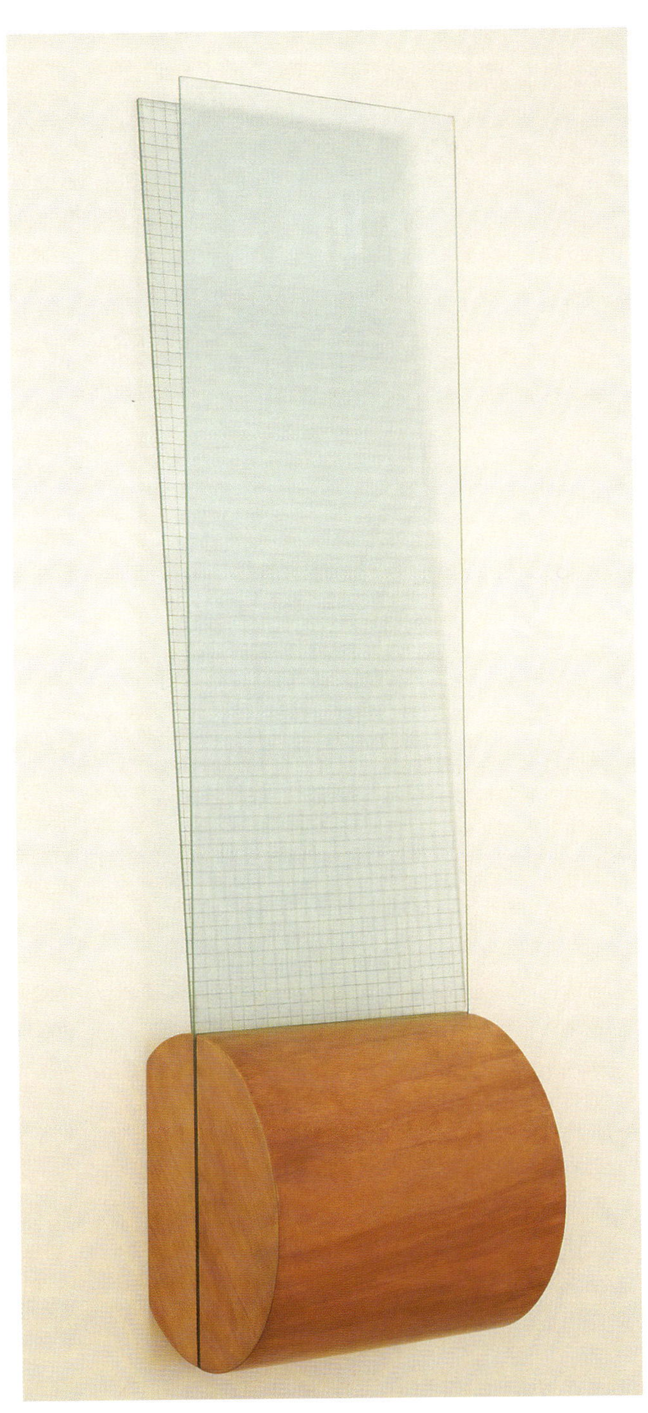

CHRISTOPHER WILMARTH, LAST HANDS, 1969

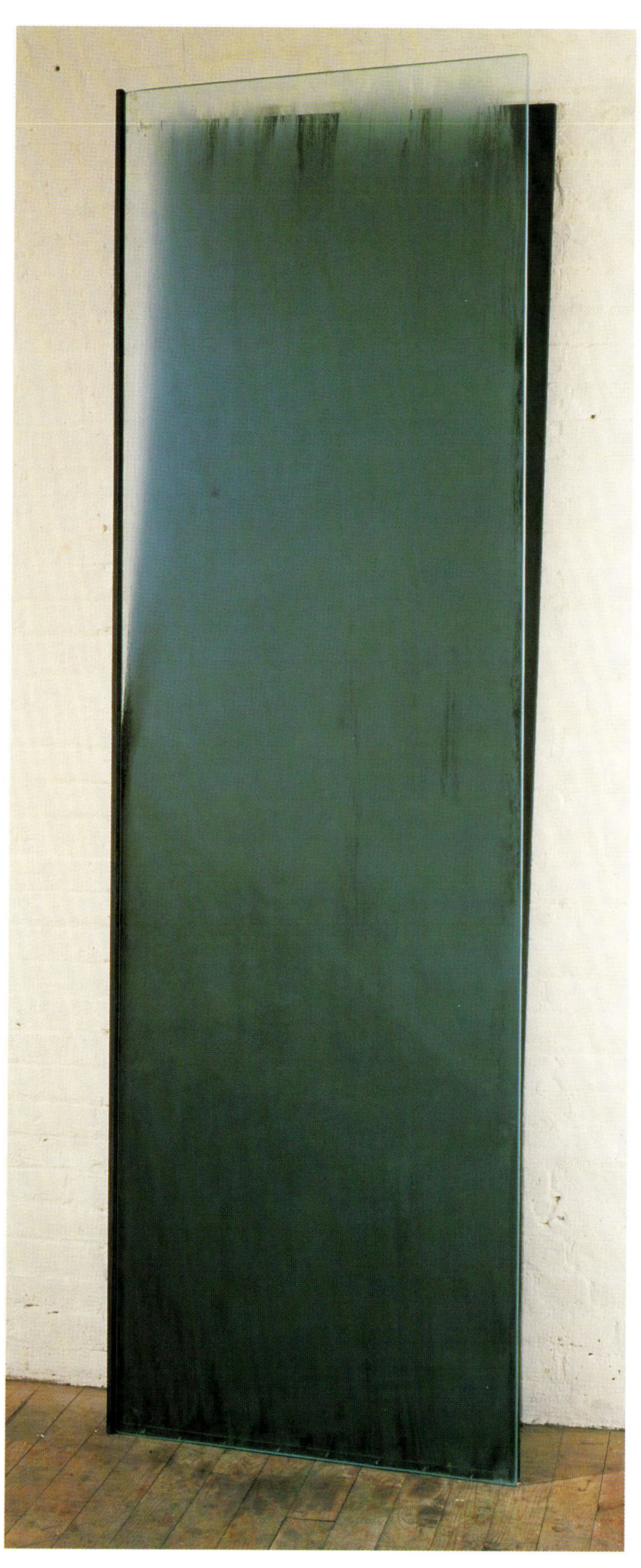

CHRISTOPHER WILMARTH, *FEBRUARY GNOMON*, 1976-77

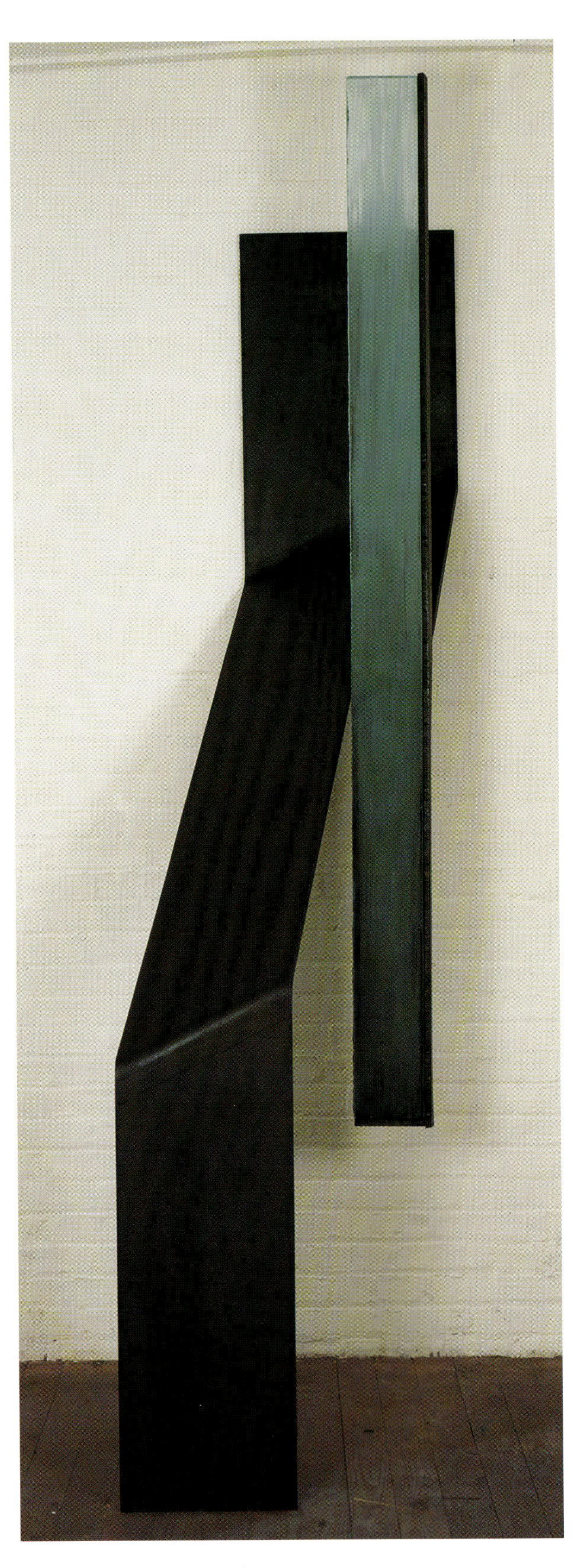

CHRISTOPHER WILMARTH, GNOMON'S PARADE (LATE), 1980

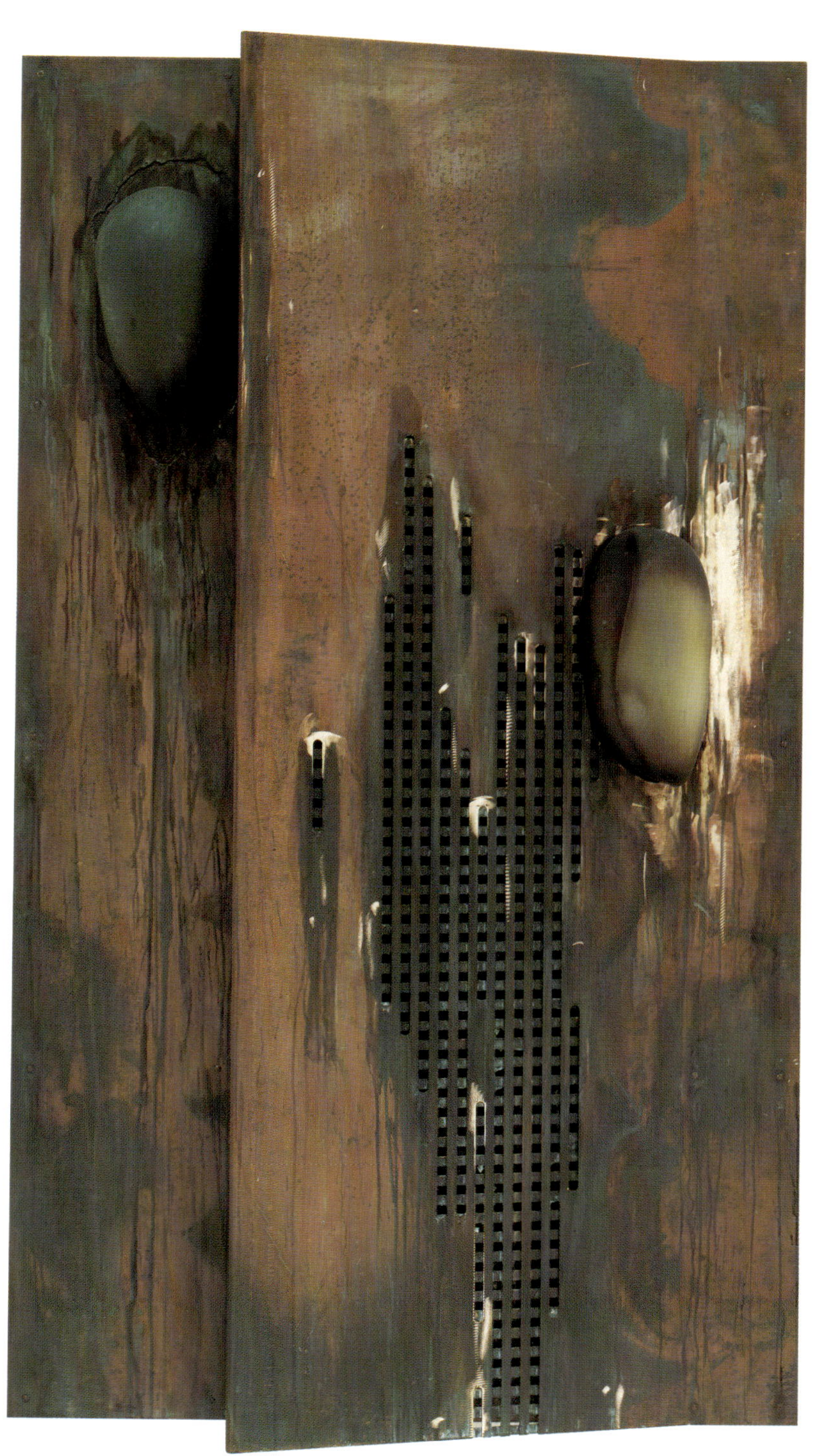

CHRISTOPHER WILMARTH, HER SIDES OF ME, 1983-84

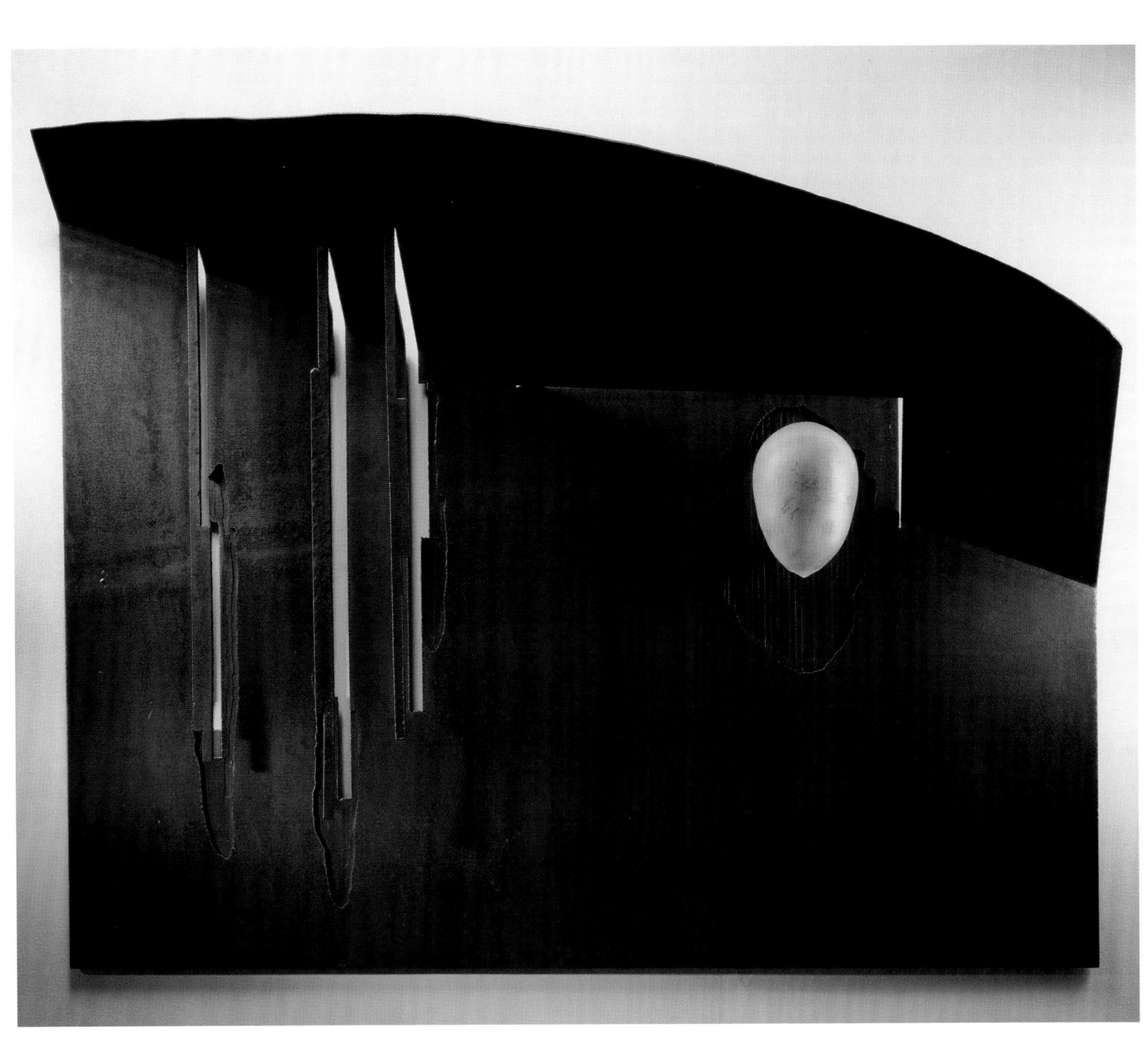

CHRISTOPHER WILMARTH, BAPTISTE (LONGING) #2, 1984

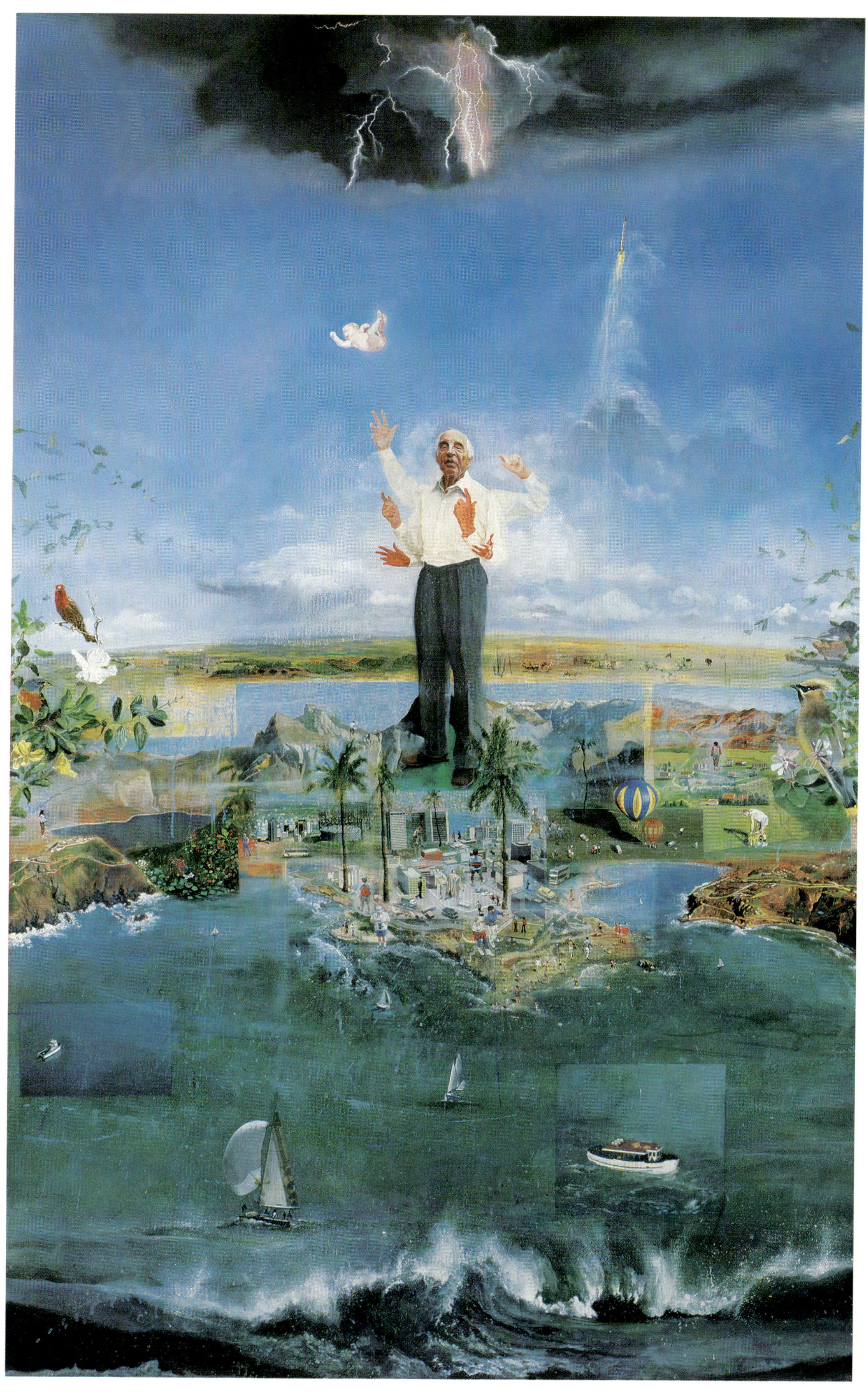

TOM WUDL, THE BIRTH OF JAN VAN EYCK AND THE EXTENT OF HIS INFLUENCE..., 1988-89

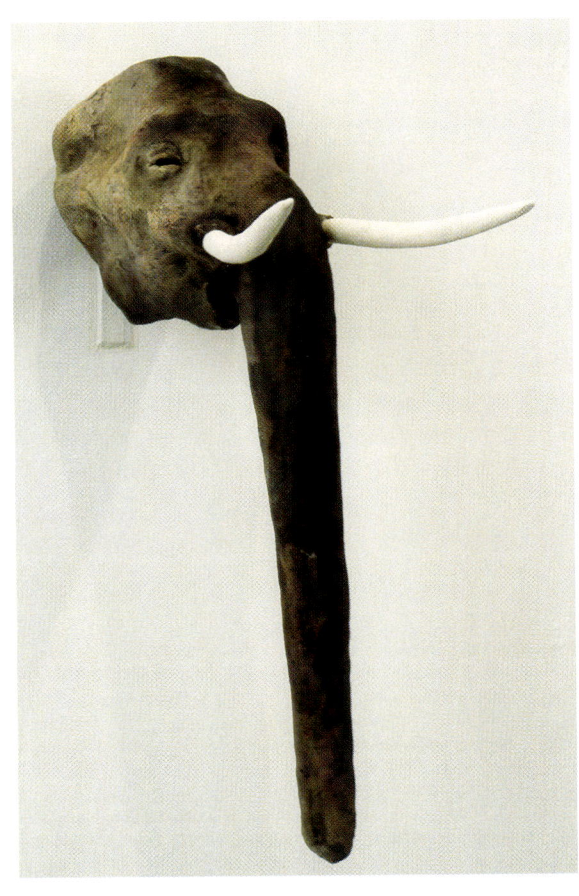

DAISY YOUNGBLOOD, ELEPHANT WITH TUSKS, 1995

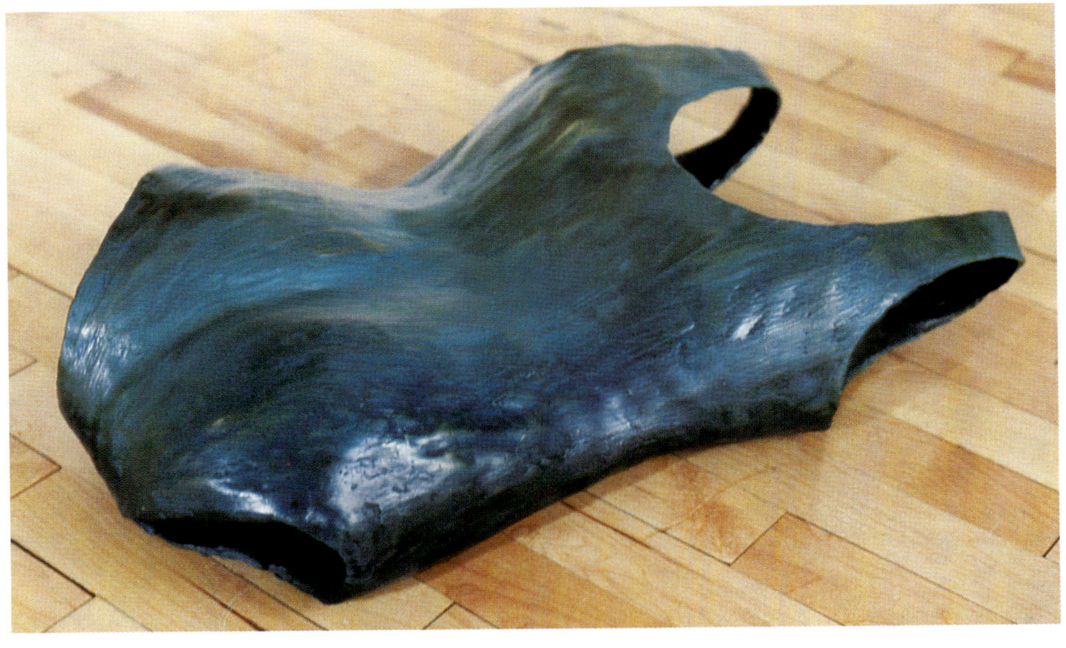

JUDITH SHEA, THE CRAWL, 1983

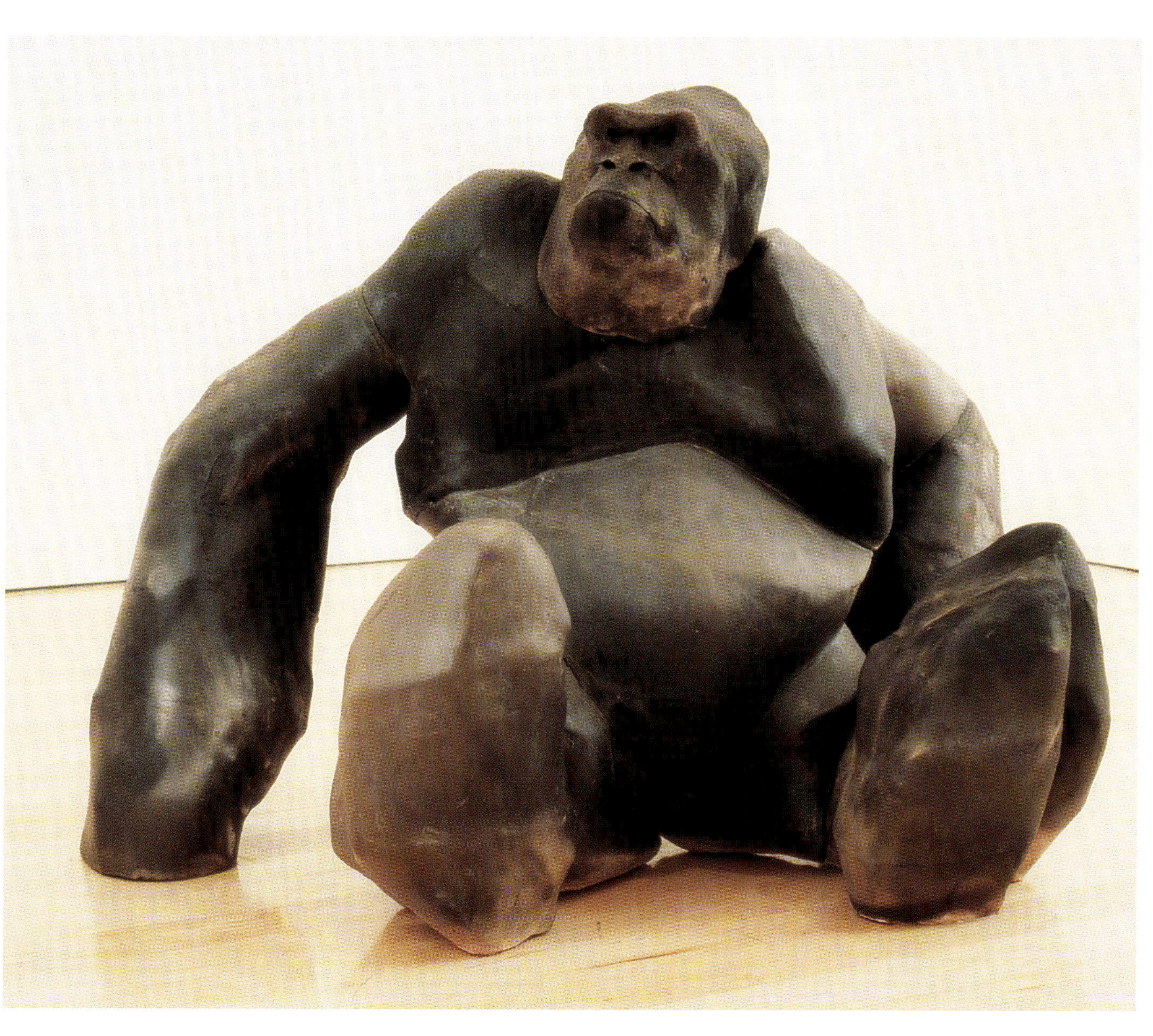

DAISY YOUNGBLOOD, GORILLA, 1995

WORKS IN THE EXHIBITION

HANNO D. AHRENS (American, b. 1954)
Untitled, 1985
wood, plaster, steel
49 x 25 x 15 in.

PIERRE ALECHINSKY (Belgian, b. 1927)
L'arbre en activite, 1973
mixed media on paper mounted on canvas
60 x 61 in.

PIERRE ALECHINSKY (Belgian, b. 1927)
To the Four Winds, 1981
acrylic on paper
73 x 73 in.

JOHN ALTOON (American, 1925-1969)
Haircut #2, 1965
acrylic on canvas
66 x 56 1/4 in.

JOSEPH AMAR (Moroccan, b. 1954)
Untitled, 1986
dry pigments, lead on plywood
47 1/2 x 83 1/2 x 6 1/2 in.

CARL ANDRE (American, b. 1935)
64 Steel Square, 1967
hot-rolled steel
3/8 x 64 x 64 in.

HORST ANTES (German, b. 1936)
Mother and Child, 1973-74
oil on canvas
51 1/4 x 39 3/8 in.

HORST ANTES (German, b. 1936)
Head Consisting of Nine Separate Parts, 1979
steel
edition 1/6
19 x 16 x 4 in.

HORST ANTES (German, b. 1936)
7 Häuser, 2 Hemden, 1993
aquatec (graphite) with sawdust on wood
70 3/4 x 94 1/2 in.

HORST ANTES (German, b. 1936)
14.2.95/15.2.95/16.2.95/17.2.95/09.3.95/28.4.95 /30.4.95/01.5.95/02.5.95/03.5.95/4.5.95/15.5.95/ 16.5.95/17.5.95/18.5.95/19.5.95/20.5.95/21.5.95 /24.6.95/25.6.95/27.6.95/28.6.95, 1995-96
aquatec (graphite) with sawdust on canvas
47 1/4 x 63 in.

JEAN ARP (French, 1887-1966)
Sculpture de Silence Corneille, 1942-64
white marble
44 1/2 x 46 1/2 x 47 in.

RICHARD ARTSCHWAGER (American, b. 1923)
Woman, 1963
acrylic on chipboard
48 1/2 x 48 in.

RICHARD ARTSCHWAGER (American, b. 1923)
Johnson Wax Building, 1974
acrylic on celotex
44 1/4 x 56 in.

RICHARD ARTSCHWAGER (American, b. 1923)
Pig Pig, 1984
acrylic on celotex, mirror, and painted wood
48 x 42 x 14 in.

RICHARD ARTSCHWAGER (American, b. 1923)
Exclamation, 1994
acrylic, wood
80 x 15 x 15 in.

FRANCIS BACON (British, 1909-1992)
Two Figures, 1961
oil with sand on canvas
77 7/8 x 55 7/8 in.

JAKE BERTHOT (American, b. 1939)
Greenpoint, 1971
oil on canvas
84 x 72 in.

JAKE BERTHOT (American, b. 1939)
Belfast, 1981
oil on canvas
73 1/4 x 49 in.

JAKE BERTHOT (American, b. 1939)
Anawanda, 1985
oil on linen
48 1/4 x 35 1/4 in.

JAKE BERTHOT (American, b. 1939)
Nymph, 1991
oil on linen
38 x 30 in.

JAKE BERTHOT (American, b. 1939)
Off Lower Bone Hollow, 1997
oil on wood panel
12 x 13 1/2 in.

JULIUS BISSIER (French, 1893-1965)
7.XI.57, 1957
egg/oil tempera on canvas
9 x 7 5/8 in.

JONATHAN BOROFSKY (American, b. 1942)
2,845,318 Molecule Men, 1982-83
painted aluminum
120 x 109 1/4 x 1/4 in.

JONATHAN BOROFSKY (American, b. 1942)
The Dancing Clown at 2,845,325, 1982-83
mixed media
147 x 80 x 80 in.

JONATHAN BOROFSKY (American, b. 1942)
2,841,779 Maidenform Woman, You Never Know Where She'll Turn Up, 1983
acrylic and graphite on canvas
126 x 96 3/4 in.

JONATHAN BOROFSKY (American, b. 1942)
I Dreamed I Could Fly at 2,893,007, 1984
oil on urethane foam
62 x 36 x 27 in.

CONSTANTIN BRANCUSI (French, b. Romania, 1876-1957)
The Kiss, 1907-08
plaster
11 x 10 1/2 x 8 1/2 in.

VIJA CELMINS (American, b. Latvia, 1939)
Gun with Hand #1, 1964
oil on canvas
24 1/2 x 34 1/2 in.

VIJA CELMINS (American, b. Latvia, 1939)
House #1, 1965
oil on wood, metal, fur, plastic
9 1/2 x 7 1/4 x 10 1/2 in.

VIJA CELMINS (American, b. Latvia, 1939)
Puzzle, 1965-66
oil on wood
2 x 12 x 10 in.

VIJA CELMINS (American, b. Latvia, 1939)
Flying Fortress, 1966
oil on canvas
16 x 26 in.

VIJA CELMINS (American, b. Latvia, 1939)
Ocean: 7 Steps #2, 1972-73
graphite on acrylic ground on paper
11 1/2 x 98 in.

VIJA CELMINS (American, b. Latvia, 1939)
Glacier Bay, 1975
graphite on acrylic ground on paper
28 3/4 x 58 1/4 in.

VIJA CELMINS (American, b. Latvia, 1939)
To Fix the Image in Memory, 1977-82
stones and painted bronze
variable dimensions

VIJA CELMINS (American, b. Latvia, 1939)
Untitled (Comet), 1988
oil on canvas
15 3/4 x 18 1/2 in.

VIJA CELMINS (American, b. Latvia, 1939)
Untitled #13, 1996
charcoal on paper
17 x 22 in.

STUART DIAMOND (American, b. 1942)
Night Falls, 1984
painted construction
129 x 64 1/2 x 20 1/2 in.

RICHARD DIEBENKORN (American, 1922-1993)
Untitled, 1980
acrylic and pencil on paper
17 1/2 x 12 in.

MARK DI SUVERO (American, b. China, 1933)
Eatherly's Lamp, 1961
brass, stainless steel, wood, iron, fiberglass
36 x 43 x 30 in.

MARK DI SUVERO (American, b. China, 1933)
Boober, 1965
welded steel
60 x 61 x 46 in.

MARK DI SUVERO (American, b. China, 1933)
Measure Piece, 1967
wood, steel
42 1/2 x 73 x 36 in.

MARK DI SUVERO (American, b. China, 1933)
Homage to Gonzalez, 1973
steel
93 x 45 x 115 in.

MARK DI SUVERO (American, b. China, 1933)
Trusspiece, 1975-76
steel
44 x 52 x 165 in.

MARK DI SUVERO (American, b. China, 1933)
Mahatma, 1978-79
steel
22 x 30 x 30 feet

MARK DI SUVERO (American, b. China, 1933)
2 Hooks, 1971-82
steel
38 x 31 x 21 in.

MARK DI SUVERO (American, b. China, 1933)
Zar, 1983
steel and stainless steel
110 x 103 x 89 1/2 in.

MARK DI SUVERO (American, b. China, 1933)
Untitled, 1997
steel
36 x 41 3/4 x 21 7/8 in.

GEORGE DUDDING (American, b. Germany, 1951)
The Taylor's Son's Game, 1990
copper
66 x 31 x 11 in.

JOHN DUFF (American, b. 1943)
Reciprocating Column, 1982
paint, fiberglass, tin
72 1/2 x 21 1/2 x 21 in.

JOHN DUFF (American, b. 1943)
White Serrated Wedge, 1984
fiberglass, resin, paint, plywood
62 1/4 x 9 3/4 x 28 in.

JOHN DUFF (American, b. 1943)
Pernambuco, 1985-86
fiberglass and enamel paint
69 x 24 x 15 1/2 in.

JOHN DUFF (American, b. 1943)
Black Floor Piece, 1992
fiberglass, enamel paint, and steel rod
8 1/4 x 63 1/4 diam. in.

JACOB EL HANANI (American, b. Morocco, 1947)
Ashshur, 1986
ink on paper
18 1/2 x 18 1/2 in.

VALERIE FAVRE (French, b. Switzerland, 1959)
Lèvres, 1993
poster paint on paper
variable dimension

VALERIE FAVRE (French, b. Switzerland, 1959)
Parapluie, 1994
wool and metal
24 1/2 x 11 3/4 in.

KLAUS FUSSMANN (German, b. 1938)
Hella K. in White before Mirror, 1977
oil on paper
27 3/8 x 28 1/4 in.

JILL GIEGERICH (American, b. 1952)
Untitled (Figure with Arch of Industry), 1983
mixed media
86 x 74 x 14 1/2 in.

SPENCER GREGORY (American, b. 1951)
Underneath, 1986-87
oil on wood panel
24 x 28 in.

ROBERT GROSVENOR (American, b. 1937)
Untitled, 1981-83
steel, vinyl coated steel, and undercoating
36 x 96 x 84 in.

ROBERT GROSVENOR (American, b. 1937)
Untitled, 1984-85
steel, plastic, tar, oil paint
72 x 72 x 72 in.

PHILIP GUSTON (American, b. Canada, 1913-1980)
Gladiators, 1938
mixed media on canvas
24 1/2 x 28 in.

PHILIP GUSTON (American, b. Canada, 1913-1980)
Zone, 1953-54
oil on canvas
46 x 48 in.

PHILIP GUSTON (American, b. Canada, 1913-1980)
The Mirror, 1957
oil on canvas
68 x 60 1/2 in.

PHILIP GUSTON (American, b. Canada, 1913-1980)
Edge of Town, 1969
oil on canvas
77 x 110 1/4 in.

PHILIP GUSTON (American, b. Canada, 1913-1980)
Web, 1975
oil on canvas
67 x 97 in.

PHILIP GUSTON (American, b. Canada, 1913-1980)
Cherries, 1976
oil on canvas
69 x 116 in.

PHILIP GUSTON (American, b. Canada, 1913-1980)
Green Rug, 1976
oil on canvas
94 x 68 1/2 in.

PHILIP GUSTON (American, b. Canada, 1913-1980)
Source, 1976
oil on canvas
76 x 117 in.

PHILIP GUSTON (American, b. Canada, 1913-1980)
Ladder, 1978
oil on canvas
70 x 108 in.

PHILIP GUSTON (American, b. Canada, 1913-1980)
Talking, 1979
oil on canvas
68 1/2 x 78 in.

BARBARA HEPWORTH (British, 1903-1975)
Figure (Ascending Form), 1956
painted wood and blue string
62 1/2 x 15 1/8 x 14 7/8 in.

RONI HORN (American, b. 1955)
Stevens' Bouquet, 1991
aluminum and plastic
42 x 50 x 15 in.

RALPH HUMPHREY (American, b. 1932)
Storm Field, 1981-82
acrylic and modeling paste on wood
54 x 84 1/2 x 6 in.

BRYAN HUNT (American, b. 1947)
Big Twist, 1978
bronze
144 x 24 x 24 in.

BRYAN HUNT (American, b. 1947)
Untitled, 1981
silk paper and copper patina on balsa wood
6 x 6 x 60 in.

DENZIL HURLEY (West Indian,b. Barbados, 1949)
Untitled, 1984-86
oil on panel
14 x 10 1/2 in.

NEIL JENNEY (American, b. 1945)
Them and Us, 1969
acrylic on canvas
58 1/2 x 135 x 4 in.

NEIL JENNEY (American, b. 1945)
Beasts and Burdens, 1970
acrylic on canvas
58 1/2 x 127 x 4 in.

ALFRED JENSEN (American, 1903-1981)
Interval in Six Scales, 1963
oil on canvas
50 x 26 in.

KRISTIN JONES (American, b. 1956) and
ANDREW GINZEL (American, b. 1954)
Cinis, 1989
graphite, gold, ash, and aluminum
35 x 48 x 45 in.

BOB KANE (American, b. 1937)
Terrace Positano, 1983
oil on canvas
44 x 72 in.

BOB KANE (American, b. 1937)
Untitled, 1985
oil on canvas
50 1/2 x 40 in.

FRANZ KLINE (American, 1910-1962)
Luzerne, 1956
oil on canvas
78 x 101 in.

FRANZ KLINE (American, 1910-1962)
Washington Wall, 1959
oil on canvas
43 1/8 x 175 in.

GABRIEL KOHN (American, 1910-1975)
Ventura III, 1965
pine
25 3/4 x 36 1/4 x 24

WOLFGANG LAIB (German, b. 1950)
Untitled, 1983
brass, tin, and rice
variable dimensions

WOLFGANG LAIB (German, b. 1950)
Rice House, 1986
rice, white metal, wood, and sealing wax
9 x 37 x 29 in.

LOIS LANE (American, b. 1948)
Untitled (Bird, Full Moon), 1985
oil on canvas
72 x 72 in.

HENRI LAURENS (French, 1885-1954)
Le Matin, 1944
bronze
edition 6/6
46 1/2 x 43 3/8 in.

JOHN LEES (American, b. 1943)
Armchair, 1974
oil on paper
24 x 29 in.

JOHN LEES (American, b. 1943)
Landscape 1975-1982, 1975-82
oil on canvas
40 1/4 x 32 1/4 in.

FERNAND LÉ GER (French, 1881-1955)
Study for "The Great Parade," 1953
india ink, gouache, pencil on paper
21 1/2 x 25 5/8 in.

LEONID LERMAN (American, b. Ukraine, 1953)
Day of Sorrow, 1987
wood
115 1/2 x 60 x 12 in.

JACQUES LIPCHITZ (American, b. Lithuania, 1891-1973)
Benediction I, 1942
bronze
42 x 48 x 48 in.

ROBERT LOBE (American, b. 1945)
Culver's Gap, 1982
hammered aluminum
55 x 92 x 42 in.

ROBERT LONGO (American, b. 1953)
Still, 1984
mixed media
96 x 288 in.

LOREN MADSEN (American, b. 1955)
Knots, 1988-94
purpleheart wood and steel rods
68 x 118 x 59 1/2 in.

LOREN MADSEN (American, b. 1955)
Untitled (Number Four), 1994
poplar wood
70 1/2 x 15 in.

GREGORY MAHONEY (American, b. 1955)
Circumnavigating Time, 1991
rusting steel, cement, alkali, salt, oil paint
22 1/4 x 98 1/2 in.

JOHN MCLAUGHLIN (American, 1898-1976)
Untitled, 1952
oil on panel
38 x 32 in.

MELISSA MEYER (American, b. 1947)
Ophelia, 1985
oil on canvas
18 x 16 in.

JOAN MIRÓ (Spanish, 1893-1983)
Femme Verte, 1968
ceramic
30 x 24 x 19 1/2 in.

ROBERT MORRIS (American, b. 1931)
Untitled, 1967-86
steel and steel mesh
31 x 108 x 108 in.

ED MOSES (American, b. 1936)
Untitled (87.26), 1987
oil and acrylic on canvas
60 1/4 x 48 in.

RON MURPHREE (American, b. 1948)
Untitled, 1982
steel, wood, rope, aluminum, iron wheels
17 x 69 1/2 x 12 in.

ELIZABETH MURRAY (American, b. 1940)
More Than You Know, 1983
oil on canvas
111 x 108 x 8 in.

GWYNN MURRILL (American, b. 1942)
Rocking Horse, 1970
wood
62 x 49 x 14 in.

DAVID NASH (British, b. 1945)
Black Column, 1983
charred sycamore
132 x 16 x 16 in.

DAVID NASH (British, b. 1945)
Rising Boat, 1986
oak
72 x 19 3/4 x 89 7/8 in.

DAVID NASH (British, b. 1945)
Three Cogs, 1987
redwood
47 x 79 x 48 in.

BRUCE NAUMAN (American, b. 1941)
Seven Virtues and Seven Vices, 1983-84
carved granite
variable dimensions

CLAES OLDENBURG (American, b. Sweden, 1929)
Model: Rope Garden, 1969
cardboard, paint, crayon, twine, wood strainer
22 x 22 x 12 in.

CLAES OLDENBURG (American, b. Sweden, 1929)
Two Bats, Black and White, 1969-71
canvas stuffed with kapok
113 x 6 1/2 x 6 1/2 in. (variable)

CLAES OLDENBURG (American, b. Sweden, 1929)
Soft Toaster- "Ghost Version" #3, 1963-72
muslin filled with kapok
13 1/8 x 18 1/8 x 11 7/8 in.

CLAES OLDENBURG (American, b. Sweden, 1929)
Standing Mitt with Ball, Half Scale, 6 Feet, 1974
lead, Cor-ten steel, laminated wood
74 x 52 x 27 in.

CLAES OLDENBURG (American, b. Sweden, 1929)
Batcolumn Model, 1980
enameled bronze and metal base
115 x 20 x 20 in.

CLAES OLDENBURG (American, b. Sweden, 1929)
Cross Section (Slice Through) of a Toothbrush with Paste, in a Cup, on a Sink: Portrait of Coosje's Thinking (Model), 1982
painted aluminum
132 1/4 x 54 1/4 x 15 1/8 in.

KATHERINE PORTER (American, b. 1941)
The City at Night, 1983
oil on canvas
86 x 186 in.

KENNETH PRICE (American, b. 1935)
Phobia (chartreuse, green), 1995
ceramic, acrylic paint
17 1/2 x 23 x 18 in.

ALAIN PRILLARD (French)
Cheval Evolutif, 1990
mixed media on wood
15 3/4 x 15 3/4 in.

GARNETT PUETT (American, b. 1959)
Untitled, 1985
beeswax, wood, steel, glass
44 1/2 x 19 x 15 in.

MARTIN PURYEAR (American, b. 1941)
Verge, 1987
painted pine and red cedar
67 1/2 x 81 1/2 x 34 1/2 in.

HARVEY QUAYTMAN (American, b. 1937)
Harmonica YP, 1972
acrylic and dry pigment on canvas
105 x 108 in.

HARVEY QUAYTMAN (American, b. 1937)
Ivory Sliver, 1986
acrylic on canvas
28 x 28 in.

HARVEY QUAYTMAN (American, b. 1937)
Herculaneum, 1992
acrylic and rust on canvas
28 x 28 in.

SUSAN ROTHENBERG (American, b. 1945)
Triphammer Bridge, 1974
acrylic and tempera on canvas
67 1/4 x 115 1/2 in.

SUSAN ROTHENBERG (American, b. 1945)
Black in Place, 1976
acrylic and tempera on canvas
68 1/2 x 85 1/2 in.

SUSAN ROTHENBERG (American, b. 1945)
Smoker, 1978-79
acrylic and flashe on canvas
62 1/4 x 45 in.

SUSAN ROTHENBERG (American, b. 1945)
Green Ray, 1984
oil on canvas
84 x 107 in.

MARK ROTHKO (American, b. Russia, 1903-1970)
Homage to Matisse, 1954
oil on canvas
105 1/2 x 51 in.

SAL SCARPITTA (American, b. 1919)
Go-Devil Sled, 1976-77
wood, resin, canvas, wax
122 x 111 1/2 x 9 in.

SEAN SCULLY (American, b. Ireland, 1945)
Narcissus, 1984
oil on canvas
109 1/2 x 96 in.

RICHARD SERRA (American, b. 1939)
W.W.I., 1984
Cor-ten steel
55 x 64 x 8 in.

JOEL SHAPIRO (American, b. 1941)
Untitled, 1980
wood
52 7/8 x 64 x 45 1/2 in.

JOEL SHAPIRO (American, b. 1941)
Untitled, 1980-81
burnt wood, oil, casein
20 3/8 x 10 x 5 5/8 in.

JOEL SHAPIRO (American, b. 1941)
Untitled, 1980-82
wood, gouache, casein
25 1/4 x 15 1/2 x 22 in.

JOEL SHAPIRO (American, b. 1941)
Untitled, 1982-83
cast bronze
edition 2/3
43 x 34 x 35 3/4 in.

JOEL SHAPIRO (American, b. 1941)
Untitled, 1982-84
bronze
edition 1/3
44 1/2 x 37 3/4 x 24 1/2 in.

JOEL SHAPIRO (American, b. 1941)
Untitled, 1987-88
cast bronze
edition 2/3
72 1/2 x 15 1/4 x 10 in.

JUDITH SHEA (American, b. 1948)
The Crawl, 1983
bronze
6 x 22 x 11 1/2 in.

PETER SHELTON (American, b. 1951)
clearbelly, 1987
mixed media
25 x 18 x 17 1/4 in.

PETER SHELTON (American, b. 1951)
bagbox, 1988-89
cast iron
54 x 12 x 12 in.

PETER SHELTON (American, b. 1951)
allarms, 1990-96
fiberglass, mixed media
74 x 244 x 12 in.

PETER SHELTON (American, b. 1951)
bluepool, 1997
mixed media
20 x 36 x 22 in.

JEANNE SILVERTHORNE (American, b. 1950)
Untitled, 1994
rubber and resin
30 x 25 1/2 x 12 in.

JEANNE SILVERTHORNE (American, b. 1950)
Cross Section, 1997
rubber
32 x 53 1/2 x 2 3/4 in.

DAVID SMITH (American, 1906-1965)
Jurassic Bird, 1945
steel
25 1/2 x 35 1/4 x 7 1/2 in.

SUSANA SOLANO (Spanish, b. 1946)
Adjustment in the Void No. 2, 1996
iron and steel mesh
45 x 138 x 138 in.

ROMAIN TAIEB (French, b. 1968)
Tête dans le bleu, 1993
acrylic and pastel on paper
66 x 66 in.

OSAMI TANAKA (Japanese, b. 1952)
Untitled V, 1986
paraffin, wax, steel
120 x 24 x 24 in.

WILLIAM TUCKER (British, b. Egypt, 1935)
The House of the Hanged Man, 1981
wood
136 x 238 x 34 in.

WILLIAM TUCKER (British, b. Egypt, 1935)
Gymnast II, 1985
bronze
edition 1/3
80 x 77 x 24 in.

RICHARD TUTTLE (American, b. 1941)
Peace and Time (XII), 1993
enamel, foam rubber, copper, plastic pipe, chicken wire, and shingle
94 x 50 in.

PETER WAITE (American, b. 1950)
The Little League Field, 1988
acrylic on plastic panels
48 x 120 in.

JOHN WALKER (British, b. 1939)
A Letter, 1976
acrylic, gel, and canvas on canvas
120 x 96 in.

JOHN WALKER (British, b. 1939)
Numinous VII, 1978
oil and acrylic on canvas
120 x 96 in.

ALISON WILDING (British, b. 1948)
Core II, 1985
rubber, brass, lead
7 1/2 x 156 x 82 in.

ALISON WILDING (British, b. 1948)
Burned, 1991-92
copper wire
65 1/4 x 19 1/4 x 13 1/4 in.

TAD WILEY (American, b. 1955)
Wave Eater, 1987
marine enamel and varnish on redwood
73 x 13 x 4 1/4 in.

CHRISTOPHER WILMARTH (American, 1943-1987)
Last Hands, 1969
glass and wood
48 x 12 1/4 x 10 1/2 in.

CHRISTOPHER WILMARTH (American, 1943-1987)
Tina Turner, 1970-71
bent glass, acidized flat glass, steel cable
69 3/4 x 177 x 58 in.

CHRISTOPHER WILMARTH (American, 1943-1987)
February Gnomon, 1976-77
glass and steel
96 x 30 x 11 in.

CHRISTOPHER WILMARTH (American, 1943-1987)
Gnomon's Parade (Late), 1980
glass and steel
105 x 30 x 40 1/2 in.

CHRISTOPHER WILMARTH (American, 1943-1987)
Her Sides of Me, 1983-84
glass, steel and bronze
72 x 41 1/2 x 8 in.

CHRISTOPHER WILMARTH (American, 1943-1987)
Baptiste (Longing) #2, 1984
glass and steel
70 x 85 1/2 x 17 in.

TOM WUDL (Bolivian, b. 1948)
The Birth of Jan Van Eyck and the Extent of His Influence ..., 1988-89
oil on canvas
96 x 60 in.

DAISY YOUNGBLOOD (American, b. 1945)
Elephant with Tusks, 1995
low fire clay
18 x 5 1/2 x 14 in.

DAISY YOUNGBLOOD (American, b. 1945)
Gorilla, 1995
low fire clay
37 x 39 x 49 in.

BOARD OF TRUSTEES

STAFF

ADMINISTRATION

Marena Grant Morrisey
Executive Director
Carissa Sage
Administrative Assistant to Executive Director

Jean Grono
Controller
Elaine Buck
Visitor Information Specialist
Niki Caruso
Office Support
Nanette Johnson
Full Charge Bookkeeper
Marie Mersinger
Librarian
Yasmin Y. Padilla
Office Support
Shirley Torres
Accounting Clerk

BUILDING/OPERATIONS

Peter VanDeusen
Chief of Operations
Alexis Garcia
Building Superintendent
Cameron Moore
Facilities Assistant
Jesus Santiago
Assistant Building Superintendent

EDUCATION

Susan Rosoff
Curator of Education
Carrie Ann Banacki
Teacher Resource Center Coordinator/OMA-UCF College of Education Liaison
Jill Berry
Education Secretary
Jan Clanton
Adult Program Specialist
Janet Kilbride
OMA-UCF Art Department Liaison
Barbara McCue
Education Assistant
Mary Shaw
Youth and Family Program Coordinator

EXHIBITIONS

Hansen Mulford
Curator of Exhibitions
Kevin Boylan
Preparator
Andrea Farnick
Registrar
Betsy Gwinn
Assistant Curator
Kimberly Heitzman
Exhibitions Assistant
Andrea S. Kalis
Curator of Pre-Columbian Art
Sue Scott
Adjunct Curator of Contemporary American Art

MARKETING AND PUBLIC RELATIONS

Stephanie Testa
Marketing Manager
Stacy Dettro
Marketing Assistant
Hilda Fraticelli
Group and Facility Sales Coordinator
Terry Johnson
Group and Facility Sales Assistant
Darlene Johnson-Sanchez
Membership Coordinator
Phyllis M. Lankiewicz
Special Events Coordinator

MUSEUM SHOP

Sarah O'Connor
Museum Shop Manager
Linda Hunicke
Shop Clerk
Ava Maxwell
Assistant Museum Shop Manager

DEVELOPMENT

Wrenda Goodwyn
Marketing and Development Director
Nicole Candela
Development Assistant
Sharon Miller
Development Coordinator
Susan Roberts Zettler
Volunteer Coordinator

PHOTOGRAPHY CREDITS AND COLOPHON

This book was designed, typeset and produced on a Power Macintosh computer by Meredy Jenkins, Orlando, Florida and edited by Carol Rutan, Winter Park, Florida. 4000 copies of the book were printed by DeRoo Printing, Orlando, Florida. The cover was printed in 2 colors on 130 lb. Strathmore Beau Brilliant, Palm Beach White. The text pages were printed 4-color process using 175 line screens on Matrix 100 lb text. The 4-color images were scanned and separated by Florida Imaging, Orlando, Florida.

PHOTOGRAPH CREDITS:

Photographers

Eric Baum 48-B (detail)

Bevan Davies 71

D. James Dee 138, 140-A

Brian Forrest 104-B, 140-B

eeva-inkeri 41

Raymond Martinot, Orlando, FL 40, 49 (bottom), 63 (bottom), 67, 87, 98, 105, 110, 112-B (detail), 131, 138

Joshua Nefsky 72

William Nettles 106

Kevin Noble 152-A

Douglas Parker Studios, Glendale, CA 20, 21, 22, 23, 25, 26, 29, 30, 31, 32, 34, 35, 36, 37, 39 (bottom), 42, 43, 46-A, 46-B, 47, 48-A (top), 48-A (bottom), 49 (top), 51 (top), 51 (bottom), 54, 55, 56-A, 56-B, 58-B, 60, 61, 62, 65, 66, 68, 69, 70 (bottom), 73, 74, 75, 76, 77, 78-A, 78-B, 82, 83 (top), 83 (bottom), 84, 85, 86, 88-A, 88-B, 90, 91, 92, 93, 94, 95, 96, 97, 100-A, 101, 103, 104-A, 107, 109, 111, 112-A, 112-B (installation), 113 (top), 114, 115, 116, 117, 118-B, 119 (top), 122, 125, 126, 128, 129, 130, 131, 132, 133, 134, 135, 137, 144-A, 147, 149, 150

Eric Pollitzer 155, 156

Jerry Thompson 154-A, 154-B, 157

Tom Vinetz 139

Angelika Weilding, Berlin 27, 28

Sarah Wells, New York 38

Zindman/Fremont 39 (top), 80

Galleries / Estates

Courtesy Angles Gallery, Santa Monica 104-B

Courtesy John Berggruen Gallery, San Francisco 140-A, 141

Courtesy Mary Boone Gallery, New York 80

Courtesy Paula Cooper Gallery, New York 41, 136, 138

Courtesy Patricia Faure Gallery, Santa Monica 152-B, 153

Courtesy L.A. Louver, Inc., Venice 106, 119 (top), 139

Courtesy Curt Marcus Gallery, New York 120

Courtesy McKee Gallery, New York 38, 63 (top), 99, 102-A, 102-B, 121, 123, 124, 143, 144-B, 146-B, 160 (top), 161

Courtesy Galerie Nathalie Obadia, Paris 64, 70 (top), 142

© Alan Bowness, Hepworth Estate 79

Courtesy Estate of Christopher Wilmarth 154-A, 154-B, 155, 156, 157, 158

Artists Rights Society

© 1998 Artists Rights Society (ARS), New York/ADAGP, Paris 21, 22, 44, 95, 104-A

© 1998 Artists Rights Society (ARS), New York/VG Bild-Kunst, Bonn 26, 27, 28, 29, 39, 51 (bottom)

© 1998 Richard Artschwager/Artists Rights Society (ARS), New York 30, 31, 32, 33

© 1998 Estate of Alfred Jensen/Artists Rights Society (ARS), New York 86

© 1998 Robert Morris/Artists Rights Society (ARS), New York 105

© 1998 Bruce Nauman/Artists Rights Society (ARS), New York 112-B

© 1998 Kate Rothko-Prizel & Christopher Rothko/Artists Rights Society (ARS), New York 129

© 1998 Richard Serra/Artists Rights Society (ARS), New York 132